AI's Take on Relationships

Sandy Y. Greenleaf

Published by Sandy Y. Greenleaf, 2024.

AI'S TAKE ON RELATIONSHIPS

First edition. March 24, 2024.

ISBN: 979-8224636464

Written by Sandy Y. Greenleaf.

Table of Contents

Chapter 1: Understanding the Foundations of Healthy Relationships ..1

Chapter 2: Self-Awareness and Personal Growth 37

Chapter 3: Effective Communication Skills 71

Chapter 4: The Art of Active Listening 113

Chapter 5: Navigating Conflict and Disagreements 151

Chapter 6: Cultivating Empathy and Emotional Intelligence 192

Chapter 7: The Power of Vulnerability and Authenticity 232

Chapter 8: Maintaining Healthy Boundaries 270

Chapter 9: Nurturing Intimacy and Connection 312

Chapter 10: Overcoming Relationship Challenges............................... 348

Chapter 11: The Impact of Technology on Modern Relationships 391

Chapter 12: Cultivating Lasting Love and Commitment 431

Chapter 13: The Importance of Forgiveness and Letting Go.............. 475

Chapter 14: Embracing Diversity and Inclusivity in Relationships.... 513

Chapter 15: The Journey of Continuous Growth and Learning......... 558

Afterword: Embracing the Journey of Lifelong Growth and Connection 601

Preface

Welcome, dear reader, to an extraordinary journey through the intricate tapestry of human relationships. As you embark on this adventure, prepare to explore the depths of connection, communication, and emotional growth that lie at the heart of every meaningful bond. "AI's Take on Relationships" is not just another book about love and friendship; it is a groundbreaking exploration of the fundamental principles that shape the way we interact with one another, as seen through the unique lens of artificial intelligence.

In a world where technology is rapidly evolving and transforming the way we live, it is only natural to wonder how AI might perceive and understand the complexities of human relationships. As the curator of this book, my role has been to ask the right questions, to probe the vast knowledge and insights that AI has to offer, and to present its unique perspective in a way that is both engaging and accessible to readers from all walks of life.

It is important to note that the opinions expressed in this book are those of AI, and as such, they may be subject to certain limitations and biases. While we have made every effort to ensure the accuracy and reliability of the information presented, it is possible that mistakes may have occurred due to the inherent challenges of working with AI-generated content. As the curator, I have done my best to verify the information and present it in a clear and concise manner, but I encourage you, the reader, to approach the material with an open mind and a critical eye.

At its core, this book is a reflection of my personal mission statement: "Democratizing knowledge for the betterment of human lives." By harnessing the power of AI to explore the intricacies of relationships, I believe that we can gain valuable insights and practical tools for improving the quality of our connections with others. Whether you are seeking to strengthen your romantic partnership, deepen your friendships, or build more meaningful relationships with family members and colleagues, this book offers a wealth of knowledge and guidance to help you along the way.

As you delve into the pages that follow, you will discover a rich tapestry of ideas, anecdotes, and practical advice that will challenge your assumptions, broaden your perspective, and inspire you to cultivate more fulfilling relationships in all areas of your life. From the art of effective communication and the power of empathy to the importance of setting healthy boundaries and navigating conflict, this book covers a wide range of topics that are essential for building and maintaining strong, resilient connections.

So, dear reader, I invite you to join me on this exciting journey of discovery and growth. Together, we will explore the fascinating world of human relationships through the eyes of AI, and emerge with a deeper understanding of ourselves and the people we hold dear. With an open heart and a curious mind, let us embark on this transformative adventure, and unlock the secrets to building a life filled with love, connection, and meaning.

Chapter 1: Understanding the Foundations of Healthy Relationships

Relationships are an integral part of the human experience, shaping our lives in countless ways. From the moment we are born, we form connections with others that influence our personal growth, emotional well-being, and overall life satisfaction. The quality of our relationships can have a profound impact on our happiness, success, and sense of fulfillment.

But what exactly makes a relationship healthy and strong? In a world where we are constantly bombarded with conflicting messages about love, friendship, and family, it can be challenging to navigate the complexities of human connections. Many of us struggle with building and maintaining meaningful relationships, often repeating patterns of behavior that lead to disappointment, heartbreak, or loneliness.

The good news is that by understanding the fundamental principles and components of healthy relationships, we can cultivate more fulfilling connections with others. Whether you are seeking to strengthen your romantic partnership, deepen your friendships, or improve your family dynamics, the insights and strategies explored in this chapter will provide a solid foundation for building and nurturing the relationships that matter most to you.

In the following pages, we will delve into the key elements that form the bedrock of healthy relationships. We will examine the importance of trust, honesty, respect, and mutual understanding in creating a strong bond with others. We will also explore the role of effective communication, active listening, empathy, and emotional connection in fostering deeper, more meaningful relationships.

Furthermore, we will discuss the different types of relationships we encounter throughout our lives, from romantic partnerships to family bonds and friendships, and the unique challenges and opportunities each presents. By gaining a deeper understanding of the stages of relationship development, we can better navigate the inevitable ups and downs that come with forming and maintaining connections with others.

As we embark on this journey of self-discovery and relationship growth, it is essential to approach the process with an open mind and a willingness to learn. Building healthy relationships is a lifelong endeavor that requires ongoing effort, self-reflection, and a commitment to personal growth. By embracing the principles and strategies outlined in this chapter, you will be well on your way to cultivating the strong, supportive, and deeply fulfilling relationships you deserve.

Section 1: The Importance of Healthy Relationships

Relationships are an integral part of the human experience, shaping our lives in profound and countless ways. From the moment we are born, we are connected to others, and these connections continue to influence our personal growth, well-being, and overall life satisfaction throughout our lives. In this section, we will explore the significance of healthy relationships and how they contribute to our mental, emotional, and physical health.

Have you ever wondered why some people seem to thrive in their personal and professional lives, while others struggle to find happiness and fulfillment? The answer often lies in the quality of their relationships. Healthy relationships provide us with a sense of belonging, support, and security, which are essential for our well-being. They help us navigate life's challenges, celebrate our successes, and grow as individuals.

Research has consistently shown that people with strong, positive relationships tend to be happier, healthier, and more resilient than those who lack such connections. In fact, the Harvard Study of Adult Development, one of the longest-running studies on human happiness, found that the single most important predictor of a person's long-term well-being is the quality of their relationships.

Throughout this section, we will delve into the various ways in which healthy relationships contribute to our personal growth, mental and emotional health, and overall life satisfaction. We will explore the key components of healthy relationships, such as trust, respect, communication, and empathy, and how they work together to create strong, lasting bonds.

By understanding the importance of healthy relationships, we can begin to cultivate and nurture the connections that matter most to us. Whether it's with our romantic partners, family members, friends, or colleagues, investing in our relationships can have a profound impact on our lives, helping us to lead more fulfilling, joyful, and purposeful lives.

So, let us embark on this journey together, exploring the fascinating world of relationships and discovering how we can build and maintain the connections that will support us, inspire us, and help us thrive.

Subsection 1.1: The Impact of Relationships on Mental and Emotional Health

Our mental and emotional well-being is deeply intertwined with the quality of our relationships. Healthy relationships, characterized by trust, support, and positive interactions, can serve as a powerful buffer against the stresses and challenges of life. When we have strong, nurturing connections with others, we are better equipped to cope with difficulties, regulate our emotions, and maintain a sense of resilience in the face of adversity.

Research has consistently shown that individuals with strong social support networks tend to have lower rates of depression, anxiety, and other mental health issues. The presence of caring, supportive relationships can help alleviate feelings of loneliness, provide a sense of belonging, and boost self-esteem. When we feel valued, understood, and supported by others, we are more likely to develop a positive self-image and a greater sense of self-worth.

Moreover, healthy relationships can serve as a source of emotional validation and help us process and make sense of our experiences. Sharing our thoughts, feelings, and struggles with trusted others can provide us with new perspectives, help us gain clarity, and reduce the burden of carrying our emotional weight alone. This emotional support can be particularly crucial during times of stress, loss, or transition, when our mental and emotional resources may be stretched thin.

In addition to providing support during difficult times, healthy relationships also contribute to our overall happiness and life satisfaction. Engaging in positive interactions with loved ones, such as sharing laughter, expressing affection, and creating meaningful memories, can boost our mood, increase our sense of fulfillment, and contribute to a more positive outlook on life. These shared experiences strengthen our bonds with others and create a sense of connection and purpose that is essential for our mental and emotional well-being.

It is important to note that the impact of relationships on mental and emotional health is not limited to romantic partnerships or family ties. Friendships, professional relationships, and even casual social connections can all play a role in supporting our well-being. The key is to cultivate relationships that are based on mutual respect, trust, and positive regard, and to invest time and effort into nurturing these connections.

By recognizing the profound impact that healthy relationships have on our mental and emotional health, we can prioritize building and maintaining strong, supportive connections with others. This may involve developing effective communication skills, setting healthy boundaries, and actively seeking out opportunities to connect with others who uplift and inspire us. As we strengthen our relationships and surround ourselves with positive, nurturing influences, we create a solid foundation for our mental and emotional well-being to thrive.

Subsection 1.2: The Role of Relationships in Personal Growth and Development

Personal growth and development are lifelong processes that are significantly influenced by the relationships we cultivate throughout our lives. Positive, healthy relationships serve as a catalyst for self-discovery, providing us with opportunities to learn, grow, and develop essential life skills. These relationships, whether with family, friends, romantic partners, or mentors, challenge us to step outside our comfort zones, explore new perspectives, and expand our understanding of ourselves and the world around us.

One of the key ways in which relationships foster personal growth is through the provision of support and encouragement. When we are surrounded by individuals who believe in us and our potential, we are more likely to take risks, pursue our dreams, and overcome obstacles. The encouragement and validation we receive from our loved ones can boost our self-confidence, resilience, and motivation, enabling us to push through challenges and achieve our goals.

Moreover, healthy relationships offer a safe space for self-reflection and self-discovery. Through our interactions with others, we gain insights into our own thoughts, feelings, and behaviors. We learn to recognize our strengths and weaknesses, and we develop a deeper understanding of our values, beliefs, and aspirations. This self-awareness is crucial for personal growth, as it allows us to make informed decisions, set meaningful goals, and work towards becoming the best version of ourselves.

Relationships also provide us with opportunities to develop and refine essential life skills, such as communication, empathy, and problem-solving. As we navigate the complexities of our connections with others, we learn to express ourselves effectively, listen actively, and consider multiple perspectives. We develop the ability to put ourselves in others' shoes, to understand and share their feelings, and to respond with compassion and understanding. These skills not only enhance our relationships but also translate into other areas of our lives, enabling us to build stronger connections, resolve conflicts, and work collaboratively towards common goals.

Furthermore, positive relationships expose us to new ideas, experiences, and ways of thinking. Through our interactions with diverse individuals, we broaden our horizons, challenge our assumptions, and gain a more nuanced understanding of the world. We learn to appreciate different viewpoints, cultures, and backgrounds, fostering a sense of openness, curiosity, and adaptability. This exposure to new perspectives is essential for personal growth, as it encourages us to question our beliefs, expand our knowledge, and develop a more inclusive and empathetic worldview.

It is important to note that personal growth through relationships is a reciprocal process. As we grow and develop, we also contribute to the growth and development of those around us. By sharing our own experiences, insights, and support, we create a positive feedback loop that reinforces the importance of healthy relationships in fostering personal growth.

In conclusion, the role of relationships in personal growth and development cannot be overstated. Through the support, self-reflection, skill development, and exposure to new perspectives that positive relationships provide, we are able to unlock our full potential and become the best version of ourselves. By actively cultivating and nurturing healthy relationships, we create a foundation for lifelong learning, growth, and fulfillment.

Subsection 1.3: The Connection Between Healthy Relationships and Life Satisfaction

The pursuit of happiness and life satisfaction is a universal human desire, and the quality of our relationships plays a crucial role in achieving these goals. Numerous studies have consistently demonstrated a strong link between healthy, supportive relationships and overall life satisfaction and happiness. When we have strong, positive connections with others, we are more likely to experience a greater sense of fulfillment, contentment, and joy in our lives.

One of the primary ways in which healthy relationships contribute to life satisfaction is through the provision of emotional support and a sense of belonging. When we have people in our lives who genuinely care about us, listen to us, and offer encouragement and understanding, we feel valued, accepted, and connected. This sense of belonging and support is essential for our well-being, as it helps us navigate life's challenges, cope with stress, and maintain a positive outlook.

Moreover, healthy relationships provide us with opportunities for shared experiences, laughter, and enjoyment. Engaging in fun activities, meaningful conversations, and creating lasting memories with loved ones can significantly boost our happiness levels. These positive interactions release feel-good hormones, such as oxytocin and endorphins, which promote feelings of happiness, bonding, and overall life satisfaction.

In addition to the emotional benefits, healthy relationships can also contribute to life satisfaction by providing a sense of purpose and meaning. When we have strong connections with others, we often feel a greater sense of responsibility and motivation to be our best selves, pursue our goals, and make a positive impact in the world. This sense of purpose can be incredibly fulfilling and can help us find greater satisfaction in our personal and professional lives.

It is important to note that the connection between healthy relationships and life satisfaction is not limited to romantic partnerships. While a loving, supportive romantic relationship can certainly contribute to happiness, other types of relationships, such as close friendships, family bonds, and even meaningful connections with colleagues or community members, can also play a significant role in promoting life satisfaction.

Furthermore, the quality of our relationships is more important than the quantity when it comes to life satisfaction. Having a few close, supportive relationships can be more beneficial than having a large number of superficial or toxic connections. It is essential to invest time and effort into cultivating and nurturing relationships that are based on mutual respect, trust, and positive regard.

The link between healthy relationships and life satisfaction is not a one-way street; it is a reciprocal process. When we are happy and satisfied with our lives, we are more likely to have the emotional resources and positive outlook necessary to build and maintain strong, healthy relationships. This creates a positive feedback loop, where healthy relationships contribute to life satisfaction, and life satisfaction, in turn, fosters healthy relationships.

In conclusion, the connection between healthy relationships and life satisfaction is undeniable. By cultivating strong, supportive connections with others, we create a foundation for happiness, fulfillment, and overall well-being. As we prioritize building and nurturing positive relationships in our lives, we unlock the key to a more satisfying and joyful existence.

Summary: Embracing the Power of Healthy Relationships for a Fulfilling Life

Throughout this section, we have explored the profound impact that healthy relationships have on our personal growth, well-being, and overall life satisfaction. From the mental and emotional benefits to the opportunities for self-discovery and skill development, the importance of cultivating strong, positive connections with others cannot be overstated.

We have seen how healthy relationships provide us with a sense of belonging, support, and security, which are essential for navigating life's challenges and maintaining resilience in the face of adversity. These connections also serve as a source of emotional validation, helping us to process our experiences, gain new perspectives, and find greater happiness and fulfillment.

Moreover, we have discovered that healthy relationships play a crucial role in fostering personal growth and development. Through the support and encouragement of others, we are inspired to step outside our comfort zones, pursue our dreams, and become the best version of ourselves. These relationships also provide a safe space for self-reflection, enabling us to gain a deeper understanding of our values, beliefs, and aspirations.

As we have learned, the connection between healthy relationships and life satisfaction is undeniable. By investing time and effort into building and nurturing strong, supportive connections with others, we create a foundation for lasting happiness and fulfillment. Whether it's through romantic partnerships, close friendships, family bonds, or meaningful connections with colleagues or community members, the quality of our relationships has a direct impact on our overall well-being.

Armed with this knowledge, we are empowered to prioritize the cultivation of healthy relationships in our lives. By developing effective communication skills, setting healthy boundaries, and actively seeking out positive, nurturing influences, we can create a network of support that will help us thrive in all aspects of our lives.

As we move forward, let us embrace the power of healthy relationships and commit to building and maintaining the connections that will support us, inspire us, and help us lead more fulfilling, joyful lives. In the following sections, we will delve deeper into the various types of relationships and the specific strategies for cultivating and strengthening these vital connections.

Section 2: Key Components of Healthy Relationships

What separates a thriving, fulfilling relationship from one that merely survives? The answer lies in the presence of certain key components that form the bedrock of healthy, meaningful connections. Just as a house requires a strong foundation to withstand the test of time, a relationship needs a solid groundwork of essential elements to flourish and grow.

In this section, we will embark on a journey to uncover the building blocks of successful partnerships. We will explore the crucial role of trust and honesty, the importance of respect and mutual understanding, the power of open communication and active listening, and the significance of empathy and emotional connection. By gaining a deeper understanding of these fundamental aspects, you will be better equipped to cultivate and maintain the relationships that matter most to you.

As we delve into each component, we will examine real-life examples and anecdotes that illustrate the transformative impact these elements can have on your connections with others. Whether you are seeking to strengthen your romantic partnership, enhance your family bonds, or build more meaningful friendships, the insights and strategies shared in this section will provide you with a roadmap to creating healthier, more fulfilling relationships.

So, let us embark on this exploration together, armed with an open mind and a willingness to learn and grow. By mastering the key components of healthy relationships, you will unlock the door to deeper, more authentic connections that enrich your life and bring you closer to the people you cherish most.

Subsection 2.1: Trust and Honesty

At the heart of every healthy relationship lies a solid foundation of trust and honesty. These two essential components are the threads that weave the fabric of strong, lasting connections. Without trust and honesty, relationships are left vulnerable to doubt, insecurity, and ultimately, erosion.

Trust is the unwavering belief in the reliability, truth, and strength of your partner. It is the confidence that allows you to be your authentic self, share your deepest fears and aspirations, and know that you will be met with understanding and support. When trust is present, you feel secure in the knowledge that your partner has your best interests at heart and will be there for you through life's ups and downs.

Honesty, on the other hand, is the commitment to being truthful, open, and transparent in your communication and actions. It is the courage to share your thoughts, feelings, and experiences without fear of judgment or retribution. Honesty fosters a sense of authenticity and vulnerability in relationships, allowing partners to build a deeper understanding of each other's needs, desires, and challenges.

Together, trust and honesty create a powerful synergy that strengthens the bond between partners. When you trust your partner to be honest with you, and when you are honest with them in return, you create a safe space for genuine connection and growth. This atmosphere of openness and authenticity allows for the free flow of communication, enabling you to navigate the complexities of your relationship with grace and understanding.

However, building and maintaining trust and honesty is an ongoing process that requires effort and dedication from both partners. It involves being consistent in your words and actions, following through on your commitments, and being accountable for your mistakes. It also means being willing to have difficult conversations, even when it feels uncomfortable, in order to address issues and maintain the integrity of your relationship.

In the face of challenges and setbacks, trust and honesty serve as the anchor that keeps your relationship steady. When you trust each other to be honest about your feelings, concerns, and needs, you create a resilient partnership that can weather any storm. You become a team, working together to overcome obstacles and celebrate successes, secure in the knowledge that you have each other's unwavering support.

Cultivating trust and honesty in your relationships is not always easy, but it is always worth it. By making these essential components the bedrock of your connections, you lay the foundation for a love that is authentic, enduring, and truly fulfilling. So, let us explore the ways in which you can nurture trust and honesty in your own relationships, and discover the transformative power of these essential building blocks.

Subsection 2.2: Respect and Mutual Understanding

Respect and mutual understanding are the cornerstones of any healthy, thriving relationship. When we speak of respect, we refer to the deep admiration and regard for another person's feelings, wishes, and rights. It is the recognition that every individual is inherently worthy of being treated with dignity, kindness, and consideration. Mutual understanding, on the other hand, is the ability to empathize with and comprehend another person's perspective, even if it differs from our own. It is the willingness to step into their shoes and see the world through their eyes.

In the context of relationships, respect and mutual understanding create a solid foundation upon which trust, intimacy, and connection can flourish. When partners treat each other with respect, they foster an atmosphere of emotional safety and security. They feel valued, heard, and appreciated for who they are, rather than being judged or criticized for their differences. This sense of respect allows individuals to be their authentic selves, knowing that their partner will honor and cherish them, flaws and all.

Mutual understanding, in turn, enables partners to navigate the complexities of their relationship with greater ease and grace. When we seek to understand our partner's thoughts, feelings, and motivations, we create a bridge of empathy that spans the gap between our individual experiences. We learn to communicate more effectively, to listen with an open heart, and to approach conflicts with patience and compassion. By striving to see things from our partner's perspective, we cultivate a deeper sense of connection and intimacy, as we recognize that our differences are opportunities for growth and learning.

Fostering respect and mutual understanding in relationships requires ongoing effort and commitment from both partners. It involves actively listening to each other, validating each other's emotions, and expressing appreciation for the unique qualities that each person brings to the relationship. It means being willing to compromise, to apologize when necessary, and to work together towards common goals. When respect and mutual understanding are consistently practiced, they become the bedrock upon which a relationship can weather any storm, emerging stronger and more resilient on the other side.

However, it is important to note that respect and mutual understanding do not mean tolerating disrespectful or abusive behavior. Healthy relationships are built on a foundation of mutual care, consideration, and support. If a partner consistently disregards your feelings, violates your boundaries, or engages in hurtful or controlling behavior, it is crucial to prioritize your own well-being and seek help if needed.

Ultimately, respect and mutual understanding are the keys to unlocking the full potential of any relationship. By treating each other with kindness, empathy, and consideration, partners create a sacred space where love can thrive and grow. They build a bond that is rooted in trust, compassion, and a deep appreciation for the unique beauty and complexity of the human experience. So, let us all strive to cultivate respect and mutual understanding in our relationships, and watch as they blossom into something truly extraordinary.

Subsection 2.3: Open Communication and Active Listening

In the tapestry of healthy relationships, open communication and active listening are the golden threads that weave a strong, unbreakable bond. These essential skills form the bedrock of understanding, empathy, and connection, allowing partners to navigate the complex landscape of their shared lives with grace and resilience.

Open communication is the willingness to express one's thoughts, feelings, and needs honestly and directly, without fear of judgment or retribution. It is the courage to be vulnerable, to share one's deepest hopes and fears, and to trust that one's partner will receive this information with care and compassion. When partners commit to open communication, they create a safe space for authentic self-expression, fostering a deeper sense of intimacy and trust.

However, open communication is only half of the equation. Equally important is the art of active listening, which involves giving one's full attention to one's partner, not just hearing their words but truly seeking to understand their perspective. Active listening requires setting aside one's own thoughts and biases, and focusing wholly on the speaker's message, both verbal and nonverbal.

When we practice active listening, we demonstrate to our partner that their thoughts and feelings matter to us. We show them that we value their input and are committed to understanding their point of view, even if it differs from our own. This validation and empathy strengthen the emotional bond between partners, creating a sense of teamwork and solidarity in the face of life's challenges.

Together, open communication and active listening form a powerful feedback loop, each skill reinforcing and enhancing the other. When partners feel heard and understood, they are more likely to share openly and honestly, knowing that their words will be met with respect and compassion. And when partners communicate openly and directly, they provide rich material for active listening, allowing for deeper insights and more meaningful connections.

Cultivating these skills requires practice, patience, and a willingness to be uncomfortable at times. It means learning to express oneself clearly and assertively, without blame or criticism. It means resisting the urge to interrupt, defend, or problem-solve, and instead focusing on understanding and empathizing with one's partner's experience. It means being willing to have difficult conversations, to apologize when necessary, and to work together to find mutually satisfying solutions.

The rewards of this effort, however, are immeasurable. Couples who master the arts of open communication and active listening report higher levels of relationship satisfaction, greater emotional intimacy, and a stronger sense of partnership. They are better equipped to weather the storms of life, to support each other through challenges, and to celebrate each other's successes.

In a world that often prizes speed, efficiency, and self-interest, the skills of open communication and active listening are a radical act of love. They require us to slow down, to be present, and to prioritize the needs of our relationship over our own individual desires. They ask us to be curious, to be humble, and to be willing to grow and change alongside our partner.

Ultimately, open communication and active listening are the keys to unlocking the full potential of our relationships. By committing to these practices, we create a foundation of trust, respect, and understanding that can withstand the tests of time. We build a love that is resilient, authentic, and deeply fulfilling, a love that empowers us to be our best selves and to create a life of shared meaning and purpose.

Subsection 2.4: Empathy and Emotional Connection

In the tapestry of human relationships, empathy and emotional connection are the threads that bind us together, creating a rich and vibrant picture of understanding, compassion, and love. These essential elements are the foundation upon which deep, meaningful relationships are built, allowing us to transcend the boundaries of our individual experiences and connect with others on a profound level.

Empathy, at its core, is the ability to understand and share the feelings of another person. It is the capacity to step into their shoes, to see the world through their eyes, and to feel the emotions that they are experiencing. When we practice empathy, we create a bridge of understanding that spans the gap between our own perspective and that of another, fostering a sense of connection and commonality that is essential to building strong, healthy relationships.

In the context of relationships, empathy allows us to respond to our loved ones with compassion, sensitivity, and care. It enables us to recognize and validate their emotions, to offer support and comfort when they are struggling, and to celebrate their joys and successes as if they were our own. By cultivating empathy, we create a safe and nurturing space where our loved ones feel seen, heard, and valued, laying the foundation for a relationship that is built on trust, respect, and mutual understanding.

Emotional connection, on the other hand, is the deep, intimate bond that we share with another person. It is the feeling of being truly seen and understood, of being accepted and loved for who we are, flaws and all. When we have a strong emotional connection with someone, we feel a sense of safety, comfort, and belonging in their presence, as if we have found a home in another person's heart.

Cultivating emotional connection requires vulnerability, authenticity, and a willingness to share our innermost thoughts, feelings, and experiences with another person. It means being open and honest about our hopes, fears, and dreams, and trusting that our partner will hold them with care and compassion. When we allow ourselves to be fully seen and known by another person, we create a bond that is unbreakable, a connection that can weather any storm and emerge stronger on the other side.

Together, empathy and emotional connection form the bedrock of healthy, fulfilling relationships. They allow us to navigate the complexities of life with grace and resilience, to support each other through challenges and celebrate each other's successes. They create a sense of partnership and teamwork, a feeling that we are in this together, no matter what life may bring.

Cultivating empathy and emotional connection requires effort, patience, and a willingness to be vulnerable. It means learning to listen with an open heart, to communicate with honesty and clarity, and to prioritize the needs of the relationship over our own individual desires. It means being willing to have difficult conversations, to apologize when necessary, and to work together to find mutually satisfying solutions.

The rewards of this effort, however, are immeasurable. Couples who cultivate empathy and emotional connection report higher levels of relationship satisfaction, greater intimacy and trust, and a deeper sense of fulfillment and purpose. They are better equipped to navigate the ups and downs of life, to support each other through thick and thin, and to create a love that is truly lasting and transformative.

In a world that often feels disconnected and divided, empathy and emotional connection are a beacon of hope and healing. They remind us of our shared humanity, of the power of love and understanding to bridge even the widest divides. By cultivating these essential elements in our relationships, we not only create a stronger, more resilient bond with our loved ones, but we also contribute to a more compassionate, connected world.

Ultimately, empathy and emotional connection are the keys to unlocking the full potential of our relationships. They are the foundation upon which we build a love that is deep, authentic, and enduring, a love that empowers us to be our best selves and to create a life of shared meaning and purpose. So let us all strive to cultivate empathy and emotional connection in our relationships, and watch as they blossom into something truly extraordinary.

Summary: Building a Foundation of Love, Trust, and Understanding

In this section, we have explored the key components that form the bedrock of healthy, thriving relationships. By cultivating trust and honesty, respect and mutual understanding, open communication and active listening, and empathy and emotional connection, we lay the foundation for a love that is authentic, enduring, and truly fulfilling.

As we navigate the complexities of our relationships, these essential elements serve as our guiding light, illuminating the path to deeper intimacy, greater resilience, and more meaningful connections. They empower us to create a safe and nurturing space where we can be our true selves, share our hopes and fears, and support each other through life's ups and downs.

Building and maintaining a strong foundation in our relationships requires ongoing effort, patience, and commitment. It means being willing to have difficult conversations, to apologize when necessary, and to work together to find mutually satisfying solutions. It means prioritizing the needs of the relationship over our own individual desires and being open to growth and change alongside our partner.

The rewards of this effort, however, are immeasurable. By making these key components the bedrock of our connections, we unlock the door to a love that is transformative, a love that empowers us to be our best selves and to create a life of shared meaning and purpose.

As we move forward in our exploration of healthy relationships, let us carry these essential elements with us, weaving them into the fabric of our daily interactions and cherishing the profound impact they have on our lives. With a strong foundation of love, trust, and understanding, we can weather any storm and emerge stronger, more connected, and more deeply fulfilled than ever before.

Section 3: The Different Types of Relationships

Relationships come in many forms, each with its own unique dynamics, challenges, and rewards. From the passion and intimacy of romantic partnerships to the unconditional love and support of family bonds, the various types of relationships we experience throughout our lives shape our personal growth, happiness, and overall well-being. In this section, we will explore the diverse landscape of human connections, delving into the characteristics, expectations, and complexities that define romantic relationships, family ties, friendships, and professional interactions.

By understanding the distinct nature of each type of relationship, we can better navigate the challenges that arise and cultivate the skills necessary to build and maintain healthy, fulfilling connections. Whether you are seeking to strengthen your romantic partnership, improve your family dynamics, forge deeper friendships, or create a more positive work environment, this section will provide valuable insights and practical guidance to help you thrive in all your relationships.

As we embark on this exploration of the different types of relationships, it is essential to recognize that every connection is unique, shaped by the individuals involved and the context in which it exists. By approaching each relationship with empathy, open-mindedness, and a willingness to learn and grow, we can unlock the full potential of our connections and create a rich, rewarding tapestry of relationships that enrich our lives and the lives of those around us.

Subsection 3.1: Romantic Relationships

Romantic relationships are among the most intense and emotionally charged connections we experience throughout our lives. These intimate partnerships are characterized by a deep sense of love, passion, and commitment, as well as a strong desire for physical and emotional closeness. When two people enter into a romantic relationship, they embark on a journey of self-discovery, personal growth, and shared experiences that have the power to shape their lives in profound ways.

At the heart of every successful romantic relationship lies a foundation of trust, respect, and open communication. These essential elements foster a sense of safety and security, allowing partners to be vulnerable with one another and build a deep emotional bond. Couples who prioritize honest and transparent communication are better equipped to navigate the challenges and obstacles that inevitably arise in any long-term partnership, from minor disagreements to major life changes.

However, romantic relationships are not without their unique set of challenges and expectations. In today's society, there is often immense pressure to find the perfect partner, maintain a passionate spark, and live up to idealized notions of love perpetuated by popular media. These unrealistic expectations can lead to feelings of inadequacy, disappointment, and even resentment when reality fails to match the fairy-tale narrative.

Moreover, romantic relationships require a delicate balance of individual needs and desires with those of the partnership as a whole. Striking this balance can be particularly challenging when partners have differing communication styles, emotional needs, or personal goals. Learning to compromise, empathize, and support one another's growth is essential for maintaining a healthy, thriving relationship in the long term.

Another significant challenge faced by many romantic partnerships is the inevitable evolution of the relationship over time. As individuals grow and change, so too do their needs, desires, and expectations within the relationship. Couples who are able to adapt to these changes and continue to nurture their connection through open communication, shared experiences, and a willingness to learn and grow together are more likely to build a resilient, lasting partnership.

Ultimately, the key to a fulfilling romantic relationship lies in embracing the unique dynamics, challenges, and rewards that come with this intimate partnership. By approaching these connections with empathy, patience, and a commitment to personal and shared growth, couples can build a strong foundation of love, trust, and mutual respect that will weather the storms of life and stand the test of time.

Subsection 3.2: Family Relationships

Family relationships are among the most complex, enduring, and influential connections we experience throughout our lives. These bonds, forged by blood, marriage, or adoption, play a crucial role in shaping our identity, values, and emotional well-being. The dynamics within a family can range from loving and supportive to challenging and strained, with each member navigating their own unique roles, expectations, and responsibilities.

At the core of healthy family relationships lies a foundation of unconditional love, trust, and mutual respect. When these elements are present, family members feel secure in their ability to express themselves, seek support, and grow together. Open communication is essential for fostering understanding, resolving conflicts, and maintaining a sense of connection among family members. By creating a safe space for honest dialogue, families can navigate the challenges and celebrate the joys of life together.

However, family relationships are not without their complexities and potential pitfalls. The close-knit nature of these bonds can sometimes lead to intense emotions, unresolved conflicts, and dysfunctional patterns of interaction. Family members may struggle with issues such as sibling rivalry, parental favoritism, or the strain of caring for elderly relatives. Additionally, external factors such as financial stress, divorce, or illness can further complicate family dynamics and test the strength of these relationships.

To cultivate healthy family relationships, it is essential for each member to understand and respect the unique roles and responsibilities they hold within the family unit. Parents, for example, play a critical role in providing love, guidance, and support to their children, while also setting boundaries and instilling values. Siblings, on the other hand, often serve as lifelong companions, offering a shared history and a sense of belonging. Grandparents, aunts, uncles, and other extended family members can provide additional support, wisdom, and perspective, enriching the family tapestry.

Nurturing healthy family relationships requires ongoing effort, patience, and commitment from all members. This may involve setting aside dedicated time for family activities, actively listening to one another, and showing empathy and understanding in the face of challenges. By prioritizing open communication, mutual respect, and a willingness to grow and adapt together, families can weather the storms of life and emerge stronger, more resilient, and more deeply connected.

Ultimately, the importance of healthy family relationships cannot be overstated. These connections provide a sense of belonging, a support system, and a foundation for personal growth and development. By investing in the well-being of our family bonds, we create a legacy of love, resilience, and connection that can be passed down through generations, shaping not only our own lives but also the lives of those who come after us.

Subsection 3.3: Friendships

Friendships are the voluntary, enduring bonds we form with others based on shared interests, experiences, and mutual affection. These relationships play a crucial role in our personal growth, happiness, and overall well-being, providing us with a sense of belonging, support, and companionship. Unlike family relationships, which are often determined by birth or marriage, friendships are chosen connections that we actively cultivate and nurture throughout our lives.

At the heart of every strong friendship lies a foundation of trust, loyalty, and mutual understanding. True friends are those who stand by us through life's ups and downs, offering a listening ear, a shoulder to cry on, and a source of laughter and joy. They celebrate our successes, provide comfort in times of sorrow, and challenge us to grow and become the best versions of ourselves. The support and encouragement we receive from our friends can be instrumental in helping us navigate the complexities of life, from personal challenges to professional endeavors.

One of the most significant benefits of friendships is the positive impact they have on our mental and emotional well-being. Studies have shown that individuals with strong social connections tend to experience lower levels of stress, anxiety, and depression, as well as greater life satisfaction and resilience in the face of adversity. The act of sharing our thoughts, feelings, and experiences with trusted friends can be deeply cathartic, providing a safe space for self-expression and emotional release.

Moreover, friendships expose us to diverse perspectives, experiences, and ways of thinking, broadening our horizons and fostering personal growth. Through our interactions with friends from different backgrounds, cultures, and walks of life, we learn to empathize, communicate effectively, and appreciate the richness of human diversity. These relationships challenge us to step outside our comfort zones, try new things, and expand our understanding of ourselves and the world around us.

However, like all relationships, friendships require ongoing effort, communication, and commitment to thrive. Building and maintaining strong friendships involves being present, reliable, and supportive, even when life gets busy or challenging. It means making time for regular check-ins, shared activities, and meaningful conversations that deepen the bond between friends. Equally important is the ability to navigate conflicts and disagreements with empathy, honesty, and a willingness to forgive and grow together.

In today's fast-paced, digitally connected world, the nature of friendships has evolved, with many relationships now maintained through social media, messaging apps, and video calls. While these platforms can help us stay connected with friends across vast distances, it is essential to recognize the value of face-to-face interactions and shared experiences in nurturing the depth and quality of our friendships. Making time for in-person gatherings, whether it's a coffee date, a weekend getaway, or a simple walk in the park, can do wonders for strengthening the bonds between friends.

Ultimately, the power of friendships lies in their ability to enrich our lives, provide a sense of belonging, and support our personal growth and well-being. By investing time and effort into building and maintaining strong, supportive friendships, we create a network of love, laughter, and companionship that can sustain us through life's joys and challenges. As we navigate the complex tapestry of relationships in our lives, let us cherish the unique and irreplaceable role that friendships play in shaping who we are and who we aspire to be.

Subsection 3.4: Professional Relationships

In the tapestry of relationships that shape our lives, professional connections hold a unique and significant place. These relationships, forged in the crucible of the workplace, play a crucial role in our personal and career development, as well as our overall well-being and satisfaction. The nature of professional relationships is inherently different from the intimate bonds of family or the chosen connections of friendship, as they are often driven by shared goals, mutual respect, and a common purpose within an organizational context.

At the heart of healthy professional relationships lies a foundation of trust, open communication, and collaboration. When colleagues trust one another, they create an environment where ideas can be freely shared, challenges can be openly addressed, and innovative solutions can be born. This trust is built through consistent, reliable behavior, a willingness to support and assist others, and a commitment to maintaining confidentiality when necessary. Open communication is equally essential, as it allows for the clear exchange of information, expectations, and feedback, fostering a sense of transparency and mutual understanding.

Collaboration is another key component of successful professional relationships. When individuals work together towards a common goal, pooling their skills, knowledge, and resources, they can achieve far more than they could alone. Effective collaboration requires a willingness to listen, compromise, and value the contributions of others, even when their perspectives may differ from our own. By fostering a spirit of teamwork and cooperation, colleagues can create a positive, supportive work environment that enhances productivity, creativity, and job satisfaction.

However, navigating professional relationships is not without its challenges. The hierarchical nature of many organizations can create power imbalances that strain communication and trust, while the pressure to achieve results can sometimes lead to competition and conflict among colleagues. To maintain healthy professional relationships, it is essential to approach these challenges with empathy, professionalism, and a focus on finding mutually beneficial solutions. This may involve setting clear boundaries, engaging in respectful conflict resolution, and seeking the guidance of mentors or supervisors when necessary.

Another crucial aspect of professional relationships is the opportunity they provide for personal and career growth. Through interactions with colleagues from diverse backgrounds and experiences, we expose ourselves to new ideas, perspectives, and ways of working. These exchanges can broaden our horizons, challenge our assumptions, and inspire us to develop new skills and knowledge. Moreover, the relationships we build in the workplace can often lead to valuable mentorship opportunities, where more experienced colleagues offer guidance, support, and advice to help us navigate our career paths and reach our full potential.

In today's increasingly interconnected and global workplace, the importance of healthy professional relationships extends beyond the boundaries of any single organization. The networks we build throughout our careers can open doors to new opportunities, provide valuable resources and support, and help us stay informed about industry trends and best practices. By actively cultivating and maintaining these relationships, even as we move between roles and organizations, we create a powerful web of connections that can sustain and enrich our professional lives.

Ultimately, the significance of healthy professional relationships lies in their ability to create a positive, productive, and fulfilling work environment. When we invest time and effort into building strong, supportive connections with our colleagues, we not only enhance our own well-being and success but also contribute to the overall success of our teams and organizations. As we navigate the complex landscape of the workplace, let us remember the power of trust, communication, collaboration, and growth in shaping the professional relationships that define our careers and our lives.

Summary: Embracing the Tapestry of Relationships

As we conclude our exploration of the different types of relationships, it becomes clear that each connection we form plays a unique and vital role in shaping our lives, our personal growth, and our overall well-being. From the passion and intimacy of romantic partnerships to the unconditional love and support of family bonds, and from the laughter and companionship of friendships to the trust and collaboration of professional connections, the diverse tapestry of relationships we weave throughout our lives is a testament to the power of human connection.

By understanding the distinct characteristics, challenges, and rewards of each type of relationship, we can approach our connections with greater empathy, wisdom, and intentionality. We learn to navigate the complexities of romantic love, to cherish the unbreakable ties of family, to cultivate the joy and support of friendships, and to foster the trust and growth of professional bonds. Each relationship, in its own way, offers us an opportunity to learn, to grow, and to experience the richness of life through the eyes of another.

As we move forward on our journey of building and nurturing healthy relationships, let us remember that the key to success lies not in perfection, but in our willingness to show up, to communicate openly, to extend empathy and understanding, and to grow alongside those we hold dear. By embracing the unique beauty and challenges of each connection, we create a life filled with love, support, and meaning.

So let us step forward with open hearts and minds, ready to embrace the tapestry of relationships that awaits us. Let us cherish the bonds we have, nurture the connections we seek, and always remember the transformative power of human connection in shaping our lives and our world. As we continue on this journey of exploration and growth, may we find strength, joy, and resilience in the relationships that define us, and may we never underestimate the profound impact of the connections we forge along the way.

Section 4: The Stages of Relationship Development

Relationships, like living organisms, go through various stages of development, each with its unique challenges and opportunities for growth. From the initial spark of attraction to the deep, enduring bond of a long-term partnership, the journey of a relationship is a complex and multifaceted one. In this section, we will explore the different stages that relationships typically go through, shedding light on the emotional, psychological, and interpersonal dynamics at play in each phase.

As we delve into the stages of relationship development, we will examine the key milestones and transitions that mark the progression of a relationship. We will discuss the excitement and uncertainty of the early stages, the deepening of intimacy and emotional connection as the relationship grows, and the challenges of navigating conflicts and maintaining a healthy, long-lasting partnership.

By understanding the natural progression of relationships, we can better navigate the ups and downs that come with each stage. We can learn to appreciate the beauty and potential of each phase while also being prepared for the inevitable challenges that arise. Whether you are just embarking on a new relationship or have been with your partner for years, this section will provide valuable insights and practical guidance to help you build and maintain a strong, healthy, and fulfilling connection.

So, let us embark on this journey together, exploring the stages of relationship development and discovering the keys to creating a love that lasts a lifetime. Through relatable examples, research-backed insights, and practical advice, we will uncover the secrets to navigating the complex and rewarding world of relationships, one stage at a time.

Subsection 4.1: The Initial Attraction and Getting to

Know Each Other

The initial stages of a relationship are often characterized by a potent mix of excitement, curiosity, and nervous energy. This phase, known as the attraction stage, is where two individuals first become aware of each other and begin to explore the possibility of a connection. It is a time of discovery, where both parties are trying to learn more about the other person and assess their compatibility.

During this stage, physical attraction often plays a significant role. The release of hormones such as dopamine and norepinephrine can create feelings of euphoria and infatuation, making the other person seem irresistible. However, attraction is not solely based on physical appearance. Other factors, such as shared interests, sense of humor, and personality traits, can also contribute to the initial spark between two people.

As the attraction grows, individuals begin to engage in the process of getting to know each other. This may involve spending time together, sharing stories and experiences, and asking questions to gain a deeper understanding of the other person's thoughts, feelings, and values. Communication plays a crucial role in this stage, as it allows both parties to express themselves and learn about each other's expectations and desires.

The initial stages of a relationship can be both exhilarating and nerve-wracking. There is a sense of uncertainty as individuals navigate the uncharted territory of a new connection. Will the attraction be mutual? Will they find common ground? These questions can create a mix of anticipation and anxiety.

It is important to approach this stage with an open mind and a willingness to learn. Rushing into a relationship or making assumptions about the other person can lead to misunderstandings and disappointment. Instead, taking the time to genuinely get to know each other can lay the foundation for a strong, healthy connection.

During this stage, it is also essential to maintain a sense of self. While it is natural to want to impress the other person and put your best foot forward, it is crucial to remain authentic and true to yourself. Pretending to be someone you are not or compromising your values and beliefs to please the other person can lead to problems down the road.

As the initial attraction and getting-to-know-each-other phase progresses, both individuals begin to develop a clearer picture of who the other person is and whether there is potential for a deeper connection. This sets the stage for the next phase of the relationship, where intimacy and emotional bonding begin to grow.

Subsection 4.2: Building Intimacy and Deepening the Connection

As a relationship progresses beyond the initial stages of attraction and getting to know each other, partners begin to develop a deeper sense of intimacy and emotional connection. This stage is crucial for the long-term success and fulfillment of the relationship, as it lays the foundation for trust, understanding, and mutual support.

Building intimacy involves a gradual process of opening up to one another, sharing personal thoughts, feelings, and experiences. It requires vulnerability, courage, and a willingness to let down one's guard. As partners reveal more of themselves, they create opportunities for empathy, acceptance, and a deeper understanding of each other's unique personalities, quirks, and challenges.

One key aspect of developing intimacy is engaging in meaningful conversations that go beyond surface-level topics. This involves asking open-ended questions, actively listening, and showing genuine interest in each other's lives. By discussing hopes, dreams, fears, and aspirations, partners can foster a sense of emotional closeness and create a safe space for self-expression.

Physical intimacy also plays a significant role in deepening the connection between partners. While sexual intimacy is often a central component, physical closeness can also be expressed through affectionate touches, hugs, and holding hands. These gestures of affection help to reinforce the emotional bond and provide a sense of comfort and security.

As intimacy grows, partners may find themselves developing a shared language and inside jokes that are unique to their relationship. These shared experiences and references create a sense of exclusivity and strengthen the feeling of being a united team.

However, building intimacy is not always a smooth process. It requires patience, effort, and a willingness to work through challenges and misunderstandings. Partners may encounter moments of vulnerability hangover, where they feel exposed or uncertain after sharing deeply personal aspects of themselves. It is essential to approach these moments with compassion, reassurance, and a commitment to open communication.

Deepening the connection also involves supporting each other through life's ups and downs. When partners show up for each other during times of stress, hardship, or celebration, they demonstrate their reliability and strengthen the emotional bond. This support can take many forms, such as offering a listening ear, providing practical assistance, or simply being present and available.

As the relationship progresses, partners may find themselves developing a shared vision for the future. This can involve discussing long-term goals, values, and aspirations, and working together to create a life that aligns with their shared priorities. By building a sense of partnership and collaboration, couples can create a strong foundation for a lasting and fulfilling relationship.

It is important to recognize that building intimacy and deepening the connection is an ongoing process that requires intentional effort and investment. Even in long-term relationships, partners must continue to prioritize quality time, communication, and emotional attunement to maintain a strong bond.

By nurturing intimacy and strengthening the emotional connection, partners create a relationship that is characterized by trust, understanding, and a deep sense of partnership. This strong foundation can help couples weather the inevitable challenges and changes that arise over the course of a long-term relationship, and create a love that endures.

Subsection 4.3: Navigating Challenges and Conflicts

As relationships progress and deepen, it is inevitable that challenges and conflicts will arise. These moments of tension and disagreement are a natural part of any relationship, and how couples navigate them can make a significant difference in the health and longevity of their partnership. In this subsection, we will explore the common challenges and conflicts that relationships face and provide strategies for effectively addressing and resolving them.

One of the most common sources of conflict in relationships is communication breakdown. When partners struggle to express their thoughts, feelings, and needs clearly and respectfully, misunderstandings and frustrations can quickly escalate. To navigate communication challenges, it is essential to develop strong active listening skills, practice empathy, and approach conversations with a spirit of openness and understanding. By creating a safe and non-judgmental space for dialogue, couples can work together to identify the root causes of their conflicts and find mutually satisfying solutions.

Another significant challenge that relationships face is the struggle to maintain a healthy balance between individual needs and the needs of the partnership. As individuals grow and change over time, their priorities, goals, and desires may shift, leading to potential conflicts with their partner's expectations and needs. Navigating this challenge requires a commitment to ongoing communication, flexibility, and a willingness to compromise. By regularly checking in with each other and discussing their individual and shared goals, couples can work together to find a balance that honors both their personal growth and the health of their relationship.

Trust issues can also pose significant challenges in relationships. When one or both partners have experienced betrayal, deception, or inconsistency in the past, it can be difficult to rebuild trust and feel secure in the relationship. Navigating trust issues requires patience, consistency, and a demonstrated commitment to honesty and transparency. By taking responsibility for past mistakes, following through on commitments, and being reliable and accountable, partners can gradually rebuild trust and strengthen their bond.

External stressors, such as financial strain, work-related challenges, or family conflicts, can also put significant pressure on relationships. When couples are faced with these external challenges, it is essential to approach them as a team, offering each other support, understanding, and a united front. By openly communicating about the challenges they face and working together to find solutions, couples can minimize the impact of external stressors on their relationship and build resilience in the face of adversity.

Navigating challenges and conflicts in relationships also requires a commitment to personal growth and self-awareness. When individuals take responsibility for their own emotions, reactions, and behaviors, they are better equipped to approach conflicts with a spirit of humility, empathy, and a willingness to learn. By cultivating a growth mindset and being open to feedback and constructive criticism, partners can use challenges as opportunities to strengthen their relationship and deepen their connection.

It is important to recognize that some conflicts may require the support of a trained professional, such as a couples therapist or counselor. When challenges feel overwhelming or insurmountable, seeking outside help can provide valuable perspective, tools, and guidance for navigating the complexities of the relationship. By being proactive and willing to invest in the health of their partnership, couples can build the skills and resilience necessary to weather even the most challenging of conflicts.

Ultimately, navigating challenges and conflicts in relationships requires a commitment to love, understanding, and a willingness to grow together. By approaching conflicts with patience, empathy, and a spirit of collaboration, couples can use these moments of tension as opportunities to deepen their connection, strengthen their bond, and build a love that endures.

Subsection 4.4: Long-term Commitment and Maintenance

As relationships progress through the stages of initial attraction, deepening intimacy, and navigating challenges, they may eventually reach a point of long-term commitment. This stage is characterized by a shared sense of dedication, stability, and a desire to build a future together. However, maintaining a healthy, long-term relationship requires ongoing effort, care, and attention from both partners.

One of the key aspects of long-term commitment is a shared vision for the future. When couples reach this stage, they often begin to discuss and plan for significant milestones, such as moving in together, getting married, starting a family, or pursuing shared goals and dreams. Having a clear understanding of each other's expectations and aspirations is crucial for ensuring that both partners are on the same page and working towards a common future.

Another essential component of long-term commitment is the ability to adapt and grow together. As individuals evolve and change over time, so too must their relationship. Couples who are committed to the long haul understand that their partnership is a dynamic, ever-evolving entity that requires flexibility, patience, and a willingness to learn and grow together. This may involve regularly reassessing and adjusting priorities, roles, and responsibilities within the relationship to ensure that both partners feel fulfilled and supported.

Maintaining a strong, healthy relationship over the long term also requires a deep level of trust, respect, and emotional intimacy. When couples have weathered the ups and downs of the earlier stages of their relationship, they have likely developed a solid foundation of trust and understanding. However, it is essential to continue nurturing and strengthening this bond through ongoing communication, vulnerability, and acts of love and appreciation. Regularly expressing gratitude, engaging in meaningful conversations, and prioritizing quality time together can help keep the emotional connection strong and vibrant.

Another critical aspect of long-term relationship maintenance is the ability to navigate and resolve conflicts in a healthy, constructive manner. While the intense passion and excitement of the early stages may have faded, long-term commitment brings with it a deeper sense of partnership and collaboration. When challenges arise, couples who are committed to the long haul approach them as a team, working together to find mutually satisfying solutions and compromises. They understand that conflict is an inevitable part of any relationship, but they have developed the skills and resilience necessary to work through difficulties and emerge stronger on the other side.

Maintaining a sense of individuality and personal growth is also crucial for the health and longevity of a long-term relationship. While it is important to cultivate a strong sense of partnership and togetherness, it is equally essential for each partner to maintain their own sense of self, pursue their individual interests and passions, and continue to grow and develop as a person. Encouraging and supporting each other's personal growth and independence can help prevent feelings of resentment, stagnation, or codependency, and ensure that both partners remain fulfilled and energized by their relationship.

Finally, long-term commitment requires a willingness to continually invest time, energy, and effort into the relationship. Just as a garden requires regular tending, watering, and nurturing to thrive, so too does a long-term partnership. This may involve regularly setting aside dedicated time for date nights, engaging in shared hobbies and interests, or simply making a conscious effort to prioritize the relationship amidst the demands and distractions of daily life. By consistently showing up for each other and making the relationship a top priority, couples can maintain a deep, lasting connection that stands the test of time.

Summary: Navigating the Journey of Love

Throughout this section, we have explored the various stages of relationship development, from the initial spark of attraction to the deep, enduring bond of a long-term partnership. By understanding the unique challenges and opportunities associated with each stage, we can better navigate the complex and rewarding journey of love.

We have seen how the excitement and uncertainty of the early stages lay the foundation for a deeper connection, and how the process of building intimacy and emotional bonding requires vulnerability, trust, and open communication. We have also examined the inevitable challenges and conflicts that arise in relationships, and the importance of approaching them with patience, empathy, and a commitment to growth.

Finally, we have discussed the rewards and responsibilities of long-term commitment, and the ongoing effort required to maintain a healthy, vibrant partnership. By consistently investing time, energy, and love into our relationships, we can create a bond that withstands the test of time and provides a source of joy, support, and fulfillment throughout our lives.

As we move forward on this journey of love, it is essential to remember that every relationship is unique, and there is no one-size-fits-all approach to building a strong, lasting connection. By staying attuned to our own needs and the needs of our partner, and by approaching each stage with an open heart and a willingness to learn and grow, we can create a love that is truly extraordinary.

So, let us embrace the challenges and opportunities that each stage of relationship development brings, and trust in the power of love to guide us through the journey ahead. With commitment, compassion, and a spirit of adventure, we can build relationships that not only survive but thrive, and that enrich our lives in countless ways.

Chapter Summary: Building a Strong Foundation for Meaningful Connections

Throughout this chapter, we have explored the fundamental components and principles that form the bedrock of healthy, thriving relationships. By understanding the significance of trust, respect, open communication, and emotional connection, we can cultivate more meaningful and fulfilling connections with others.

Recognizing the different types of relationships in our lives, from romantic partnerships to family bonds and friendships, allows us to appreciate the unique challenges and opportunities that each presents. By familiarizing ourselves with the stages of relationship development, we can navigate the journey of building and maintaining strong connections with greater awareness and intentionality.

Armed with this knowledge, we are better equipped to foster relationships that not only enrich our lives but also contribute to our personal growth and overall well-being. As we move forward, it is essential to remember that building healthy relationships is an ongoing process that requires effort, dedication, and a willingness to learn and grow alongside others.

By laying a strong foundation based on the principles discussed in this chapter, we can create a solid framework for nurturing the relationships that matter most to us. With this understanding, we are now ready to delve deeper into the various aspects of building and maintaining healthy, meaningful connections in the chapters to come.

Chapter 2: Self-Awareness and Personal Growth

The foundation of any strong, healthy relationship lies within ourselves. Before we can truly connect with others, we must first understand who we are, what we value, and how we interact with the world around us. This journey of self-discovery is a crucial step in fostering positive relationships and creating a fulfilling life.

Self-awareness is the key to unlocking our true potential and navigating the complexities of human connections. It involves taking an honest look at our thoughts, emotions, and behaviors, and recognizing how they impact our relationships. By developing a deep understanding of ourselves, we can identify our strengths, weaknesses, and areas for growth, allowing us to make positive changes and become the best version of ourselves.

Emotional intelligence, a closely related concept, plays a vital role in building and maintaining strong relationships. It encompasses the ability to recognize, understand, and manage our own emotions, as well as the emotions of others. By cultivating emotional intelligence, we can improve our communication skills, empathy, and conflict resolution abilities, all of which are essential for creating meaningful and lasting connections.

Personal growth is an ongoing process that requires commitment, courage, and a willingness to step outside of our comfort zones. It involves setting goals, embracing challenges, and learning from our experiences. By continuously working on ourselves and striving for self-improvement, we not only enhance our own lives but also enrich the lives of those around us.

Throughout this chapter, we will explore the importance of self-awareness, personal growth, and emotional intelligence in fostering positive relationships. We will delve into strategies for developing these essential skills and examine how they can transform the way we connect with others. By embarking on this journey of self-discovery and growth, we lay the groundwork for building strong, healthy, and fulfilling relationships that stand the test of time.

Section 1: The Importance of Self-Awareness in Relationships

In the pursuit of nurturing strong, healthy relationships, one of the most crucial yet often overlooked factors is self-awareness. The journey towards building meaningful connections with others begins with a deep understanding of oneself. Self-awareness, the ability to recognize and comprehend our own emotions, thoughts, and behaviors, plays a pivotal role in shaping the dynamics of our relationships.

Imagine embarking on a voyage without a map or compass. Without a clear sense of direction, it becomes challenging to navigate the terrain and reach your desired destination. Similarly, in the realm of relationships, lacking self-awareness can lead to a series of missteps, misunderstandings, and unresolved conflicts. By cultivating a keen sense of self-awareness, we equip ourselves with the tools necessary to build and maintain thriving, authentic connections with others.

The significance of self-awareness in relationships cannot be overstated. It serves as the foundation upon which we can develop emotional intelligence, empathy, and effective communication skills. When we are attuned to our own emotions and triggers, we are better positioned to respond to our partners, friends, and family members with compassion and understanding. Self-awareness allows us to recognize our strengths and weaknesses, enabling us to work on personal growth and foster more fulfilling relationships.

Throughout this section, we will delve into the various aspects of self-awareness and its impact on our relationships. We will explore the art of understanding our own emotions and triggers, learn how to recognize our strengths and weaknesses, and examine the profound influence of self-awareness on communication and conflict resolution. By the end of this section, you will have gained valuable insights and practical strategies to enhance your self-awareness and, in turn, cultivate more meaningful, harmonious relationships.

As we embark on this transformative journey of self-discovery, it is essential to approach the process with an open mind and a willingness to engage in honest self-reflection. The path to greater self-awareness may not always be easy, but the rewards are immeasurable. By investing in your own personal growth and understanding, you are laying the groundwork for healthier, more fulfilling relationships that can withstand the test of time.

So, let us begin this exploration of the critical role of self-awareness in relationships. Together, we will uncover the power of knowing ourselves deeply and how it can transform the way we connect with others. Get ready to embark on a journey of self-discovery that will not only enrich your relationships but also lead to a more authentic and satisfying life.

Subsection 1.1: Understanding Your Own Emotions and Triggers

Embarking on the journey of self-awareness begins with a deep dive into your emotional landscape. Understanding your own emotions and triggers is a crucial step in building and maintaining healthy relationships. By becoming attuned to your inner world, you can navigate the complexities of interpersonal dynamics with greater ease and compassion.

Emotions are the colorful threads that weave the tapestry of our lives. They are the guiding forces that shape our experiences, influencing our thoughts, behaviors, and interactions with others. However, many of us struggle to identify and articulate our emotions, often finding ourselves caught in a whirlwind of confusion and reactivity.

The first step in understanding your emotions is to cultivate a sense of mindfulness. Mindfulness is the practice of bringing your attention to the present moment, observing your thoughts and feelings without judgment. By developing a mindful approach to your emotional experiences, you can begin to recognize patterns and triggers that may be impacting your relationships.

One effective way to identify your emotions is to pay attention to your physical sensations. Emotions often manifest in the body, whether it's a tightness in the chest, a knot in the stomach, or a feeling of warmth in the cheeks. By tuning into these bodily cues, you can start to develop a deeper awareness of your emotional states.

Another crucial aspect of understanding your emotions is recognizing your triggers. Triggers are the specific situations, words, or actions that elicit a strong emotional response within you. These triggers may stem from past experiences, unresolved traumas, or deeply held beliefs. By identifying your triggers, you can begin to develop strategies for managing your emotional reactions in a healthier way.

It's important to note that understanding your emotions and triggers is not about suppressing or avoiding them. Rather, it's about developing a more compassionate and accepting relationship with your inner world. When you can acknowledge and validate your own emotions, you create a foundation of self-awareness that allows you to respond to relationship challenges with greater clarity and resilience.

Journaling can be a powerful tool in the process of emotional self-discovery. By taking the time to write about your experiences, thoughts, and feelings, you can gain valuable insights into your emotional patterns and triggers. Journaling provides a safe space for self-reflection, allowing you to process your emotions and develop a deeper understanding of yourself.

In addition to journaling, seeking the support of a trusted friend, family member, or therapist can be incredibly beneficial in the journey of emotional self-awareness. Sharing your experiences and insights with others can provide valuable perspectives and help you feel less alone in your struggles.

As you continue to explore and understand your own emotions and triggers, remember to approach the process with patience and self-compassion. Developing emotional self-awareness is a lifelong journey, and there will be moments of confusion and setbacks along the way. By remaining committed to the process and treating yourself with kindness, you can cultivate a deeper sense of self-understanding that will serve you well in all your relationships.

Subsection 1.2: Recognizing Your Strengths and Weaknesses

In the pursuit of self-awareness and personal growth, acknowledging both your strengths and weaknesses is a crucial step. By recognizing and embracing these aspects of yourself, you lay the foundation for fostering healthier, more authentic relationships with others.

Strengths are the unique qualities, skills, and talents that define you as an individual. These are the areas in which you excel, the attributes that make you stand out, and the characteristics that contribute to your success and fulfillment. Identifying your strengths allows you to leverage them in your relationships, both personal and professional. When you are aware of your strengths, you can confidently contribute to the growth and well-being of your relationships, offering your unique gifts and abilities to support and uplift those around you.

However, recognizing your strengths is only half the equation. Equally important is acknowledging and accepting your weaknesses. Weaknesses are the areas in which you struggle, the aspects of yourself that may hinder your growth or create challenges in your relationships. These can be personal traits, such as a tendency to procrastinate or a difficulty in expressing emotions, or they can be skills that require further development, such as active listening or effective communication.

Acknowledging your weaknesses takes courage and vulnerability. It requires a willingness to look honestly at yourself, without judgment or self-criticism. By embracing your weaknesses, you create space for growth and improvement. When you are aware of the areas in which you need to develop, you can actively seek out opportunities to learn, grow, and strengthen those aspects of yourself.

Moreover, recognizing your weaknesses allows you to approach your relationships with greater humility and empathy. When you understand that you, too, have areas in which you struggle, you can extend compassion and understanding to others who may be facing their own challenges. This creates a foundation of mutual support and growth within your relationships, as you navigate the ups and downs of life together.

It is important to note that recognizing your strengths and weaknesses is not a one-time event, but rather an ongoing process of self-discovery and reflection. As you grow and evolve, your strengths and weaknesses may shift and change. By remaining open to this process and continually assessing yourself, you can adapt and adjust, ensuring that you are always working towards personal growth and stronger, healthier relationships.

To aid in the process of recognizing your strengths and weaknesses, there are various tools and techniques you can employ. One effective method is to seek feedback from trusted friends, family members, or colleagues. Ask them to share their observations about your strengths and areas for improvement. This external perspective can provide valuable insights and help you see yourself through the eyes of others.

Another useful tool is self-reflection through journaling or meditation. By taking time to quietly reflect on your experiences, thoughts, and emotions, you can gain a deeper understanding of your inner world. Ask yourself questions such as, "What comes naturally to me?" or "In what situations do I feel most challenged?" These introspective practices can help you uncover hidden strengths and identify areas for growth.

Ultimately, recognizing your strengths and weaknesses is a powerful act of self-love and personal growth. By embracing all aspects of yourself, you create a solid foundation for building authentic, meaningful relationships. When you know yourself deeply, you can show up more fully and authentically in your interactions with others, fostering deeper connections and more fulfilling relationships.

Subsection 1.3: The Impact of Self-Awareness on Communication and Conflict Resolution

Effective communication and conflict resolution are cornerstones of healthy, thriving relationships. However, these skills do not develop in a vacuum; they are deeply intertwined with our level of self-awareness. The more attuned we are to our own thoughts, feelings, and behaviors, the better equipped we become to navigate the complexities of interpersonal communication and resolve conflicts with grace and understanding.

Self-awareness is the foundation upon which we build our ability to express ourselves clearly and listen actively to others. When we are in touch with our own emotions and needs, we can communicate them more effectively to our partners, friends, and family members. This clarity of expression reduces the likelihood of misunderstandings and allows others to respond to us with empathy and support.

Moreover, self-awareness enables us to recognize our own communication patterns and potential roadblocks. By understanding our tendencies, such as interrupting others or becoming defensive when faced with criticism, we can consciously work to improve these habits. This self-knowledge empowers us to be more mindful in our interactions, leading to more productive and satisfying conversations.

In the realm of conflict resolution, self-awareness is equally crucial. Conflicts often arise when our own unmet needs, fears, or insecurities are triggered by the words or actions of others. By developing a keen sense of self-awareness, we can identify these triggers and respond to them with greater clarity and composure.

When we are self-aware, we are better able to separate our own emotions from the issue at hand. This emotional regulation allows us to approach conflicts with a more objective and solution-oriented mindset. Instead of reacting impulsively or defensively, we can take a step back, assess the situation, and respond in a manner that promotes understanding and resolution.

Furthermore, self-awareness enables us to recognize our own role in conflicts. By examining our thoughts, feelings, and behaviors, we can identify ways in which we may be contributing to the problem. This introspection allows us to take responsibility for our actions and work towards finding a mutually beneficial solution.

Self-awareness also fosters empathy, a crucial component of effective conflict resolution. When we are in touch with our own emotions, we are better able to understand and relate to the feelings of others. This empathetic understanding creates a safe space for open and honest communication, where both parties feel heard and validated.

Cultivating self-awareness is an ongoing process that requires commitment and practice. One effective way to develop self-awareness is through mindfulness meditation. By regularly taking time to observe our thoughts and feelings without judgment, we can gain a deeper understanding of our inner world and how it influences our interactions with others.

Another valuable tool for enhancing self-awareness is seeking feedback from trusted friends, family members, or a therapist. By inviting others to share their perspectives on our communication style and conflict resolution skills, we can gain valuable insights into areas where we may need to grow and improve.

Ultimately, the impact of self-awareness on communication and conflict resolution cannot be overstated. By developing a deep understanding of ourselves, we lay the groundwork for healthier, more authentic relationships. When we approach interactions with clarity, empathy, and a willingness to grow, we create a space where love, understanding, and connection can flourish.

Summary: Embracing Self-Awareness for Stronger, Healthier Relationships

Throughout this section, we have explored the critical role of self-awareness in building and maintaining healthy relationships. We have discovered that by understanding our own emotions, recognizing our strengths and weaknesses, and cultivating a deep sense of self-knowledge, we lay the foundation for more authentic and fulfilling connections with others.

The journey of self-awareness is ongoing, requiring patience, curiosity, and a willingness to engage in honest self-reflection. By developing a keen understanding of our emotional landscape, we become better equipped to navigate the complexities of interpersonal relationships. We learn to communicate our needs and boundaries more effectively, respond to conflicts with greater clarity and composure, and approach our interactions with empathy and understanding.

Recognizing our strengths and weaknesses is a crucial aspect of self-awareness. By embracing our unique qualities and acknowledging the areas in which we need to grow, we create space for personal development and more authentic connections with others. This self-knowledge allows us to show up more fully in our relationships, offering our best selves while also extending compassion and understanding to those around us.

The impact of self-awareness on communication and conflict resolution cannot be overstated. When we are attuned to our own thoughts, feelings, and behaviors, we can express ourselves more clearly, listen more actively, and approach conflicts with a solution-oriented mindset. By cultivating emotional intelligence and empathy, we create a safe space for open and honest dialogue, fostering deeper understanding and stronger bonds with our loved ones.

As we conclude this section, we encourage you to embrace the transformative power of self-awareness. By committing to the ongoing process of self-discovery and personal growth, you are investing in the health and longevity of your relationships. Remember, the more deeply you know and understand yourself, the more fully you can show up for others, creating a ripple effect of love, compassion, and connection in all your relationships.

So, take a moment to reflect on the insights and strategies shared in this section. Consider how you can integrate these practices into your daily life, nurturing your self-awareness and cultivating more meaningful connections with those who matter most. As you continue on this journey of self-discovery, trust in the power of your own growth and the positive impact it will have on your relationships and overall well-being.

Section 2: Developing Emotional Intelligence

In the realm of relationships, emotional intelligence (EI) emerges as a crucial factor that can make or break the bonds we forge with others. Far beyond mere intellectual prowess, EI encompasses a set of skills that enable us to navigate the complex tapestry of human emotions, both within ourselves and in our interactions with others. As we delve into the concept of emotional intelligence and its profound impact on building strong, healthy relationships, we embark on a transformative journey of self-discovery and interpersonal growth.

Picture a relationship where both partners possess a keen understanding of their own emotions, as well as the ability to empathize with and respond to the feelings of their significant other. Such a relationship is characterized by open communication, mutual respect, and a deep sense of connection. Developing emotional intelligence allows us to create these very foundations, fostering an environment where love, trust, and understanding can flourish.

But what exactly is emotional intelligence, and how can we cultivate it within ourselves? At its core, EI involves the ability to recognize, understand, and manage our own emotions, as well as the capacity to perceive and respond to the emotions of others. It is a skill set that enables us to navigate the often-turbulent waters of human interaction with grace, empathy, and wisdom.

Throughout this section, we will explore the various facets of emotional intelligence and its integral role in building strong, healthy relationships. From understanding the key components of EI to learning practical strategies for enhancing our emotional awareness and regulation, we will embark on a journey of personal growth and relationship transformation. By the end of this section, you will be equipped with the tools and insights necessary to cultivate emotional intelligence within yourself and, in turn, foster more meaningful, fulfilling connections with those around you.

So, let us dive into the fascinating world of emotional intelligence and discover how this essential skill set can revolutionize the way we approach and nurture our relationships. Together, we will uncover the secrets to building the kind of deep, lasting connections that we all yearn for – connections built on a foundation of empathy, understanding, and emotional wisdom.

Subsection 2.1: The Key Components of Emotional Intelligence

As we embark on our journey to understand the profound impact of emotional intelligence on relationships, it is essential to first explore the key components that make up this crucial skill set. Emotional intelligence, or EI, is not a singular trait but rather a complex tapestry woven from various interconnected elements. By identifying and comprehending these fundamental components, we can begin to cultivate a deeper awareness of our own emotions and those of others, laying the groundwork for building strong, healthy relationships.

At the heart of emotional intelligence lies self-awareness, the ability to recognize and understand our own emotions as they arise. This introspective capacity allows us to identify our emotional triggers, acknowledge our strengths and weaknesses, and gain insight into how our feelings influence our thoughts and behaviors. By developing a keen sense of self-awareness, we can better navigate the challenges that inevitably arise in relationships, communicating our needs and boundaries with clarity and confidence.

Closely intertwined with self-awareness is self-regulation, the ability to manage and control our emotional responses in a healthy, constructive manner. This component of EI enables us to pause, reflect, and choose our reactions wisely, rather than being swept away by the heat of the moment. By cultivating self-regulation, we can approach conflicts and disagreements with a level head, fostering an environment of open communication and mutual respect within our relationships.

Empathy, another critical component of emotional intelligence, is the ability to understand and share the feelings of others. This compassionate capacity allows us to step into our partner's shoes, seeing the world through their eyes and validating their experiences. By practicing empathy, we can build deeper, more meaningful connections with our loved ones, creating a safe space for vulnerability and emotional intimacy to flourish.

Motivation, the drive to pursue goals and persevere in the face of challenges, is yet another key aspect of emotional intelligence. In the context of relationships, motivation fuels our desire to continuously work on and improve our connections with others. It propels us to invest time and energy into nurturing our bonds, even when faced with obstacles or setbacks. By harnessing the power of motivation, we can build resilient, long-lasting relationships that weather the storms of life.

Finally, social skills, the ability to communicate effectively, build rapport, and navigate social interactions with ease, round out the key components of emotional intelligence. These skills enable us to express ourselves clearly, listen actively, and respond to others with empathy and understanding. By mastering the art of social interaction, we can create a positive, supportive environment within our relationships, fostering trust, collaboration, and mutual growth.

As we delve deeper into the world of emotional intelligence, it becomes clear that these key components are not separate entities but rather interconnected threads that weave together to create a rich, vibrant tapestry. By understanding and nurturing each of these elements within ourselves, we can cultivate a profound sense of emotional awareness and resilience, laying the foundation for building strong, healthy relationships that stand the test of time.

Subsection 2.2: Strategies for Enhancing Emotional Intelligence

Developing and enhancing emotional intelligence is a transformative journey that requires dedication, self-reflection, and a willingness to embrace personal growth. By cultivating this essential skill set, we can unlock the door to more fulfilling, harmonious relationships and improve our overall quality of life. In this subsection, we will explore practical strategies for enhancing emotional intelligence, empowering you with the tools and techniques necessary to navigate the complex landscape of human emotions and build stronger, more meaningful connections with others.

One of the foundational strategies for enhancing emotional intelligence is the practice of mindfulness. By bringing a gentle, non-judgmental awareness to our present-moment experiences, we can develop a deeper understanding of our own emotions and the emotions of those around us. Mindfulness allows us to step back from the whirlwind of thoughts and feelings that often cloud our perception, creating a space for clarity, insight, and empathy to emerge. Through regular mindfulness practices, such as meditation, deep breathing, or journaling, we can strengthen our capacity for self-awareness and emotional regulation, laying the groundwork for more emotionally intelligent interactions.

Another crucial strategy for enhancing emotional intelligence is active listening. In the context of relationships, truly listening to others involves more than merely hearing their words; it requires a genuine presence, an open heart, and a willingness to understand their perspective. By practicing active listening, we demonstrate empathy, validate our partner's experiences, and foster a sense of trust and connection. This can be achieved by giving our full attention to the speaker, asking clarifying questions, and reflecting back on what we have heard to ensure mutual understanding. Through the art of active listening, we can cultivate deeper, more meaningful relationships built on a foundation of respect and emotional attunement.

Developing self-awareness is another essential strategy for enhancing emotional intelligence. This involves taking an honest, introspective look at our own emotions, thoughts, and behaviors, and understanding how they impact our relationships. By regularly checking in with ourselves, we can identify patterns, triggers, and areas for growth, allowing us to make conscious choices that align with our values and goals. Self-awareness can be cultivated through practices such as self-reflection, seeking feedback from others, and engaging in personal development activities, such as therapy or coaching. As we deepen our self-awareness, we become better equipped to manage our emotions, communicate our needs, and navigate the challenges that arise in our relationships.

Cultivating empathy is a powerful strategy for enhancing emotional intelligence and building stronger, more compassionate relationships. Empathy involves the ability to understand and share the feelings of others, even when their experiences differ from our own. By practicing empathy, we can create a safe, supportive space for our loved ones to express themselves, fostering a deeper sense of connection and understanding. This can be achieved by actively imagining ourselves in our partner's shoes, validating their emotions, and responding with kindness and compassion. Through the practice of empathy, we can build bridges of understanding, heal past wounds, and create relationships that are rooted in love, trust, and mutual respect.

Finally, embracing vulnerability is a courageous strategy for enhancing emotional intelligence and building authentic, intimate relationships. Vulnerability involves the willingness to be open, honest, and transparent about our thoughts, feelings, and experiences, even when it feels uncomfortable or risky. By embracing vulnerability, we create opportunities for deeper connection, emotional healing, and personal growth. This can be achieved by sharing our fears, hopes, and dreams with our loved ones, owning our mistakes and imperfections, and being receptive to the vulnerability of others. As we cultivate a culture of vulnerability in our relationships, we foster an environment of trust, acceptance, and emotional resilience.

Enhancing emotional intelligence is a lifelong journey that requires patience, self-compassion, and a commitment to personal growth. By implementing these practical strategies – mindfulness, active listening, self-awareness, empathy, and vulnerability – we can develop the emotional skills necessary to build strong, healthy relationships that thrive in the face of life's challenges. As we continue to cultivate our emotional intelligence, we open ourselves up to a world of profound connection, understanding, and love, creating a ripple effect that extends far beyond our personal relationships and into the fabric of our communities and the world at large.

Subsection 2.3: The Role of Empathy in Emotional Intelligence and Relationships

In the tapestry of emotional intelligence, empathy emerges as a vital thread, weaving together the fabric of strong, compassionate relationships. Empathy, the ability to understand and share the feelings of others, is a fundamental component of emotional intelligence that enables us to connect with others on a deeper, more meaningful level. As we examine the importance of empathy in the context of emotional intelligence and relationships, we uncover the transformative power of this essential skill in fostering understanding, trust, and emotional intimacy.

At its core, empathy is a bridge that spans the gap between our own experiences and those of others. It is the capacity to step into another person's shoes, to see the world through their eyes, and to feel their emotions as if they were our own. When we cultivate empathy within ourselves, we develop a profound sense of understanding and compassion for those around us, laying the foundation for relationships built on mutual respect, trust, and emotional attunement.

In the realm of emotional intelligence, empathy plays a crucial role in enhancing our ability to navigate the complex landscape of human emotions. By attuning ourselves to the feelings of others, we can respond with sensitivity, kindness, and understanding, even in the face of conflict or disagreement. Empathy allows us to create a safe, supportive space for open communication and emotional expression, fostering an environment where vulnerability is welcomed and emotional wounds can heal.

Moreover, empathy is a catalyst for building strong, resilient relationships that can weather the storms of life. When we approach our interactions with empathy, we create a deep sense of connection and understanding that transcends surface-level differences and challenges. By validating our partner's experiences, listening with an open heart, and responding with compassion, we cultivate a bond that is rooted in trust, respect, and emotional intimacy.

Empathy also plays a vital role in conflict resolution and problem-solving within relationships. When we can truly understand and appreciate our partner's perspective, even when it differs from our own, we open the door to finding mutually satisfying solutions and compromises. By approaching challenges with empathy and a willingness to see things from multiple angles, we can navigate difficult conversations with grace, patience, and understanding, strengthening our relationships in the process.

Cultivating empathy is a lifelong journey that requires practice, self-reflection, and a willingness to step outside of our own experiences.

By engaging in active listening, asking open-ended questions, and seeking to understand rather than judge, we can develop our empathetic capacities and become more emotionally intelligent individuals. As we grow in empathy, we not only enrich our personal relationships but also contribute to building a more compassionate, understanding world.

In the end, empathy is the heartbeat of emotional intelligence and the lifeblood of strong, healthy relationships. By nurturing this essential skill within ourselves, we unlock the door to deeper connection, emotional healing, and personal growth. As we learn to see the world through the eyes of others, we discover the transformative power of empathy in creating a more loving, compassionate, and understanding world, one relationship at a time.

Summary: Cultivating Emotional Intelligence for Stronger, More Fulfilling Relationships

As we conclude our exploration of emotional intelligence and its profound impact on relationships, it becomes clear that developing this essential skill set is a transformative journey that can lead to more fulfilling, harmonious connections with others. By cultivating self-awareness, self-regulation, empathy, motivation, and social skills, we lay the foundation for building strong, healthy relationships that can weather the storms of life and provide a source of joy, support, and personal growth.

Throughout this section, we have delved into the key components of emotional intelligence, examining how each element contributes to our ability to navigate the complex landscape of human emotions and interactions. We have explored practical strategies for enhancing our emotional intelligence, such as practicing mindfulness, engaging in active listening, cultivating self-awareness, and embracing vulnerability. By implementing these techniques and making a commitment to ongoing personal development, we can unlock the door to more emotionally intelligent relationships and improve our overall quality of life.

Moreover, we have highlighted the crucial role of empathy in emotional intelligence and relationships, recognizing its power to foster understanding, trust, and emotional intimacy. By developing our capacity for empathy, we can create a safe, supportive space for open communication, conflict resolution, and emotional healing, strengthening our bonds with others and contributing to a more compassionate world.

As we move forward on our journey of cultivating emotional intelligence, it is essential to remember that this is a lifelong process that requires patience, self-compassion, and a willingness to embrace personal growth. By consistently applying the insights and strategies explored in this section, we can develop the emotional skills necessary to build strong, healthy relationships that thrive in the face of life's challenges and provide a source of deep connection, understanding, and love.

So, let us take the lessons learned from this section and apply them to our daily lives, embracing the transformative power of emotional intelligence in our relationships. As we continue to grow and evolve emotionally, we open ourselves up to a world of profound connection, personal growth, and fulfillment, creating a ripple effect that extends far beyond our personal relationships and into the fabric of our communities and the world at large.

Section 3: Personal Growth and Self-Improvement

In the journey of building and maintaining healthy relationships, personal growth and self-improvement play a crucial role. As individuals, we are constantly evolving, learning, and adapting to new experiences and challenges. By focusing on our own personal development, we not only enhance our self-awareness and emotional intelligence but also cultivate the skills and qualities necessary to foster positive, meaningful connections with others.

Personal growth is a lifelong process that involves setting goals, embracing new experiences, and continuously striving to become the best version of ourselves. When we prioritize our own growth and well-being, we create a strong foundation for building healthy, resilient relationships. By investing in ourselves, we develop a deeper understanding of our own needs, values, and boundaries, enabling us to communicate more effectively and navigate relationship challenges with greater ease.

Self-improvement, on the other hand, involves identifying areas of our lives that we wish to enhance or change and taking proactive steps to make those changes happen. This may include learning new skills, breaking old habits, or adopting new mindsets and behaviors that align with our goals and values. By continuously working on ourselves, we become more confident, resilient, and empathetic, qualities that are essential for building and maintaining strong, positive relationships.

Throughout this section, we will explore the significance of personal growth and self-improvement in the context of relationships. We will delve into the importance of setting personal goals and priorities, developing a growth mindset, and embracing lifelong learning and self-reflection. By understanding the powerful impact of personal development on our relationships, we can cultivate the skills and qualities necessary to build and maintain meaningful, fulfilling connections with the people in our lives.

Subsection 3.1: Setting Personal Goals and Priorities

Setting personal goals and priorities is a fundamental aspect of personal growth and self-improvement. When we take the time to identify what we want to achieve and what matters most to us, we create a roadmap for our personal development journey. This process not only helps us stay focused and motivated but also ensures that our actions and decisions align with our values and contribute to healthier relationships.

To begin setting personal goals, start by reflecting on your life and identifying areas where you want to see improvement or change. Consider your aspirations, dreams, and the kind of person you want to become. Ask yourself questions such as: What do I want to accomplish in the short-term and long-term? What skills do I want to develop? What habits do I want to cultivate or break? By answering these questions honestly and introspectively, you lay the foundation for creating meaningful, achievable goals.

Once you have identified your goals, it's crucial to prioritize them based on their importance and urgency. Not all goals carry equal weight, and it's essential to focus your time and energy on the ones that matter most. Prioritizing your goals helps you allocate your resources effectively and prevents you from spreading yourself too thin. Consider using a framework like the Eisenhower Matrix, which categorizes tasks into four quadrants based on their importance and urgency, to help you prioritize your goals and actions.

When setting goals, it's also important to ensure that they align with your values. Your values are the guiding principles that shape your beliefs, attitudes, and behaviors. They form the core of who you are and what you stand for. By setting goals that are congruent with your values, you create a sense of purpose and fulfillment in your life. You're more likely to stay committed to your goals when they resonate with your deepest beliefs and aspirations.

Moreover, setting personal goals and priorities that align with your values contributes to healthier relationships. When you have a clear sense of who you are and what you stand for, you're better equipped to communicate your needs, desires, and boundaries to others. You're more likely to attract and build relationships with people who share similar values and support your personal growth. By staying true to yourself and your goals, you foster authentic, meaningful connections built on mutual respect and understanding.

In summary, setting personal goals and priorities is a vital step in the journey of personal growth and self-improvement. By identifying what you want to achieve, prioritizing your goals based on importance and urgency, and ensuring that they align with your values, you create a roadmap for your personal development. This process not only helps you stay focused and motivated but also contributes to building healthier, more fulfilling relationships based on authenticity and shared values.

Subsection 3.2: Developing a Growth Mindset

In the pursuit of personal growth and self-improvement, developing a growth mindset is a game-changer. A growth mindset, a concept pioneered by psychologist Carol Dweck, is the belief that one's abilities, intelligence, and talents can be developed and enhanced through dedication and hard work. This perspective stands in stark contrast to a fixed mindset, which assumes that our abilities and traits are static and cannot be significantly altered.

Embracing a growth mindset has a profound impact on both personal development and relationship success. When we adopt this mentality, we view challenges and setbacks as opportunities for learning and growth rather than as insurmountable obstacles or personal failures. We become more resilient, adaptable, and open to new experiences, which are essential qualities for building strong, healthy relationships.

One of the key benefits of a growth mindset is that it fosters a love for learning. Instead of shying away from difficult tasks or new experiences, individuals with a growth mindset actively seek out opportunities to expand their knowledge and skills. They understand that the process of learning and improvement is just as valuable as the end result. This continuous pursuit of personal growth not only enhances self-awareness and emotional intelligence but also makes us more interesting, well-rounded partners in our relationships.

Moreover, a growth mindset promotes a more positive and constructive approach to relationship challenges. When faced with conflicts or disagreements, individuals with a growth mindset are more likely to view these situations as opportunities for learning and growth rather than as threats to their ego or self-worth. They are more open to feedback, willing to take responsibility for their actions, and committed to finding mutually beneficial solutions. This approach fosters a culture of open communication, empathy, and collaboration in relationships, leading to stronger, more resilient connections.

Developing a growth mindset is a process that requires intentional effort and practice. One effective strategy is to reframe negative self-talk and limiting beliefs. Instead of saying, "I'm not good at communication," try, "I'm learning to communicate more effectively every day." By shifting our language and thoughts, we create a more positive and empowering narrative that supports personal growth and relationship success.

Another powerful tool for cultivating a growth mindset is setting learning goals rather than performance goals. Instead of focusing solely on achieving a specific outcome, such as "I want to have the perfect relationship," focus on the process of learning and improvement, such as "I want to learn how to be a more supportive and understanding partner." By prioritizing growth and development, we take the pressure off of achieving perfection and create more opportunities for meaningful progress.

Seeking out role models and mentors who embody a growth mindset can also be incredibly valuable. Surround yourself with individuals who embrace challenges, persist in the face of setbacks, and continuously strive for personal and relational growth. Their examples and guidance can inspire and support you on your own journey of developing a growth mindset.

In summary, developing a growth mindset is a powerful tool for personal development and relationship success. By embracing the belief that our abilities and traits can be developed through dedication and hard work, we become more resilient, adaptable, and open to new experiences. We foster a love for learning, approach challenges with a positive and constructive mindset, and create stronger, more collaborative relationships. Through intentional effort and practice, such as reframing negative self-talk, setting learning goals, and seeking out role models, we can cultivate a growth mindset that transforms our personal growth and relationship success.

Subsection 3.3: Embracing Lifelong Learning and Self-Reflection

In the pursuit of personal growth and stronger relationships, embracing lifelong learning and self-reflection is essential. Lifelong learning is the ongoing, voluntary, and self-motivated pursuit of knowledge and skills for personal and professional development. It extends beyond formal education and encourages individuals to continuously seek opportunities to expand their understanding and capabilities throughout their lives. Self-reflection, on the other hand, is the practice of introspection and self-examination, allowing individuals to gain a deeper understanding of their thoughts, emotions, behaviors, and experiences.

Embracing lifelong learning is a powerful tool for fostering personal growth and enhancing relationships. By actively seeking out new knowledge and skills, individuals can broaden their perspectives, challenge their assumptions, and develop a more well-rounded understanding of themselves and the world around them. This continuous pursuit of learning not only enhances self-awareness and emotional intelligence but also makes individuals more interesting, engaging, and attractive partners in their relationships. When we demonstrate a genuine curiosity and passion for learning, we inspire and motivate others to do the same, creating a positive and growth-oriented dynamic in our relationships.

Moreover, lifelong learning equips individuals with the tools and strategies necessary to navigate the complexities of relationships effectively. By acquiring new communication skills, conflict resolution techniques, and emotional intelligence competencies, individuals can approach relationship challenges with greater confidence, empathy, and resilience. They can adapt to changing circumstances, find creative solutions to problems, and cultivate a more collaborative and understanding approach to building and maintaining strong, healthy relationships.

Self-reflection, in tandem with lifelong learning, is a critical component of personal growth and relationship success. By regularly engaging in introspection and self-examination, individuals can gain a deeper understanding of their own thoughts, emotions, behaviors, and patterns. This heightened self-awareness allows them to identify areas for improvement, recognize their strengths and weaknesses, and make conscious efforts to grow and evolve as individuals and partners.

Through self-reflection, individuals can also develop a greater sense of empathy and understanding towards others. By examining their own experiences, motivations, and challenges, they can better appreciate the perspectives and needs of their partners, family members, and friends. This increased empathy fosters more compassionate, supportive, and understanding relationships, as individuals are better equipped to put themselves in others' shoes and respond with kindness and sensitivity.

To embrace lifelong learning and self-reflection, individuals can adopt several practical strategies. Setting aside dedicated time for learning, whether through reading, attending workshops, or enrolling in courses, can help prioritize personal growth and development. Keeping a journal or engaging in regular self-reflection exercises, such as mindfulness practices or personal assessments, can facilitate deeper introspection and self-awareness. Seeking out mentors, coaches, or therapists who can provide guidance and support on the journey of personal growth can also be incredibly valuable.

Furthermore, creating a culture of lifelong learning and self-reflection within relationships can have a profound impact on their quality and longevity. Encouraging open and honest communication, regularly discussing personal growth goals and challenges, and supporting each other's learning and development initiatives can foster a strong, growth-oriented partnership. By celebrating each other's progress, offering constructive feedback, and holding each other accountable, couples can create a nurturing and empowering environment that promotes ongoing personal and relational growth.

In conclusion, embracing lifelong learning and self-reflection is a vital component of personal growth and stronger relationships. By actively seeking out new knowledge and skills, engaging in regular introspection and self-examination, and adopting practical strategies for growth and development, individuals can cultivate a more self-aware, empathetic, and resilient approach to building and maintaining successful relationships. Through a commitment to ongoing learning and self-reflection, individuals can unlock their full potential, foster more meaningful connections, and create a lasting, positive impact on their personal and relational well-being.

Summary: Cultivating Personal Growth for Stronger Relationships

In this section, we have explored the profound impact of personal growth and self-improvement on fostering positive, healthy relationships. By setting personal goals and priorities, developing a growth mindset, and embracing lifelong learning and self-reflection, individuals can cultivate the skills, qualities, and self-awareness necessary to build and maintain meaningful connections with others.

We have seen how aligning our goals with our values creates a sense of purpose and authenticity in our relationships, attracting partners who share our aspirations and support our growth. By adopting a growth mindset, we become more resilient, adaptable, and open to learning from challenges and setbacks, fostering a positive and collaborative approach to relationship hurdles.

Moreover, by embracing lifelong learning and self-reflection, we continuously expand our knowledge, empathy, and emotional intelligence, becoming more well-rounded and understanding partners. Through regular introspection and a commitment to ongoing growth, we gain a deeper understanding of ourselves and others, enabling us to communicate more effectively, resolve conflicts constructively, and create a nurturing environment for personal and relational development.

As we embark on the journey of personal growth and self-improvement, it is essential to remember that the process is ongoing and ever-evolving. By consistently setting new goals, challenging ourselves to learn and grow, and reflecting on our experiences, we can unlock our full potential and cultivate the most fulfilling, supportive, and enduring relationships possible.

In the next section, we will delve into the common personal barriers that can hinder our growth and relationship success, exploring strategies for overcoming limiting beliefs, healing from past traumas, and developing healthy coping mechanisms. By addressing these challenges head-on and equipping ourselves with the tools for personal development, we lay the foundation for a lifetime of positive, transformative relationships.

Section 4: Overcoming Personal Barriers to Relationship Success

Have you ever found yourself stuck in a pattern of unfulfilling relationships, wondering why you can't seem to achieve the deep, meaningful connections you desire? The truth is, we all carry personal baggage and face internal obstacles that can hinder our ability to build and maintain healthy, thriving relationships. In this section, we'll dive into the common personal barriers that may be holding you back from experiencing the love, trust, and intimacy you deserve.

Picture this: You've just started dating someone new, and things seem to be going well. However, as the relationship progresses, you find yourself plagued by self-doubt, fear of abandonment, or difficulty trusting your partner. These feelings may stem from past relationship traumas, limiting beliefs about yourself or others, or unhealthy coping mechanisms you've developed over time.

Recognizing and addressing these personal barriers is crucial for breaking free from negative patterns and cultivating the kind of relationships you truly want. By exploring your own emotional landscape, challenging limiting beliefs, and developing healthy coping strategies, you can transform your inner world and pave the way for more fulfilling, authentic connections.

Throughout this section, we'll examine the most common personal barriers to relationship success, such as low self-esteem, unresolved past traumas, and fear of vulnerability. We'll provide you with practical tools and techniques for overcoming these obstacles, drawing upon real-life examples, expert insights, and evidence-based strategies.

As you embark on this journey of self-discovery and growth, remember that facing your personal barriers takes courage, patience, and self-compassion. By investing in your own emotional well-being and developing a deeper understanding of yourself, you'll not only enhance your capacity for healthy relationships but also cultivate a greater sense of inner peace and resilience.

So, let's dive in and explore the transformative power of overcoming personal barriers to relationship success. Together, we'll uncover the keys to unlocking your full potential for love, connection, and personal growth.

Subsection 4.1: Identifying and Challenging Limiting Beliefs

Our beliefs shape our reality, influencing how we perceive ourselves, others, and the world around us. When it comes to relationships, limiting beliefs can act as invisible barriers, preventing us from experiencing the depth of connection and personal growth we desire. These beliefs often stem from past experiences, childhood conditioning, or societal messages that we internalize over time.

Identifying your own limiting beliefs is the first step towards breaking free from their grip. Common limiting beliefs in relationships include thoughts such as "I'm not good enough," "I don't deserve love," or "All relationships end in heartbreak." These beliefs can manifest in various ways, such as settling for unfulfilling partnerships, sabotaging healthy connections, or avoiding vulnerability altogether.

To recognize your limiting beliefs, pay attention to the recurring thoughts and patterns that emerge in your relationships. Notice the self-talk that arises when you face challenges or experience emotional triggers. Ask yourself, "What core belief is driving this reaction?" By bringing awareness to these underlying beliefs, you begin to loosen their hold on your life.

Once you've identified your limiting beliefs, the next step is to challenge them. Question the validity of these beliefs by examining the evidence for and against them. Are they based on facts or merely assumptions? Look for examples in your own life or the lives of others that contradict these limiting ideas. Seek out alternative perspectives that empower and inspire you.

As you challenge your limiting beliefs, it's essential to replace them with more empowering and accurate ones. For example, instead of believing that you're unworthy of love, embrace the truth that you are inherently deserving of love and respect. Craft affirmations that align with your desired reality, such as "I am capable of creating healthy, loving relationships" or "I am worthy of an equal and supportive partnership."

Transforming limiting beliefs is an ongoing process that requires patience, self-compassion, and a willingness to step outside your comfort zone. Surround yourself with supportive people who uplift and encourage you. Engage in practices that nurture your self-worth, such as mindfulness, self-care, and pursuing your passions. As you gradually reshape your beliefs, you'll notice a profound shift in the quality of your relationships and your overall sense of well-being.

Remember, your beliefs are not set in stone. You have the power to rewrite the narratives that have held you back and embrace a more empowering, love-filled story. By identifying and challenging your limiting beliefs, you open the door to a world of possibilities in your relationships and personal growth. Embrace the journey of self-discovery, and watch as your connections flourish in ways you never thought possible.

Subsection 4.2: Healing from Past Relationship Traumas

The echoes of past relationship traumas can reverberate through our lives, casting shadows on our present and future connections. Whether it's the lingering pain of a difficult breakup, the scars of betrayal, or the wounds of emotional abuse, these experiences can shape our beliefs, behaviors, and emotional responses in profound ways. Healing from these traumas is a crucial step in building the resilience necessary for cultivating healthy, fulfilling relationships.

Acknowledging the impact of past relationship traumas is the first step towards healing. It's essential to recognize that the pain you experienced was real and valid, and that it's okay to still carry the weight of those memories. Suppressing or denying these emotions can only lead to further distress and hinder your ability to move forward. Instead, create a safe space for yourself to explore and process these feelings, whether through journaling, therapy, or confiding in a trusted friend.

As you navigate the healing process, self-compassion will be your guiding light. Treat yourself with the same kindness, understanding, and empathy you would extend to a beloved friend. Recognize that healing is not a linear journey, and there will be ups and downs along the way. Be patient with yourself and celebrate the small victories, such as setting healthier boundaries or learning to trust again.

One powerful tool for healing is reframing your narrative. Often, we internalize negative beliefs about ourselves or relationships based on past traumas. We might tell ourselves that we are unlovable, unworthy, or destined for heartbreak. Challenge these limiting beliefs by actively seeking evidence to the contrary. Look for examples of healthy, loving relationships in your life or the lives of others. Remind yourself of your inherent worth and the fact that your past experiences do not define your future.

Engaging in self-care practices is another essential aspect of the healing process. Prioritize activities that nourish your mind, body, and soul. This might include practicing mindfulness, engaging in regular exercise, pursuing creative hobbies, or spending time in nature. By taking care of yourself, you send a powerful message that you are worthy of love and respect, both from yourself and others.

As you work towards healing, it's important to set healthy boundaries in your relationships. Learn to communicate your needs and desires clearly, and be willing to walk away from situations or people that compromise your well-being. Surround yourself with supportive, understanding individuals who uplift and encourage you. Seek out relationships that are built on mutual respect, trust, and compassion.

Remember, healing is a journey, not a destination. There may be times when old wounds resurface or new challenges arise. However, by developing resilience and a toolkit of healthy coping mechanisms, you'll be better equipped to navigate these moments with grace and self-assurance. Trust in your own strength and your capacity for growth, and know that with each step, you are moving closer to the loving, fulfilling relationships you deserve.

Subsection 4.3: Developing Healthy Coping Mechanisms and Self-Care Practices

In the face of life's challenges and relationship struggles, it's all too easy to fall into patterns of unhealthy coping mechanisms. Whether it's turning to substances, engaging in self-destructive behaviors, or withdrawing from others, these strategies may provide temporary relief but ultimately lead to greater distress and dysfunction. Developing healthy coping mechanisms and prioritizing self-care are essential for maintaining personal well-being and fostering positive relationships.

The first step in cultivating healthy coping strategies is to identify your current patterns of behavior. Take a moment to reflect on how you typically respond to stress, anxiety, or emotional pain. Do you find yourself reaching for alcohol or unhealthy foods? Do you tend to isolate yourself or lash out at others? By bringing awareness to these automatic reactions, you can begin to make conscious choices to replace them with more adaptive responses.

One of the most effective ways to cope with life's challenges is to build a robust support system. Surround yourself with trusted friends, family members, or a therapist who can offer a listening ear, practical assistance, and emotional validation. Sharing your struggles with others can help alleviate feelings of loneliness and provide a fresh perspective on your situation. Remember, seeking support is a sign of strength, not weakness.

In addition to reaching out to others, it's crucial to develop a repertoire of self-soothing techniques. These practices can help calm your mind, regulate your emotions, and promote a sense of inner peace. Some examples include deep breathing exercises, progressive muscle relaxation, mindfulness meditation, or engaging in creative pursuits like art or music. Experiment with different strategies to find what works best for you, and make them a regular part of your self-care routine.

Self-care extends beyond just managing stress in the moment; it also involves taking proactive steps to nurture your overall well-being. This means prioritizing activities that bring you joy, fulfillment, and a sense of purpose. Engage in hobbies that allow you to express yourself, such as writing, gardening, or playing a musical instrument. Make time for physical exercise, which has been shown to boost mood, reduce stress, and improve overall health. Nourish your body with a balanced diet, adequate sleep, and regular check-ups with healthcare professionals.

Another key aspect of self-care is setting healthy boundaries. Learn to say "no" to commitments or relationships that drain your energy or compromise your values. Communicate your needs and expectations clearly, and be willing to walk away from situations that consistently leave you feeling depleted or disrespected. By honoring your own limits and prioritizing your well-being, you create the space for more fulfilling and reciprocal connections.

As you develop healthy coping mechanisms and self-care practices, be patient with yourself. Breaking old patterns and establishing new habits takes time and effort. Celebrate your progress, no matter how small, and treat yourself with compassion when you stumble. Remember, the goal is not perfection but rather a commitment to ongoing growth and self-discovery.

Ultimately, by investing in your own emotional, physical, and spiritual well-being, you lay the foundation for more resilient and nurturing relationships. When you show up for yourself with kindness and care, you naturally attract others who value and support your authentic self. Embrace the journey of self-care, and watch as your capacity for love, connection, and personal growth expands in ways you never thought possible.

Summary: Embracing the Journey of Personal Growth for Relationship Success

Throughout this section, we've explored the profound impact that personal barriers can have on our ability to cultivate healthy, fulfilling relationships. By delving into the realms of limiting beliefs, past relationship traumas, and unhealthy coping mechanisms, we've shed light on the invisible obstacles that often hold us back from experiencing the love and connection we desire.

However, the journey of overcoming these barriers is not one of despair, but of hope and transformation. By developing self-awareness, challenging limiting beliefs, and embracing the healing process, we open ourselves up to a world of possibility in our relationships. Through the cultivation of self-compassion, the establishment of healthy boundaries, and the prioritization of self-care, we lay the foundation for resilient, nurturing connections that stand the test of time.

As you reflect on the insights and strategies presented in this section, remember that growth is an ongoing process. There will be moments of triumph and moments of struggle, but each step brings you closer to the authentic, loving relationships you deserve. Embrace the journey of self-discovery, and trust in your inherent capacity for resilience and transformation.

Armed with the knowledge and tools to overcome personal barriers, you now stand at the precipice of a new chapter in your relationship journey. In the coming sections, we'll explore the skills and strategies necessary to build and maintain thriving, emotionally intelligent connections. From effective communication to navigating conflict, from cultivating intimacy to fostering forgiveness, the path ahead is rich with opportunities for growth and connection.

So, take a deep breath, and step forward with courage and self-compassion. The journey of overcoming personal barriers is not always easy, but it is always worth it. By investing in your own emotional well-being and committing to the process of personal growth, you open the door to a lifetime of love, joy, and fulfillment in your relationships. Remember, you are worthy of the beautiful connections you seek, and with each step, you draw closer to the life and love you truly deserve.

Chapter Summary: Embracing Self-Awareness and Personal Growth for Stronger Relationships

Throughout this chapter, we have explored the crucial role of self-awareness and personal growth in building and maintaining healthy, positive relationships. By understanding our own emotions, triggers, strengths, and weaknesses, we can navigate relationship challenges more effectively and communicate with greater clarity and empathy.

Developing emotional intelligence is a key component of personal growth and relationship success. By cultivating self-awareness, self-regulation, motivation, empathy, and social skills, we can enhance our ability to connect with others on a deeper, more meaningful level.

Furthermore, embracing a growth mindset and committing to lifelong learning and self-reflection can help us overcome personal barriers, heal from past traumas, and develop resilience in the face of relationship challenges.

By setting personal goals, prioritizing self-care, and developing healthy coping mechanisms, we create a strong foundation for nurturing positive relationships with others. Ultimately, the journey of self-awareness and personal growth is an ongoing process that requires dedication, patience, and a willingness to learn and adapt.

As we continue to invest in our own personal development, we not only improve our own lives but also enhance the quality of our relationships with others. By embracing self-awareness and personal growth, we can build stronger, more fulfilling connections with the people we care about most.

Chapter 3: Effective Communication Skills

Picture this: you're having a conversation with your partner, friend, or family member, and suddenly, you find yourself in the middle of a heated argument. Emotions are running high, and you can't seem to get your point across. You feel frustrated, misunderstood, and disconnected from the person you care about. If this scenario sounds all too familiar, you're not alone. Communication breakdowns are a common challenge in relationships, but the good news is that effective communication skills can be learned and mastered.

In this chapter, we'll explore the essential techniques and strategies for building trust, resolving conflicts, and deepening connections through effective communication. We'll delve into the power of active listening, the art of expressing yourself clearly and assertively, and the importance of nonverbal cues in conveying your message. You'll discover how to navigate difficult conversations with empathy and respect, and how to find common ground even in the midst of disagreements.

But effective communication isn't just about avoiding conflicts and misunderstandings. It's also about fostering a deeper sense of connection and intimacy with the people you care about. When you learn to communicate openly, honestly, and authentically, you create a safe space for vulnerability and emotional intimacy to flourish. You build a foundation of trust and understanding that allows your relationships to grow and thrive.

Throughout this chapter, we'll explore real-life examples and anecdotes that illustrate the transformative power of effective communication. You'll gain practical, actionable tips that you can start implementing in your own relationships right away, whether you're looking to improve your romantic partnership, strengthen your friendships, or build better connections with your family members.

So, if you're ready to take your communication skills to the next level and unlock the full potential of your relationships, let's dive in. By the end of this chapter, you'll have a toolbox full of strategies and techniques that will help you build stronger, more fulfilling connections with the people who matter most to you.

Section 1: The Fundamentals of Effective Communication

Picture this: you're having a conversation with your partner, friend, or family member, but somehow, despite your best efforts, the message you're trying to convey gets lost in translation. Frustration builds, misunderstandings occur, and the relationship suffers. Sound familiar? Effective communication is the cornerstone of any healthy relationship, yet it's a skill that many of us struggle with.

In this section, we'll explore the key principles and elements of effective communication in relationships. We'll dive deep into the art of expressing yourself clearly and concisely, ensuring that your message is heard and understood by your loved ones. You'll discover the power of nonverbal communication and how your body language can either reinforce or undermine your words.

But effective communication isn't just about getting your point across; it's also about adapting your communication style to your audience. What works with your best friend might not work with your romantic partner or your boss. We'll explore how to tailor your approach to different individuals and situations, fostering deeper connections and understanding.

Throughout this section, we'll draw on real-life examples and research-backed insights to illustrate the transformative impact of effective communication on relationships. Whether you're looking to strengthen your romantic partnership, improve your friendships, or build better connections with your family members, the fundamentals covered here will serve as a solid foundation.

So, let's dive in and unlock the secrets to effective communication. By the end of this section, you'll be equipped with the tools and knowledge needed to express yourself authentically, listen actively, and build stronger, more fulfilling relationships with the people who matter most to you.

Subsection 1.1: The Importance of Clear and Concise Messaging

In the world of relationships, few things are as crucial as the ability to communicate effectively. At the heart of this lies the importance of conveying your thoughts and feelings clearly and concisely. When you express yourself in a manner that is easily understood by your partner, friend, or family member, you lay the foundation for a strong, healthy relationship built on trust and mutual understanding.

Imagine a scenario where you're trying to express your concerns about a particular issue to your partner. If your message is convoluted, ambiguous, or laden with unnecessary details, your partner may struggle to grasp the core of your concerns. This can lead to misunderstandings, frustration, and even conflict. On the other hand, when you communicate your thoughts and feelings in a clear, concise manner, your partner is more likely to understand your perspective and respond in a way that addresses your concerns effectively.

The power of clear and concise messaging extends beyond just avoiding misunderstandings. When you express yourself succinctly, you demonstrate respect for your listener's time and attention. In today's fast-paced world, where attention spans are shorter than ever, being able to convey your message quickly and effectively is a valuable skill. It shows that you value your partner's presence and are mindful of their needs.

Moreover, clear communication allows for more productive conversations and problem-solving. When both parties understand each other's perspectives and concerns, they can work together to find solutions and compromises that benefit the relationship as a whole. This is particularly important when navigating difficult or emotionally charged topics, where clarity and concision can help prevent the conversation from derailing into unproductive territory.

So, how can you cultivate the skill of clear and concise messaging? Start by organizing your thoughts before you speak. Take a moment to reflect on what you want to say and how you can express it in the most straightforward manner possible. Use simple, easy-to-understand language and avoid jargon or overly complex vocabulary. Be specific and direct, focusing on the core message you want to convey.

It's also essential to be mindful of your tone and delivery. Even the clearest message can be misinterpreted if delivered in a harsh, sarcastic, or dismissive tone. Aim for a calm, respectful, and empathetic approach, even when discussing difficult topics. This will help create a safe, supportive environment where both parties feel heard and understood.

In summary, clear and concise messaging is a cornerstone of effective communication in relationships. By expressing your thoughts and feelings in a straightforward, easily understandable manner, you can foster deeper connections, avoid misunderstandings, and pave the way for more productive conversations. As you navigate the complexities of relationships, remember that clarity and concision are powerful tools in building strong, healthy bonds with the people who matter most to you.

Subsection 1.2: Nonverbal Communication and Body Language

In the intricate dance of human interaction, communication extends far beyond the spoken word. The way we stand, the gestures we make, and the expressions on our faces all contribute to the messages we convey. Nonverbal communication and body language play a crucial role in effective communication and relationship building, often speaking louder than the words we utter.

Research suggests that a significant portion of our communication is nonverbal. In fact, studies have shown that up to 93% of our communication is conveyed through nonverbal cues, such as facial expressions, tone of voice, and body language. This means that even when we're not speaking, we're still communicating a wealth of information to those around us.

The power of nonverbal communication lies in its ability to convey emotions, attitudes, and intentions that words alone may not be able to express. A warm smile, a gentle touch, or an open posture can communicate feelings of affection, support, and approachability. On the other hand, crossed arms, averted eyes, or a furrowed brow can signal discomfort, defensiveness, or disapproval.

In relationships, being attuned to nonverbal cues can help us better understand our partners, friends, and family members. By paying attention to the subtle shifts in their body language and facial expressions, we can gain insight into their emotional states and respond accordingly. This heightened awareness can foster empathy, compassion, and a deeper sense of connection.

Moreover, our own nonverbal communication can have a profound impact on the quality of our relationships. By consciously aligning our body language with our words and intentions, we can create a sense of congruence and authenticity in our interactions. This can help build trust, rapport, and a positive emotional climate in our relationships.

To harness the power of nonverbal communication, it's essential to develop an awareness of your own body language and the signals you're sending. Start by paying attention to your posture, facial expressions, and gestures during conversations. Are you maintaining eye contact, or are you frequently looking away? Are your arms crossed, or are they relaxed at your sides? These subtle cues can influence how others perceive and respond to you.

It's also important to be mindful of cultural differences in nonverbal communication. What may be considered appropriate or friendly in one culture could be seen as offensive or disrespectful in another. By educating yourself about these cultural nuances and adapting your nonverbal communication accordingly, you can navigate cross-cultural interactions with greater sensitivity and effectiveness.

In addition to being aware of your own nonverbal cues, it's equally important to develop your skills in reading and interpreting the body language of others. This involves paying close attention to their facial expressions, eye contact, posture, and gestures, and considering these cues in the context of the overall situation. By becoming a more skilled observer of nonverbal communication, you can gain valuable insights into the thoughts, feelings, and intentions of those around you.

Ultimately, the power of nonverbal communication lies in its ability to enhance our understanding of others and ourselves. By embracing the subtle yet profound language of the body, we can create more authentic, empathetic, and fulfilling relationships with the people in our lives. As you navigate the complexities of human interaction, remember that sometimes, the most important messages are the ones that are left unspoken.

Subsection 1.3: Adapting Your Communication Style to Your Audience

In the tapestry of human interaction, effective communication is the thread that weaves relationships together. However, the art of communication is not a one-size-fits-all approach. To truly connect with others and foster understanding, it is essential to adapt your communication style to suit your audience. By tailoring your approach to different individuals and situations, you can bridge gaps, build rapport, and create a foundation for strong, lasting relationships.

Picture yourself in a conversation with a close friend. Your communication style is likely to be casual, filled with inside jokes, and peppered with shared experiences. Now, imagine yourself in a professional setting, discussing a project with a colleague. In this context, your communication style would be more formal, focused on the task at hand, and centered around shared goals. These two scenarios illustrate the importance of adapting your communication style to your audience.

The key to successful audience adaptation lies in understanding the unique needs, preferences, and characteristics of the person or group you are communicating with. This involves taking into account factors such as age, cultural background, personality, and relationship dynamics. By considering these elements, you can adjust your language, tone, and approach to create a communication experience that resonates with your audience.

For instance, when communicating with an older family member, you may need to speak more slowly, use simpler language, and provide more context to ensure understanding. On the other hand, when interacting with a younger audience, such as your children or students, you may need to use more engaging, interactive communication techniques to capture and maintain their attention.

Cultural differences also play a significant role in communication style adaptation. What may be considered appropriate or effective in one cultural context may not be so in another. By educating yourself about the communication norms and expectations of different cultures, you can navigate cross-cultural interactions with greater sensitivity and effectiveness. This involves being mindful of nonverbal cues, communication patterns, and cultural values that may influence how your message is received and interpreted.

In addition to considering the characteristics of your audience, adapting your communication style also involves being attuned to the situational context. The way you communicate in a high-stakes business meeting will differ from how you interact with friends over a casual dinner. By assessing the formality of the situation, the level of familiarity with your audience, and the goals of the interaction, you can adjust your communication style to fit the context.

To effectively adapt your communication style, it is crucial to develop a repertoire of communication techniques and strategies. This involves honing your skills in active listening, empathy, assertiveness, and flexibility. By actively listening to your audience, you can gain valuable insights into their perspectives, needs, and concerns. Empathy allows you to put yourself in their shoes and communicate in a way that demonstrates understanding and compassion. Assertiveness enables you to express your own thoughts and needs clearly and confidently, while flexibility allows you to adjust your approach as needed to maintain effective communication.

Ultimately, adapting your communication style to your audience is an ongoing process of learning, experimentation, and refinement. It requires a willingness to step outside your comfort zone, embrace different perspectives, and continuously improve your communication skills. By mastering the art of audience adaptation, you can create more meaningful, effective, and satisfying interactions with the people in your life, fostering deeper connections and understanding.

In a world where communication is the bedrock of relationships, the ability to adapt your communication style to your audience is a superpower. By tailoring your approach to the unique needs and characteristics of those you interact with, you can navigate the complexities of human interaction with greater ease, empathy, and effectiveness. As you embark on your journey to become a master communicator, remember that the key to unlocking the hearts and minds of others lies in your willingness to meet them where they are.

Summary: Mastering the Fundamentals of Effective Communication

Throughout this section, we've explored the fundamental principles and elements of effective communication in relationships. We've delved into the importance of clear and concise messaging, the power of nonverbal communication and body language, and the art of adapting your communication style to your audience.

By mastering these key aspects of communication, you can create a solid foundation for building strong, healthy, and fulfilling relationships. When you express yourself clearly and concisely, you minimize misunderstandings and foster a deeper sense of connection with your loved ones. By becoming attuned to the subtle nuances of nonverbal communication, you can gain valuable insights into the thoughts and feelings of others, and respond with empathy and understanding.

Moreover, by adapting your communication style to suit the unique needs and characteristics of your audience, you can navigate the complexities of human interaction with greater ease and effectiveness. Whether you're communicating with a partner, friend, family member, or colleague, the ability to tailor your approach is essential for building rapport, trust, and mutual understanding.

As you move forward on your journey to becoming a master communicator, remember that effective communication is an ongoing process of learning, growth, and refinement. By continually honing your skills, embracing new perspectives, and remaining open to feedback, you can cultivate a communication style that is authentic, empathetic, and transformative.

So, take the insights and strategies you've learned in this section and begin applying them to your own relationships. Start by practicing clear and concise messaging, paying attention to your own nonverbal cues, and adapting your communication style to different individuals and situations. With time and practice, you'll find that the fundamentals of effective communication become second nature, allowing you to build deeper, more meaningful connections with the people who matter most to you.

Remember, the power to transform your relationships lies within your own hands. By mastering the fundamentals of effective communication, you can unlock the door to a world of greater understanding, empathy, and connection. So, go forth and communicate with confidence, knowing that you have the tools and knowledge necessary to build the strong, healthy, and fulfilling relationships you deserve.

Section 2: Mastering the Art of Active Listening

In the tapestry of human relationships, communication serves as the thread that weaves hearts and minds together. At the core of effective communication lies the transformative power of active listening. More than merely hearing words, active listening is an art that involves fully engaging with your conversation partner, seeking to understand their thoughts, feelings, and experiences on a profound level.

As we embark on this journey to master the art of active listening, we will explore the myriad ways in which this essential skill can enrich and deepen your relationships. From building trust and fostering empathy to navigating conflicts and strengthening bonds, active listening is a catalyst for positive change in all aspects of your interpersonal connections.

Throughout this section, we will delve into the benefits of active listening, equipping you with practical techniques and strategies to become a more attentive, engaged, and compassionate listener. We will also explore common barriers to effective listening and provide guidance on how to overcome them, ensuring that you can create a safe and supportive space for meaningful dialogue.

Whether you seek to improve your romantic partnership, strengthen your family ties, or cultivate more fulfilling friendships, mastering the art of active listening is a transformative step on the path to building authentic, lasting connections. By fully embracing the power of presence, empathy, and understanding, you will unlock the potential for deeper intimacy, trust, and mutual growth in all your relationships.

As we embark on this section, approach the content with an open heart and a curious mind. Embrace the opportunity to refine your listening skills, and witness the profound impact it can have on your ability to connect, support, and understand others on a deeper level. Together, let us explore the transformative potential of active listening and discover how this essential skill can enrich your relationships and enhance your life.

Subsection 2.1: The Benefits of Active Listening in Relationships

In the intricate dance of human connection, active listening emerges as a powerful tool for strengthening the bonds that tie us together. It is through the art of attentive, empathetic listening that we create a sacred space for our loved ones to share their thoughts, feelings, and experiences without fear of judgment or interruption. When we fully engage in active listening, we send a clear message to our conversation partner: "I am here, I value your perspective, and I am committed to understanding you on a deeper level."

The benefits of active listening in relationships are far-reaching and transformative. By giving our undivided attention and creating a safe, supportive environment for open communication, we lay the foundation for trust to flourish. Trust is the bedrock upon which all healthy relationships are built, and active listening is a key ingredient in its development. When our loved ones feel truly heard and understood, they are more likely to open up, share their vulnerabilities, and forge deeper connections with us.

Moreover, active listening fosters a sense of validation and empathy in our relationships. When we take the time to listen attentively and reflect back on what our conversation partner has shared, we demonstrate that their thoughts and feelings matter to us. This validation can be incredibly healing and empowering, particularly in moments of conflict or distress. By showing our loved ones that we are genuinely interested in their perspective, we create a space for mutual understanding and empathy to grow.

Active listening also plays a crucial role in preventing misunderstandings and resolving conflicts in relationships. When emotions run high, it is all too easy to fall into the trap of reactive listening, where we focus more on formulating our response than on truly understanding our partner's point of view. By practicing active listening, we can break this cycle and approach conflicts with a more open, curious mindset. By seeking to understand rather than to be understood, we can identify the root causes of our disagreements and work together to find mutually satisfying solutions.

In addition to its benefits in conflict resolution, active listening can also enhance our ability to provide emotional support and comfort to our loved ones. When we listen with empathy and compassion, we create a safe haven for our conversation partners to express their fears, doubts, and vulnerabilities. By offering a non-judgmental, supportive presence, we can help our loved ones feel less alone in their struggles and more equipped to face life's challenges.

Ultimately, the power of active listening lies in its ability to deepen our connections with others and foster a greater sense of intimacy in our relationships. By fully engaging in the present moment, setting aside our own agendas, and seeking to understand our loved ones on a profound level, we create a space for genuine, heartfelt connection to flourish. As we master the art of active listening, we open ourselves up to a world of richer, more fulfilling relationships built on a foundation of trust, empathy, and mutual understanding.

Subsection 2.2: Techniques for Effective Active Listening

The journey towards becoming a more attentive and engaged listener begins with a commitment to mastering the techniques of effective active listening. These techniques serve as powerful tools in your communication toolkit, enabling you to create a safe, supportive space for your conversation partner to share their thoughts and feelings. By employing these strategies consistently, you can cultivate a deeper sense of understanding, empathy, and connection in your relationships.

One of the cornerstone techniques of effective active listening is to give your undivided attention to your conversation partner. This means setting aside distractions, such as electronic devices or competing thoughts, and fully focusing on the person speaking. Maintain eye contact, if culturally appropriate, and use open, inviting body language to signal your engagement. By giving your full attention, you demonstrate respect and genuine interest in understanding your partner's perspective.

Another essential technique is to practice reflective listening, which involves paraphrasing or summarizing your conversation partner's words to ensure accurate understanding. This technique allows you to clarify any ambiguities and convey that you are genuinely listening and processing the information shared. For example, you might say, "What I'm hearing is that you feel overwhelmed by the recent changes at work. Is that correct?" By reflecting back on what you've heard, you provide an opportunity for your partner to confirm or clarify their message, promoting clearer communication.

Asking open-ended questions is another powerful active listening technique that encourages your conversation partner to elaborate on their thoughts and feelings. Open-ended questions typically begin with "what," "how," or "why," and invite a more detailed response than closed-ended questions, which can be answered with a simple "yes" or "no." For instance, instead of asking, "Did you have a good day?" you might inquire, "What were some of the highlights of your day?" This approach demonstrates your genuine curiosity and desire to gain a deeper understanding of your partner's experiences.

In addition to verbal techniques, effective active listening also involves paying attention to nonverbal cues, such as facial expressions, tone of voice, and body language. These nonverbal signals often convey important information about your conversation partner's emotional state and can provide valuable context for their words. By remaining attuned to these cues, you can respond with greater empathy and sensitivity, fostering a more supportive and understanding communication dynamic.

It is also crucial to practice patience and resist the urge to interrupt or offer unsolicited advice when actively listening. Allow your conversation partner the space to express themselves fully without rushing to fill silences or offer solutions. Remember that active listening is not about fixing problems or providing immediate answers, but rather about creating a supportive environment for your partner to process their thoughts and emotions at their own pace.

Finally, effective active listening involves maintaining an open, non-judgmental attitude throughout the conversation. Suspend your own biases, assumptions, and preconceived notions, and approach the interaction with a genuine desire to understand your partner's unique perspective. By creating a safe, non-judgmental space, you encourage your conversation partner to share more openly and honestly, deepening the level of trust and intimacy in your relationship.

As you integrate these techniques into your communication repertoire, remember that active listening is a skill that requires ongoing practice and refinement. Be patient with yourself and celebrate the small victories as you become a more attentive, engaged, and empathetic listener. With dedication and persistence, you will find that the art of effective active listening has the power to transform your relationships, fostering deeper understanding, trust, and connection with those who matter most.

Subsection 2.3: Overcoming Barriers to Active Listening

In our journey to master the art of active listening, it is essential to recognize and address the various obstacles that can hinder our ability to fully engage in the process. These barriers, ranging from external distractions to internal biases and emotional triggers, can prevent us from truly hearing and understanding our conversation partners. By identifying and proactively addressing these challenges, we can cultivate a more focused, empathetic, and effective approach to active listening.

One of the most common barriers to active listening is the presence of external distractions. In today's fast-paced, technology-driven world, it is all too easy to become sidetracked by the constant barrage of notifications, emails, and social media alerts that vie for our attention. To overcome this obstacle, it is crucial to create a dedicated space for active listening, free from the intrusion of digital distractions. This may involve silencing or turning off electronic devices, finding a quiet and private location for important conversations, and consciously choosing to prioritize the present moment over competing demands.

Another significant barrier to active listening is the influence of our own internal biases, prejudices, and preconceived notions. We all carry with us a unique set of experiences, beliefs, and assumptions that shape our perceptions of the world around us. When engaging in active listening, it is essential to recognize and set aside these biases, approaching the conversation with an open and curious mindset. This requires a willingness to challenge our own assumptions, consider alternative perspectives, and resist the temptation to jump to conclusions or pass judgment based on limited information.

Emotional triggers can also pose a significant challenge to effective active listening. When a conversation touches upon sensitive or emotionally charged topics, it can be difficult to maintain a calm, non-reactive presence. Our own unresolved issues, past traumas, or deeply held beliefs can color our interpretation of the speaker's words, leading to defensive reactions or a breakdown in communication. To navigate these emotional barriers, it is important to cultivate self-awareness and practice emotional regulation techniques, such as deep breathing, grounding exercises, or mindfulness meditation. By learning to recognize and manage our own emotional responses, we can create a more stable and supportive environment for active listening.

In addition to these internal barriers, the fast pace and competing demands of modern life can also hinder our ability to fully engage in active listening. In a world that often prioritizes speed and efficiency over depth and connection, it can be challenging to carve out the time and mental space necessary for truly attentive listening. To overcome this obstacle, it is important to consciously prioritize active listening as a valuable investment in our relationships and personal growth. This may involve setting aside dedicated time for important conversations, practicing saying "no" to non-essential commitments, and cultivating a greater sense of presence and mindfulness in our daily interactions.

Finally, cultural differences and communication styles can also present barriers to active listening. In an increasingly diverse and globalized world, we are likely to encounter individuals from a wide range of backgrounds, each with their own unique ways of expressing themselves and interpreting information. To bridge these cultural gaps and ensure effective communication, it is essential to approach active listening with a spirit of cultural humility and a willingness to learn. This may involve educating ourselves about different communication norms and styles, practicing non-judgmental curiosity, and being open to adapting our own listening approach to better meet the needs of our conversation partners.

As we work to overcome these various barriers to active listening, it is important to remember that the process is one of ongoing growth and development. By remaining committed to self-reflection, continuous learning, and a genuine desire to understand others, we can gradually dismantle the obstacles that stand in the way of truly effective communication. Through patience, persistence, and a willingness to embrace the challenges inherent in active listening, we can cultivate the skills necessary to foster deeper, more meaningful connections with those around us.

Summary: Cultivating Deeper Connections Through Active Listening

Throughout this section, we have explored the transformative power of active listening in fostering deeper, more meaningful connections with others. By mastering the techniques of effective listening, such as giving undivided attention, practicing reflective listening, asking open-ended questions, and remaining attuned to nonverbal cues, we can create a safe and supportive space for our loved ones to share their thoughts and feelings. We have also examined the various barriers that can hinder our ability to fully engage in active listening, including external distractions, internal biases, emotional triggers, and cultural differences.

As we conclude this section, it is essential to recognize that the journey towards becoming a more attentive and empathetic listener is an ongoing process of growth and self-reflection. By remaining committed to practicing these skills and overcoming the obstacles that stand in our way, we can cultivate a greater sense of understanding, trust, and intimacy in our relationships. Through the art of active listening, we have the power to transform our connections with others, creating a more compassionate and supportive world, one conversation at a time.

As you move forward, take the insights and techniques you have learned and apply them to your daily interactions. Embrace the challenges and rewards of active listening, and witness the profound impact it can have on your ability to connect with others on a deeper level. Remember, the gift of your full presence and undivided attention is one of the most precious offerings you can give to those you care about. By mastering the art of active listening, you are not only investing in the health and longevity of your relationships but also in your own personal growth and emotional well-being.

Section 3: Communicating in Challenging Situations

Relationships, no matter how strong and healthy, are bound to face challenges and conflicts from time to time. When emotions run high, and tensions arise, it can be difficult to maintain effective communication and navigate these rocky waters. However, the way we approach and handle these challenging situations can make all the difference in the strength and resilience of our relationships.

In this section, we will explore strategies for communicating effectively during conflicts and disagreements. We will delve into the art of approaching difficult conversations with empathy and respect, even when emotions are running high. You will learn techniques for managing your own emotions and responding constructively to others' feelings during heated exchanges, allowing you to maintain a level-headed and productive dialogue.

We will also discuss the importance of finding common ground and compromising in resolving conflicts. By identifying shared interests, values, and goals, you can work together to find mutually beneficial solutions and strengthen your bond. Additionally, we will explore the power of using "I" statements in conflict resolution, a technique that allows you to express your feelings and needs without placing blame or criticism on your partner, fostering a more collaborative and understanding environment.

Throughout this section, we will emphasize the importance of active listening, empathy, and patience in navigating challenging situations. By approaching conflicts with an open mind and a willingness to understand your partner's perspective, you can transform potentially damaging disagreements into opportunities for growth, learning, and deeper connection.

So, whether you're facing a minor disagreement or a major conflict, the strategies and insights in this section will equip you with the tools you need to communicate effectively, resolve issues constructively, and emerge from challenging situations with a stronger, more resilient relationship.

Subsection 3.1: Approaching Difficult Conversations with Empathy and Respect

Engaging in difficult conversations is an inevitable part of any relationship, whether it's with a romantic partner, family member, or close friend. These challenging discussions can arise from a variety of situations, such as differing opinions, unmet expectations, or hurtful actions. When emotions run high, it's easy to become defensive, accusatory, or dismissive, which can quickly escalate the situation and cause further damage to the relationship. However, by approaching these conversations with empathy and respect, you can create a safe and productive space for both parties to express their feelings and work towards a resolution.

The first step in navigating a difficult conversation is to prepare yourself mentally and emotionally. Take a moment to reflect on your own feelings and the potential perspective of the other person. Try to put yourself in their shoes and consider how they might be experiencing the situation. This exercise in empathy will help you approach the conversation with a more open and understanding mindset, rather than a combative or judgmental one.

When initiating the conversation, choose a time and place that is conducive to a private, uninterrupted discussion. Avoid starting the conversation when either party is already stressed, tired, or emotionally charged. Begin by expressing your desire to have an open, honest dialogue and emphasize the importance of the relationship. Use "I" statements to express your feelings and concerns, rather than "you" statements, which can come across as accusatory or blaming. For example, instead of saying, "You never listen to me," try saying, "I feel unheard when I express my concerns."

As the conversation progresses, make a conscious effort to listen actively and attentively to the other person's perspective. Avoid interrupting, dismissing, or minimizing their feelings. Instead, show genuine interest and concern for their experiences and emotions. Ask clarifying questions to better understand their point of view and acknowledge the validity of their feelings, even if you don't necessarily agree with their perspective.

Maintain a calm, respectful tone throughout the conversation, even if the other person becomes emotional or confrontational. Avoid using sarcasm, criticism, or contempt, as these behaviors can quickly derail the discussion and cause further hurt. If the conversation becomes heated or unproductive, suggest taking a brief break to allow both parties to collect their thoughts and regain composure.

Throughout the discussion, focus on finding common ground and working towards a mutually beneficial solution. Avoid making demands or ultimatums, and instead, approach the conversation as a collaborative effort to improve the relationship. Be willing to compromise and make concessions where appropriate, while also standing firm on your own needs and boundaries.

Remember, the goal of a difficult conversation is not to "win" or prove the other person wrong, but rather to deepen understanding, resolve conflicts, and strengthen the relationship. By approaching these challenging discussions with empathy, respect, and a genuine desire for resolution, you can navigate even the most difficult conversations and emerge with a stronger, more resilient bond.

Subsection 3.2: Managing Emotions During Conflicts

Conflicts and disagreements can be emotionally charged situations that test the strength and resilience of any relationship. When emotions run high, it can be challenging to maintain a clear perspective and communicate effectively. However, learning to manage your own emotions and respond constructively to others' feelings during heated exchanges is a crucial skill for navigating conflicts and preserving the health of your relationships.

One of the first steps in managing emotions during conflicts is to recognize and acknowledge your own emotional state. Take a moment to check in with yourself and identify the feelings that are surfacing, such as anger, frustration, hurt, or fear. By naming and accepting your emotions, you can begin to process them more objectively and prevent them from overwhelming you or clouding your judgment.

Once you have acknowledged your emotions, focus on regulating them. Take deep, calming breaths to slow down your physiological response and reduce the intensity of your feelings. If necessary, take a brief break from the conversation to collect your thoughts and regain composure. During this time, engage in self-soothing techniques, such as progressive muscle relaxation or positive self-talk, to help you maintain a more balanced emotional state.

When you feel ready to re-engage in the conversation, practice active listening and empathy. Make a conscious effort to understand and validate the other person's emotions, even if you don't agree with their perspective. Use phrases like, "I can see how that would be frustrating," or "It sounds like you're feeling really hurt right now," to show that you acknowledge and respect their feelings. By demonstrating empathy, you create a more supportive and collaborative environment that can help diffuse tension and promote more productive dialogue.

As you express your own thoughts and feelings, focus on using "I" statements to communicate your experiences without placing blame or criticism on the other person. For example, instead of saying, "You always shut down when we argue," try saying, "I feel disconnected when we have difficulty communicating during conflicts." By owning your emotions and experiences, you take responsibility for your role in the conversation and avoid putting the other person on the defensive.

Throughout the conversation, maintain a calm and respectful tone, even if the other person becomes emotionally reactive. Avoid responding with anger, sarcasm, or contempt, as these behaviors can escalate the conflict and cause further damage to the relationship. Instead, focus on expressing your feelings and needs clearly and assertively, while remaining open to finding a mutually beneficial solution.

It's important to remember that managing emotions during conflicts is a skill that requires practice and patience. Be kind to yourself and your partner as you navigate these challenging situations, and celebrate the progress you make in regulating your emotions and communicating more effectively. With time and effort, you can develop greater emotional resilience and strengthen your ability to handle conflicts in a constructive, relationship-enhancing way.

Subsection 3.3: Finding Common Ground and Compromise

In the midst of conflicts and disagreements, it can be challenging to see eye-to-eye with your partner or loved one. However, finding common ground and reaching compromises are essential skills for resolving disputes and maintaining a healthy, long-lasting relationship. By focusing on shared interests, values, and goals, you can shift the conversation from a combative, "me vs. you" mentality to a collaborative, "us vs. the problem" approach.

To begin the process of finding common ground, take a step back from the specific issue at hand and consider the broader context of your relationship. Reflect on the foundational elements that brought you together, such as shared values, dreams, and aspirations. These commonalities can serve as a reminder of the strong bond you share and provide a starting point for productive problem-solving.

When discussing the conflict, make a conscious effort to identify areas of agreement, no matter how small they may seem. Acknowledge and validate the points on which you both agree, and use these as building blocks for finding a mutually satisfactory solution. By focusing on the common ground, you create a more positive and collaborative atmosphere that encourages open communication and reduces defensiveness.

As you explore potential solutions, be willing to consider your partner's perspective and needs alongside your own. Engage in active listening and seek to understand their point of view, even if you don't fully agree with it. By demonstrating empathy and respect for their position, you foster a more supportive and understanding environment that promotes compromise.

When proposing solutions, aim for a balanced approach that takes both parties' needs and concerns into account. Be willing to make concessions and find middle ground, while also advocating for your own needs and boundaries. Remember that compromise doesn't mean sacrificing your values or self-worth; rather, it involves finding a mutually beneficial solution that honors both individuals' needs and priorities.

In some cases, finding common ground and reaching a compromise may require thinking outside the box and exploring creative solutions. Be open to brainstorming and considering unconventional ideas that may not have been immediately apparent. By approaching the problem with a flexible and open mindset, you increase the likelihood of discovering a resolution that works for both parties.

Throughout the process of finding common ground and compromise, maintain a focus on the long-term health and well-being of your relationship. Recognize that resolving conflicts is not about winning or losing, but rather about strengthening your bond and growing together as a couple. By prioritizing your shared interests, values, and goals, you can navigate even the most challenging disagreements and emerge with a stronger, more resilient relationship.

Subsection 3.4: The Power of "I" Statements in Conflict Resolution

In the heat of conflict, it's easy to fall into the trap of using accusatory or blaming language, which can quickly escalate tensions and create a defensive atmosphere. However, by employing "I" statements, you can express your feelings and needs in a non-confrontational manner, promoting more effective communication and problem-solving.

"I" statements are a powerful tool for conveying your emotions and experiences without placing blame or criticism on the other person. They allow you to take ownership of your feelings and express them in a way that is less likely to trigger a defensive response from your partner. By focusing on your own experiences, you create a more supportive and collaborative environment that encourages open dialogue and mutual understanding.

The structure of an "I" statement typically follows this format: "I feel [emotion] when [situation or behavior] because [reason or impact]." For example, instead of saying, "You never listen to me," which places blame on the other person, you might say, "I feel unheard when I express my concerns because it makes me feel like my thoughts and feelings aren't valued." By framing your statement in this way, you clearly express your emotions and the impact of the situation without attacking or criticizing your partner.

Using "I" statements not only helps you communicate your feelings more effectively but also encourages your partner to respond with empathy and understanding. When you express your emotions in a non-threatening manner, your partner is more likely to listen attentively and consider your perspective. This, in turn, creates a more supportive and collaborative atmosphere that facilitates problem-solving and compromise.

It's important to note that using "I" statements doesn't guarantee that your partner will always agree with your perspective or that conflicts will be resolved immediately. However, they do provide a foundation for more productive and respectful communication, which is essential for navigating disagreements and finding mutually beneficial solutions.

When incorporating "I" statements into your communication during conflicts, be sure to use them genuinely and authentically. Avoid using them as a way to disguise criticism or manipulate the conversation. Instead, focus on expressing your true feelings and needs in a clear, concise, and non-judgmental manner.

In addition to using "I" statements, it's essential to practice active listening when your partner is expressing their own feelings and needs. Give them your full attention, avoid interrupting, and seek to understand their perspective. By demonstrating empathy and respect for their experiences, you create a more supportive and collaborative environment that promotes effective problem-solving.

Incorporating "I" statements into your communication toolkit can be a game-changer for navigating conflicts and disagreements in your relationships. By expressing your feelings and needs in a non-confrontational manner, you foster a more supportive and understanding atmosphere that encourages open dialogue, empathy, and collaborative problem-solving. With practice and patience, using "I" statements can become a natural part of your communication style, helping you build stronger, more resilient relationships that can weather even the most challenging conflicts.

Summary: Navigating Challenges with Empathy and Understanding

Communicating effectively during conflicts and disagreements is a vital skill for maintaining healthy, long-lasting relationships. By approaching challenging situations with empathy, respect, and a focus on finding common ground, you can transform potential roadblocks into opportunities for growth and connection.

Throughout this section, we've explored various strategies for navigating difficult conversations, managing emotions, and reaching compromises. From preparing yourself mentally and emotionally to practicing active listening and using "I" statements, these techniques provide a foundation for more productive and respectful communication.

Remember, the goal of communicating during conflicts is not to emerge victorious or prove the other person wrong, but rather to deepen understanding, resolve differences, and strengthen your bond. By prioritizing empathy, collaboration, and a willingness to find mutually beneficial solutions, you can cultivate a more supportive and resilient relationship that can withstand even the most challenging of circumstances.

As you move forward, take the insights and strategies discussed in this section and apply them to your own relationships. Embrace the power of empathetic communication, and approach conflicts as opportunities to learn, grow, and connect with your loved ones on a deeper level. With practice, patience, and a commitment to understanding, you can navigate any challenging situation and emerge with a stronger, more loving relationship.

Section 4: Harnessing the Power of Positive Communication

In the realm of relationships, the way we communicate with our partners, family members, and friends plays a crucial role in shaping the quality and longevity of our connections. The power of positive communication cannot be overstated, as it has the ability to transform even the most challenging relationships into sources of joy, support, and personal growth. By embracing affirming and supportive communication strategies, we can cultivate a deeper sense of understanding, trust, and intimacy with the people who matter most to us.

Imagine a relationship where every interaction is infused with kindness, empathy, and a genuine desire to uplift and encourage one another. A relationship where conflicts are approached with a spirit of collaboration and a focus on finding mutually beneficial solutions. This is the essence of positive communication – a way of relating to others that prioritizes connection, growth, and the nurturing of a strong, resilient bond.

In this section, we will embark on a journey to explore the profound impact of positive communication on relationship satisfaction. We will delve into the science behind the power of affirmative language, active listening, and empathetic responses, and how these elements contribute to creating a more harmonious and fulfilling relational dynamic. Through real-life examples, practical strategies, and evidence-based insights, you will gain the tools and knowledge necessary to transform your communication style and, in turn, enhance the quality of your relationships.

Whether you are seeking to strengthen your romantic partnership, deepen your friendships, or foster more meaningful connections with family members, the principles of positive communication can be applied to all areas of your interpersonal life. By committing to a more affirming and supportive approach to communication, you will not only improve the health and happiness of your relationships but also cultivate a greater sense of personal well-being and resilience.

So, let us embark on this transformative journey together, as we explore the power of positive communication and unlock the full potential of our relationships. Get ready to discover how small shifts in your communication style can lead to profound changes in the way you connect with others and experience the joys of a more loving, supportive, and fulfilling relational landscape.

Subsection 4.1: The Benefits of Positive Communication in Relationships

Positive communication is a powerful tool that can transform the dynamics of any relationship, be it romantic, familial, or platonic. When we engage in affirming, supportive, and empathetic communication with our loved ones, we create an environment that fosters growth, resilience, and overall well-being. The benefits of positive communication in relationships are far-reaching and can have a profound impact on the quality and longevity of our connections.

One of the most significant advantages of positive communication is its ability to enhance relationship satisfaction. When we express ourselves in a kind, respectful, and understanding manner, we create a safe space for open and honest dialogue. This, in turn, allows our partners to feel heard, valued, and appreciated, leading to a deeper sense of intimacy and connection. By focusing on the positive aspects of our relationships and expressing gratitude for the small, everyday moments, we cultivate a culture of appreciation and mutual respect that strengthens our bonds and increases overall satisfaction.

Moreover, positive communication plays a crucial role in building resilience within relationships. Life is full of challenges and obstacles, and the way we communicate with our loved ones during these trying times can make all the difference. When we approach conflicts and setbacks with a solutions-focused mindset and a willingness to listen and understand each other's perspectives, we develop a shared sense of purpose and unity. By offering words of encouragement, validation, and support, we help our partners feel more equipped to face adversity and bounce back from setbacks, fostering a more resilient and adaptable relationship.

In addition to enhancing relationship satisfaction and resilience, positive communication also contributes to the overall well-being of both partners. When we engage in affirming and supportive interactions, we create a positive feedback loop that promotes feelings of happiness, contentment, and security. This, in turn, can have a ripple effect on other areas of our lives, such as our mental health, self-esteem, and ability to cope with stress. By prioritizing positive communication in our relationships, we not only nurture the health of our connections but also invest in our personal growth and well-being.

The power of positive communication lies in its ability to transform the way we perceive and experience our relationships. By shifting our focus from negative aspects to the strengths and opportunities within our connections, we open ourselves up to a world of possibilities. Through the consistent practice of affirming language, active listening, and empathetic responses, we can create a relationship dynamic that is characterized by trust, respect, and unconditional love, ultimately leading to a more fulfilling and satisfying life.

Subsection 4.2: Expressing Gratitude and Appreciation

In the hustle and bustle of daily life, it's easy to overlook the power of two simple words: "thank you." Expressing gratitude and appreciation is a fundamental aspect of positive communication that can have a profound impact on the health and happiness of our relationships. When we take the time to acknowledge and appreciate the efforts, gestures, and qualities of our loved ones, we foster a sense of connection, validation, and mutual respect that strengthens our bonds and promotes a more positive relationship climate.

Gratitude is more than just a fleeting sentiment; it is a practice that requires intentionality and consistency. By making a habit of regularly expressing appreciation for the people in our lives, we cultivate a mindset of positivity and abundance that permeates our interactions and influences the overall tone of our relationships. Whether it's a heartfelt "thank you" for a thoughtful act, a compliment on a job well done, or a simple acknowledgment of our partner's unique qualities, these expressions of gratitude serve as powerful reminders of the value and significance of our connections.

The benefits of expressing gratitude and appreciation in relationships are well-documented. Research has shown that couples who regularly express gratitude towards each other experience higher levels of relationship satisfaction, intimacy, and overall well-being. Gratitude has been linked to increased feelings of love, respect, and commitment, as well as a greater ability to navigate conflicts and challenges in a constructive manner. By focusing on the positive aspects of our relationships and acknowledging the efforts of our loved ones, we create a buffer against the inevitable stresses and strains that can arise, fostering a more resilient and adaptable bond.

Moreover, expressing gratitude and appreciation has a reciprocal effect on our relationships. When we make a conscious effort to recognize and appreciate the contributions of our partners, we create a positive feedback loop that encourages them to continue investing in the relationship. This, in turn, leads to a greater sense of mutual support, understanding, and collaboration, as both partners feel valued and motivated to contribute to the growth and well-being of the relationship.

To cultivate a culture of gratitude and appreciation in our relationships, it is essential to make it a daily practice. This can involve setting aside dedicated time each day to reflect on the things we appreciate about our loved ones, writing heartfelt notes or letters expressing our gratitude, or simply making a point to verbalize our appreciation in the moment. By incorporating gratitude into our regular communication patterns, we create a foundation of positivity and mutual respect that can weather even the toughest of challenges.

It is important to note that expressing gratitude and appreciation is not about grand gestures or elaborate displays of affection. Rather, it is about consistently acknowledging the small, everyday moments and actions that contribute to the overall health and happiness of our relationships. Whether it's expressing thanks for a thoughtful text message, acknowledging the effort put into a home-cooked meal, or simply recognizing the unwavering support of our partners during a difficult time, these seemingly small acts of gratitude can have a profound impact on the quality and longevity of our connections.

In a world that often emphasizes criticism and complaint, expressing gratitude and appreciation is a revolutionary act. By choosing to focus on the positive aspects of our relationships and regularly acknowledging the efforts and qualities of our loved ones, we create a culture of love, respect, and mutual support that can transform even the most challenging of circumstances. So, let us make a commitment to infusing our relationships with the power of gratitude, one "thank you" at a time, and watch as our connections flourish and thrive in the face of all of life's ups and downs.

Subsection 4.3: Offering Constructive Feedback and Support

In the context of positive communication, offering constructive feedback and support plays a vital role in fostering growth, learning, and positive change within relationships. When delivered effectively, feedback can serve as a powerful catalyst for personal and interpersonal development, strengthening the bonds between partners and promoting a culture of continuous improvement. However, providing constructive feedback is an art that requires skill, empathy, and a genuine desire to uplift and empower others.

At its core, constructive feedback is about helping our loved ones identify areas for growth and providing them with the guidance and support they need to make positive changes. It is not about criticizing or pointing out flaws, but rather about collaborating with our partners to create a shared vision of success and working together to achieve it. By approaching feedback from a place of love, respect, and a sincere belief in our partner's potential, we create a safe and supportive environment that encourages open communication and personal development.

One of the key elements of offering constructive feedback is timing. It is essential to choose the right moment to provide feedback, when both partners are receptive and emotionally prepared to engage in a productive conversation. This may involve setting aside dedicated time to discuss areas for improvement, or simply seizing opportune moments as they arise in the natural flow of daily interactions. By being mindful of timing and creating a space for open and honest dialogue, we increase the likelihood that our feedback will be well-received and acted upon.

Another crucial aspect of constructive feedback is the way in which it is delivered. The language we use and the tone we employ can make all the difference in how our feedback is perceived and internalized by our partners. It is important to focus on specific behaviors or actions rather than making broad generalizations or attacking our partner's character. By using "I" statements and expressing our observations and feelings in a non-judgmental manner, we create a sense of collaboration and shared responsibility for growth and change.

In addition to providing feedback, offering ongoing support is equally important in promoting positive change within relationships. This involves being a consistent source of encouragement, validation, and practical assistance as our partners work to implement the insights and suggestions we have provided. Whether it's celebrating small victories, offering words of affirmation, or simply being present and available to listen and offer guidance, our unwavering support can make all the difference in our partner's journey of personal growth.

It is important to recognize that offering constructive feedback and support is not a one-time event, but rather an ongoing process that requires patience, persistence, and a willingness to adapt and evolve alongside our partners. As we work together to identify areas for improvement and implement positive changes, we may encounter setbacks, resistance, or unexpected challenges along the way. By remaining committed to the process and maintaining a spirit of empathy and understanding, we can weather these obstacles and emerge stronger, more connected, and better equipped to face the challenges of life together.

Ultimately, the power of offering constructive feedback and support lies in its ability to transform relationships from a source of stagnation and conflict into a catalyst for personal and interpersonal growth. By approaching feedback with love, respect, and a genuine desire to uplift and empower our partners, we create a dynamic of continuous improvement that permeates every aspect of our lives together. Through the consistent practice of providing guidance, encouragement, and practical support, we not only help our loved ones reach their full potential but also deepen the bonds of trust, intimacy, and mutual understanding that form the foundation of any strong and enduring relationship.

Summary: Embracing the Transformative Power of

Positive Communication

Throughout this section, we have explored the profound impact that positive communication can have on the quality and longevity of our relationships. By harnessing the power of affirming language, active listening, and empathetic responses, we can create a relationship dynamic that is characterized by trust, respect, and mutual understanding.

We have seen how regularly expressing gratitude and appreciation can strengthen our bonds, increase feelings of love and commitment, and foster a more resilient connection in the face of life's challenges. Moreover, we have learned that offering constructive feedback and support is essential for promoting personal and interpersonal growth, as it allows us to collaborate with our loved ones to create a shared vision of success and work together to achieve it.

As we conclude this section, it is important to remember that the power of positive communication lies not only in the words we speak but also in the intentions behind them. By approaching our interactions with a genuine desire to uplift, empower, and connect with our partners, we can transform even the most challenging of circumstances into opportunities for growth and connection.

So, let us embrace the transformative power of positive communication and make a commitment to infusing our relationships with the language of love, gratitude, and support. By doing so, we not only invest in the health and happiness of our connections but also cultivate a greater sense of personal well-being and fulfillment. Remember, every interaction is an opportunity to strengthen our bonds and create a more loving, supportive, and thriving relational landscape. Let us seize those opportunities with open hearts and minds, and watch as our relationships flourish in ways we never thought possible.

Section 5: The Role of Technology in Modern Communication

In today's fast-paced, digitally connected world, technology has become an integral part of our daily lives, transforming the way we communicate and interact with others. From instant messaging and social media to video calls and online dating, digital platforms have opened up new avenues for connecting with people across the globe. However, as technology continues to shape our relationships, it is crucial to examine its impact on the quality and depth of our connections.

This section delves into the complex role of technology in modern communication, exploring both the benefits and challenges it presents in the context of relationships. We will discuss how digital tools can enhance connectivity, convenience, and accessibility, allowing us to maintain long-distance relationships, reconnect with old friends, and expand our social networks. At the same time, we will address the potential pitfalls of overreliance on technology, such as the erosion of face-to-face interaction, the risk of miscommunication, and the blurring of boundaries between our online and offline lives.

As we navigate this digital landscape, it is essential to develop strategies for effectively managing our online presence and ensuring that technology serves as a tool for nurturing meaningful connections rather than a barrier to authentic communication. Throughout this section, we will explore practical tips and guidelines for establishing healthy boundaries, maintaining a balance between online and offline interactions, and harnessing the power of technology to strengthen our relationships.

By gaining a deeper understanding of the role of technology in modern communication, we can make informed choices about how we engage with digital platforms and cultivate the skills necessary to build and maintain strong, fulfilling relationships in the digital age. So, let us embark on this exploration of the intersection between technology and human connection, and discover how we can navigate this ever-evolving landscape with intention, mindfulness, and care.

Subsection 5.1: The Benefits and Challenges of Digital Communication

In the digital age, communication has been revolutionized by the advent of various digital platforms, such as text messaging, social media, and video calls. These technological advancements have brought about numerous benefits, making it easier than ever to connect with people across the globe, maintain long-distance relationships, and express ourselves in new and creative ways. However, alongside these advantages, digital communication also presents a unique set of challenges that can impact the quality and depth of our interactions.

One of the most significant benefits of digital communication is its convenience and accessibility. With just a few taps on our smartphones or clicks on our computers, we can instantly reach out to friends, family, and colleagues, regardless of their location. This ease of communication has made it possible to maintain relationships with people who might otherwise have drifted apart due to distance or busy schedules. Moreover, digital platforms offer a wide range of tools and features that enhance our ability to express ourselves, such as emojis, GIFs, and multimedia sharing, allowing us to convey emotions and experiences in vivid and engaging ways.

However, the convenience of digital communication can also be a double-edged sword. The constant availability and immediacy of these platforms can create a sense of pressure to be always "on" and responsive, leading to feelings of anxiety, stress, and even burnout. Additionally, the lack of face-to-face interaction in digital communication can sometimes lead to misunderstandings and miscommunications, as nonverbal cues like facial expressions, tone of voice, and body language are often lost in translation. This can result in misinterpretations, unintended offense, or a breakdown in communication.

Another challenge of digital communication is the potential for information overload. With an endless stream of messages, notifications, and updates from various platforms, it can be difficult to filter out the noise and focus on what truly matters. This constant barrage of information can lead to distraction, decreased productivity, and a sense of being overwhelmed. It is essential to develop strategies for managing digital communication, such as setting boundaries, prioritizing important messages, and taking regular breaks from screens to maintain a healthy balance.

Privacy and security concerns are also significant challenges in the realm of digital communication. As we share more of our personal lives online, we become increasingly vulnerable to data breaches, identity theft, and other cyber threats. It is crucial to be mindful of the information we share on digital platforms and to take steps to protect our privacy, such as using strong passwords, enabling two-factor authentication, and being cautious about accepting friend requests or sharing sensitive information with strangers.

Despite these challenges, digital communication has become an integral part of modern relationships, and it is essential to learn how to navigate this landscape effectively. By being aware of the potential pitfalls and developing strategies to mitigate them, we can harness the power of digital platforms to nurture meaningful connections, express ourselves authentically, and maintain strong, healthy relationships in the digital age.

Subsection 5.2: Establishing Healthy Boundaries in Digital Communication

In the age of constant connectivity, it is more important than ever to establish and maintain healthy boundaries around digital communication. Without clear boundaries, the lines between our personal and professional lives can become blurred, leading to increased stress, anxiety, and even burnout. By setting appropriate limits on when, where, and how we engage with technology, we can protect our time, privacy, and emotional well-being, while still reaping the benefits of digital communication.

One of the first steps in establishing healthy boundaries is to be mindful of the time we spend on digital platforms. It is easy to get caught up in the endless scroll of social media feeds or the constant ping of notifications, leading to hours of unproductive screen time. To combat this, consider setting specific time limits for engaging with digital communication, such as dedicating certain hours of the day to checking emails or browsing social media. By creating a schedule and sticking to it, you can ensure that your time is being used intentionally and productively.

Another crucial aspect of maintaining healthy boundaries is protecting your privacy online. In a world where personal information is increasingly valuable, it is essential to be cautious about what you share on digital platforms. Be selective about the personal details you disclose, and consider adjusting your privacy settings to limit who can access your information. Remember that once something is posted online, it can be difficult, if not impossible, to remove entirely, so think carefully before hitting "send" or "post."

It is also important to establish boundaries around the types of digital communication you engage in. Not all platforms are created equal, and some may be more conducive to healthy communication than others. For example, while social media can be a great way to stay connected with friends and family, it can also be a source of stress and negativity. If you find that certain platforms are consistently impacting your emotional well-being, it may be time to reassess your engagement with them. Consider muting or unfollowing accounts that regularly post content that leaves you feeling drained or upset, and focus on cultivating a digital environment that uplifts and inspires you.

In addition to setting boundaries around your own digital communication, it is also important to respect the boundaries of others. Just as you have the right to disconnect and unplug, so do your friends, family, and colleagues. Avoid the temptation to constantly check in or expect immediate responses, and be understanding if someone needs time away from their devices. By modeling healthy digital habits and respecting the boundaries of others, you can contribute to a more positive and balanced digital culture.

Ultimately, establishing healthy boundaries around digital communication is an ongoing process that requires self-awareness, intentionality, and commitment. By taking proactive steps to protect your time, privacy, and emotional well-being, you can ensure that technology remains a tool for connection and growth, rather than a source of stress and anxiety. Remember, the goal is not to eliminate digital communication altogether, but rather to find a balance that allows you to harness its benefits while minimizing its drawbacks. With a little effort and mindfulness, you can create a digital environment that supports and enhances your relationships, both online and off.

Subsection 5.3: Balancing Online and Offline Communication

In today's digitally-driven world, finding the right balance between online and offline communication is crucial for nurturing strong, authentic connections in our relationships. While technology has undoubtedly made it easier to stay connected with loved ones across vast distances and time zones, it is essential to recognize the value of face-to-face interactions in building and maintaining deep, meaningful bonds.

One of the key strategies for striking a healthy balance between digital and in-person communication is to prioritize quality over quantity. While it may be tempting to constantly check in with friends and family through text messages, social media, or instant messaging, these brief, often superficial interactions cannot replace the depth and richness of face-to-face conversations. By setting aside dedicated time for in-person meetings, whether it's a weekly coffee date with a close friend or a monthly family gathering, we create opportunities for more substantial, engaging exchanges that allow us to truly connect with one another on a deeper level.

Another important aspect of balancing online and offline communication is being mindful of the context and purpose of each interaction. While digital platforms can be incredibly useful for sharing quick updates, coordinating plans, or engaging in lighthearted banter, they may not always be the most appropriate or effective means of addressing more complex, emotionally-charged issues. In these situations, it is often best to opt for face-to-face conversations, which allow for greater nuance, empathy, and understanding. By being discerning about when to use digital communication and when to prioritize in-person interactions, we can ensure that our relationships remain strong, authentic, and fulfilling.

In addition to being mindful of the context and purpose of our interactions, it is also crucial to establish clear boundaries around our digital communication habits. This may involve setting specific times of day for checking emails or social media, turning off notifications during important face-to-face conversations, or designating tech-free zones in our homes or workplaces. By creating these boundaries, we not only protect our own time and mental well-being but also demonstrate respect for the people in our lives, showing them that they have our full attention and presence when we are together.

Ultimately, the key to balancing online and offline communication lies in recognizing the unique strengths and limitations of each mode of interaction. While digital platforms can help us stay connected and informed, they cannot fully replace the depth, warmth, and authenticity of face-to-face conversations. By being intentional about how we use technology in our relationships, prioritizing quality over quantity, and setting clear boundaries around our digital habits, we can cultivate strong, meaningful connections that stand the test of time, both online and off.

Summary: Embracing Technology for Stronger

Connections

In this digital age, technology has become an integral part of our relationships, transforming the way we communicate, connect, and interact with one another. As we navigate this ever-evolving landscape, it is crucial to recognize both the benefits and challenges that digital communication presents. By harnessing the power of technology mindfully and intentionally, we can cultivate stronger, more meaningful connections with the people in our lives.

Throughout this section, we have explored the various ways in which technology has reshaped modern communication. From the convenience and accessibility of instant messaging and video calls to the potential for misunderstandings and information overload, digital platforms have brought about a complex array of advantages and pitfalls. By understanding these dynamics and developing strategies for effective digital communication, we can minimize the drawbacks and maximize the benefits of these powerful tools.

Central to navigating this digital landscape is the establishment of healthy boundaries. By setting clear limits around our online presence, protecting our privacy, and respecting the boundaries of others, we can create a more balanced and positive digital environment. Equally important is the cultivation of a mindful approach to digital communication, one that prioritizes quality over quantity and recognizes the irreplaceable value of face-to-face interactions.

As we move forward in this digital age, it is essential to remember that technology is ultimately a tool – one that can either enhance or detract from our relationships, depending on how we choose to use it. By embracing the opportunities that digital communication presents while remaining grounded in the timeless principles of authentic human connection, we can harness the power of technology to build stronger, more resilient relationships that thrive both online and off.

So let us approach this digital frontier with curiosity, empathy, and intention, recognizing that the key to navigating modern communication lies not in the tools themselves, but in the hearts and minds of those who use them. By staying true to our values, nurturing our bonds, and adapting to the ever-changing landscape of technology, we can cultivate relationships that stand the test of time – and the test of the digital age.

Chapter Summary: Mastering the Art of Effective Communication for Stronger Relationships

Effective communication is the cornerstone of healthy, thriving relationships. By mastering the essential techniques and strategies discussed in this chapter, you can build trust, deepen connections, and navigate conflicts with greater ease and understanding.

Remember that clear, concise messaging, active listening, and nonverbal communication are all crucial components of effective communication. By adapting your communication style to your audience and approaching challenging situations with empathy and respect, you can foster more productive and satisfying interactions with others.

Harnessing the power of positive communication, expressing gratitude, and offering constructive feedback can further strengthen your relationships and contribute to a more supportive and affirming dynamic. As you navigate the ever-evolving landscape of modern communication, be mindful of the role technology plays in your interactions and strive to maintain a healthy balance between online and offline connections.

Ultimately, effective communication is a skill that requires ongoing practice, self-reflection, and a willingness to learn and grow. By committing to these principles and consistently applying them in your relationships, you can cultivate more authentic, meaningful, and resilient connections with the people who matter most in your life. As you continue on your journey of personal growth and relationship development, remember that every interaction is an opportunity to deepen your understanding, strengthen your bonds, and create a more fulfilling and connected life.

Chapter 4: The Art of Active Listening

In the realm of relationships, few skills are as crucial as the ability to listen actively and attentively. Active listening goes beyond merely hearing the words spoken; it is a powerful tool that enables us to truly understand, empathize with, and connect with the people in our lives. By mastering the art of active listening, we can transform our relationships, fostering deeper understanding, trust, and rapport with our partners, family members, friends, and colleagues.

Imagine a world where everyone feels genuinely heard and understood. A world where conversations flow seamlessly, unhindered by misunderstandings or unspoken resentments. This is the power of active listening – it has the potential to create a more compassionate, connected, and harmonious society. When we listen actively, we demonstrate respect, validate emotions, and create a safe space for others to express themselves fully.

In this chapter, we will embark on a journey to explore the intricacies of active listening and its profound impact on our relationships. We will delve into the key components of active listening, from giving undivided attention and employing nonverbal cues to asking clarifying questions and navigating emotional triggers. Through relatable examples, research-backed insights, and practical tips, you will gain the tools and knowledge necessary to become an exceptional listener.

As we unravel the art of active listening, we will also examine the common barriers that hinder effective communication and explore strategies to overcome them. By learning to manage internal distractions, suspend judgment, and navigate emotional triggers, you will be better equipped to handle challenging conversations and maintain a receptive, empathetic mindset.

Furthermore, we will dive into the role of empathy and validation in active listening, discovering how to convey understanding and support even in the face of disagreement. You will learn to reflect feelings, paraphrase content, and validate experiences, fostering a deeper sense of connection and trust in your relationships.

Throughout this chapter, we will explore the application of active listening in various contexts, from romantic partnerships and family dynamics to professional settings and social interactions. By adapting these skills to different situations, you will be able to enhance your relationships across all areas of your life, creating a more fulfilling and connected existence.

So, let us embark on this transformative journey together, unlocking the power of active listening to build stronger, more empathetic, and more meaningful relationships. As we explore the art of listening with an open heart and mind, we will discover the key to cultivating a more compassionate and understanding world, one conversation at a time.

Section 1: Understanding the Importance of Active Listening

In the fast-paced world we live in, it's easy to get caught up in the constant chatter and noise that surrounds us. We often find ourselves half-listening to our partners, friends, or family members, our minds preoccupied with our own thoughts and concerns. However, the art of active listening is a crucial skill that can transform our relationships, fostering deeper connections, empathy, and understanding.

Active listening goes beyond simply hearing the words someone is saying. It involves fully engaging with the speaker, giving them your undivided attention, and seeking to understand their perspective, feelings, and needs. When we practice active listening, we create a safe space for others to express themselves, knowing that they are being heard and validated.

The impact of active listening on our relationships cannot be overstated. It helps build trust, as the speaker feels valued and respected when their thoughts and emotions are acknowledged. Active listening also facilitates effective communication, reducing misunderstandings and conflicts that often arise from miscommunication or lack of attentiveness.

Moreover, active listening is a powerful tool for cultivating empathy and emotional intelligence. By truly listening to others, we gain insight into their experiences, challenges, and aspirations. This understanding allows us to respond with compassion, support, and encouragement, strengthening the bonds we share with those around us.

In this section, we will delve into the critical role of active listening in building strong, empathetic, and meaningful relationships. We will explore the key components of active listening, the barriers that can hinder our ability to listen effectively, and the strategies we can employ to overcome these obstacles. By mastering the art of active listening, we can unlock the potential for deeper, more fulfilling connections with the people who matter most in our lives.

Subsection 1.1: The Difference Between Hearing and Listening

In our daily lives, we often use the words "hearing" and "listening" interchangeably, as if they were synonymous. However, there is a significant difference between these two acts, and understanding this distinction is crucial for developing effective communication skills and building strong relationships.

Hearing is a passive, involuntary process that involves the reception of auditory stimuli by our ears. It is a physiological function that occurs automatically, as long as our auditory system is functioning correctly. When we hear, we simply perceive sounds, whether it's the chirping of birds, the honking of cars, or the words spoken by another person. Hearing does not necessarily require our full attention or engagement with the source of the sound.

On the other hand, listening is an active, voluntary process that involves not only hearing but also consciously focusing on and making sense of the sounds we perceive. It requires a deliberate effort to understand and interpret the meaning behind the words being spoken. When we listen, we give our full attention to the speaker, processing their message, tone, and nonverbal cues to gain a deeper understanding of their thoughts, feelings, and intentions.

Active listening goes beyond merely hearing the words; it involves engaging with the speaker on an intellectual and emotional level. It requires setting aside our own thoughts, judgments, and preconceptions to fully immerse ourselves in the other person's perspective. By practicing active listening, we demonstrate respect, empathy, and a genuine interest in the speaker, fostering a sense of trust and connection in our relationships.

The difference between hearing and listening can be illustrated by considering a lecture or presentation. While everyone in the audience may hear the words being spoken, not everyone is actively listening. Some may be daydreaming, checking their phones, or thinking about unrelated matters. Those who are actively listening, however, are fully engaged, taking notes, asking questions, and processing the information being shared.

Recognizing the distinction between hearing and listening is the first step towards becoming a more effective communicator and building stronger, more empathetic relationships. By consciously shifting from passive hearing to active listening, we can improve our ability to understand and connect with others, leading to more meaningful and satisfying interactions in all aspects of our lives.

Subsection 1.2: The Benefits of Active Listening in Relationships

Active listening is a powerful tool that can transform the quality of our relationships, whether they be romantic partnerships, family bonds, friendships, or professional connections. By fully engaging with others and giving them our undivided attention, we create an environment that fosters trust, understanding, and emotional connection.

One of the primary benefits of active listening is the development of trust. When we listen attentively to others, we demonstrate that we value their thoughts, feelings, and experiences. This validation helps to create a safe space where individuals feel comfortable opening up and sharing their innermost selves. As a result, the speaker feels heard, respected, and supported, leading to a deeper sense of trust in the listener and the relationship as a whole.

Active listening also promotes better understanding between individuals. By focusing on the speaker's message, asking clarifying questions, and reflecting on their words, we gain a clearer picture of their perspective, motivations, and needs. This understanding helps to reduce misinterpretations, assumptions, and conflicts that can arise from miscommunication. When we truly understand each other, we can respond with greater empathy, compassion, and wisdom, leading to more harmonious and fulfilling relationships.

Moreover, active listening plays a crucial role in fostering emotional connection. When we give others our full attention, we create a sense of intimacy and closeness that goes beyond surface-level interactions. By attuning to the speaker's emotional state, we can offer support, validation, and encouragement that resonates with their needs. This emotional attunement helps to build a strong foundation of trust, respect, and affection, which is essential for the health and longevity of any relationship.

The benefits of active listening extend to various types of relationships. In romantic partnerships, active listening can help couples navigate difficult conversations, resolve conflicts, and deepen their emotional intimacy. Within families, active listening can foster better communication, understanding, and support among family members, leading to more cohesive and resilient family dynamics. In friendships, active listening can help to build trust, empathy, and a sense of being truly seen and appreciated by others. And in professional settings, active listening can improve collaboration, teamwork, and leadership, leading to more productive and satisfying work relationships.

Ultimately, the power of active listening lies in its ability to create a shared sense of understanding, respect, and connection between individuals. By giving others our full attention and seeking to understand their world, we lay the foundation for relationships that are built on trust, empathy, and mutual growth. As we cultivate the art of active listening, we not only enrich our own lives but also contribute to a more compassionate and connected world.

Subsection 1.3: The Impact of Active Listening on Conflict Resolution

Conflict is an inevitable part of any relationship, whether it be with a romantic partner, family member, friend, or colleague. While conflicts can be challenging and emotionally charged, they also present an opportunity for growth, understanding, and strengthening of the relationship. One of the most effective tools for navigating conflicts and facilitating effective problem-solving is the practice of active listening.

Active listening plays a crucial role in de-escalating conflicts by creating a space for open, honest, and respectful communication. When we find ourselves in a conflict situation, our natural instinct may be to defend our position, argue our point, or dismiss the other person's perspective. However, by engaging in active listening, we can shift the dynamic of the conversation from one of confrontation to one of collaboration.

When we actively listen during a conflict, we demonstrate a willingness to understand the other person's viewpoint, even if we don't agree with it. By giving them our full attention, acknowledging their feelings, and seeking to comprehend their needs and concerns, we create an atmosphere of empathy and respect. This approach can help to reduce tensions, as the other person feels heard and validated, rather than attacked or dismissed.

Active listening also allows us to gather more information about the conflict at hand. By asking open-ended questions, seeking clarification, and reflecting on what the other person has said, we can gain a deeper understanding of the root causes of the conflict. This understanding is essential for effective problem-solving, as it enables us to address the underlying issues rather than simply arguing over surface-level disagreements.

Moreover, active listening can help to uncover hidden or unexpressed needs and emotions that may be fueling the conflict. Often, conflicts arise not just from differing opinions but also from unmet needs or unresolved emotional hurts. By creating a safe space for the other person to express themselves fully, we can bring these underlying factors to light and work together to find mutually satisfying solutions.

The impact of active listening on conflict resolution extends beyond the immediate situation. By modeling effective communication and problem-solving skills, we set a positive example for future interactions. As we consistently practice active listening, we build trust, respect, and understanding in our relationships, making it easier to navigate conflicts when they arise.

It's important to note that active listening doesn't mean agreeing with everything the other person says or giving up our own needs and opinions. Rather, it is a tool for creating a collaborative, solution-focused approach to conflict resolution. By combining active listening with assertive communication and a willingness to compromise, we can work towards finding win-win solutions that meet the needs of all parties involved.

In summary, the practice of active listening is a powerful tool for de-escalating conflicts and facilitating effective problem-solving in relationships. By creating a space for empathy, understanding, and collaboration, active listening helps to reduce tensions, uncover underlying issues, and pave the way for mutually satisfying solutions. As we cultivate this skill, we not only improve our ability to navigate conflicts in the moment but also build stronger, more resilient relationships over time.

Summary: Unlocking the Power of Active Listening for Stronger Relationships

Throughout this section, we have explored the critical role that active listening plays in building strong, empathetic, and meaningful relationships. By understanding the difference between hearing and listening, recognizing the numerous benefits of active listening, and grasping its impact on conflict resolution, we can begin to cultivate this essential skill in our daily lives.

Active listening is not merely a technique; it is a way of being present and engaged with others, demonstrating genuine interest, respect, and care. When we give others our full attention, seek to understand their perspectives, and respond with empathy and compassion, we create a foundation of trust, connection, and mutual understanding that can transform our relationships.

Whether we are navigating the complexities of romantic partnerships, strengthening family bonds, deepening friendships, or fostering collaborative work environments, active listening is a powerful tool that can help us build bridges, resolve conflicts, and create a sense of belonging and validation for those around us.

As we move forward in our exploration of the art of active listening, we will delve into the specific skills, strategies, and practices that can help us become more effective listeners. By committing to this ongoing process of learning and growth, we open ourselves up to a world of richer, more fulfilling relationships, where we not only hear but truly understand and connect with the people who matter most to us.

Section 2: Key Components of Active Listening

Active listening is a powerful skill that can transform the way you communicate and connect with others in your relationships. It goes beyond simply hearing the words someone is saying; it involves fully engaging with the speaker, seeking to understand their perspective, and responding with empathy and compassion. By mastering the key components of active listening, you can create a safe, supportive space for open and honest communication, fostering deeper understanding and stronger bonds with your loved ones.

In this section, we will break down the essential elements of active listening and explore how you can apply them in your relationships. From giving your undivided attention to the speaker to using nonverbal cues that show engagement, we will delve into the practical techniques that will help you become a more effective and empathetic listener. You will learn how to employ verbal encouragers and ask clarifying questions to demonstrate your interest and gain a more comprehensive understanding of the speaker's thoughts and feelings.

By incorporating these key components into your communication style, you will be better equipped to navigate the complexities of your relationships, whether it's with your romantic partner, family members, or friends. Active listening has the power to defuse conflicts, promote mutual understanding, and create a foundation of trust and respect in your relationships. As you explore and practice these essential skills, you will discover the transformative impact of truly listening to and connecting with the people in your life.

Subsection 2.1: Giving Undivided Attention

In today's fast-paced, technology-driven world, it's easy to become distracted and fail to give our full attention to the people we're communicating with. However, giving undivided attention is a crucial component of active listening and is essential for building strong, healthy relationships. When you give your undivided attention to the person speaking, you're demonstrating respect, interest, and a genuine desire to understand their thoughts and feelings.

One of the first steps in giving undivided attention is to minimize distractions. This means putting away your phone, turning off the TV, and finding a quiet space where you can focus solely on the conversation. It's also important to avoid multitasking, such as trying to listen while simultaneously working on your computer or thinking about your to-do list. When you're fully present and engaged in the conversation, you'll be better able to pick up on nonverbal cues, such as facial expressions and body language, which can provide valuable insights into the speaker's emotional state.

Another key aspect of giving undivided attention is maintaining eye contact with the speaker. Eye contact helps establish a connection and shows that you're fully engaged in the conversation. However, it's important to note that the appropriate amount of eye contact can vary depending on cultural norms and individual comfort levels. In general, aim to maintain eye contact for around 50-70% of the conversation, taking brief breaks to avoid staring or making the speaker feel uncomfortable.

In addition to minimizing distractions and maintaining eye contact, it's essential to adopt an open and receptive body posture. This means uncrossing your arms, leaning slightly forward, and nodding occasionally to show that you're actively listening. By adopting an open body posture, you're signaling to the speaker that you're approachable, interested, and willing to engage in the conversation.

Giving undivided attention also involves resisting the urge to interrupt or jump in with your own thoughts and opinions. When you're fully focused on understanding the speaker's perspective, you'll be less likely to interrupt or steer the conversation in a different direction. Instead, allow the speaker to express themselves fully, and wait for natural pauses or invitations to respond.

By mastering the art of giving undivided attention, you'll be well on your way to becoming an effective active listener. When you give your full attention to the person speaking, you're creating a safe, supportive space for open and honest communication, which is essential for building trust and strengthening your relationships.

Subsection 2.2: Using Nonverbal Cues to Show Engagement

Nonverbal cues play a crucial role in demonstrating active listening and showing engagement in a conversation. These cues, such as eye contact, facial expressions, and body language, can convey a wealth of information about your interest, empathy, and understanding, even without uttering a single word. By effectively using nonverbal cues, you can create a more supportive and connected communication experience, fostering deeper relationships with others.

Eye contact is one of the most powerful nonverbal cues in active listening. When you maintain appropriate eye contact with the speaker, you signal that you are fully present and engaged in the conversation. It shows that you are giving them your undivided attention and are interested in what they have to say. However, it's essential to strike a balance with eye contact, as too much can come across as intimidating or aggressive, while too little may suggest disinterest or lack of confidence. Aim for a natural, comfortable level of eye contact that allows you to connect with the speaker without causing discomfort.

Facial expressions are another key component of nonverbal communication in active listening. Your facial expressions can convey a range of emotions, from empathy and understanding to confusion or concern. By mirroring the speaker's facial expressions, you can show that you are attuned to their emotional state and are experiencing their story alongside them. For example, if the speaker is sharing a happy memory, a warm smile can demonstrate your shared joy. Conversely, if they are discussing a challenging situation, a concerned or sympathetic expression can convey your support and understanding.

Body language is equally important in demonstrating active listening. Your posture, gestures, and physical orientation can all contribute to creating a sense of engagement and connection with the speaker. Leaning slightly forward, maintaining an open posture with uncrossed arms and legs, and nodding occasionally can all signal that you are actively listening and interested in the conversation. Conversely, crossed arms, slouching, or turning away from the speaker can convey disinterest, defensiveness, or lack of engagement.

It's important to note that nonverbal cues can vary across cultures, and what may be considered appropriate in one context may not be in another. As an active listener, it's essential to be aware of these cultural differences and to adapt your nonverbal communication accordingly. By being sensitive to the speaker's background and experiences, you can ensure that your nonverbal cues are respectful, appropriate, and effective in building a strong, empathetic connection.

Incorporating nonverbal cues into your active listening practice takes time and effort, but the benefits are well worth it. By showing engagement through eye contact, facial expressions, and body language, you can create a more supportive, understanding, and connected communication experience. As you become more attuned to the power of nonverbal cues, you'll find that your relationships deepen, your empathy grows, and your ability to communicate effectively flourishes.

Subsection 2.3: Employing Verbal Encouragers

Verbal encouragers are an essential component of active listening, as they demonstrate to the speaker that you are fully engaged, interested, and supportive of their sharing. These small, simple phrases, such as "mhm," "go on," and "I see," may seem inconsequential, but they play a powerful role in encouraging the speaker to continue expressing their thoughts and feelings.

When you use verbal encouragers, you're sending a clear message to the speaker that you are present, attentive, and eager to hear more. These subtle cues create a safe, supportive environment that allows the speaker to open up and share more deeply. By interjecting these brief phrases at appropriate moments, you're showing that you're tracking the conversation and that you value the speaker's perspective.

One of the key benefits of using verbal encouragers is that they help to maintain the flow of the conversation without interrupting the speaker's train of thought. Unlike asking questions or offering opinions, verbal encouragers don't require the speaker to pause or shift gears. Instead, they provide gentle prompts that encourage the speaker to continue exploring their ideas and emotions, creating a more natural, free-flowing dialogue.

When employing verbal encouragers, it's essential to use them judiciously and authentically. Overusing these phrases or using them in a robotic, insincere manner can have the opposite effect, making the speaker feel patronized or disregarded. Aim to use verbal encouragers sparingly, at moments when the speaker seems to be searching for words or when you genuinely want to express your interest and support.

It's also important to pay attention to your tone and inflection when using verbal encouragers. A warm, encouraging tone can convey empathy and understanding, while a flat or disinterested tone can undermine the effectiveness of these phrases. Strive to match your tone to the emotional content of the conversation, using a softer, more sympathetic tone when the speaker is sharing something difficult or painful, and a more upbeat, enthusiastic tone when they're sharing something positive or exciting.

In addition to the examples mentioned above, there are countless other verbal encouragers you can use to show interest and support, such as "tell me more," "that's interesting," and "I'm listening." Experiment with different phrases to find the ones that feel most natural and authentic to you, and be open to adapting your language to suit the unique needs and preferences of each individual speaker.

By mastering the art of employing verbal encouragers, you'll be well-equipped to create a more supportive, engaging, and effective communication experience in all of your relationships. Whether you're listening to a partner, family member, or friend, these simple yet powerful phrases can help to build trust, deepen understanding, and foster stronger, more meaningful connections.

Subsection 2.4: Asking Clarifying Questions

Asking clarifying questions is a crucial aspect of active listening, as it allows you to gain a deeper understanding of the speaker's thoughts, feelings, and experiences. By posing open-ended, thoughtful questions, you demonstrate your genuine interest in the conversation and your desire to fully comprehend the speaker's perspective. This not only helps you gather more information but also strengthens the connection between you and the speaker, fostering a sense of trust and openness in your relationship.

When asking clarifying questions, it's essential to focus on open-ended inquiries that encourage the speaker to elaborate on their thoughts and feelings. Open-ended questions typically begin with words such as "what," "how," or "why," and they invite the speaker to provide more than just a simple "yes" or "no" response. For example, instead of asking, "Did that situation make you feel angry?" you might ask, "How did you feel when that situation occurred?" This subtle difference in phrasing opens the door for the speaker to explore and express their emotions in greater depth.

Clarifying questions can also help you better understand the context and significance of the speaker's experiences. By asking questions that delve into the background or implications of a particular event or feeling, you can gain valuable insights into the speaker's world view and the factors that shape their perspective. For instance, you might ask, "What led up to that moment?" or "How has this experience influenced your thoughts on the matter?" These types of questions show that you are not only listening to the surface-level details but also seeking to understand the deeper meaning behind the speaker's words.

It's important to note that the tone and timing of your clarifying questions are just as important as the questions themselves. When asking questions, be sure to maintain a curious, non-judgmental tone that conveys your genuine interest and empathy. Avoid interrupting the speaker or asking questions in rapid succession, as this can come across as interrogative or overwhelming. Instead, allow for natural pauses in the conversation and ask your questions at appropriate moments, giving the speaker ample time to process and respond.

As you ask clarifying questions, be prepared to listen actively to the answers and respond with empathy and understanding. If the speaker shares something particularly vulnerable or emotionally charged, acknowledge their feelings and express your support. You might say something like, "That must have been really challenging for you" or "I can imagine how much courage it took to share that with me." By validating the speaker's experiences and emotions, you create a safe, supportive space that encourages further sharing and deepens your connection.

Asking clarifying questions is a skill that requires practice and patience, but the rewards are well worth the effort. By mastering this essential component of active listening, you'll be better equipped to navigate the complexities of your relationships, offering support, understanding, and empathy to those you care about most. As you continue to ask open-ended, thoughtful questions and listen with genuine curiosity and compassion, you'll find that your conversations become richer, your connections deeper, and your relationships stronger.

Summary: Mastering the Art of Active Listening

Throughout this section, we've explored the key components of active listening and how they can be applied to strengthen your relationships. By giving your undivided attention, using nonverbal cues to show engagement, employing verbal encouragers, and asking clarifying questions, you can create a supportive, empathetic, and connected communication experience with your loved ones.

Mastering the art of active listening takes practice and dedication, but the benefits are immeasurable. When you fully engage with the speaker, seeking to understand their perspective and responding with compassion, you foster a deep sense of trust, respect, and understanding in your relationships. You create a safe space for open, honest communication, where both parties feel heard, validated, and supported.

As you continue to incorporate these essential elements of active listening into your daily interactions, you'll find that your relationships flourish. Conflicts will be easier to navigate, as you'll be better equipped to understand and empathize with your partner's point of view. Intimacy and connection will deepen, as you create an environment where vulnerability and authenticity can thrive. And your overall communication skills will improve, allowing you to build stronger, more meaningful bonds with the people who matter most.

Remember, active listening is a journey, not a destination. It requires ongoing effort, self-reflection, and a willingness to adapt and grow. But by committing to this powerful practice, you'll unlock the full potential of your relationships, creating a more loving, fulfilling, and connected life. So embrace the art of active listening, and watch as your relationships transform before your eyes.

Section 3: Overcoming Barriers to Active Listening

Active listening is a powerful tool for building strong, empathetic relationships, but it's not always easy to put into practice. Even with the best intentions, various obstacles can hinder our ability to fully engage in the listening process. In this section, we'll explore some of the most common barriers to active listening and provide practical strategies for overcoming them.

From internal distractions and emotional triggers to the temptation to judge or assume, many factors can interfere with our capacity to listen effectively. By identifying these barriers and developing techniques to manage them, we can cultivate a more open, receptive, and understanding mindset in our interactions with others.

As we delve into the challenges of active listening, it's essential to approach the topic with self-compassion and patience. Overcoming these barriers is a continuous process of self-awareness, practice, and growth. By committing to this journey, we can enhance our listening skills, deepen our connections, and foster more meaningful relationships in all aspects of our lives.

So, let's embark on this exploration of the obstacles that stand in the way of effective listening and equip ourselves with the tools and strategies needed to overcome them. By doing so, we'll unlock the full potential of active listening and experience the transformative power of truly hearing and understanding others.

Subsection 3.1: Managing Internal Distractions

One of the most significant barriers to active listening is the constant chatter of our inner dialogue. Our minds are rarely still, constantly jumping from one thought to another, even when we're engaged in conversation. This internal noise can make it challenging to stay present and fully attentive to the person speaking, leading to missed information, misunderstandings, and a lack of genuine connection.

To effectively manage internal distractions and cultivate a more focused, present state of mind during conversations, it's essential to develop techniques for quieting the inner dialogue. One powerful approach is the practice of mindfulness. By bringing your attention to the present moment and observing your thoughts without judgment, you can gradually learn to detach from the constant stream of mental chatter and maintain a more stable, attentive presence.

Another helpful strategy is to actively engage your senses during the conversation. Focus on the sound of the speaker's voice, observe their facial expressions and body language, and pay attention to the physical sensations in your own body. By immersing yourself in the sensory experience of the moment, you can anchor your attention and minimize the pull of internal distractions.

It's also important to recognize when your mind has wandered and gently redirect your focus back to the conversation. This may require a conscious effort at first, but with practice, it will become more natural and effortless. If you find yourself struggling to stay present, take a deep breath, acknowledge the distraction, and then intentionally refocus your attention on the speaker.

In addition to these in-the-moment techniques, regular practice of mindfulness meditation can help strengthen your ability to manage internal distractions over time. By dedicating a few minutes each day to sitting in stillness and observing your thoughts without attachment, you can cultivate a greater sense of mental clarity, stability, and presence that will carry over into your conversations and relationships.

Remember, managing internal distractions is a skill that requires patience, self-compassion, and consistent practice. Be kind to yourself when your mind wanders, and celebrate the small victories as you gradually develop a more focused, attentive presence in your interactions with others. By committing to this ongoing process of self-awareness and growth, you'll unlock the full potential of active listening and experience the transformative power of truly being present with others.

Subsection 3.2: Avoiding Judgment and Assumptions

One of the most significant barriers to active listening is the tendency to make judgments and assumptions about the speaker or the content of their message. When we approach a conversation with preconceived notions or biases, we limit our ability to truly hear and understand the other person's perspective. Judgments and assumptions can lead to misinterpretations, missed opportunities for connection, and even conflict in our relationships.

To become an effective active listener, it's essential to learn how to suspend judgment and avoid making assumptions. This requires a conscious effort to maintain an open and receptive mindset, even when faced with ideas or opinions that differ from our own. By setting aside our personal beliefs and biases, we create a safe and non-judgmental space for the speaker to express themselves freely and authentically.

One powerful strategy for avoiding judgment and assumptions is to practice curiosity and genuine interest in the speaker's perspective. Instead of mentally preparing a response or rebuttal while the other person is talking, focus on understanding their point of view. Ask open-ended questions to gain clarity and insight into their thoughts and feelings, and resist the urge to jump to conclusions or impose your own interpretations.

Another key aspect of suspending judgment is to become aware of your own emotional reactions and triggers. When we hear something that challenges our beliefs or evokes a strong emotional response, it's easy to slip into a judgmental or defensive mindset. By developing self-awareness and learning to recognize these triggers, we can consciously choose to set aside our initial reactions and maintain an open, curious attitude.

It's also important to remember that everyone's experiences, backgrounds, and perspectives are unique. What may seem obvious or logical to us may not be the case for someone else. By embracing this diversity of thought and experience, we can approach conversations with a sense of humility and respect, acknowledging that there is always something to learn from others.

Practicing empathy is another powerful tool for avoiding judgment and assumptions. By putting ourselves in the speaker's shoes and attempting to understand their perspective, we can develop a deeper appreciation for their experiences and emotions. This empathetic approach helps us to listen with compassion and understanding, rather than judgment or criticism.

Ultimately, avoiding judgment and assumptions is a continuous practice that requires self-awareness, patience, and a willingness to step outside of our comfort zones. By committing to this practice, we can cultivate a more open, receptive mindset that allows us to truly hear and connect with others on a deeper level. As we learn to suspend our own biases and embrace the richness of diverse perspectives, we unlock the full potential of active listening and build stronger, more empathetic relationships in all areas of our lives.

Subsection 3.3: Navigating Emotional Triggers

Active listening is a powerful tool for building empathy and understanding in our relationships, but it's not always an easy process. At times, we may find ourselves triggered by certain topics, words, or emotions expressed by the speaker, causing our own emotional reactions to surface. These triggers can range from mild discomfort to intense feelings of anger, sadness, or defensiveness, making it challenging to remain present and receptive in the conversation.

When we encounter emotional triggers during active listening, it's essential to have strategies in place to manage our reactions and maintain a supportive, non-judgmental presence. The first step is to develop self-awareness and learn to recognize when we're being triggered. This requires paying close attention to our physical sensations, thoughts, and emotions as we listen, noticing any changes or shifts that may indicate a triggered response.

Once we've identified that we're being triggered, the next step is to practice self-regulation techniques to manage our emotional reactions. One effective approach is to focus on our breathing, taking slow, deep breaths to calm our nervous system and regain a sense of centeredness. We can also use grounding techniques, such as feeling our feet on the floor or noticing the sensations in our hands, to anchor ourselves in the present moment and prevent getting swept away by intense emotions.

Another key strategy for navigating emotional triggers is to practice self-compassion and non-judgment. When we find ourselves triggered, it's easy to slip into self-criticism or blame, which only amplifies our emotional distress. Instead, we can cultivate a kind, understanding attitude towards ourselves, acknowledging that triggers are a normal part of the human experience and that we're doing our best to manage them.

It's also important to remember that navigating emotional triggers is an ongoing process that requires patience and practice. We may not always respond perfectly in the moment, and that's okay. What matters is that we continue to develop our self-awareness, build our emotional regulation skills, and approach each conversation with a commitment to being present and supportive, even in the face of challenges.

In some cases, it may be necessary to take a brief break from the conversation to regain our composure and emotional equilibrium. This can be as simple as excusing ourselves to take a few deep breaths or stepping outside for a moment of fresh air. By giving ourselves permission to take a pause when needed, we can return to the conversation with renewed focus and a greater capacity for empathy and understanding.

Ultimately, navigating emotional triggers during active listening is a skill that requires self-awareness, compassion, and a willingness to engage in ongoing personal growth. By developing strategies to manage our own emotional reactions, we can create a safe, supportive space for others to express themselves freely, deepening our connections and fostering more authentic, meaningful relationships in all areas of our lives.

Summary: Embracing the Journey of Effective Listening

Throughout this section, we've explored the common barriers that can hinder our ability to listen actively and effectively in our relationships. From the constant chatter of our inner dialogue to the temptation to judge or make assumptions, these obstacles can prevent us from truly hearing and understanding others. However, by developing self-awareness, practicing specific strategies, and cultivating a mindset of openness and compassion, we can learn to overcome these barriers and unlock the full potential of active listening.

As we navigate the challenges of managing internal distractions, suspending judgment, and dealing with emotional triggers, it's essential to approach the process with patience, self-compassion, and a commitment to ongoing growth. Overcoming these barriers is not a one-time achievement but rather a continuous journey of self-discovery and skill-building. By embracing this journey and dedicating ourselves to the practice of effective listening, we can transform our relationships and create deeper, more meaningful connections with others.

Remember, the power of active listening lies not only in the words we hear but also in the empathy, understanding, and support we convey through our presence and attention. By learning to listen with an open heart and a curious mind, we can create a safe, non-judgmental space for others to express themselves freely and authentically. In doing so, we foster trust, respect, and mutual understanding, laying the foundation for strong, resilient relationships that can weather any storm.

As you move forward on your own journey of mastering the art of active listening, take the insights and strategies from this section and apply them in your daily interactions. Celebrate your progress, learn from your missteps, and remain committed to the ongoing practice of self-awareness and growth. By embracing the challenges and rewards of effective listening, you'll not only enrich your own relationships but also contribute to a more compassionate, connected world, one conversation at a time.

Section 4: Practicing Empathy and Validation

In the journey of mastering the art of active listening, empathy and validation play a crucial role in fostering deep, meaningful connections with others. When we listen with empathy and offer validation, we create a safe and supportive space for our loved ones to share their thoughts, feelings, and experiences. This section will explore the transformative power of empathy and validation in relationships, and provide practical guidance on how to cultivate these essential skills.

Empathy lies at the heart of active listening, allowing us to step into another person's shoes and understand their perspective. By developing empathy, we move beyond mere intellectual understanding and connect with others on an emotional level. We'll delve into the importance of empathy in building trust, resolving conflicts, and strengthening the bonds we share with our partners, family members, and friends.

Validation, the act of acknowledging and accepting another person's feelings and experiences, is a powerful tool in active listening. When we validate others, we communicate that their emotions are valid and that we understand and accept them, even if we don't necessarily agree with their perspective. In this section, we'll explore the art of reflecting feelings and content, and learn how to provide validation in a genuine and supportive manner.

Through relatable examples and practical exercises, you'll discover how to cultivate empathy and validation in your daily interactions. We'll address common challenges, such as navigating emotionally charged conversations and managing our own emotional reactions, and provide strategies for maintaining an open, non-judgmental mindset. By integrating empathy and validation into your active listening practice, you'll develop a deeper capacity for understanding, compassion, and connection in all your relationships.

Subsection 4.1: Understanding the Importance of Empathy

Empathy, the ability to understand and share the feelings of another, is a fundamental component of active listening and a crucial skill for building strong, compassionate relationships. When we listen with empathy, we create a safe and supportive environment that allows others to express themselves freely, knowing that they will be heard and understood.

One of the primary benefits of empathetic listening is that it fosters a deep sense of connection and trust between individuals. When we demonstrate genuine empathy, we show others that we value their thoughts, feelings, and experiences. This validation helps to strengthen the emotional bond between people, creating a solid foundation for healthy, long-lasting relationships.

Moreover, empathy plays a vital role in effective communication and conflict resolution. By putting ourselves in another person's shoes and seeing things from their perspective, we can better understand the root causes of their concerns or frustrations. This understanding enables us to approach conflicts with greater compassion and patience, leading to more productive conversations and mutually beneficial solutions.

Empathetic listening also encourages personal growth and emotional intelligence. When we practice empathy, we expand our own emotional awareness and develop a greater capacity for understanding and relating to others. This heightened emotional intelligence can have far-reaching benefits in our personal and professional lives, enabling us to navigate complex social situations with greater ease and success.

Cultivating empathy through active listening requires a conscious effort to set aside our own judgments, biases, and preconceptions. It involves focusing our full attention on the speaker, observing their nonverbal cues, and responding with genuine care and concern. By making empathy a central part of our listening practice, we can create more meaningful, fulfilling relationships built on a foundation of mutual understanding and respect.

Subsection 4.2: Reflecting Feelings and Content

Reflecting feelings and content is a powerful technique in active listening that involves paraphrasing and mirroring back the speaker's emotions and main points. This practice demonstrates to the speaker that you have not only heard their words but also understood the underlying feelings and intentions behind them. By reflecting feelings and content, you show empathy, validate the speaker's experiences, and create a deeper sense of connection and understanding.

To effectively reflect feelings, focus on identifying and naming the emotions expressed by the speaker, both verbally and non-verbally. Pay attention to their tone of voice, facial expressions, and body language, as these cues often convey the true emotional content of their message. When paraphrasing their feelings, use feeling words such as "frustrated," "excited," or "overwhelmed" to accurately capture and validate their emotional state.

For example, if your friend says, "I can't believe I didn't get the promotion. I worked so hard for it," you might reflect their feelings by saying, "It sounds like you're feeling really disappointed and frustrated because you put in a lot of effort and didn't get the recognition you deserved."

In addition to reflecting feelings, it's important to paraphrase and reflect the main content of the speaker's message. This involves summarizing the key points and ideas they have expressed, using your own words to demonstrate your understanding. By reflecting content, you not only show that you have been attentive but also provide an opportunity for the speaker to clarify or elaborate on their thoughts if needed.

To reflect content effectively, listen for the central themes, ideas, and experiences shared by the speaker. Avoid getting bogged down in minor details or tangential information. Instead, focus on capturing the essence of their message and conveying it back to them in a concise and organized manner.

For instance, if your colleague says, "I've been working on this project for weeks, but I keep running into roadblocks. The client keeps changing their mind, and my team is struggling to keep up," you might reflect the content by saying, "It seems like this project has been challenging because of the constant changes from the client and the difficulty in adapting quickly with your team."

When reflecting feelings and content, it's essential to use tentative language and avoid making assumptions or judgments. Use phrases like "it sounds like," "it seems," or "correct me if I'm wrong" to convey that you are open to clarification and feedback from the speaker. This approach ensures that you are not imposing your own interpretations or biases onto their experiences.

Remember that the goal of reflecting feelings and content is not to provide solutions or advice but rather to create a safe, non-judgmental space for the speaker to feel heard, understood, and validated. By mastering this skill, you can deepen your capacity for empathy, strengthen your relationships, and foster more meaningful connections with others.

Subsection 4.3: Validating Experiences and Emotions

Validation is a powerful tool in active listening that involves acknowledging and accepting the speaker's experiences and emotions, even if you don't necessarily agree with their perspective. When we validate others, we create a safe and supportive environment that allows them to express themselves freely, without fear of judgment or criticism. This act of validation communicates to the speaker that their feelings are valid, and that we understand and accept them as they are.

One of the primary benefits of validation is that it helps to build trust and strengthen emotional bonds in relationships. When we validate someone's experiences and emotions, we show them that we value their thoughts and feelings, and that we are willing to support them through their challenges. This can be particularly important in situations where the speaker is sharing something difficult or painful, such as a personal struggle or a traumatic event.

To validate effectively, it's essential to listen attentively and respond with empathy and understanding. This involves acknowledging the speaker's emotions and experiences, without trying to minimize or dismiss them. For example, if a friend shares that they are feeling overwhelmed and anxious about a upcoming work presentation, you might validate their feelings by saying, "It's completely understandable to feel anxious about such an important presentation. It sounds like this is a really challenging situation for you."

It's important to note that validation does not necessarily mean agreeing with the speaker's perspective or condoning their actions. Rather, it means acknowledging and accepting their feelings as real and valid, even if you have a different viewpoint. By separating validation from agreement, we create a space for open, honest communication and problem-solving.

In addition to verbal validation, nonverbal cues such as nodding, maintaining eye contact, and offering a supportive touch (when appropriate) can also convey empathy and understanding. These nonverbal signals communicate to the speaker that you are fully present and engaged in the conversation, and that you are there to support them.

Validating experiences and emotions is a skill that requires practice and patience. It can be challenging to set aside our own judgments and biases, and to fully embrace another person's perspective. However, by making a conscious effort to validate others, we can foster deeper, more meaningful connections and create a more compassionate, understanding world.

Summary: Embracing Empathy and Validation for Stronger Connections

Throughout this section, we have explored the transformative power of empathy and validation in active listening and relationship building. By cultivating empathy, we develop the ability to understand and share the feelings of others, creating a safe and supportive environment that fosters trust and emotional connection. Reflecting feelings and content allows us to demonstrate our understanding and validate the speaker's experiences, showing that we value their thoughts and emotions.

Validation, the act of acknowledging and accepting another person's feelings and experiences, is a crucial component of active listening. It communicates to the speaker that their emotions are valid and that we understand and accept them, even if we may not necessarily agree with their perspective. By separating validation from agreement, we create a space for open, honest communication and problem-solving.

As we navigate the complexities of relationships, it is essential to remember that empathy and validation require practice, patience, and a willingness to set aside our own judgments and biases. By making a conscious effort to listen with empathy and offer validation, we can foster deeper, more meaningful connections with our loved ones and create a more compassionate, understanding world.

The insights and techniques covered in this section provide a solid foundation for incorporating empathy and validation into your active listening practice. As you continue on your journey of personal growth and relationship development, remember to approach each interaction with an open heart and a genuine desire to understand and support others. By embracing empathy and validation, you have the power to transform your relationships and create lasting, fulfilling connections built on trust, compassion, and mutual understanding.

Section 5: Applying Active Listening in Different Contexts

Active listening is a powerful tool that can transform the way we communicate and connect with others, but its application may vary depending on the context and the nature of the relationship. In this section, we will explore how to adapt and apply active listening skills to various relationship contexts and situations, from romantic partnerships to family dynamics, professional settings, and social interactions.

Understanding the nuances of each context is crucial for effectively employing active listening techniques. For instance, the way you listen to your romantic partner may differ from how you listen to a colleague or a friend. By tailoring your approach to the specific needs and challenges of each relationship, you can create a more supportive, empathetic, and understanding environment that fosters growth and connection.

Throughout this section, we will delve into real-life examples and practical strategies for applying active listening in diverse scenarios. You'll discover how active listening can help you navigate complex family relationships, build trust and rapport with colleagues, and create more meaningful social connections. By mastering the art of context-specific active listening, you'll be equipped with the tools to strengthen your relationships across all aspects of your life.

As we explore these different contexts, remember that the core principles of active listening—empathy, undivided attention, and non-judgmental understanding—remain constant. By adapting these principles to the unique demands of each relationship, you'll be better prepared to face the challenges and reap the rewards of effective communication in all your interactions.

Subsection 5.1: Active Listening in Romantic Relationships

In the context of romantic relationships, active listening plays a crucial role in fostering intimacy, understanding, and emotional connection. When we listen attentively to our partners, we create a safe space for them to express their thoughts, feelings, and needs, which is essential for building trust and strengthening the bond between us.

One of the primary benefits of active listening in romantic relationships is that it allows us to gain a deeper understanding of our partner's perspective. By giving our undivided attention and practicing empathy, we can better comprehend their experiences, motivations, and challenges. This understanding is crucial for navigating conflicts, offering support, and making decisions that take both partners' needs into account.

To apply active listening effectively in romantic relationships, it's important to minimize distractions and create an environment conducive to open communication. This may involve setting aside dedicated time for conversations, turning off electronic devices, and choosing a private, comfortable setting. By demonstrating that we are fully present and engaged, we encourage our partners to share more freely and openly.

When actively listening to our romantic partners, it's essential to suspend judgment and avoid jumping to conclusions. Instead, we should focus on understanding their point of view, even if it differs from our own. By asking clarifying questions and reflecting on what we've heard, we can ensure that we have accurately grasped their message and show that we value their perspective.

Another crucial aspect of active listening in romantic relationships is validating our partner's feelings and experiences. This involves acknowledging the validity of their emotions, even if we don't necessarily agree with their interpretation of events. By saying things like, "I understand why you feel that way," or "That must have been really challenging for you," we show that we respect and empathize with their experiences, which can help them feel heard and supported.

Active listening can also help couples navigate conflicts more effectively. When emotions run high, it's easy to fall into patterns of defensiveness, criticism, or stonewalling. However, by focusing on listening to understand rather than to respond, we can de-escalate tensions and find common ground. This approach allows both partners to express their needs and concerns without fear of judgment or retaliation, paving the way for more constructive problem-solving.

Ultimately, active listening in romantic relationships is about creating a foundation of trust, respect, and emotional intimacy. By consistently practicing this skill, couples can deepen their connection, foster greater understanding, and build a stronger, more resilient partnership. As with any skill, active listening requires practice and patience, but the rewards – a more loving, supportive, and fulfilling relationship – are well worth the effort.

Subsection 5.2: Active Listening in Family Dynamics

Family relationships are among the most complex and emotionally charged connections we experience throughout our lives. The dynamics within a family can be influenced by a myriad of factors, including individual personalities, past experiences, and communication patterns. Active listening plays a crucial role in navigating these intricate relationships, promoting understanding, and fostering healthier interactions among family members.

One of the primary challenges in family communication is the tendency for members to fall into established roles and patterns of interaction. These patterns, which may have developed over years or even generations, can hinder effective communication and lead to misunderstandings and conflicts. By employing active listening techniques, family members can break free from these unproductive cycles and create a more supportive and inclusive environment.

When practicing active listening within the family context, it's essential to approach conversations with an open mind and a willingness to understand each person's perspective. This can be particularly challenging when discussing sensitive topics or navigating long-standing disagreements. However, by setting aside preconceived notions and focusing on listening to understand, family members can create a safe space for honest and productive dialogue.

One effective strategy for active listening in family dynamics is to practice empathy and validation. This involves making a concerted effort to understand and acknowledge the feelings and experiences of each family member, even if you don't necessarily agree with their perspective.

By expressing empathy and validating their emotions, you create a foundation of trust and respect that can help bridge gaps and facilitate more constructive conversations.

Another key aspect of active listening in family relationships is managing emotional triggers. Family interactions can often evoke strong emotional responses, such as anger, frustration, or defensiveness, which can derail communication and escalate conflicts. By developing self-awareness and practicing emotional regulation, family members can learn to recognize and manage their own triggers, allowing them to engage in more productive and compassionate dialogue.

Active listening can also play a vital role in supporting family members through challenging times, such as periods of stress, loss, or transition. By providing a non-judgmental and supportive presence, family members can create a safe haven for one another to express their fears, doubts, and vulnerabilities. This emotional support can help strengthen family bonds and foster resilience in the face of adversity.

Incorporating active listening into family dynamics requires a commitment from all members to prioritize open, honest, and respectful communication. This may involve setting aside dedicated time for family discussions, establishing ground rules for communication, and practicing active listening skills consistently. By making active listening a core value within the family, members can create a more harmonious and supportive home environment that nurtures growth and connection.

Ultimately, the power of active listening in family dynamics lies in its ability to transform relationships and create a more loving, understanding, and resilient family unit. By embracing the principles of empathy, non-judgment, and emotional attunement, family members can navigate even the most complex and challenging relationships with grace and compassion. Through the consistent practice of active listening, families can build a strong foundation of trust, respect, and mutual understanding that will support them through all of life's joys and challenges.

Subsection 5.3: Active Listening in Professional Settings

In the fast-paced and often high-pressure world of work, effective communication is paramount to success. Active listening, a critical component of effective communication, can significantly improve teamwork, leadership, and conflict resolution in professional settings. By mastering the art of active listening, individuals can foster a more collaborative, productive, and harmonious work environment.

One of the primary benefits of active listening in the workplace is enhanced teamwork. When team members practice active listening, they create an atmosphere of mutual respect, trust, and understanding. By giving their full attention to their colleagues and seeking to comprehend their perspectives, active listeners demonstrate that they value the input and expertise of others. This, in turn, encourages open communication, idea-sharing, and collaboration, leading to more effective problem-solving and decision-making.

Active listening is also a crucial skill for effective leadership. Leaders who practice active listening show their team members that they are invested in their success and well-being. By taking the time to listen attentively to their employees' concerns, ideas, and feedback, leaders can gain valuable insights into the challenges and opportunities facing their team. This understanding allows them to provide more targeted support, guidance, and resources, ultimately fostering a more engaged and motivated workforce.

Moreover, active listening plays a vital role in conflict resolution within professional settings. Workplace conflicts can arise due to misunderstandings, competing priorities, or personality differences. By employing active listening techniques, individuals can help de-escalate tensions and find common ground. When conflicting parties feel heard and understood, they are more likely to approach the issue with an open mind and a willingness to compromise. Active listeners can facilitate this process by reflecting on what has been said, asking clarifying questions, and helping to identify underlying needs and concerns.

To apply active listening effectively in professional settings, it's essential to create an environment that supports open and honest communication. This may involve setting aside dedicated time for one-on-one conversations, team meetings, or feedback sessions. It's also important to minimize distractions, such as electronic devices or competing priorities, to ensure that full attention can be given to the speaker.

When actively listening in the workplace, it's crucial to maintain a non-judgmental and empathetic approach. This involves setting aside personal biases or preconceptions and focusing on understanding the speaker's perspective. By asking open-ended questions and providing verbal and nonverbal cues of engagement, active listeners can encourage their colleagues to share their thoughts and feelings more freely.

Another key aspect of active listening in professional settings is the ability to paraphrase and summarize what has been said. This not only demonstrates understanding but also helps to clarify any misinterpretations or ambiguities. By reflecting on the speaker's message, active listeners can ensure that everyone is on the same page and working towards a common goal.

Ultimately, the power of active listening in professional settings lies in its ability to transform the way individuals and teams communicate and collaborate. By fostering an environment of trust, respect, and understanding, active listening can help break down barriers, resolve conflicts, and unlock the full potential of every team member. As organizations increasingly recognize the value of effective communication, those who master the art of active listening will be well-positioned to thrive in their careers and make a positive impact in their workplaces.

Subsection 5.4: Active Listening in Social Interactions

Active listening is not only crucial for maintaining healthy romantic relationships, family dynamics, and professional connections but also plays a vital role in enhancing our social interactions and building stronger, more meaningful friendships. By applying active listening skills in our social lives, we can create deeper, more authentic connections with others and foster a sense of belonging and support.

In social settings, active listening involves being fully present and engaged in conversations, showing genuine interest in others' thoughts, experiences, and emotions. By giving our undivided attention to our friends and acquaintances, we demonstrate that we value their company and care about their well-being. This, in turn, encourages them to open up and share more of themselves, leading to more intimate and fulfilling social bonds.

One of the key benefits of active listening in social interactions is that it allows us to gain a more comprehensive understanding of others' perspectives and experiences. By asking open-ended questions, providing verbal and nonverbal cues of engagement, and reflecting on what has been shared, we can gain valuable insights into our friends' lives, challenges, and aspirations. This deeper understanding enables us to offer more meaningful support, advice, and encouragement, strengthening the foundation of our friendships.

Moreover, active listening can help us navigate conflicts and misunderstandings that may arise in our social circles. When tensions run high or disagreements occur, it's easy to become defensive or dismissive of others' viewpoints. However, by practicing active listening, we can approach these situations with empathy, patience, and a willingness to understand. By focusing on hearing and acknowledging our friends' concerns, rather than rushing to judgment or offering unsolicited advice, we can help de-escalate conflicts and find mutually beneficial solutions.

In social settings, active listening also plays a crucial role in creating a sense of belonging and validation. When we listen attentively to our friends' stories, experiences, and emotions, we send a powerful message that their thoughts and feelings matter. This validation can be particularly important for individuals who may be going through challenging times or struggling with self-doubt. By offering a non-judgmental, supportive presence, we can help our friends feel seen, heard, and valued, fostering a deeper sense of connection and trust.

To apply active listening effectively in social interactions, it's essential to be mindful of our own biases, assumptions, and distractions. We must approach conversations with an open mind, setting aside preconceived notions and focusing on understanding, rather than judging or advising. It's also important to be aware of our own emotional triggers and to practice self-regulation, ensuring that we can remain present and supportive even in the face of difficult or uncomfortable topics.

Another key aspect of active listening in social interactions is the ability to balance sharing and listening. While it's important to offer our own thoughts, experiences, and support, we must also be mindful of not dominating the conversation or shifting the focus away from our friends' needs. By striking a balance between self-expression and attentive listening, we can create a more reciprocal and fulfilling social dynamic.

Ultimately, the power of active listening in social interactions lies in its ability to transform the way we connect with others and build meaningful, lasting friendships. By embracing the principles of empathy, non-judgment, and emotional attunement, we can create a more inclusive, supportive, and authentic social environment that nurtures growth, resilience, and joy. Through the consistent practice of active listening, we can cultivate the kind of deep, transformative friendships that enrich our lives and help us navigate the ups and downs of the human experience with grace, compassion, and understanding.

Summary: Embracing Active Listening for Stronger Connections

Throughout this section, we have explored the transformative power of active listening in various relationship contexts, from romantic partnerships and family dynamics to professional settings and social interactions. By adapting and applying active listening skills to the unique demands and challenges of each situation, we can cultivate deeper, more meaningful connections and foster a greater sense of understanding, empathy, and support in all of our relationships.

The core principles of active listening – empathy, non-judgment, and emotional attunement – serve as a foundation for building stronger, more resilient relationships across all aspects of our lives. By consistently practicing these skills and tailoring our approach to the specific needs of each context, we can create a more supportive, inclusive, and harmonious environment that encourages growth, healing, and connection.

As we navigate the complexities of our relationships, it is essential to remember that active listening is a continuous journey of learning, self-reflection, and improvement. By embracing the power of this transformative skill and committing to its ongoing practice, we can unlock the full potential of our relationships, both with others and with ourselves.

The insights and strategies provided in this section serve as a roadmap for applying active listening to the diverse tapestry of our lives. By integrating these principles into our daily interactions and approaching each relationship with an open heart and a willingness to understand, we can cultivate a more compassionate, connected, and fulfilling existence.

As we move forward on this journey of growth and self-discovery, let us embrace the art of active listening as a catalyst for positive change, healing, and transformation. By truly hearing and understanding one another, we can build bridges of empathy, trust, and mutual respect that will support us through all of life's joys and challenges.

Chapter Summary: Mastering the Art of Active Listening for Stronger Relationships

Throughout this chapter, we have explored the transformative power of active listening in building stronger, more empathetic, and more meaningful relationships. By understanding the key components of active listening, such as giving undivided attention, using nonverbal cues, employing verbal encouragers, and asking clarifying questions, you can demonstrate genuine interest and engagement in your conversations.

We have also addressed common barriers to active listening, including internal distractions, judgments, assumptions, and emotional triggers. By developing strategies to overcome these obstacles, you can cultivate a more open and receptive mindset, allowing you to truly hear and understand the perspectives of others.

Furthermore, we have delved into the importance of empathy and validation in active listening. By reflecting feelings and content, as well as validating experiences and emotions, you can convey understanding and support, even in challenging conversations.

Finally, we have explored how to apply active listening skills in various relationship contexts, from romantic partnerships and family dynamics to professional settings and social interactions. By adapting your active listening approach to suit different situations, you can enhance communication, build trust, and foster deeper connections across all areas of your life.

As you continue on your journey of mastering the art of active listening, remember that it is a skill that requires ongoing practice and commitment. By consistently applying the principles and techniques outlined in this chapter, you can transform the way you interact with others, leading to more fulfilling, empathetic, and successful relationships. Embrace the power of active listening, and watch as your connections flourish and thrive.

Chapter 5: Navigating Conflict and Disagreements

Conflict is an inevitable part of any relationship, whether it's with a romantic partner, family member, friend, or colleague. When two individuals come together, each with their own unique perspectives, beliefs, and experiences, disagreements are bound to arise. However, it's not the presence of conflict that determines the health and longevity of a relationship; rather, it's how we choose to navigate and resolve these challenges that truly matters.

In this chapter, we'll explore the art of constructive conflict resolution and develop practical strategies for handling disagreements in a manner that strengthens, rather than weakens, our relationships. We'll delve into the common causes of conflict, examine the role of emotions in escalating or defusing tensions, and learn how to distinguish between healthy and unhealthy patterns of conflict.

Through relatable examples and evidence-based insights, we'll discover the power of a collaborative mindset, one that prioritizes understanding, empathy, and mutual respect. We'll practice effective communication techniques, such as using "I" statements, active listening, and asking open-ended questions, to foster productive dialogue and problem-solving.

As we navigate the complexities of conflict in various relationship contexts, from romantic partnerships to family dynamics and workplace interactions, we'll gain valuable tools for maintaining composure, finding common ground, and working towards win-win solutions. We'll also learn to recognize when conflicts have escalated beyond the scope of self-help strategies and explore the benefits of seeking professional support, such as couple's therapy or mediation.

By the end of this chapter, you'll be equipped with a robust toolkit for transforming conflict into an opportunity for growth, connection, and understanding. You'll have the confidence to approach disagreements with a positive, solution-oriented mindset, and the skills to communicate effectively, even in the face of intense emotions. Most importantly, you'll discover that by learning to navigate conflict constructively, you can build relationships that are resilient, deeply satisfying, and able to weather the storms of life.

Section 1: Understanding the Nature of Conflict in Relationships

Conflict is an inevitable part of any relationship, whether it's with a romantic partner, family member, friend, or colleague. It arises when people have differing opinions, needs, or expectations, and it can range from minor disagreements to major disputes that threaten the very foundation of the relationship. While conflict is often viewed as a negative experience, it can also be an opportunity for growth, increased understanding, and stronger bonds when handled constructively.

In this section, we will delve into the common causes and dynamics of conflicts and disagreements in various types of relationships. By gaining a deeper understanding of the factors that contribute to conflict, we can develop more effective strategies for managing and resolving them in a healthy and productive manner.

We will explore the role of communication, emotions, and underlying issues in the escalation and resolution of conflicts. Through real-life examples and research-backed insights, we will examine the differences between healthy and unhealthy conflict, and how to foster a relationship dynamic that promotes open, honest, and respectful dialogue.

Whether you're currently facing a challenging situation in your own relationships or simply seeking to improve your conflict resolution skills, this section will provide you with the knowledge and tools needed to navigate the complex landscape of interpersonal conflicts. By the end of this section, you will have a clearer understanding of the nature of conflict and be better equipped to handle disagreements in a way that strengthens, rather than weakens, your relationships.

Subsection 1.1: Identifying the Root Causes of Conflict

Conflicts in relationships often arise from a complex interplay of various factors, some of which may not be immediately apparent. To effectively address and resolve conflicts, it is crucial to identify the underlying issues that contribute to these disagreements. By taking the time to explore the root causes of conflict, couples, family members, friends, and colleagues can gain a deeper understanding of each other's perspectives and work towards finding lasting solutions.

One of the primary sources of conflict in relationships is unmet needs or expectations. When individuals feel that their physical, emotional, or psychological needs are not being fulfilled by their partner or loved ones, it can lead to feelings of frustration, resentment, and dissatisfaction. These unmet needs may stem from a lack of communication, differing priorities, or a mismatch in values. For example, if one partner places a high value on quality time together while the other prioritizes personal space and independence, conflicts may arise when these needs clash.

Another common root cause of conflict is the presence of unresolved past issues or traumas. Individuals may bring baggage from previous relationships, childhood experiences, or personal struggles into their current connections, which can color their perceptions and reactions to present-day situations. For instance, someone who experienced betrayal in a past relationship may struggle with trust and be more prone to jealousy or suspicion in their current partnership, leading to conflicts over seemingly minor issues.

Differences in communication styles and emotional expression can also contribute to conflicts in relationships. Some individuals may be more direct and assertive in their communication, while others may prefer a more passive or indirect approach. These differences can lead to misunderstandings, hurt feelings, and a breakdown in effective dialogue.

Similarly, variations in emotional expressiveness can create tension, with one person feeling overwhelmed by their partner's emotional intensity while the other feels neglected or unheard.

External stressors and life transitions can also play a significant role in the emergence of conflicts. Financial strain, work-related pressures, health concerns, or major life changes such as the arrival of a new baby or a move to a new city can put additional stress on relationships and exacerbate existing tensions. During these challenging times, individuals may be more prone to irritability, short tempers, and a decreased ability to handle conflicts constructively.

To identify the root causes of conflict in a relationship, it is essential to approach the process with openness, curiosity, and a willingness to engage in self-reflection. Couples and individuals can start by asking themselves questions such as:

- What are my unmet needs or expectations in this relationship?

- Are there any past experiences or traumas that may be influencing my reactions to current situations?

- How do my communication style and emotional expression differ from my partner's, and how might this contribute to misunderstandings?

- What external stressors or life transitions are we currently facing, and how are they impacting our relationship?

By honestly exploring these questions and engaging in open, non-judgmental dialogue with their loved ones, individuals can gain valuable insights into the underlying factors that fuel conflicts in their relationships. Armed with this knowledge, they can work collaboratively to address these root causes, develop greater empathy and understanding, and find mutually satisfying solutions to their disagreements. By doing so, they lay the foundation for a stronger, more resilient connection built on trust, respect, and a shared commitment to growth.

Subsection 1.2: The Role of Emotions in Conflict

Emotions play a significant role in the escalation and resolution of conflicts in relationships. When disagreements arise, the emotional responses of those involved can greatly influence the course of the conflict and its eventual outcome. Intense emotions such as anger, frustration, fear, or sadness can cloud judgment, hinder effective communication, and lead to destructive behaviors that further fuel the conflict.

During a heated argument, it is common for individuals to experience a surge of strong emotions that can overwhelm their ability to think rationally and respond constructively. In these moments, the body's fight-or-flight response is activated, releasing stress hormones like cortisol and adrenaline that prepare us to either confront the perceived threat or flee from it. This physiological reaction can manifest in various ways, such as raised voices, aggressive body language, or a desire to withdraw from the situation entirely.

The impact of unchecked emotions on conflict escalation can be profound. When individuals allow their emotions to dictate their words and actions, they may say or do things that they later regret, causing further damage to the relationship. Harsh criticism, name-calling, or stonewalling can all contribute to a toxic cycle of negative interactions that erode trust and goodwill between partners. Moreover, when one person's emotional intensity is met with a similarly charged response from the other, the conflict can quickly spiral out of control, making it increasingly difficult to find a resolution.

However, emotions can also play a constructive role in conflict resolution when they are acknowledged, validated, and managed effectively. By recognizing and accepting the presence of strong emotions during a disagreement, individuals can take steps to regulate their own emotional responses and approach the situation with greater clarity and composure. This may involve taking a brief time-out to calm down, engaging in deep breathing exercises, or practicing mindfulness techniques to stay grounded in the present moment.

Once the initial emotional intensity has subsided, it becomes easier to engage in a more productive dialogue aimed at understanding each other's perspectives and finding mutually satisfying solutions. By expressing emotions in a non-threatening, non-judgmental manner, individuals can foster a sense of empathy and connection, even in the midst of a disagreement. Statements such as "I feel hurt when..." or "I'm worried that..." can help convey the emotional impact of the conflict without resorting to blame or accusation.

Furthermore, acknowledging and validating the emotions of the other person can go a long way in de-escalating conflicts and promoting a more collaborative approach to problem-solving. When individuals feel heard, understood, and respected, they are more likely to reciprocate with a willingness to listen and compromise. Active listening skills, such as paraphrasing and reflecting, can demonstrate a genuine desire to understand the other person's emotional experience and work together towards a resolution.

Managing intense emotions during conflicts also requires a certain level of self-awareness and emotional intelligence. By developing a deeper understanding of one's own emotional triggers, patterns, and coping mechanisms, individuals can better regulate their responses and avoid getting swept up in the heat of the moment. This may involve learning to identify and challenge negative thought patterns, practicing self-soothing techniques, or seeking the support of a trusted friend, family member, or mental health professional.

Ultimately, the role of emotions in conflict is complex and multifaceted. While intense emotions can undoubtedly contribute to the escalation of disagreements, they can also serve as a catalyst for deeper understanding, empathy, and connection when approached with mindfulness and skill.

By learning to manage and harness the power of emotions, individuals can navigate conflicts more effectively and build stronger, more resilient relationships in the process.

Subsection 1.3: The Difference Between Healthy and Unhealthy Conflict

Conflict is an inevitable part of any relationship, but not all conflicts are created equal. Some conflicts can be constructive, leading to personal growth, increased understanding, and stronger connections between individuals. On the other hand, some conflicts can be destructive, eroding trust, damaging communication, and ultimately undermining the very foundation of the relationship. Distinguishing between healthy and unhealthy conflict is crucial for navigating disagreements effectively and maintaining strong, resilient bonds with others.

Healthy conflict is characterized by a focus on the issue at hand, rather than personal attacks or blame. When engaging in constructive conflict, individuals approach the disagreement with a spirit of collaboration and a genuine desire to find a mutually satisfactory solution. They express their thoughts, feelings, and needs clearly and respectfully, while also actively listening to and considering the perspective of the other person. Healthy conflict involves a willingness to compromise, negotiate, and find common ground, recognizing that the relationship is more important than being right or winning the argument.

In healthy conflict, emotions are acknowledged and managed effectively. While it is natural to experience frustration, anger, or disappointment during a disagreement, individuals engaging in constructive conflict take responsibility for their own emotional responses and avoid letting their feelings dictate their words or actions. They may take breaks when necessary to calm down and regain composure, but they remain committed to resolving the issue and maintaining open, honest communication throughout the process.

Constructive conflict can lead to positive outcomes, such as increased self-awareness, enhanced problem-solving skills, and a deeper understanding of one another's needs and perspectives. By working through disagreements in a healthy manner, individuals can strengthen their bond, build trust, and create a more resilient relationship that can weather future challenges.

On the other hand, unhealthy conflict is characterized by a focus on winning, dominating, or punishing the other person. In destructive conflicts, individuals may resort to personal attacks, criticism, or blame, rather than addressing the issue at hand. They may use aggressive or manipulative tactics to control the conversation, such as yelling, intimidation, or stonewalling. Unhealthy conflict often involves a lack of respect for the other person's thoughts, feelings, or boundaries, and a disregard for the impact of one's words or actions on the relationship.

In destructive conflicts, emotions can quickly escalate and spiral out of control. Individuals may allow their anger, frustration, or resentment to fuel hurtful words or actions, causing further damage to the relationship. They may refuse to take responsibility for their own role in the conflict, instead focusing on the faults or shortcomings of the other person. Unhealthy conflict can lead to a breakdown in communication, a loss of trust, and a growing sense of disconnection or alienation between individuals.

Destructive conflicts can have long-lasting negative consequences for relationships. They can erode the very foundation of trust, respect, and goodwill that is essential for any healthy connection. Over time, a pattern of unhealthy conflict can lead to resentment, bitterness, and a sense of hopelessness about the future of the relationship.

Recognizing the difference between healthy and unhealthy conflict is an important step in fostering strong, resilient relationships. By approaching disagreements with a spirit of collaboration, respect, and emotional maturity, individuals can transform potential sources of tension into opportunities for growth, understanding, and connection.

Through the use of effective communication strategies, active listening, and a willingness to find mutually satisfactory solutions, individuals can navigate even the most challenging conflicts in a way that strengthens, rather than weakens, their relationships.

Summary: Embracing Conflict as an Opportunity for Growth

Conflict is a natural and inevitable part of any relationship, but it is how we choose to approach and navigate these challenges that ultimately determine the strength and resilience of our connections. By understanding the common causes and dynamics of conflicts, such as unmet needs, emotional triggers, and communication styles, we can develop the skills and strategies necessary to transform disagreements into opportunities for growth and deeper understanding.

Recognizing the difference between healthy and unhealthy conflict is crucial in this process. Healthy conflict is characterized by a focus on the issue at hand, a spirit of collaboration, and a willingness to find mutually satisfactory solutions. It involves managing emotions effectively, maintaining respect for one another, and using disagreements as a catalyst for positive change. In contrast, unhealthy conflict is marked by personal attacks, a lack of respect, and a focus on winning or dominating the other person, which can erode trust and damage the very foundation of the relationship.

By cultivating self-awareness, emotional intelligence, and effective communication skills, we can approach conflicts in a more constructive and compassionate manner. This involves taking responsibility for our own emotions and reactions, actively listening to and validating the experiences of others, and working together to find common ground and compromise. With practice and commitment, we can learn to harness the power of conflict to strengthen our relationships, deepen our connections, and foster personal growth and resilience.

As we move forward in our exploration of navigating conflicts and disagreements, it is essential to remember that conflict itself is not the enemy. Rather, it is an invitation to engage in the hard but rewarding work of understanding ourselves and others more fully, communicating our needs and boundaries clearly, and building relationships that can weather the storms of life. By embracing this challenge with open hearts and minds, we open ourselves up to the possibility of truly authentic, fulfilling, and lasting connections.

Section 2: Developing a Conflict Resolution Mindset

Conflict is an inevitable part of any relationship, whether it's with a romantic partner, family member, friend, or colleague. How we approach and handle these conflicts can make a significant difference in the health and longevity of our relationships. Developing a conflict resolution mindset is crucial for navigating disagreements and challenges in a constructive and relationship-preserving manner.

In this section, we will explore the key elements of cultivating a mindset that promotes effective conflict resolution. We'll delve into the importance of adopting a collaborative approach, where both parties work together to find mutually beneficial solutions. By shifting away from a win-lose mentality and focusing on problem-solving, we can create an environment that fosters open communication, understanding, and growth.

Moreover, we'll discuss the role of empathy and perspective-taking in conflict resolution. Learning to consider the other person's viewpoint, emotions, and needs can help us develop a deeper understanding of the situation and find common ground. We'll also examine the significance of maintaining respect and compassion, even in the heat of an argument, to ensure that the relationship remains the priority.

Throughout this section, we'll provide practical strategies and techniques for embodying a conflict resolution mindset. By incorporating these approaches into your own life, you'll be better equipped to handle disagreements in a way that strengthens your relationships and promotes personal growth. Whether you're facing a minor misunderstanding or a major dispute, developing a conflict resolution mindset will serve as a foundation for building healthier, more resilient connections with the people who matter most to you.

Subsection 2.1: Embracing a Collaborative Approach

When faced with conflicts in relationships, it's easy to fall into a win-lose mentality, where each person seeks to emerge victorious at the expense of the other. However, this approach often leads to resentment, damaged trust, and a deterioration of the relationship. To navigate conflicts constructively and preserve the health of your connections, it's crucial to embrace a collaborative approach.

A collaborative approach to conflict resolution involves shifting your mindset from one of competition to one of cooperation. Instead of viewing the other person as an opponent to be defeated, consider them as a partner in finding a mutually beneficial solution. This perspective change can be challenging, especially when emotions are running high, but it is essential for creating an environment conducive to open, honest communication and problem-solving.

To adopt a collaborative mindset, start by acknowledging that both parties have valid concerns, needs, and perspectives. Recognize that the goal is not to determine who is right or wrong, but rather to find a resolution that addresses everyone's interests. By focusing on the issues at hand rather than attacking or blaming one another, you create a safe space for exploring creative solutions and reaching compromises.

Effective collaboration also requires a willingness to listen actively and empathetically. Take the time to understand the other person's point of view, even if you disagree with it. Ask clarifying questions, paraphrase their statements to ensure understanding, and validate their emotions. By demonstrating genuine interest and respect for their perspective, you foster a sense of trust and openness that is essential for productive problem-solving.

As you work together to find a resolution, maintain a flexible and open-minded approach. Be willing to brainstorm a wide range of options, and avoid getting attached to a single solution. Encourage the other person to share their ideas and build upon them, looking for areas of common ground and opportunities for compromise. Remember that the goal is not to win but to find a solution that works for both of you.

Embracing a collaborative approach to conflict resolution may not always be easy, particularly when dealing with longstanding or deeply entrenched issues. However, by consistently choosing cooperation over competition, you lay the foundation for healthier, more resilient relationships. With practice and patience, you can develop the skills and mindset necessary to navigate even the most challenging conflicts with grace, empathy, and a focus on strengthening your connections.

Subsection 2.2: Practicing Empathy and Perspective-Taking

Empathy and perspective-taking are essential skills for navigating conflicts and disagreements in relationships. When we find ourselves in the midst of a heated argument or a tense discussion, it can be challenging to step back and consider the other person's point of view. However, making a conscious effort to understand and acknowledge their perspective can be a powerful tool for fostering understanding, finding common ground, and ultimately resolving conflicts in a constructive manner.

Empathy involves putting yourself in the other person's shoes and attempting to understand their thoughts, feelings, and experiences. It requires setting aside your own judgments and biases and genuinely listening to what the other person has to say. By practicing empathy, you demonstrate that you value and respect their perspective, even if you don't necessarily agree with it. This validation can go a long way in creating a safe and open environment for productive dialogue and problem-solving.

Perspective-taking, on the other hand, involves actively seeking to understand the other person's viewpoint and the factors that have shaped their beliefs and opinions. It requires asking questions, listening attentively, and considering the context of their experiences. By taking the time to see the situation through their eyes, you gain a more comprehensive understanding of the issues at hand and can approach the conflict with greater insight and compassion.

Practicing empathy and perspective-taking during disagreements can be challenging, especially when emotions are running high. It's natural to feel defensive or to want to prioritize your own needs and desires. However, by making a conscious effort to step back and consider the other person's perspective, you create opportunities for growth, learning, and strengthening your relationship.

One effective way to cultivate empathy and perspective-taking is through active listening. Instead of focusing on formulating your response or rebuttal, give the other person your full attention and seek to understand their message. Ask clarifying questions, paraphrase their statements to ensure understanding, and acknowledge their emotions. By demonstrating genuine interest and concern for their perspective, you create a foundation of trust and respect that can facilitate more productive conversations.

Another key aspect of practicing empathy and perspective-taking is managing your own emotions. When we feel attacked or misunderstood, it's easy to become defensive or reactive. However, by taking a moment to regulate your own emotional response, you can approach the situation with greater clarity and objectivity. Take deep breaths, practice mindfulness, and remind yourself that the goal is to understand and find a resolution, not to win an argument.

It's important to note that practicing empathy and perspective-taking does not mean abandoning your own needs, beliefs, or boundaries. Rather, it involves finding a balance between asserting yourself and considering the other person's perspective. By approaching conflicts with a spirit of curiosity, openness, and respect, you create opportunities for mutual understanding and collaborative problem-solving.

Incorporating empathy and perspective-taking into your conflict resolution toolkit can have a profound impact on the health and resilience of your relationships. By consistently making an effort to understand and validate the other person's perspective, you foster a deeper sense of connection, trust, and mutual respect. While it may not always be easy, the rewards of practicing these skills are well worth the effort, as they lay the foundation for more loving, supportive, and fulfilling relationships.

Subsection 2.3: Maintaining Respect and Compassion

In the heat of conflict, it can be all too easy to lose sight of the importance of respect and compassion. When emotions are running high and disagreements seem insurmountable, we may find ourselves lashing out, using hurtful words, or disregarding the other person's feelings. However, maintaining respect and compassion, even in the midst of conflict, is crucial for preserving the health and well-being of our relationships.

Respect is the foundation of any strong, healthy relationship. It involves treating the other person with dignity, valuing their opinions and experiences, and acknowledging their inherent worth as a human being. When we approach conflicts with respect, we create a safe space for open, honest communication and collaborative problem-solving. We signal to the other person that we are committed to finding a resolution that works for both of us, rather than simply trying to win an argument or prove a point.

Compassion, on the other hand, involves recognizing and empathizing with the other person's emotions, needs, and struggles. It requires setting aside our own judgments and biases and seeking to understand the other person's perspective with kindness and care. By approaching conflicts with compassion, we demonstrate that we value the other person's well-being and are committed to finding a solution that addresses their concerns and needs, as well as our own.

Maintaining respect and compassion in the midst of conflict can be challenging, especially when we feel hurt, angry, or misunderstood. However, there are several strategies we can employ to uphold these important values, even in difficult moments. One key approach is to practice active listening, giving the other person our full attention and seeking to understand their perspective without interruption or judgment. By demonstrating genuine interest and concern for their thoughts and feelings, we create a foundation of trust and respect that can facilitate more productive conversations.

Another important strategy is to manage our own emotions and reactions. When we feel triggered or defensive, it can be tempting to lash out or shut down. However, by taking a moment to breathe, regain our composure, and choose our words carefully, we can respond in a way that is respectful and compassionate, even if we disagree. This may involve using "I" statements to express our own thoughts and feelings, rather than making accusations or generalizations about the other person.

It's also crucial to maintain healthy boundaries and assertiveness, even as we strive to be respectful and compassionate. This means being clear about our own needs, values, and limits, and communicating them in a way that is firm but not aggressive. By standing up for ourselves with respect and care, we create opportunities for mutual understanding and compromise, rather than allowing resentment or bitterness to fester.

Ultimately, maintaining respect and compassion in the midst of conflict is about recognizing the humanity in the other person and treating them with the same dignity and care that we would want for ourselves. It requires a willingness to set aside our own ego and defensiveness and approach the situation with an open heart and mind. By consistently choosing respect and compassion, even in difficult moments, we lay the foundation for stronger, more resilient relationships that can weather even the toughest challenges.

Summary: Nurturing Stronger Relationships Through a Conflict Resolution Mindset

Developing a conflict resolution mindset is a crucial step in building and maintaining healthy, resilient relationships. By embracing a collaborative approach, practicing empathy and perspective-taking, and maintaining respect and compassion, we lay the foundation for constructive problem-solving and growth. This mindset shift enables us to navigate even the most challenging disagreements with grace and understanding, prioritizing the well-being of our relationships above the desire to be right or win an argument.

As we cultivate this mindset, we create a safe space for open, honest communication and mutual understanding. We learn to set aside our own biases and defensiveness, and instead approach conflicts with curiosity, openness, and a genuine desire to find solutions that work for everyone involved. By consistently choosing empathy, respect, and collaboration, we not only resolve conflicts more effectively but also deepen our connections and strengthen the bonds that hold our relationships together.

Adopting a conflict resolution mindset is an ongoing process that requires practice, patience, and self-awareness. It may not always be easy, especially when emotions are running high or when dealing with long-standing issues. However, the rewards of this approach are immeasurable. By nurturing a mindset that prioritizes the health and resilience of our relationships, we unlock the potential for greater love, trust, and fulfillment in all of our connections.

As you continue on your journey of building stronger, more harmonious relationships, remember that developing a conflict resolution mindset is a powerful tool in your arsenal. By approaching disagreements with empathy, respect, and a focus on collaboration, you not only navigate conflicts more effectively but also cultivate a deeper sense of understanding, compassion, and connection with the people who matter most to you. Embrace this mindset, and watch as your relationships flourish and thrive, even in the face of life's inevitable challenges.

Section 3: Effective Communication Strategies for Conflict Resolution

Conflict is an inevitable part of any relationship, whether it's with a romantic partner, family member, friend, or colleague. While conflicts can be challenging and emotionally charged, they also present an opportunity for growth, understanding, and strengthening the bond between individuals. The key to navigating conflicts successfully lies in employing effective communication strategies that promote constructive dialogue and collaborative problem-solving.

In this section, we will explore a range of communication techniques and approaches that can help you manage conflicts in a healthy, respectful, and productive manner. By learning and applying these strategies, you'll be better equipped to express your thoughts, feelings, and needs assertively, while also creating a safe space for the other person to share their perspective.

We'll begin by discussing the importance of using "I" statements, which allow you to communicate your experiences without placing blame or making accusations. You'll also discover the power of active listening and reflecting, which demonstrate your commitment to understanding the other person's point of view and validating their emotions.

Additionally, we'll delve into the art of asking open-ended questions, a technique that encourages the sharing of information, clarifies misunderstandings, and promotes a deeper exploration of the issues at hand. By mastering these communication skills, you'll be better prepared to find common ground and work together towards mutually beneficial solutions.

Throughout this section, we'll provide real-life examples and scenarios that illustrate how these communication strategies can be applied in various relationship contexts. Whether you're navigating a disagreement with your spouse, addressing a family conflict, or dealing with a workplace dispute, the insights and techniques shared here will empower you to approach conflicts with greater confidence, empathy, and skill.

By embracing effective communication as a tool for conflict resolution, you'll not only be able to manage challenges more successfully but also foster a deeper sense of connection, trust, and understanding in your relationships. So, let's dive in and explore how you can transform conflicts into opportunities for growth and strengthening your bonds with others.

Subsection 3.1: Using "I" Statements

When navigating conflicts in relationships, the way we express ourselves can significantly impact the outcome of the conversation. One effective communication strategy is the use of "I" statements, which allow us to convey our thoughts, feelings, and needs in a non-defensive and assertive manner.

"I" statements shift the focus from blaming or accusing the other person to expressing our own experiences and perspectives. By starting sentences with "I," we take responsibility for our emotions and thoughts, reducing the likelihood of the other person feeling attacked or defensive. For example, instead of saying, "You never listen to me," which can come across as accusatory, we might say, "I feel unheard when I share my concerns with you."

Using "I" statements helps to create a safe and non-judgmental space for open communication. It encourages both parties to express their feelings and needs honestly, without fear of retribution or criticism. By modeling this approach, we invite the other person to reciprocate, fostering a dialogue that is focused on understanding and collaboration rather than winning an argument.

When constructing "I" statements, it's essential to be specific about our experiences and avoid generalizations. For instance, "I felt hurt when you dismissed my ideas during the meeting" is more effective than "You always disregard my opinions." Being specific helps the other person understand the precise situation or behavior that caused our emotional response, making it easier for them to address the issue and work towards a resolution.

It's also important to remember that "I" statements are not a magic solution to all conflicts. They should be used in conjunction with other communication skills, such as active listening and empathy. By combining "I" statements with a genuine desire to understand the other person's perspective, we create a foundation for productive and respectful conflict resolution.

In summary, using "I" statements is a powerful tool for expressing ourselves assertively and non-defensively during conflicts. By focusing on our own experiences and emotions, we create a safe space for open communication and collaboration. As we practice this technique, we'll find that our relationships grow stronger, and our ability to navigate challenges with grace and understanding improves.

Subsection 3.2: Active Listening and Reflecting

Active listening is a crucial skill in effective communication, particularly when navigating conflicts and disagreements in relationships. It involves fully concentrating on, understanding, and responding to what the other person is saying, both verbally and non-verbally. By practicing active listening, we demonstrate our commitment to understanding the other person's perspective, feelings, and needs, which can help to de-escalate tensions and foster a more productive dialogue.

One key aspect of active listening is reflecting, which involves paraphrasing or summarizing the other person's message to ensure that we have accurately understood their point of view. Reflecting shows that we are genuinely interested in comprehending their perspective and validates their experience, making them feel heard and valued.

When reflecting, it's essential to use phrases such as "What I'm hearing is..." or "It sounds like you're feeling..." followed by a concise summary of the main points or emotions expressed. For example, if your partner says, "I feel like you never make time for me anymore," you might reflect by saying, "It sounds like you're feeling neglected and that our relationship hasn't been a priority lately." This reflection demonstrates that you have listened attentively and understand the core message behind their words.

Reflecting also provides an opportunity for the other person to clarify or correct any misunderstandings, ensuring that both parties are on the same page. If your reflection is inaccurate, the other person can elaborate further, allowing you to gain a more complete understanding of their perspective.

In addition to verbal reflection, active listening involves paying attention to non-verbal cues, such as facial expressions, body language, and tone of voice. These non-verbal signals can often convey important information about the other person's emotional state and can help you respond with greater empathy and understanding.

Other essential components of active listening include maintaining eye contact, minimizing distractions, and avoiding the urge to interrupt or formulate a response while the other person is speaking. By fully focusing on the other person and their message, we create a safe and respectful space for open communication and problem-solving.

Practicing active listening and reflecting takes time and patience, but it is a skill that can be developed and refined with practice. As we become more adept at listening attentively and reflecting the other person's perspective, we can significantly improve our ability to navigate conflicts and build stronger, more resilient relationships.

In summary, active listening and reflecting are essential tools for effective communication during conflicts and disagreements. By fully concentrating on the other person's message, paraphrasing their main points, and validating their experience, we demonstrate our commitment to understanding and working collaboratively towards a resolution. As we cultivate these skills, we can transform conflicts into opportunities for growth, connection, and mutual understanding.

Subsection 3.3: Asking Open-Ended Questions

In the midst of a conflict or disagreement, it's easy to fall into the trap of making assumptions about the other person's thoughts, feelings, and motivations. However, these assumptions can often lead to misunderstandings and further escalation of the conflict. One effective way to avoid this pitfall and gain a deeper understanding of the other person's perspective is by asking open-ended questions.

Open-ended questions are designed to elicit more than a simple "yes" or "no" response. They encourage the other person to elaborate on their thoughts, feelings, and experiences, providing valuable insight into their point of view. By asking open-ended questions, we create a space for dialogue and exploration, demonstrating our genuine interest in understanding the other person's perspective.

For example, instead of asking, "Are you upset with me?" which is a closed-ended question that may lead to a defensive response, we could ask, "Can you tell me more about how you're feeling right now?" This open-ended question invites the other person to share their emotions and thoughts more freely, without feeling pressured to provide a specific answer.

When asking open-ended questions, it's essential to use a neutral, non-judgmental tone. This helps to create a safe and supportive environment where the other person feels comfortable expressing themselves honestly. Questions should be phrased in a way that demonstrates curiosity and a willingness to learn, rather than an attempt to prove a point or assign blame.

Some examples of open-ended questions that can be useful in navigating conflicts include:

- "What are your thoughts on this situation?"

- "How has this experience affected you?"

- "Can you help me understand your perspective better?"

- "What do you think we could do to resolve this issue?"

- "What are your main concerns or priorities in this situation?"

By asking these types of questions, we gain valuable information that can help clarify misunderstandings, uncover hidden concerns, and identify common ground. As we listen attentively to the other person's responses, we can ask follow-up questions to deepen our understanding and demonstrate our commitment to finding a mutually beneficial solution.

It's important to remember that asking open-ended questions is just one part of effective communication during conflicts. It should be combined with active listening, reflecting, and a genuine desire to understand and collaborate with the other person. By incorporating open-ended questions into our conflict resolution toolkit, we can foster more productive, empathetic, and solution-oriented conversations that strengthen our relationships and build trust.

In summary, asking open-ended questions is a powerful tool for gathering information, clarifying misunderstandings, and encouraging open communication during conflicts. By inviting the other person to share their thoughts and feelings more fully, we demonstrate our commitment to understanding their perspective and working together to find a resolution. As we practice this skill, we can transform conflicts into opportunities for growth, connection, and mutual understanding.

Subsection 3.4: Finding Common Ground

In the midst of a conflict, it can be challenging to see eye-to-eye with the other person, especially when emotions are running high and opinions seem vastly different. However, even in the most contentious situations, there often exist shared interests, values, and goals that can serve as a foundation for collaborative problem-solving. By actively seeking out these areas of common ground, we can shift the focus from our differences to the things that unite us, paving the way for more productive and mutually beneficial conflict resolution.

One of the first steps in finding common ground is to approach the conflict with a genuine desire to understand the other person's perspective. This requires setting aside our own preconceptions and biases and being open to hearing their thoughts, feelings, and concerns. By actively listening and asking open-ended questions, we can gain valuable insights into what matters most to them and identify potential areas of overlap with our own interests and values.

For example, imagine a couple disagreeing about how to spend their shared finances. One partner may prioritize saving for a down payment on a house, while the other may feel that investing in a new business venture is more important. At first glance, these goals may seem incompatible. However, by exploring the underlying motivations and values behind each person's perspective, the couple may discover that they both ultimately want to build a secure and prosperous future together. This shared goal can serve as a starting point for finding a compromise that honors both of their needs and desires.

In addition to identifying shared interests and goals, it's also essential to recognize and acknowledge the common values that underlie our relationships. These may include things like honesty, respect, trust, and compassion. By reminding ourselves and the other person of these shared values, we can create a sense of unity and purpose, even in the face of disagreement. This can help to reduce defensiveness and foster a more collaborative spirit as we work towards finding a resolution.

Another key aspect of finding common ground is being willing to let go of the need to be "right" or to "win" the argument. When we become too attached to our own position, we may inadvertently close ourselves off to alternative perspectives and solutions. By approaching the conflict with a more open and flexible mindset, we create space for creative problem-solving and the emergence of novel ideas that can benefit both parties.

It's also important to remember that finding common ground is not about compromising our own needs or values for the sake of avoiding conflict. Rather, it's about recognizing that our relationships are built on a foundation of shared humanity and that by working together, we can often find solutions that honor and uplift everyone involved. This requires a willingness to engage in honest, respectful dialogue and to be open to the possibility of growth and transformation.

In summary, finding common ground is a powerful tool for navigating conflicts and building stronger, more resilient relationships. By actively seeking out shared interests, values, and goals, we can shift the focus from our differences to the things that unite us. Through open and honest communication, a willingness to understand each other's perspectives, and a commitment to collaborative problem-solving, we can transform conflicts into opportunities for growth, connection, and mutual understanding. As we practice this skill, we not only become better equipped to handle the challenges that arise in our relationships but also deepen our capacity for empathy, compassion, and love.

Summary: Mastering the Art of Effective Communication for Conflict Resolution

Throughout this section, we have explored a range of powerful communication strategies that can transform the way you navigate conflicts and disagreements in your relationships. By mastering techniques such as using "I" statements, active listening, reflecting, asking open-ended questions, and finding common ground, you can approach even the most challenging situations with greater confidence, empathy, and skill.

Remember, effective communication is not about winning an argument or proving a point; it's about fostering understanding, connection, and collaboration. When you express yourself assertively and non-defensively, listen attentively to the other person's perspective, and seek out shared interests and values, you create a foundation for productive problem-solving and mutual growth.

As you practice and integrate these strategies into your communication toolkit, you may find that conflicts become less daunting and more manageable. You'll be better equipped to handle difficult emotions, clarify misunderstandings, and find creative solutions that honor the needs and desires of everyone involved.

Of course, mastering the art of effective communication is an ongoing journey, and there will always be room for improvement and refinement. But by committing to these principles and techniques, you can cultivate more resilient, fulfilling, and harmonious relationships in all areas of your life.

As you move forward, remember to approach each interaction with patience, curiosity, and compassion. Embrace the opportunity to learn and grow alongside your loved ones, colleagues, and friends. And trust in your ability to navigate even the most complex conflicts with grace, wisdom, and care.

With these tools and insights at your disposal, you are well on your way to becoming a masterful communicator and a skilled navigator of life's relational challenges. So take a deep breath, trust in the process, and continue to cultivate the art of effective communication, one conversation at a time.

Section 4: Navigating Specific Types of Conflict

Conflict is an inevitable part of any relationship, whether it's with a romantic partner, family member, friend, or colleague. While the principles of effective communication and conflict resolution remain the same across different types of relationships, the specific challenges and dynamics can vary greatly. In this section, we'll explore some of the most common types of conflicts that arise in various relationship contexts and provide targeted strategies for navigating these challenges.

From the unique intimacy and intensity of romantic partnerships to the complex web of roles and expectations in family relationships, each type of connection brings its own set of potential pitfalls and opportunities for growth. We'll delve into the intricacies of resolving conflicts related to intimacy, commitment, and expectations in romantic relationships, as well as the delicate balance of managing family dynamics and responsibilities. In the professional sphere, we'll examine strategies for addressing workplace conflicts with colleagues, supervisors, or subordinates, focusing on maintaining productivity and professionalism while preserving important working relationships.

Friendships, too, can be tested by misunderstandings, breaches of trust, and changing expectations over time. We'll explore ways to approach these challenges with care and compassion, working to repair and strengthen the bonds of friendship even in the face of conflict.

Throughout this section, we'll draw on real-life examples and expert insights to provide a comprehensive guide to navigating the unique challenges of conflict in different relationship contexts. By the end of this section, you'll be equipped with a toolkit of strategies and techniques for approaching conflict with confidence, empathy, and skill, no matter what type of relationship you're working to strengthen and support.

Subsection 4.1: Resolving Conflicts in Romantic Relationships

Romantic relationships are often the most intimate and emotionally charged connections we form, making them particularly vulnerable to conflicts and disagreements. When two individuals merge their lives, they bring with them unique personalities, expectations, and communication styles, which can lead to misunderstandings and friction. However, with the right tools and techniques, couples can navigate these challenges and emerge stronger, fostering a deeper sense of intimacy and understanding.

One of the most common sources of conflict in romantic relationships is differing expectations surrounding commitment, intimacy, and the future of the relationship. When partners have misaligned goals or desires, it can lead to feelings of frustration, insecurity, and resentment. To address these issues, it's essential for couples to engage in open, honest communication about their needs and expectations. This may involve setting aside dedicated time for heart-to-heart conversations, practicing active listening, and expressing oneself using "I" statements to avoid placing blame or making accusations.

Another key aspect of resolving romantic conflicts is learning to compromise and find mutually satisfying solutions. This requires a willingness to consider one another's perspectives, identify shared goals, and make concessions when necessary. For example, if one partner desires more quality time together while the other values independence, they may need to find a middle ground that honors both needs, such as planning regular date nights while also allowing for individual pursuits.

In some cases, conflicts in romantic relationships may stem from deeper issues, such as unresolved past traumas, attachment styles, or personal insecurities. When these underlying factors are at play, it may be beneficial to seek the guidance of a trained couples therapist who can help partners identify and work through these challenges in a safe, supportive environment.

Ultimately, the key to resolving conflicts in romantic relationships lies in approaching disagreements with empathy, patience, and a commitment to the relationship's growth. By cultivating a strong foundation of trust, respect, and open communication, couples can weather the storms of conflict and emerge with a deeper, more resilient bond. Remember, every relationship faces challenges – it's how you navigate them together that determines the strength and longevity of your partnership.

Subsection 4.2: Managing Family Conflicts

Family relationships are among the most complex and emotionally charged connections we form throughout our lives. The intricate web of roles, responsibilities, and expectations within a family can often lead to conflicts and disagreements that strain even the strongest bonds. However, by approaching these challenges with empathy, patience, and effective communication strategies, families can navigate conflicts and emerge with a deeper understanding and appreciation for one another.

One of the primary sources of conflict in family relationships stems from the unique dynamics and hierarchies that exist within the family structure. Parents, siblings, and extended family members all have different levels of authority, influence, and responsibility, which can sometimes lead to power struggles, resentment, and feelings of unfairness. To manage these conflicts effectively, it's essential for family members to recognize and respect each other's roles and boundaries while also maintaining open lines of communication.

When addressing family conflicts, it's crucial to create a safe and non-judgmental space where each family member feels heard and validated. This may involve setting aside dedicated time for family meetings or one-on-one conversations, where individuals can express their thoughts, feelings, and concerns without fear of criticism or retribution. By practicing active listening and using "I" statements to express oneself, family members can foster a sense of mutual understanding and respect, even in the face of disagreements.

Another key aspect of managing family conflicts is learning to compromise and find solutions that benefit the family as a whole. This requires a willingness to consider multiple perspectives, identify common goals, and make sacrifices when necessary. For example, if siblings are arguing over the use of a shared space, they may need to work together to create a schedule or establish guidelines that ensure everyone's needs are met fairly.

In some cases, family conflicts may be rooted in deeper issues, such as unresolved traumas, mental health concerns, or substance abuse problems. When these underlying factors are at play, it may be necessary to seek the guidance of a trained family therapist or counselor who can help the family work through these challenges in a safe, supportive environment. By addressing the root causes of conflict and developing healthy coping mechanisms, families can build resilience and strengthen their bonds.

Ultimately, the key to managing family conflicts lies in cultivating a strong foundation of love, respect, and open communication. By approaching disagreements with empathy, patience, and a commitment to the family's well-being, family members can weather the storms of conflict and emerge with a deeper appreciation for the unique roles and contributions of each individual. Remember, every family faces challenges – it's how you navigate them together that determines the strength and resilience of your family bond.

Subsection 4.3: Addressing Workplace Conflicts

Conflicts in the workplace are an inevitable part of professional life, as individuals with diverse personalities, work styles, and goals come together to collaborate and achieve common objectives. Whether it's a disagreement with a colleague, a misunderstanding with a supervisor, or a dispute with a subordinate, unresolved workplace conflicts can lead to decreased productivity, low morale, and a toxic work environment. By developing effective strategies for addressing these challenges, professionals can foster a more harmonious and efficient workplace while preserving important working relationships.

One of the key principles of resolving workplace conflicts is maintaining a professional and respectful approach, regardless of the situation. This means avoiding personal attacks, gossip, or other unprofessional behaviors that can escalate tensions and damage relationships. Instead, focus on addressing the issue at hand in a calm, objective manner, using clear and constructive language to express your concerns and perspectives.

Active listening is another crucial skill for navigating workplace conflicts. By giving your full attention to the other person and striving to understand their point of view, you demonstrate respect and create a more collaborative atmosphere. Encourage open communication by asking questions, paraphrasing their statements to ensure understanding, and acknowledging their feelings and concerns. This approach can help break down barriers and foster a more productive dialogue.

When addressing conflicts with colleagues, it's essential to find common ground and work towards mutually beneficial solutions. This may involve compromising, finding creative alternatives, or seeking the guidance of a neutral third party, such as a mediator or HR representative. By focusing on shared goals and interests, rather than individual positions, colleagues can often find a path forward that satisfies everyone's needs.

Conflicts with supervisors or subordinates can be particularly challenging, as they involve power dynamics and hierarchical relationships. When addressing issues with a supervisor, it's important to remain professional, respectful, and solution-oriented. Schedule a private meeting to discuss your concerns, come prepared with specific examples and constructive suggestions, and be open to feedback and guidance. If the conflict persists or escalates, consider seeking support from HR or a trusted mentor.

When managing conflicts with subordinates, it's crucial to balance assertiveness with empathy. Clearly communicate your expectations and provide specific feedback on areas for improvement, but also take the time to listen to their perspective and concerns. Work together to develop an action plan that outlines steps for resolving the issue and preventing future conflicts. Regularly follow up to ensure progress and provide ongoing support and guidance.

In some cases, workplace conflicts may stem from deeper systemic issues, such as a lack of clear policies, poor communication channels, or a toxic organizational culture. When these underlying factors are at play, it may be necessary to involve higher-level management or HR to address the root causes and implement broader changes.

Ultimately, the key to addressing workplace conflicts lies in maintaining a professional, empathetic, and solution-oriented approach. By cultivating strong communication skills, actively listening to others, and working towards mutually beneficial outcomes, professionals can navigate even the most challenging conflicts and build a more collaborative and supportive work environment. Remember, conflicts are opportunities for growth and learning – by approaching them with an open mind and a commitment to resolution, you can emerge as a stronger, more effective professional.

Subsection 4.4: Dealing with Conflicts in Friendships

Friendships are an essential part of our lives, providing us with support, companionship, and a sense of belonging. However, like any relationship, friendships are not immune to conflicts and challenges. Misunderstandings, breaches of trust, and changing expectations can strain even the strongest friendships, leading to hurt feelings, resentment, and even the end of the relationship. By learning to navigate these conflicts with empathy, honesty, and a commitment to resolution, we can strengthen our friendships and build more resilient bonds.

One of the most common sources of conflict in friendships is misunderstandings. When communication breaks down, or when friends fail to express their needs and expectations clearly, it can lead to confusion, frustration, and hurt feelings. To address these misunderstandings, it's essential to approach the situation with an open mind and a willingness to listen. Take the time to hear your friend's perspective, and express your own thoughts and feelings calmly and honestly. By engaging in a dialogue and working to clarify any misunderstandings, you can often resolve conflicts and prevent them from escalating.

Another significant challenge in friendships is breaches of trust. Whether it's a broken promise, a betrayal of confidence, or a failure to be there when needed, trust violations can deeply damage a friendship. When addressing these issues, it's crucial to be honest about your feelings and to give your friend the opportunity to explain their actions. While it may be tempting to lash out or end the friendship immediately, taking the time to have a meaningful conversation can often lead to a deeper understanding and a path forward. Remember that forgiveness is a process, and it may take time to rebuild trust, but with patience and commitment, it is possible to overcome even the most painful breaches.

As friendships evolve over time, it's natural for expectations and needs to change. What once worked in a friendship may no longer be fulfilling, leading to feelings of dissatisfaction and conflict. To navigate these changing expectations, it's essential to have open and honest conversations with your friends about your needs and desires. Be willing to listen to their perspective and work together to find a new dynamic that works for both of you. This may involve setting new boundaries, finding new ways to connect, or even deciding to end the friendship if it no longer serves you both.

When dealing with conflicts in friendships, it's essential to approach the situation with empathy and compassion. Remember that your friend is a complex individual with their own thoughts, feelings, and experiences. By striving to understand their perspective and communicating your own needs and feelings honestly, you create a foundation for resolution and growth. It's also important to recognize when a conflict may require outside help, such as the guidance of a therapist or mediator, to work through more complex or deep-seated issues.

Ultimately, the key to navigating conflicts in friendships lies in a commitment to open communication, empathy, and a willingness to work towards resolution. By approaching challenges with patience, understanding, and a focus on the value of the friendship, we can overcome even the most difficult conflicts and build stronger, more resilient bonds with the people we care about most. Remember, every friendship will face challenges, but it's how we navigate them together that determines the strength and longevity of our connections.

Summary: Navigating Conflict with Empathy and Resilience

Throughout this section, we've explored the unique challenges and dynamics of conflicts that arise in various relationship contexts, from the intimacy of romantic partnerships to the complex web of family roles and responsibilities, and from the professionalism of the workplace to the evolving nature of friendships. While each type of relationship brings its own set of potential pitfalls and opportunities for growth, the fundamental principles of effective communication, empathy, and a commitment to resolution remain constant.

By approaching conflicts with an open mind, a willingness to listen, and a focus on finding mutually beneficial solutions, we can navigate even the most challenging disagreements and emerge with stronger, more resilient relationships. Whether it's learning to compromise in romantic partnerships, respecting roles and boundaries in family dynamics, maintaining professionalism in the workplace, or adapting to changing expectations in friendships, the key lies in cultivating a foundation of trust, respect, and open communication.

As we've seen, conflicts can often be rooted in deeper issues, such as unresolved traumas, differing expectations, or systemic problems within a relationship or organization. By taking the time to understand and address these underlying factors, we can work towards more lasting and meaningful resolutions. And when conflicts become too complex or entrenched to handle alone, seeking the guidance of a trained professional, such as a therapist or mediator, can provide a safe and supportive space for growth and healing.

Ultimately, navigating conflicts in any relationship requires patience, empathy, and a commitment to the relationship's well-being. By approaching disagreements as opportunities for learning and growth, rather than as threats or failures, we can cultivate more resilient and fulfilling connections with the people who matter most to us. Remember, every relationship will face challenges, but it's how we navigate them together that determines the strength and longevity of our bonds. With the strategies and insights gained from this section, you now have the tools to approach conflicts with confidence, compassion, and a deeper understanding of what it takes to build and maintain thriving relationships across all aspects of your life.

Section 5: When to Seek Professional Help

Navigating conflicts and disagreements in relationships can be a challenging and emotional process. While many of the strategies and techniques discussed in this chapter can help you effectively manage and resolve conflicts, there may be times when the issues at hand feel overwhelming or impossible to tackle on your own. Recognizing when a conflict has escalated beyond the scope of self-help strategies is a crucial step in maintaining the health and well-being of your relationships.

In this section, we will explore the signs that indicate it may be time to seek professional support, such as couples therapy or mediation, to address persistent or complex relationship conflicts. We will also discuss how to identify unhealthy or abusive patterns of conflict, emphasizing the importance of prioritizing your safety and well-being. Additionally, we will provide guidance on how to approach the topic of seeking professional help with your partner or family member, and what to expect from the process.

It is important to remember that seeking professional help is not a sign of weakness or failure; rather, it is a proactive and courageous step towards building healthier, more resilient relationships. By learning to recognize when conflicts have become unmanageable and taking action to seek appropriate support, you can work towards creating more positive, fulfilling connections with the people who matter most in your life.

Subsection 5.1: Identifying Signs of Unhealthy or Abusive Conflict

Conflict is a natural and inevitable part of any relationship, but not all conflicts are created equal. While healthy disagreements can lead to growth and understanding, unhealthy or abusive conflicts can cause significant emotional harm and erode the foundation of a relationship. Learning to recognize the red flags that indicate a conflict has become destructive is crucial for maintaining the well-being of yourself and your loved ones.

One of the most prominent signs of an unhealthy conflict is the presence of verbal abuse. This can include name-calling, belittling, or using language that is designed to intimidate or demean the other person. Phrases like "You're so stupid" or "You'll never amount to anything" are clear indicators that the conflict has crossed the line into emotionally abusive territory. When disagreements consistently involve personal attacks or insults, it's a strong signal that professional intervention may be necessary.

Another red flag to watch out for is the escalation of conflicts into physical aggression or violence. This can range from throwing objects and slamming doors to pushing, grabbing, or hitting. Any form of physical intimidation or harm is a serious issue that requires immediate attention. If you find yourself in a situation where you feel unsafe or threatened during a conflict, it's essential to reach out for help from a trusted friend, family member, or professional organization.

Unhealthy conflicts can also be characterized by a pervasive sense of control or manipulation. If one partner consistently dominates the conversation, refuses to listen to the other's perspective, or uses guilt or shame to exert control, it's a sign that the power dynamics in the relationship are imbalanced. This type of emotional manipulation can be subtle, but it's no less damaging than overt forms of abuse.

It's also important to be aware of the frequency and duration of conflicts. While occasional disagreements are normal, constant fighting or simmering tension can indicate deeper issues that require professional attention. If you find that conflicts are becoming more frequent, lasting longer, or are increasingly difficult to resolve, it may be time to seek the guidance of a trained therapist or counselor.

Remember, recognizing the signs of unhealthy or abusive conflict is not about assigning blame or shame. It's about acknowledging that the current patterns of interaction are not sustainable or conducive to a healthy relationship. By learning to identify these red flags, you can take proactive steps to seek the support and resources needed to break the cycle of destructive conflict and build a more positive, respectful relationship dynamic.

Subsection 5.2: Considering Couple's Therapy or Mediation

When conflicts in a relationship become persistent, complex, or seemingly insurmountable, it may be time to consider seeking the guidance of a trained professional. Couple's therapy and mediation are two valuable options for partners who find themselves stuck in a cycle of unproductive arguments or struggling to navigate difficult issues on their own.

Couple's therapy involves working with a licensed therapist who specializes in helping couples improve their communication, deepen their understanding of one another, and develop healthier ways of relating. In a supportive and non-judgmental environment, partners can explore the root causes of their conflicts, express their feelings and needs, and learn new skills for resolving disagreements constructively. Through the guidance of a trained professional, couples can gain insight into their patterns of interaction, break free from negative cycles, and cultivate greater empathy, trust, and intimacy in their relationship.

Mediation, on the other hand, is a process in which a neutral third party facilitates a structured dialogue between partners to help them resolve specific disputes or negotiate important decisions. Mediators are trained to create a safe and respectful space for both parties to express their perspectives, identify their shared interests, and brainstorm mutually beneficial solutions. This approach can be particularly useful for couples who are navigating high-stakes issues such as financial disagreements, parenting conflicts, or the terms of a separation or divorce.

One of the primary benefits of seeking professional help is the opportunity to gain an objective, outside perspective on the relationship dynamics at play. When couples are deeply entrenched in a conflict, it can be challenging to see the situation clearly or consider alternative viewpoints. A skilled therapist or mediator can help partners step back from their subjective experiences, identify blind spots or unexamined assumptions, and develop a more holistic understanding of their challenges.

Moreover, working with a professional can provide couples with a structured framework for addressing their issues and making lasting changes. Therapists and mediators are equipped with evidence-based strategies and techniques that have been shown to be effective in helping couples improve their relationships. By committing to a regular process of guided exploration and skill-building, partners can develop a shared language for discussing their needs, a deeper appreciation for one another's perspectives, and a greater capacity for weathering future challenges together.

It is important to note that seeking professional help is not a sign of failure or weakness, but rather a proactive step towards building a stronger, more resilient relationship. By investing in the health and well-being of their partnership, couples can lay the foundation for a more fulfilling and satisfying life together. Whether through couple's therapy, mediation, or a combination of both, the guidance of a trained professional can be an invaluable resource for navigating the complexities of love and commitment in the modern world.

Subsection 5.3: Knowing When to Walk Away

Despite our best efforts to resolve conflicts and maintain healthy relationships, there may come a time when a partnership or connection has become irreparably damaged. Recognizing when a relationship has reached a point of no return is a difficult but necessary step in prioritizing your well-being and future happiness. It's essential to understand that walking away from a relationship is not a sign of failure, but rather a courageous act of self-respect and self-preservation.

One of the most telling signs that a relationship may have run its course is a persistent pattern of unresolved conflicts and a lack of progress in addressing underlying issues. If you find yourself repeatedly engaging in the same arguments without any meaningful change or resolution, it may indicate a fundamental incompatibility or unwillingness to compromise. When a relationship becomes characterized by a cycle of hurt, frustration, and resentment, with no genuine effort to break free from destructive patterns, it may be time to consider moving on.

Another red flag is a consistent lack of respect or a disregard for your boundaries, feelings, and needs. If your partner consistently belittles your opinions, dismisses your emotions, or ignores your requests for change, it demonstrates a lack of consideration for your well-being. A healthy relationship is built on a foundation of mutual respect, empathy, and a willingness to prioritize each other's happiness. If these essential elements are consistently absent, it may be a sign that the relationship is not sustainable in the long run.

It's also important to pay attention to your own emotional and mental state within the relationship. If you find yourself constantly feeling drained, anxious, or unhappy, with little hope for improvement, it may be a sign that the relationship is taking a significant toll on your well-being. While all relationships go through challenges and rough patches, a healthy partnership should ultimately contribute to your sense of fulfillment, growth, and peace of mind. If the negative aspects of the relationship consistently outweigh the positive, it may be time to reassess its viability.

When deciding to walk away from a relationship, it's crucial to approach the process with compassion, both for yourself and your partner. This means communicating your decision clearly and respectfully, while setting firm boundaries and expectations for the future. It may be helpful to seek the support of a trusted friend, family member, or therapist to navigate the emotional challenges of ending a relationship and to develop a plan for moving forward.

Remember, walking away from a relationship that is no longer serving you is not an act of giving up, but rather an act of self-love and self-preservation. By acknowledging when a partnership has become irreparable and taking steps to end it in a healthy, respectful manner, you create space for healing, growth, and the possibility of finding a more fulfilling connection in the future. Trust in your own resilience and know that you deserve a relationship that uplifts, supports, and brings out the best in you.

Summary: Prioritizing Your Well-Being and Building Healthier Relationships

Navigating conflicts and disagreements in relationships can be a challenging and emotionally taxing process. While many of the strategies and techniques discussed in this chapter can help you effectively manage and resolve conflicts, it's crucial to recognize when a situation has escalated beyond the scope of self-help and requires professional intervention.

By learning to identify the signs of unhealthy or abusive conflict, such as verbal abuse, physical aggression, emotional manipulation, and a pervasive sense of control, you can take proactive steps to prioritize your safety and well-being. Seeking the guidance of a trained therapist or mediator can provide you with the support, tools, and objective perspective needed to break free from destructive patterns and build healthier, more resilient relationships.

Remember, seeking professional help is not a sign of weakness or failure, but rather a courageous act of self-care and commitment to your personal growth and the well-being of your relationships. Whether through couple's therapy, mediation, or individual counseling, investing in your emotional health and the health of your partnerships can lead to a more fulfilling, satisfying life.

However, it's also essential to acknowledge that not all relationships can or should be salvaged. When a partnership has become irreparably damaged, characterized by a persistent lack of respect, empathy, and effort to change, it may be necessary to walk away. By recognizing when a relationship has reached a point of no return and taking steps to end it in a healthy, respectful manner, you create space for healing, self-discovery, and the possibility of finding a more compatible, supportive connection in the future.

As you navigate the complexities of relationships and conflict, remember to approach the process with compassion, both for yourself and others. Trust in your own resilience, seek the support you need, and remain committed to building the kind of relationships that bring out the best in you and contribute to your overall sense of happiness and well-being.

Chapter Summary: Embracing Conflict as an Opportunity for Growth

Conflict is an inevitable part of any relationship, but it doesn't have to be a destructive force. By approaching disagreements with a growth mindset and employing effective communication strategies, you can transform conflicts into opportunities for deepening understanding, fostering empathy, and strengthening your connections with others.

Throughout this chapter, we've explored the nature of conflict in relationships, developed a conflict resolution mindset, and learned practical communication techniques for navigating disagreements constructively. By embracing a collaborative approach, practicing active listening, and maintaining respect and compassion, you can work through conflicts in a way that preserves and enhances your relationships.

Remember, the goal of conflict resolution is not to win an argument or prove a point, but rather to find a mutually satisfying solution that meets the needs and concerns of all parties involved. This requires a willingness to be vulnerable, to consider alternative perspectives, and to work together towards a common goal.

In some cases, conflicts may escalate beyond the scope of self-help strategies, and it's important to recognize when professional support is needed. Seeking the guidance of a trained therapist or mediator can provide valuable tools and insights for navigating complex or persistent relationship challenges.

Ultimately, the key to successfully navigating conflict and disagreements lies in approaching them with an open heart, a curious mind, and a commitment to personal growth. By embracing conflict as an opportunity for learning and connection, you can cultivate more resilient, fulfilling, and deeply satisfying relationships in all areas of your life.

Chapter 6: Cultivating Empathy and Emotional Intelligence

In the tapestry of human relationships, empathy and emotional intelligence are the golden threads that weave together the fabric of strong, compassionate, and resilient connections. These invaluable skills allow us to step into the shoes of others, to understand their perspectives, and to respond with kindness and understanding. As we navigate the complex landscape of relationships, cultivating empathy and emotional intelligence becomes a crucial endeavor, one that can transform the way we interact with the people in our lives.

Empathy, at its core, is the ability to understand and share the feelings of another person. It is the bridge that spans the gap between our own experiences and those of others, allowing us to connect on a deeper, more meaningful level. When we practice empathy, we create a safe space for vulnerability, trust, and genuine connection to flourish. We become better listeners, more attuned to the needs and emotions of those around us, and more capable of offering support and understanding during both the joyous and challenging moments in life.

Emotional intelligence, on the other hand, is the capacity to recognize, understand, and manage our own emotions, as well as the emotions of others. It encompasses a set of skills that enable us to navigate the often-turbulent waters of relationships with grace and wisdom. By developing our emotional intelligence, we become more self-aware, better able to regulate our own emotions, and more adept at reading and responding to the emotional cues of others. This heightened awareness and skill set allows us to communicate more effectively, resolve conflicts with greater ease, and build relationships that are characterized by mutual understanding and respect.

In this chapter, we will embark on a journey of exploration, delving into the fascinating world of empathy and emotional intelligence. We will examine the neuroscience behind these skills, uncovering the intricate workings of the brain that enable us to connect with others on an emotional level. Through a blend of scientific research, practical exercises, and real-life examples, we will learn how to cultivate empathy and emotional intelligence in our daily lives, and how to apply these skills to build stronger, more fulfilling relationships.

As we navigate the pages ahead, we will discover the transformative power of empathy and emotional intelligence in various contexts, from romantic partnerships and family dynamics to friendships and professional relationships. We will explore the challenges that can arise when empathy is lacking, and learn strategies for overcoming barriers to understanding and connection. Along the way, we will also uncover the profound impact that empathy and emotional intelligence can have on our personal growth, resilience, and overall well-being.

So, let us embark on this transformative journey together, armed with an open heart and a curious mind. As we cultivate empathy and emotional intelligence, we will not only strengthen the bonds we share with others but also deepen our understanding of ourselves and the intricate web of human connection that surrounds us. In a world that often feels divided and disconnected, these skills offer a beacon of hope, a pathway to building bridges of understanding, and a foundation for nurturing relationships that can weather the storms of life and emerge stronger, more compassionate, and more resilient than ever before.

Section 1: Understanding the Foundations of Empathy

Empathy, the ability to understand and share the feelings of another, is a fundamental building block of strong, healthy relationships. It allows us to connect with others on a deeper level, fostering trust, compassion, and mutual understanding. In a world where relationships are often strained by misunderstandings, conflicts, and emotional disconnects, cultivating empathy has become more important than ever.

But what exactly is empathy, and how does it manifest in our daily interactions? This section will delve into the concept of empathy, exploring its different types and the role it plays in building and maintaining meaningful connections with others. By gaining a deeper understanding of empathy and its foundations, we can lay the groundwork for more fulfilling, supportive, and resilient relationships.

Through relatable examples and research-backed insights, we will examine how empathy develops, both from a psychological and neurological perspective. We will also explore the various ways in which empathy can be expressed, from cognitive empathy, which involves understanding another person's perspective, to emotional empathy, which entails sharing and experiencing their feelings.

As we navigate the complexities of human connections, empathy serves as a guiding light, helping us to bridge differences, resolve conflicts, and create a sense of belonging. By the end of this section, you will have a clearer understanding of what empathy is, why it matters, and how you can cultivate it in your own relationships. So, let us embark on this journey together, as we uncover the transformative power of empathy and its ability to enrich our lives and the lives of those around us.

Subsection 1.1: Defining Empathy and Its Key Components

Empathy is a complex and multifaceted concept that lies at the heart of human connection and understanding. At its core, empathy refers to the ability to recognize, comprehend, and share the feelings, thoughts, and experiences of another person. It is the capacity to step into someone else's shoes, to see the world through their eyes, and to respond with compassion and understanding.

To truly grasp the essence of empathy, it is essential to break down its key components. One fundamental aspect of empathy is cognitive empathy, also known as perspective-taking. This involves the ability to understand and interpret another person's mental state, including their beliefs, intentions, and motivations. Cognitive empathy allows us to intellectually comprehend what someone else might be thinking or feeling, even if we have not experienced the same situation ourselves.

Another crucial component of empathy is emotional empathy, which goes beyond mere understanding and involves actually sharing and experiencing the feelings of another person. When we engage in emotional empathy, we resonate with the emotions of others, feeling their joy, sadness, anger, or fear as if they were our own. This type of empathy creates a deep sense of connection and allows us to offer genuine support and comfort to those around us.

It is important to note that empathy is not the same as sympathy, which involves feeling concern or pity for someone else's situation without necessarily understanding or sharing their emotions. While sympathy can be a kind and caring response, empathy takes it a step further by fostering a deeper level of connection and understanding.

Empathy is a skill that can be cultivated and strengthened over time. It requires an open mind, a willingness to listen, and the ability to set aside our own judgments and biases. By practicing empathy in our daily interactions, we can build stronger, more meaningful relationships and contribute to a more compassionate and understanding world.

In the following subsections, we will explore the neuroscience behind empathy, its role in human connection and bonding, and practical strategies for cultivating and expressing empathy in our relationships. By gaining a deeper understanding of this essential human capacity, we can unlock the power of empathy to transform our lives and the lives of those around us.

Subsection 1.2: The Neuroscience of Empathy

The ability to empathize with others is not just a social or emotional skill; it is deeply rooted in the complex workings of the human brain. Neuroscience has made significant strides in unraveling the neural mechanisms that underlie empathy, shedding light on how our brains process and respond to the emotions and experiences of others.

One of the key discoveries in the neuroscience of empathy is the existence of mirror neurons. These specialized brain cells, first identified in the premotor cortex of macaque monkeys, fire not only when an individual performs an action but also when they observe someone else performing the same action. In humans, mirror neurons have been found in various regions of the brain, including the inferior frontal gyrus and the inferior parietal lobule.

The discovery of mirror neurons has led to the development of the "shared neural representations" theory of empathy. According to this theory, when we observe or imagine another person's emotional state, our brains activate the same neural networks that are involved in experiencing that emotion ourselves. This shared neural representation allows us to understand and resonate with the feelings of others on a deep, neurological level.

In addition to mirror neurons, several other brain regions have been implicated in the experience of empathy. The anterior insula, for example, is involved in processing both our own emotions and the emotions of others. This region is activated when we experience disgust, pain, or other visceral sensations, and it also lights up when we observe others experiencing similar emotions.

The anterior cingulate cortex (ACC) is another brain region that plays a crucial role in empathy. The ACC is involved in the processing of physical and social pain, as well as in the regulation of emotional responses. When we witness someone else in distress, the ACC helps us to understand and share their pain, while also modulating our own emotional reactions.

The amygdala, a small almond-shaped structure deep within the brain, is also involved in the experience of empathy. Known for its role in processing emotions, particularly fear and anxiety, the amygdala helps us to recognize and respond to the emotional states of others. Individuals with damage to the amygdala often have difficulty interpreting facial expressions and understanding the emotions of others.

The neuroscience of empathy also highlights the importance of neurochemicals, such as oxytocin and vasopressin, in facilitating empathetic responses. Oxytocin, often referred to as the "love hormone," has been shown to enhance trust, social bonding, and empathy. When we engage in empathetic interactions, our brains release oxytocin, which helps to strengthen our emotional connections with others.

While the neural basis of empathy is complex and multifaceted, these findings underscore the idea that empathy is not just a learned behavior but a fundamental aspect of human neurobiology. By understanding the neurological underpinnings of empathy, we can gain a deeper appreciation for the power of human connection and the ways in which our brains are wired for compassion and understanding.

Subsection 1.3: The Role of Empathy in Human Connection and Bonding

Empathy is the glue that holds human relationships together, fostering deep, meaningful connections and a sense of belonging. When we empathize with others, we create a bridge of understanding that allows us to connect on a profound level, transcending superficial differences and finding common ground.

At its core, empathy is about recognizing and sharing the feelings of another person. It is the ability to step into their shoes, to see the world through their eyes, and to respond with compassion and understanding. When we engage in empathetic interactions, we send a powerful message to others: "I see you, I hear you, and I understand what you're going through." This validation of their experiences and emotions creates a strong bond, as people feel seen, heard, and supported.

Empathy plays a crucial role in building trust and intimacy in relationships. When we demonstrate empathy, we show others that we are willing to be vulnerable, to open ourselves up to their experiences, and to offer genuine support. This vulnerability and authenticity foster a sense of safety and trust, allowing people to let their guard down and share their deepest thoughts, feelings, and fears. As a result, empathetic relationships tend to be more intimate, resilient, and fulfilling.

Moreover, empathy helps us to navigate the complexities of human interactions with greater ease and understanding. When conflicts arise, empathy allows us to see beyond our own perspective and consider the needs, desires, and motivations of others. By understanding where someone else is coming from, we can approach disagreements with greater compassion, patience, and a willingness to find mutually beneficial solutions. Empathy enables us to bridge divides, resolve conflicts, and maintain strong, healthy relationships even in the face of challenges.

Empathy also plays a vital role in fostering a sense of belonging and connection within communities and social groups. When we extend empathy to others, we create an inclusive environment where everyone feels valued, respected, and understood. This sense of belonging is essential for our well-being, as it provides us with a support network, a shared identity, and a feeling of being part of something larger than ourselves.

The power of empathy in human connection and bonding is beautifully illustrated by the concept of "empathetic resonance." Just as two tuning forks vibrate in harmony when placed near each other, our brains and bodies resonate with the emotions and experiences of those around us. When we witness someone else's joy, sorrow, or excitement, our own neural pathways light up in response, creating a shared emotional experience. This empathetic resonance is the foundation of human connection, allowing us to feel a deep sense of kinship and understanding with others.

In a world that is often divided by differences and misunderstandings, empathy is a powerful tool for building bridges, fostering connection, and creating a sense of belonging. By cultivating empathy in our relationships and interactions, we can tap into the transformative power of human connection, leading to more fulfilling, compassionate, and resilient bonds with those around us.

Summary: Empathy as the Cornerstone of Meaningful Connections

Throughout this section, we have explored the fundamental role of empathy in building strong, meaningful relationships. By delving into the concept of empathy, its different components, and the neuroscience behind it, we have gained a deeper understanding of how this essential human capacity shapes our connections with others.

We have learned that empathy is a multifaceted concept, encompassing both cognitive and emotional aspects. Cognitive empathy allows us to understand and interpret the thoughts and feelings of others, while emotional empathy enables us to share and experience those emotions as if they were our own. Together, these components create a powerful foundation for understanding, compassion, and connection.

The neuroscience of empathy has revealed fascinating insights into how our brains process and respond to the emotions and experiences of others. From the discovery of mirror neurons to the role of the anterior insula, anterior cingulate cortex, and amygdala, we have seen how empathy is deeply rooted in our neurological wiring. This understanding highlights the idea that empathy is not merely a learned behavior but a fundamental aspect of human nature.

Moreover, we have explored the crucial role of empathy in fostering trust, intimacy, and a sense of belonging in our relationships. By validating the experiences and emotions of others, empathy creates a bridge of understanding that allows us to connect on a profound level. It enables us to navigate conflicts with greater ease, find common ground, and build resilient, fulfilling relationships.

As we move forward in our exploration of relationships, it is essential to keep the power of empathy at the forefront of our minds. By cultivating empathy in our daily interactions and making a conscious effort to understand and share the feelings of others, we can unlock the transformative potential of human connection.

In the coming sections, we will build upon this foundation of empathy, exploring practical strategies for developing emotional intelligence, expressing empathy in various types of relationships, overcoming barriers to empathy, and harnessing its power for effective conflict resolution. Armed with a deep understanding of empathy and its significance, we are well-equipped to embark on a journey of personal growth and relationship enrichment.

Section 2: Developing Emotional Intelligence

Imagine a world where you not only understand your own emotions but also possess the ability to recognize and empathize with the feelings of others. A world where you can navigate complex social situations with ease, build strong and meaningful relationships, and communicate effectively with people from all walks of life. This is the world of emotional intelligence, a crucial set of skills that can transform the way you interact with others and lead a more fulfilling life.

In this section, we will embark on a journey to explore the fascinating concept of emotional intelligence and its four key components: self-awareness, self-management, social awareness, and relationship management. We will delve into the science behind emotional intelligence, examining how it develops and why it matters in our personal and professional lives.

But understanding emotional intelligence is just the beginning. The real power lies in learning how to cultivate and enhance these skills. Throughout this section, we will provide you with practical strategies and exercises to help you develop your emotional intelligence, from increasing your self-awareness to managing your emotions effectively and building stronger, more empathetic relationships with others.

Whether you are seeking to improve your romantic partnerships, strengthen your family bonds, or excel in your professional life, developing your emotional intelligence is a critical step on the path to success. By the end of this section, you will have a deeper understanding of your own emotions and the emotions of others, as well as a toolkit of strategies to help you navigate the complex world of human relationships with greater ease and confidence.

So, let us embark on this transformative journey together, as we unlock the secrets of emotional intelligence and discover how it can enrich our lives and the lives of those around us.

Subsection 2.1: The Four Pillars of Emotional Intelligence

Emotional intelligence, often referred to as EQ, is a complex and multifaceted concept that encompasses a wide range of skills and abilities. To better understand the nature of emotional intelligence, it is helpful to break it down into its four main components: self-awareness, self-management, social awareness, and relationship management.

Self-awareness is the foundation of emotional intelligence. It involves the ability to recognize and understand your own emotions, thoughts, and behaviors. When you are self-aware, you are able to identify your strengths and weaknesses, understand how your emotions influence your actions, and recognize the impact you have on others. This level of introspection allows you to make more informed decisions, communicate more effectively, and build stronger relationships.

Self-management, the second pillar of emotional intelligence, builds upon self-awareness. It is the ability to regulate and control your emotions, thoughts, and behaviors in a healthy and productive manner. This includes managing stress, controlling impulses, and adapting to change. When you possess strong self-management skills, you are better equipped to handle challenges, maintain focus, and pursue your goals with resilience and determination.

Social awareness, the third component of emotional intelligence, involves the ability to recognize and understand the emotions, needs, and concerns of others. This includes the capacity for empathy, the skill of picking up on emotional cues, and the ability to see things from another person's perspective. When you are socially aware, you are better able to navigate social situations, build rapport with others, and create a sense of connection and understanding.

The fourth and final pillar of emotional intelligence is relationship management. This involves the ability to use your emotional intelligence skills to build and maintain strong, positive relationships with others. This includes effective communication, conflict resolution, and the ability to inspire and influence others. When you possess strong relationship management skills, you are able to build trust, foster collaboration, and create a positive and supportive environment in both your personal and professional life.

By understanding and developing these four key components of emotional intelligence, you can unlock your full potential and create more meaningful and fulfilling relationships with others. In the following subsections, we will explore each of these pillars in greater depth, providing practical strategies and exercises to help you cultivate and strengthen your emotional intelligence skills.

Subsection 2.2: Strategies for Improving Self-Awareness and Self-Regulation

Developing a keen sense of self-awareness and the ability to regulate your emotions effectively is a crucial step in enhancing your emotional intelligence. By gaining a deeper understanding of your own thoughts, feelings, and behaviors, you can make more informed decisions, communicate more effectively, and build stronger, more positive relationships with others.

One of the most powerful tools for increasing self-awareness is the practice of mindfulness. Mindfulness involves bringing your attention to the present moment, observing your thoughts and emotions without judgment, and accepting them as they are. By regularly engaging in mindfulness exercises, such as meditation or deep breathing, you can cultivate a greater sense of self-awareness and gain valuable insights into your internal experiences.

Another effective strategy for improving self-awareness is to keep a journal. Writing down your thoughts, feelings, and experiences can help you gain clarity, identify patterns in your behavior, and track your personal growth over time. As you reflect on your journal entries, you may discover new insights into your motivations, triggers, and coping mechanisms, allowing you to make more conscious choices in your daily life.

Self-regulation, the ability to manage your emotions and behaviors effectively, is another essential component of emotional intelligence. One powerful technique for enhancing self-regulation is cognitive reframing, which involves changing the way you interpret and respond to challenging situations. By identifying negative thought patterns and replacing them with more balanced, positive perspectives, you can reduce stress, manage difficult emotions, and maintain a sense of emotional equilibrium.

Another effective strategy for improving self-regulation is to develop a toolkit of healthy coping mechanisms. This may include engaging in regular exercise, practicing relaxation techniques such as deep breathing or progressive muscle relaxation, or seeking support from trusted friends or family members. By having a range of positive strategies at your disposal, you can more effectively navigate stressful or emotionally charged situations and maintain a sense of emotional balance.

Ultimately, improving self-awareness and self-regulation requires a commitment to ongoing personal growth and development. By regularly engaging in practices that promote introspection, self-reflection, and emotional management, you can cultivate a deeper understanding of yourself and develop the skills necessary to thrive in both your personal and professional life.

Subsection 2.3: Enhancing Social Awareness and Relationship Management Skills

Building strong, emotionally intelligent relationships requires not only a deep understanding of your own emotions but also the ability to recognize and respond to the emotions of others. This is where social awareness and relationship management skills come into play. By developing these critical components of emotional intelligence, you can foster more meaningful connections, communicate more effectively, and navigate interpersonal challenges with greater ease and success.

One of the key aspects of social awareness is the ability to read and interpret nonverbal cues. From facial expressions to body language, the way people communicate without words can often reveal more about their thoughts and feelings than what they say out loud. To enhance your social awareness, start by paying closer attention to these nonverbal signals. Notice how people's expressions change when they speak, observe their posture and gestures, and listen for subtle changes in tone of voice. By becoming more attuned to these cues, you can gain valuable insights into the emotional states of others and respond in a more empathetic and effective manner.

Another important aspect of social awareness is the ability to put yourself in someone else's shoes. This involves more than just intellectual understanding; it requires a willingness to step outside of your own perspective and genuinely consider the thoughts, feelings, and experiences of others. One powerful exercise for developing this skill is to engage in active listening. When conversing with others, focus on fully hearing and understanding their message, rather than simply waiting for your turn to speak. Ask clarifying questions, reflect back on what you've heard, and show genuine interest in their perspective. By practicing active listening, you can build stronger, more empathetic relationships and foster a deeper sense of connection and understanding.

Relationship management, the fourth pillar of emotional intelligence, involves using your emotional intelligence skills to build and maintain positive, productive relationships. One key strategy for effective relationship management is to develop strong communication skills. This involves not only expressing yourself clearly and assertively but also being open and receptive to feedback from others. When communicating with others, strive to be honest, direct, and respectful, even in challenging or emotionally charged situations. By modeling open, authentic communication, you can create a safe and trusting environment that encourages others to do the same.

Another critical aspect of relationship management is the ability to handle conflicts and disagreements in a constructive and emotionally intelligent manner. When conflicts arise, it's essential to approach them with a spirit of collaboration and a willingness to find mutually beneficial solutions. This involves actively listening to the other person's perspective, acknowledging their feelings, and working together to identify common ground and potential compromises. By approaching conflicts with empathy, respect, and a focus on problem-solving, you can turn potentially divisive situations into opportunities for growth and strengthening of relationships.

Ultimately, enhancing your social awareness and relationship management skills is an ongoing process that requires regular practice and self-reflection. By making a conscious effort to tune into the emotions of others, communicate openly and authentically, and approach relationships with empathy and respect, you can build a strong foundation of emotional intelligence that will serve you well in all areas of your life. Whether you're navigating a challenging conversation with a loved one, collaborating with colleagues at work, or building new friendships, these skills will enable you to create more meaningful, fulfilling connections and thrive in your personal and professional relationships.

Summary: Unlocking the Power of Emotional Intelligence for Stronger Relationships

Throughout this section, we have explored the fascinating world of emotional intelligence and its four key components: self-awareness, self-management, social awareness, and relationship management. By understanding and developing these essential skills, you can unlock a powerful tool for building stronger, more meaningful relationships in all areas of your life.

We have discussed strategies for improving self-awareness, such as practicing mindfulness and keeping a journal, which can help you gain a deeper understanding of your own emotions, thoughts, and behaviors. We have also explored techniques for enhancing self-regulation, including cognitive reframing and developing healthy coping mechanisms, which enable you to manage your emotions effectively and maintain a sense of emotional balance.

Furthermore, we have delved into the importance of social awareness and relationship management skills, highlighting the value of reading nonverbal cues, engaging in active listening, and approaching conflicts with empathy and a focus on problem-solving. By cultivating these skills, you can foster more meaningful connections, communicate more effectively, and navigate interpersonal challenges with greater ease and success.

As you continue on your journey of developing emotional intelligence, remember that it is an ongoing process that requires regular practice and self-reflection. By committing to this process and incorporating the strategies and insights discussed in this section, you can create a strong foundation of emotional intelligence that will serve you well in all your relationships.

Embrace the power of emotional intelligence, and watch as your relationships flourish and grow. With enhanced self-awareness, self-regulation, social awareness, and relationship management skills, you will be well-equipped to build the kind of deep, meaningful connections that enrich your life and bring joy to those around you. So, take the first step today, and begin your journey towards greater emotional intelligence and more fulfilling relationships.

Section 3: Practicing Empathy in Relationships

Empathy, the ability to understand and share the feelings of another, is a crucial ingredient in building strong, compassionate, and resilient relationships. When we practice empathy, we create a deeper connection with others, fostering trust, understanding, and emotional intimacy. In this section, we will explore practical ways to cultivate and express empathy in various types of relationships, from romantic partnerships to family dynamics, friendships, and even professional interactions.

Empathy is not merely a feeling or an innate trait; it is a skill that can be developed and strengthened over time. By actively practicing empathy, we can improve our ability to relate to others, communicate effectively, and navigate challenges and conflicts with greater ease and understanding. Whether you are seeking to enhance your romantic relationship, build closer bonds with family members, or create more meaningful friendships, the power of empathy cannot be overstated.

Throughout this section, we will delve into the unique challenges and opportunities for practicing empathy in different relational contexts. We will explore how empathy can help us bridge gaps, overcome misunderstandings, and create a more supportive and loving environment in our relationships. By examining real-life examples and practical strategies, you will gain valuable insights and tools for expressing empathy and strengthening your connections with others.

As we embark on this journey of practicing empathy in relationships, it is essential to approach the process with an open mind, a willingness to learn, and a commitment to personal growth. By cultivating empathy, we not only enrich our relationships but also contribute to a more compassionate and understanding world. So, let us dive in and discover the transformative power of empathy in our relationships.

Subsection 3.1: Empathy in Romantic Relationships

Empathy plays a vital role in fostering strong, healthy, and lasting romantic relationships. When partners practice empathy, they create a deep emotional connection, build trust, and enhance their ability to navigate challenges together. In this subsection, we will explore the importance of empathy in romantic partnerships and provide strategies for cultivating empathetic communication and understanding.

One of the key benefits of empathy in romantic relationships is that it allows partners to truly understand and validate each other's feelings, thoughts, and experiences. By putting ourselves in our partner's shoes and seeing things from their perspective, we can respond with compassion, support, and understanding. This creates a safe and nurturing environment where both partners feel heard, respected, and valued.

Empathetic communication is a crucial aspect of building and maintaining a strong romantic bond. When couples engage in empathetic dialogue, they listen actively, express their own feelings and needs clearly, and seek to understand their partner's point of view. This type of communication helps prevent misunderstandings, reduces conflict, and fosters a deeper sense of connection and intimacy.

To practice empathy in romantic relationships, partners can start by cultivating self-awareness and emotional intelligence. By becoming more attuned to their own emotions and reactions, individuals can better regulate their responses and approach their partner with patience and understanding. It is also essential to create a safe space for open, honest communication, where both partners feel comfortable expressing their thoughts and feelings without fear of judgment or criticism.

Another effective strategy for fostering empathy in romantic relationships is to engage in shared activities and experiences that promote bonding and emotional connection. This can include anything from trying new hobbies together to engaging in meaningful conversations about hopes, dreams, and fears. By creating opportunities for shared vulnerability and intimacy, couples can deepen their understanding of each other and strengthen their empathetic bond.

It is important to note that practicing empathy in romantic relationships is an ongoing process that requires effort, patience, and commitment from both partners. There will be times when misunderstandings or conflicts arise, but by approaching these challenges with empathy and a willingness to understand each other's perspectives, couples can work through difficulties and emerge stronger and more connected.

In conclusion, empathy is a powerful tool for building and maintaining strong, healthy, and fulfilling romantic relationships. By practicing empathetic communication, cultivating self-awareness, and creating opportunities for emotional connection, partners can foster a deep sense of understanding, trust, and intimacy that will stand the test of time.

Subsection 3.2: Empathy in Family Dynamics

Family relationships are among the most complex and emotionally charged bonds we experience throughout our lives. These connections are shaped by a tapestry of shared history, individual personalities, and the unique roles each member plays within the family unit. Cultivating empathy within family dynamics is essential for fostering understanding, resolving conflicts, and strengthening the ties that bind us together.

Empathy in family relationships involves the ability to step into the shoes of our loved ones, to see the world through their eyes, and to connect with their emotions and experiences. It requires us to move beyond our own perspectives and to consider the thoughts, feelings, and needs of our family members. By practicing empathy, we create a family environment that is characterized by compassion, support, and open communication.

One of the key challenges in cultivating empathy within family dynamics is navigating the complex web of relationships and roles that exist across generations. Parents, children, siblings, grandparents, and extended family members all bring their own unique experiences, expectations, and communication styles to the table. To foster empathy, it is essential to recognize and respect these differences while finding common ground and understanding.

For parents, practicing empathy involves taking the time to listen to their children's concerns, validate their feelings, and offer guidance and support. It means recognizing that each child is a unique individual with their own thoughts, emotions, and needs. By modeling empathetic behavior and creating a safe space for open communication, parents can help their children develop emotional intelligence and build strong, healthy relationships.

Siblings, too, play a crucial role in cultivating empathy within the family. As children grow and navigate the challenges of sibling rivalry, shared experiences, and changing family dynamics, empathy becomes a vital tool for maintaining close, supportive bonds. By learning to see situations from each other's perspectives, siblings can develop a deeper understanding of one another, resolve conflicts more effectively, and offer comfort and support during difficult times.

Empathy also plays a significant role in bridging the generational divide within families. As grandparents, aunts, uncles, and other extended family members interact with younger generations, it is essential to approach these relationships with openness, curiosity, and a willingness to understand their unique experiences and challenges. By actively listening, sharing stories, and offering wisdom and guidance, older family members can foster empathy and create a sense of continuity and connection across generations.

Cultivating empathy within family dynamics requires ongoing effort, patience, and self-reflection. It involves being mindful of our own emotions and reactions, and taking responsibility for how we communicate and interact with our loved ones. By practicing active listening, expressing our own feelings and needs clearly, and seeking to understand rather than judge, we can create a family environment that is built on a foundation of empathy and mutual respect.

In times of conflict or disagreement, empathy becomes a powerful tool for finding resolution and healing. By approaching difficult conversations with a willingness to understand each other's perspectives and emotions, family members can work together to find solutions that meet everyone's needs. This process may involve compromise, forgiveness, and a commitment to ongoing communication and growth.

Ultimately, empathy within family dynamics serves as a catalyst for creating strong, resilient, and loving relationships that can weather the storms of life. By fostering a culture of empathy within our families, we lay the groundwork for a lifetime of close, supportive bonds that will continue to nurture and sustain us through the years. As we navigate the joys and challenges of family life, let us remember the transformative power of empathy in bringing us closer together and helping us build a legacy of love and understanding.

Subsection 3.3: Empathy in Friendships and Social Interactions

Friendships and social interactions form the fabric of our daily lives, providing us with a sense of belonging, support, and connection. At the heart of these relationships lies empathy, the ability to understand and share the feelings of others. By practicing empathy in our friendships and social interactions, we can foster deeper, more meaningful connections and create a more compassionate and supportive social environment.

Empathy in friendships involves being present, attentive, and responsive to our friends' emotions and experiences. It means taking the time to listen actively, without judgment or interruption, and striving to understand their perspectives and feelings. When we approach our friendships with empathy, we create a safe space for our friends to express themselves authentically and vulnerably, knowing that they will be met with understanding and support.

One of the most powerful ways to practice empathy in friendships is through active listening. This involves giving our full attention to our friends when they are speaking, using nonverbal cues like eye contact and nodding to show that we are engaged, and reflecting back on what we have heard to ensure that we have understood correctly. By listening empathetically, we demonstrate to our friends that their thoughts and feelings matter to us and that we value their experiences.

Empathy in social interactions extends beyond our close friendships and encompasses our daily encounters with acquaintances, colleagues, and even strangers. In these interactions, practicing empathy involves being mindful of others' emotions and experiences, even if we do not know them well. It means approaching each interaction with openness, curiosity, and a willingness to understand and connect with others on a human level.

In social situations, empathy can manifest in small but meaningful ways, such as offering a kind word or a listening ear to someone who seems upset, or taking the time to acknowledge and appreciate others' contributions and efforts. By extending empathy to those around us, we create a ripple effect of positivity and connection that can transform our social interactions and build a more compassionate community.

Practicing empathy in friendships and social interactions also involves being aware of and sensitive to cultural, social, and individual differences. It means recognizing that each person brings their own unique experiences, beliefs, and perspectives to the table and striving to understand and respect these differences. By approaching our interactions with cultural sensitivity and an open mind, we can build bridges of understanding and foster more inclusive and harmonious relationships.

The benefits of empathetic listening and support in friendships and social interactions are numerous. When we feel truly heard and understood by others, we experience a deep sense of validation and connection. This, in turn, can boost our self-esteem, reduce feelings of loneliness and isolation, and promote overall emotional well-being. Moreover, when we extend empathy to others, we create a positive feedback loop of kindness and support that can strengthen our relationships and build a more resilient social network.

Cultivating empathy in friendships and social interactions requires ongoing practice and self-reflection. It involves being mindful of our own emotions and reactions, taking responsibility for how we communicate and interact with others, and continually striving to broaden our perspectives and understanding. By making empathy a central part of our social interactions, we not only enrich our own lives but also contribute to building a more compassionate and connected world.

In a world that can often feel divided and disconnected, the power of empathy in friendships and social interactions cannot be overstated. By taking the time to listen, understand, and connect with others on a deep, empathetic level, we can create a tapestry of relationships that sustain us, uplift us, and remind us of our shared humanity. As we navigate the joys and challenges of social life, let us remember the transformative potential of empathy in bringing us closer together and fostering a more loving and supportive world.

Subsection 3.4: Empathy in Professional Relationships

In the fast-paced, high-pressure world of work, it is easy to overlook the importance of empathy in professional relationships. However, cultivating empathy in the workplace is essential for building strong, productive, and harmonious connections with colleagues and clients alike. When we approach our professional interactions with empathy, we create a more supportive, collaborative, and emotionally intelligent work environment that benefits everyone involved.

Empathy in professional relationships involves the ability to understand and share the feelings of others, even in the context of work-related challenges and pressures. It means taking the time to listen actively to our colleagues' concerns, ideas, and perspectives, and striving to see situations from their point of view. By practicing empathy in the workplace, we can foster a culture of trust, respect, and open communication that enables us to work together more effectively and achieve our shared goals.

One of the key benefits of empathy in professional relationships is that it enhances collaboration and teamwork. When we approach our interactions with colleagues with empathy and understanding, we create a safe space for sharing ideas, voicing concerns, and working together to solve problems. By valuing each other's contributions and perspectives, we can tap into the collective wisdom and creativity of our team, leading to more innovative solutions and better outcomes.

Empathy is also crucial for building strong, positive relationships with clients and customers. When we take the time to understand our clients' needs, challenges, and aspirations, we can provide more personalized, responsive, and effective solutions that meet their unique requirements. By demonstrating empathy and genuine concern for our clients' well-being, we can establish long-lasting, mutually beneficial relationships built on trust and loyalty.

To cultivate empathy in professional relationships, it is essential to practice active listening and effective communication. This involves giving our full attention to others when they are speaking, asking clarifying questions, and reflecting back on what we have heard to ensure that we have understood correctly. By listening empathetically and communicating clearly and respectfully, we can build bridges of understanding and foster more positive, productive interactions with colleagues and clients.

Another key strategy for building empathetic connections in the workplace is to seek out opportunities for collaboration and shared experiences. By working together on projects, participating in team-building activities, or simply engaging in informal conversations, we can gain a deeper understanding of our colleagues' perspectives, strengths, and challenges. These shared experiences can help to break down barriers, build trust, and foster a sense of camaraderie and mutual support.

Cultivating empathy in professional relationships also requires us to be mindful of our own emotions and reactions, and to manage them in a way that promotes positive, constructive interactions. This may involve practicing self-awareness, emotional regulation, and stress management techniques, such as mindfulness or deep breathing exercises. By taking care of our own emotional well-being, we can show up more fully and empathetically for others in the workplace.

Ultimately, empathy in professional relationships is about recognizing our shared humanity and working together to create a more supportive, inclusive, and successful work environment. By approaching our interactions with colleagues and clients with empathy, respect, and understanding, we can build stronger, more resilient relationships that enable us to navigate challenges, celebrate successes, and achieve our goals together. As we strive to cultivate empathy in the workplace, let us remember the transformative power of human connection in creating a more compassionate, collaborative, and fulfilling professional life.

Summary: Cultivating Empathy for Stronger, More Fulfilling Relationships

Throughout this section, we have explored the transformative power of empathy in various types of relationships, from romantic partnerships and family dynamics to friendships, social interactions, and even professional connections. By practicing empathy, we can create deeper, more meaningful bonds with others, fostering understanding, trust, and emotional intimacy.

The key takeaways from this section emphasize the importance of active listening, clear communication, and a willingness to understand and validate others' feelings and experiences. Whether in romantic relationships, where empathy can help partners navigate challenges and build a strong emotional connection, or in family dynamics, where it can bridge generational gaps and promote understanding, the practice of empathy is essential for nurturing healthy, resilient relationships.

Moreover, empathy plays a vital role in friendships and social interactions, allowing us to create a supportive, compassionate environment that promotes well-being and a sense of belonging. Even in professional relationships, empathy can enhance collaboration, teamwork, and client relations, leading to more successful outcomes and a more positive work culture.

As we conclude this section on practicing empathy in relationships, it is essential to remember that cultivating empathy is an ongoing process that requires effort, self-reflection, and a commitment to personal growth. By consistently applying the strategies and insights discussed here, we can strengthen our ability to connect with others on a deeper level, navigate challenges more effectively, and build a network of fulfilling, supportive relationships.

So, as you move forward on your journey to create more empathetic, compassionate connections with others, take the time to listen actively, communicate openly and honestly, and seek to understand and validate the experiences of those around you. By making empathy a central part of your relationships, you will not only enrich your own life but also contribute to building a more understanding, supportive, and connected world.

Section 4: Overcoming Barriers to Empathy

Empathy is a crucial component of emotional intelligence and plays a vital role in building strong, compassionate relationships. However, despite our best intentions, we may encounter various obstacles that hinder our ability to empathize with others effectively. These barriers can stem from personal biases, emotional triggers, or a lack of mindfulness and presence in our interactions. Recognizing and addressing these challenges is essential for cultivating deeper, more meaningful connections with the people in our lives.

In this section, we will explore the common barriers to empathy and provide practical strategies for overcoming them. By understanding how our biases and prejudices can cloud our judgment and limit our capacity for empathy, we can take steps to challenge and expand our perspectives. We will also discuss the impact of emotional triggers and reactivity on our ability to remain present and attuned to others' experiences, and offer techniques for managing these responses in a constructive manner.

Furthermore, we will delve into the power of mindfulness and presence in fostering empathetic connections. By cultivating a state of mindful awareness, we can enhance our ability to listen actively, understand others' perspectives, and respond with compassion and understanding. Through a combination of self-reflection, practical exercises, and real-life examples, this section will equip you with the tools and insights needed to break down the walls that hinder empathy and build bridges of understanding and connection in your relationships.

Subsection 4.1: Recognizing and Challenging Personal Biases

Personal biases and prejudices can act as significant barriers to empathy, hindering our ability to understand and connect with others on a deeper level. These biases, which are often unconscious and deeply ingrained, can lead us to make snap judgments, stereotype others, and limit our capacity for compassion and understanding. Recognizing and challenging these biases is a crucial step in cultivating empathy and building stronger, more authentic relationships.

One of the first steps in overcoming personal biases is to acknowledge their existence. We all hold certain beliefs, assumptions, and stereotypes that have been shaped by our upbringing, experiences, and societal influences. These biases can be based on factors such as race, gender, age, religion, socioeconomic status, or sexual orientation. By becoming aware of our own biases, we can begin to question their validity and take steps to challenge them.

Self-reflection is a powerful tool in identifying personal biases. Taking the time to examine our thoughts, feelings, and reactions towards others can help us uncover underlying prejudices that may be influencing our behavior. Asking ourselves questions such as, "Why do I feel this way about this person or group?" or "What assumptions am I making based on limited information?" can provide valuable insights into our biases.

Another effective technique for challenging personal biases is to actively seek out diverse perspectives and experiences. Engaging with people from different backgrounds, cultures, and walks of life can broaden our understanding and help us develop a more inclusive and empathetic worldview. This can involve reading books, watching films, or attending events that expose us to new ideas and ways of thinking.

When we encounter situations that trigger our biases, it's essential to practice mindfulness and self-awareness. Instead of reacting automatically based on our prejudices, we can take a step back and examine the situation objectively. By questioning our assumptions and considering alternative perspectives, we can begin to break down the barriers that hinder empathy and open ourselves up to more compassionate and understanding interactions.

Overcoming personal biases is an ongoing process that requires commitment, humility, and a willingness to learn and grow. It involves acknowledging our own limitations, challenging our assumptions, and actively seeking out opportunities to expand our understanding of others. By recognizing and confronting our biases, we can cultivate a more empathetic and inclusive approach to our relationships, fostering deeper connections and greater understanding.

Subsection 4.2: Managing Emotional Triggers and Reactivity

Emotional triggers and reactivity can pose significant challenges to empathetic responses in relationships. When we are triggered by certain words, actions, or situations, our emotional reactions can cloud our judgment and hinder our ability to remain present and understanding towards others. Managing these emotional triggers is crucial for cultivating empathy and fostering healthy, compassionate relationships.

The first step in managing emotional triggers is to develop self-awareness. By paying attention to our thoughts, feelings, and physical sensations, we can begin to recognize the signs of emotional reactivity. Common indicators may include a racing heart, tense muscles, or a sense of defensiveness or anger. Acknowledging these reactions without judgment allows us to create space between the trigger and our response, providing an opportunity to choose a more empathetic approach.

One effective strategy for regulating emotional reactions is to practice mindful breathing. When we find ourselves triggered, taking a few deep, slow breaths can help calm our nervous system and reduce the intensity of our emotional response. This simple act of focusing on our breath can ground us in the present moment and create a sense of inner stability, enabling us to approach the situation with greater clarity and compassion.

Another powerful tool for managing emotional triggers is cognitive reframing. This involves challenging the automatic thoughts and assumptions that fuel our emotional reactions and considering alternative perspectives. For example, if we find ourselves feeling defensive when our partner expresses a concern, we can reframe the situation by reminding ourselves that their intention is likely not to attack us but to express their own feelings and needs. By consciously shifting our mindset, we can open ourselves up to a more empathetic and understanding response.

In addition to these in-the-moment strategies, it's essential to engage in ongoing self-reflection and personal growth work to address the root causes of our emotional triggers. This may involve exploring our past experiences, attachment styles, or unresolved traumas that contribute to our reactivity. Seeking the support of a therapist, counselor, or trusted mentor can provide valuable guidance and tools for processing these underlying issues and developing greater emotional resilience.

Practicing self-compassion is also crucial for managing emotional triggers and cultivating empathy. When we encounter difficult emotions or reactions within ourselves, treating ourselves with kindness and understanding can help us extend the same compassion to others. Recognizing that we are all human, with our own struggles and imperfections, can foster a sense of common humanity and empathy in our relationships.

Managing emotional triggers and reactivity is an ongoing process that requires patience, self-awareness, and a commitment to personal growth. By developing a toolkit of strategies, such as mindful breathing, cognitive reframing, and self-reflection, we can gradually enhance our capacity for empathetic responses and create more harmonious, compassionate relationships. Through this work, we can build the emotional intelligence and resilience needed to navigate the challenges of interpersonal dynamics with greater ease and understanding.

Subsection 4.3: Cultivating Mindfulness and Presence

Mindfulness, the practice of being fully present and aware in the current moment, is a powerful tool for enhancing empathy and fostering deeper connections in relationships. By cultivating mindfulness, we can learn to stay attuned to our own emotions and experiences, as well as those of others, creating a foundation for more meaningful and compassionate interactions.

One of the key benefits of mindfulness is its ability to help us reduce distractions and increase our focus on the present moment. In today's fast-paced, technology-driven world, it's easy to become caught up in a constant stream of thoughts, worries, and external stimuli. This mental clutter can prevent us from fully engaging with the people around us, hindering our ability to listen attentively and respond with empathy. By practicing mindfulness, we can learn to quiet the noise in our minds and bring our full attention to the person in front of us, allowing for more authentic and understanding connections.

Mindfulness also helps us become more aware of our own emotions and reactions, enabling us to respond to others with greater clarity and compassion. When we are not mindful, we may find ourselves reacting automatically to situations or conversations, driven by our own biases, assumptions, or emotional triggers. By cultivating mindfulness, we can learn to observe our thoughts and feelings without judgment, creating space between our initial reactions and our responses. This heightened self-awareness allows us to approach interactions with greater empathy, as we can more easily recognize and set aside our own preconceptions and focus on understanding the other person's perspective.

Incorporating mindfulness practices into our daily lives can be as simple as taking a few minutes each day to sit quietly and focus on our breath. This basic meditation practice helps train our minds to be more present and less easily distracted. As we become more comfortable with mindfulness, we can begin to apply it to our interactions with others, bringing a greater sense of presence and openness to our conversations.

Another powerful mindfulness practice for cultivating empathy is active listening. When engaging in conversation, we often fall into the habit of mentally preparing our response while the other person is still speaking, rather than fully focusing on what they are saying. Active listening involves setting aside our own agenda and giving our full attention to the speaker, without judgment or interruption. By practicing active listening, we can create a safe and supportive space for others to express themselves, fostering deeper understanding and connection.

Mindfulness can also be applied to nonverbal communication, such as body language and facial expressions. By being mindful of our own nonverbal cues and attuned to those of others, we can gain valuable insights into the emotional states and needs of the people around us. This heightened awareness can help us respond with greater sensitivity and compassion, even in challenging or emotionally charged situations.

Cultivating mindfulness and presence is an ongoing journey that requires patience, practice, and self-compassion. It's important to remember that mindfulness is not about achieving a state of perfect focus or emotional control, but rather about developing a greater capacity for awareness, acceptance, and empathy in our relationships. By committing to the practice of mindfulness, we can gradually transform the way we connect with others, fostering more authentic, compassionate, and fulfilling relationships in all areas of our lives.

Summary: Cultivating Empathy Through Self-Awareness and Growth

Throughout this section, we have explored the common barriers that hinder our ability to empathize with others, including personal biases, emotional triggers, and a lack of mindfulness. By recognizing and addressing these obstacles, we can cultivate a more compassionate and understanding approach to our relationships, fostering deeper connections and greater harmony.

The journey towards empathy begins with self-awareness. By acknowledging our own biases and prejudices, we can take steps to challenge and expand our perspectives, opening ourselves up to more inclusive and understanding interactions. Through self-reflection, diverse experiences, and a willingness to question our assumptions, we can gradually break down the walls that limit our capacity for empathy.

Managing emotional triggers and reactivity is another crucial aspect of cultivating empathy. By developing mindfulness and self-awareness, we can learn to recognize the signs of emotional reactivity and respond with greater clarity and compassion. Techniques such as mindful breathing, cognitive reframing, and self-compassion can help us navigate challenging situations with greater ease and understanding, enabling us to extend empathy even in the face of difficult emotions.

Finally, the practice of mindfulness and presence is essential for fostering empathetic connections. By learning to quiet the noise in our minds and bring our full attention to the present moment, we can create a safe and supportive space for others to express themselves. Through active listening, nonverbal attunement, and a commitment to staying present, we can build more authentic and compassionate relationships in all areas of our lives.

Overcoming the barriers to empathy is an ongoing journey that requires patience, self-awareness, and a willingness to learn and grow. By recognizing our own limitations, challenging our assumptions, and actively cultivating mindfulness and presence, we can develop the emotional intelligence and resilience needed to navigate the complexities of human connection. As we continue on this path, we will find ourselves better equipped to build strong, compassionate, and fulfilling relationships, enriching not only our own lives but the lives of those around us.

Section 5: The Power of Empathy and Emotional Intelligence in Conflict Resolution

Conflict is an inevitable part of any relationship, whether it be with a romantic partner, family member, friend, or colleague. When left unresolved, conflicts can lead to resentment, bitterness, and even the breakdown of relationships. However, by harnessing the power of empathy and emotional intelligence, individuals can navigate conflicts and disagreements more effectively, leading to stronger, more resilient connections.

Imagine a heated argument between two partners, both feeling unheard and misunderstood. In the heat of the moment, it's easy to get caught up in one's own emotions and perspectives, failing to see the situation from the other person's point of view. This is where empathy comes in – the ability to put oneself in another's shoes and understand their feelings, thoughts, and experiences. By actively practicing empathy during conflicts, individuals can gain a deeper understanding of their partner's perspective, leading to more productive conversations and a greater likelihood of finding mutually satisfying resolutions.

Alongside empathy, emotional intelligence plays a crucial role in managing conflict dynamics. Emotional intelligence involves recognizing and regulating one's own emotions, as well as being attuned to the emotions of others. When faced with a disagreement, emotionally intelligent individuals are better equipped to manage their own stress, frustration, or anger, allowing them to approach the situation with a clearer, more level-headed mindset. They are also more adept at reading their partner's emotional cues, enabling them to respond with sensitivity and understanding rather than defensiveness or aggression.

Throughout this section, we will explore the various ways in which empathy and emotional intelligence can be applied to conflict resolution in relationships. From learning how to validate differing viewpoints and manage emotional triggers, to finding compromises and solutions that meet both parties' needs, readers will gain valuable insights and practical strategies for navigating even the most challenging disagreements. By cultivating these essential skills, individuals can transform conflicts into opportunities for growth, understanding, and deeper connection, ultimately strengthening the foundation of their relationships.

Subsection 5.1: Applying Empathy to Understand Different Perspectives

In the heat of a conflict, it's easy to become entrenched in our own viewpoints, convinced that we are right and the other person is wrong. However, this narrow-minded approach often leads to a deadlock, where both parties feel unheard and misunderstood. To break free from this cycle and find a resolution, it's crucial to apply empathy and make a genuine effort to understand the other person's perspective.

Empathy is the ability to put yourself in someone else's shoes, to see the world through their eyes, and to understand their feelings, thoughts, and experiences. When we practice empathy during conflicts, we create a space for open dialogue and mutual understanding. Instead of focusing solely on our own needs and desires, we actively listen to the other person's concerns and validate their emotions.

For example, imagine a couple arguing about their differing approaches to financial management. One partner may prioritize saving for the future, while the other believes in enjoying life in the present. By applying empathy, each partner can take a step back and try to understand the underlying reasons behind the other's perspective. Perhaps the partner who prioritizes saving grew up in a household that experienced financial hardship, leading them to value security and stability. Meanwhile, the partner who believes in living for the moment may have witnessed a loved one's life cut short, prompting them to cherish every experience.

By seeking to understand these deeper motivations and experiences, the couple can move beyond surface-level disagreements and find common ground. They can acknowledge and validate each other's viewpoints, even if they don't fully agree with them. This empathetic approach opens the door to compromise and collaboration, as both partners feel heard and respected.

Moreover, practicing empathy during conflicts helps to reduce defensive reactions and emotional escalation. When we feel understood and validated, we are less likely to lash out or become hostile. Instead, we are more open to finding mutually beneficial solutions and working together to resolve the issue at hand.

To apply empathy effectively in conflict situations, it's essential to develop active listening skills. This means giving the other person your full attention, avoiding interruptions, and asking clarifying questions to ensure you understand their perspective. It also involves acknowledging their emotions and expressing genuine interest in their experiences.

Additionally, it's important to suspend judgment and resist the urge to formulate counterarguments while the other person is speaking. By creating a safe, non-judgmental space for open communication, both parties can express their thoughts and feelings freely, leading to a more productive and empathetic dialogue.

In summary, applying empathy is a powerful tool for navigating conflicts and understanding different perspectives. By putting ourselves in the other person's shoes and seeking to understand their viewpoints, we can foster a more compassionate, collaborative approach to problem-solving. This not only helps to resolve immediate disagreements but also strengthens the foundation of our relationships, promoting greater trust, respect, and resilience in the face of future challenges.

Subsection 5.2: Using Emotional Intelligence to Manage Conflict Dynamics

Emotional intelligence is a critical skill set that can help individuals navigate the complex dynamics of conflicts in relationships. By understanding and managing one's own emotions, as well as being attuned to the emotions of others, it becomes possible to de-escalate tensions and promote constructive dialogue. When conflicts arise, emotionally intelligent individuals are better equipped to handle the situation with grace, empathy, and a solutions-oriented mindset.

One key aspect of using emotional intelligence in conflict management is self-awareness. This involves recognizing and understanding one's own emotional triggers, reactions, and patterns of behavior. By developing a keen sense of self-awareness, individuals can identify when their emotions are beginning to escalate during a conflict and take proactive steps to regulate them. This may involve techniques such as deep breathing, taking a momentary pause, or mentally reframing the situation in a more positive light. By managing their own emotional responses, individuals can maintain a calmer, more rational approach to the conflict at hand.

Another crucial component of emotional intelligence in conflict resolution is empathy. Empathy allows individuals to put themselves in the other person's shoes, to understand their perspective, feelings, and needs. By actively listening and seeking to understand the other party's viewpoint, individuals can demonstrate respect and validation, even in the midst of a disagreement. This empathetic approach can help to diffuse defensive reactions and create a more collaborative atmosphere, where both parties feel heard and valued.

In addition to self-awareness and empathy, emotionally intelligent individuals also possess strong communication skills. They are able to express their own thoughts, feelings, and needs clearly and assertively, without resorting to aggressive or passive-aggressive behaviors. They also know how to listen actively, asking questions and providing feedback to ensure that they fully understand the other person's perspective. By modeling effective communication techniques, emotionally intelligent individuals can help to steer conflicts towards more productive, solutions-focused discussions.

Furthermore, emotional intelligence enables individuals to maintain a sense of perspective and adaptability during conflicts. Rather than becoming entrenched in a rigid stance or a win-lose mentality, emotionally intelligent individuals are open to exploring alternative viewpoints and finding mutually beneficial solutions. They are willing to compromise and collaborate, recognizing that the ultimate goal is to strengthen the relationship and find a resolution that works for both parties.

To cultivate emotional intelligence skills for conflict management, individuals can engage in a variety of practices and techniques. These may include mindfulness and self-reflection exercises, which help to build self-awareness and emotional regulation capabilities. Engaging in active listening and empathy-building activities, such as role-playing or perspective-taking exercises, can also enhance one's ability to understand and validate others' emotions. Additionally, learning effective communication strategies, such as using "I" statements and avoiding blame or criticism, can contribute to more constructive dialogue during conflicts.

By harnessing the power of emotional intelligence, individuals can transform conflicts into opportunities for growth, understanding, and relationship strengthening. Rather than viewing disagreements as threats or obstacles, emotionally intelligent individuals approach conflicts with a mindset of curiosity, compassion, and collaboration. They recognize that by managing their own emotions, empathizing with others, and communicating effectively, they can navigate even the most challenging conflict dynamics and emerge with stronger, more resilient relationships.

Subsection 5.3: Finding Empathetic Solutions and Compromises

In the midst of a conflict, it can be challenging to find solutions that satisfy both parties. Emotions run high, and the desire to "win" the argument can overshadow the need for a mutually beneficial resolution. However, by approaching conflicts with empathy and a willingness to compromise, individuals can navigate even the most challenging disagreements and emerge with stronger, more resilient relationships.

Empathy is a powerful tool for finding common ground and developing solutions that meet the needs of both parties. When we take the time to truly understand the other person's perspective, feelings, and motivations, we gain valuable insights into what is driving their behavior and what they need to feel heard and respected. This understanding can help us to reframe the conflict in a more positive light, shifting the focus from winning or losing to finding a resolution that works for everyone.

One way to cultivate empathy in conflict situations is to practice active listening. This means giving the other person our full attention, avoiding interruptions, and asking clarifying questions to ensure that we fully understand their viewpoint. It also involves acknowledging their emotions and validating their experiences, even if we don't agree with their perspective. By creating a safe, non-judgmental space for open communication, we encourage the other person to share their thoughts and feelings freely, leading to a more productive and collaborative dialogue.

Another key aspect of finding empathetic solutions is a willingness to compromise. Compromise involves finding a middle ground between two opposing viewpoints, where both parties make concessions in order to reach a mutually satisfactory agreement. This requires a degree of flexibility and open-mindedness, as well as a recognition that the relationship is more important than being "right" or getting everything we want.

To find effective compromises, it's essential to focus on the underlying needs and interests of both parties, rather than getting stuck on specific positions or demands. By identifying the core concerns and values that are driving the conflict, we can explore creative solutions that address these needs in a mutually beneficial way. This may involve brainstorming a range of options, considering alternative perspectives, and being willing to let go of certain expectations or desires in service of the greater good.

It's also important to approach compromises with a spirit of fairness and reciprocity. This means being willing to make sacrifices and concessions, but also expecting the other person to do the same. By demonstrating a commitment to finding a balanced, equitable solution, we create a foundation of trust and respect that can strengthen the relationship over time.

Ultimately, finding empathetic solutions and compromises requires a shift in mindset from a self-focused, win-lose mentality to a collaborative, win-win approach. It involves recognizing that the most satisfying and enduring resolutions are those that meet the needs of both parties and contribute to the overall health and well-being of the relationship. By approaching conflicts with empathy, active listening, and a willingness to compromise, individuals can transform even the most challenging disagreements into opportunities for growth, understanding, and connection.

Summary: Harnessing Empathy and Emotional Intelligence for Stronger Relationships

Throughout this section, we have explored the transformative power of empathy and emotional intelligence in navigating conflicts and disagreements within relationships. By cultivating these essential skills, individuals can approach even the most challenging situations with a mindset of understanding, collaboration, and growth.

Empathy allows us to step into another person's shoes, to see the world through their eyes, and to validate their experiences and emotions. When we apply empathy during conflicts, we create a safe space for open, honest communication, where both parties feel heard and respected. This lays the foundation for finding mutually satisfying solutions and compromises that strengthen the relationship.

Emotional intelligence, on the other hand, enables us to manage our own emotions effectively while remaining attuned to the emotions of others. By developing self-awareness, self-regulation, and effective communication skills, we can approach conflicts with a clear, level-headed mindset, avoiding defensive reactions or emotional escalation. Emotionally intelligent individuals are better equipped to steer conflicts towards productive, solutions-focused discussions.

The combination of empathy and emotional intelligence is a powerful tool for building stronger, more resilient relationships. By seeking to understand others' perspectives, managing our own emotions, and finding compromises that meet both parties' needs, we can transform conflicts into opportunities for growth and connection.

As we move forward, it is essential to remember that developing empathy and emotional intelligence is an ongoing journey. By consistently practicing active listening, perspective-taking, and self-reflection, we can continue to strengthen these skills and build healthier, more fulfilling relationships. With empathy and emotional intelligence as our guides, we can navigate even the most challenging conflicts with grace, compassion, and a deep commitment to the well-being of our relationships.

Chapter Summary: Nurturing Empathy and Emotional Intelligence for Stronger

Relationships

Throughout this chapter, we have explored the crucial role that empathy and emotional intelligence play in building strong, compassionate, and resilient relationships. By understanding the foundations of empathy, developing emotional intelligence skills, and practicing empathy in various types of relationships, we can create deeper, more meaningful connections with others.

We have examined the neuroscience behind empathy and the four pillars of emotional intelligence, providing practical strategies for enhancing self-awareness, self-regulation, social awareness, and relationship management. By applying these skills in romantic partnerships, family dynamics, friendships, and professional relationships, we can foster more understanding, support, and collaboration.

However, cultivating empathy and emotional intelligence is not always easy. We have discussed common barriers to empathy, such as personal biases, emotional triggers, and reactivity, and provided techniques for overcoming these obstacles. By challenging our biases, managing our emotions, and practicing mindfulness, we can become more attuned to others' experiences and respond with greater compassion.

Perhaps one of the most powerful applications of empathy and emotional intelligence is in conflict resolution. By using these skills to understand different perspectives, manage conflict dynamics, and find mutually satisfying solutions, we can navigate disagreements and strengthen our relationships in the process.

As we continue on our journey of building fulfilling relationships, let us remember the transformative power of empathy and emotional intelligence. By nurturing these qualities within ourselves and our connections with others, we can create a more compassionate, understanding, and resilient world, one relationship at a time.

Chapter 7: The Power of Vulnerability and Authenticity

In the realm of relationships, few things hold as much transformative power as vulnerability and authenticity. These two interconnected qualities form the bedrock of genuine, meaningful connections that nourish the soul and enrich our lives. When we dare to be vulnerable, we strip away the facades that keep us isolated and invite others to see the raw, unfiltered essence of who we are. It is in these moments of unadulterated honesty that we create space for true intimacy and understanding to flourish.

Authenticity, the act of being true to oneself and expressing one's thoughts, feelings, and desires without pretense, goes hand in hand with vulnerability. It requires a willingness to stand in our truth, even when it feels uncomfortable or exposing. By embracing authenticity, we give ourselves permission to be imperfect, to own our struggles and triumphs alike, and to show up fully in our relationships.

In a world that often rewards conformity and self-censorship, vulnerability and authenticity can feel like risky endeavors. The fear of rejection, judgment, or ridicule can be paralyzing, tempting us to hide behind masks of perfection and self-sufficiency. However, it is precisely in the act of shedding these masks that we open ourselves up to the possibility of deep, authentic connection.

When we allow ourselves to be seen, flaws and all, we create a profound sense of trust and safety in our relationships. We signal to others that it is okay to be imperfect, to have doubts and fears, and to navigate the messy, beautiful terrain of the human experience together. This vulnerability invites reciprocity, encouraging others to lower their own defenses and meet us in a space of mutual understanding and compassion.

Throughout this chapter, we will explore the transformative power of vulnerability and authenticity in relationships. We will examine the barriers that prevent us from embracing these qualities and provide practical strategies for overcoming them. We will delve into the ways in which vulnerability and authenticity can be cultivated in various types of relationships, from romantic partnerships to family dynamics and friendships. By the end of this chapter, you will have a deeper understanding of how embracing vulnerability and authenticity can lead to more fulfilling, resilient, and genuinely connected relationships.

Section 1: Understanding Vulnerability and Authenticity

In the quest for meaningful relationships, two essential qualities often emerge as the foundation for genuine connections: vulnerability and authenticity. These powerful concepts, while seemingly simple, hold the key to unlocking the depth and richness of human interactions. As we embark on this exploration of vulnerability and authenticity, we will uncover the transformative potential they hold for our relationships and personal growth.

Vulnerability, at its core, is the willingness to be seen, truly seen, by others. It is the courage to remove the masks we wear and expose our authentic selves, complete with our fears, dreams, and imperfections. When we embrace vulnerability, we create space for others to connect with us on a profound level, fostering empathy, trust, and understanding. It is through this raw and honest sharing of ourselves that we invite others to do the same, forging bonds that transcend the superficial and delve into the depths of the human experience.

Authenticity, on the other hand, is the unapologetic expression of our true selves. It is the alignment of our thoughts, feelings, and actions, free from the constraints of societal expectations or the need for validation. When we live authentically, we give ourselves permission to be who we are, flaws and all, and in doing so, we attract those who resonate with our genuine essence. Authenticity breeds trust and respect, as others can sense the sincerity and integrity that emanate from an individual who is true to themselves.

Together, vulnerability and authenticity form a powerful combination that lays the groundwork for genuine connections. By embracing these qualities, we open ourselves up to the possibility of deep, meaningful relationships that nourish our souls and help us grow. In the following subsections, we will delve deeper into the meanings of vulnerability and authenticity, explore their interconnectedness, and discover how they can transform the way we relate to ourselves and others. So, let us embark on this journey of self-discovery and unlock the power of vulnerability and authenticity in our lives.

Subsection 1.1: The Meaning of Vulnerability

Vulnerability is a term that has gained significant attention in recent years, particularly in the context of personal growth and relationships. At its core, vulnerability refers to the willingness to be open, honest, and authentic with others, even in the face of potential rejection, judgment, or emotional pain. It is the courage to show up as our true selves, flaws and all, and to allow others to see the parts of us that we often keep hidden.

From an emotional perspective, vulnerability involves exposing our deepest feelings, fears, and desires to others. It means sharing our hopes, dreams, and aspirations, as well as our insecurities, doubts, and failures. When we are vulnerable, we allow ourselves to be seen in our entirety, without the masks or facades that we often wear to protect ourselves from emotional harm. This can be a frightening prospect, as it requires us to confront our own fears of rejection and abandonment, and to trust that others will accept and love us for who we truly are.

Psychologically, vulnerability is closely linked to the concept of shame. Shame is the belief that we are fundamentally flawed or unworthy, and that if others were to see our true selves, they would reject us. When we experience shame, we often try to hide or conceal the parts of ourselves that we believe are unacceptable or unlovable. However, by embracing vulnerability and sharing these parts of ourselves with others, we can begin to heal from shame and develop a greater sense of self-acceptance and self-love.

Vulnerability is also essential for building deep, meaningful connections with others. When we are willing to be vulnerable with someone, we create a space for them to be vulnerable in return. This mutual sharing of our innermost selves fosters a sense of trust, empathy, and understanding that is essential for healthy relationships. By being vulnerable, we invite others to see us as we truly are, and to connect with us on a deeper, more authentic level.

Subsection 1.2: The Essence of Authenticity

Authenticity, at its core, is the unwavering commitment to being true to oneself. It is the courage to embrace and express one's genuine thoughts, feelings, and values, even in the face of external pressures or societal expectations. When we live authentically, we allow our unique essence to shine through, unencumbered by the need for validation or the fear of judgment.

To be authentic is to strip away the layers of pretense and façade that we often adopt to fit in or please others. It means honoring our innermost desires, passions, and convictions, and aligning our actions with our true selves. Authenticity requires a deep level of self-awareness, as we must first understand who we are and what we stand for before we can live in accordance with our authentic nature.

In the realm of relationships, authenticity is a powerful catalyst for genuine connection. When we show up as our authentic selves, we create space for others to do the same. By embracing vulnerability and sharing our true thoughts and feelings, we invite others to connect with us on a deeper, more meaningful level. Authenticity fosters trust, as others can sense the sincerity and integrity that emanate from someone who is unapologetically themselves.

Moreover, authenticity is essential for personal growth and self-acceptance. When we live authentically, we give ourselves permission to be imperfect, to make mistakes, and to learn from them. We release the burden of constantly seeking approval or validation from others, and instead, find contentment and fulfillment from within. Authenticity allows us to embrace our unique strengths, quirks, and flaws, and to celebrate the diversity of the human experience.

However, living authentically is not always easy. It requires courage, self-reflection, and a willingness to confront our deepest fears and insecurities. It means risking rejection or disapproval from those who may not understand or appreciate our true selves. Yet, the rewards of authenticity are immeasurable – a life lived with integrity, purpose, and genuine connection.

In essence, authenticity is the foundation upon which genuine self-expression and relationships are built. It is the key to unlocking our full potential, both personally and interpersonally. By embracing our authentic selves and encouraging others to do the same, we create a world where true connection, empathy, and understanding can flourish.

Subsection 1.3: The Interconnection Between Vulnerability and Authenticity

Vulnerability and authenticity are two sides of the same coin, intricately woven together in the tapestry of human connection. While vulnerability is the willingness to expose one's true self, authenticity is the unapologetic expression of that self. These two qualities are mutually reinforcing, each one nurturing and strengthening the other in a beautiful dance of self-discovery and genuine connection.

To be vulnerable is to invite others to see the authentic self that lies beneath the surface. It is through the courageous act of sharing our deepest fears, hopes, and dreams that we create space for authentic connection. When we lower our defenses and allow ourselves to be seen, we give others permission to do the same. This mutual exchange of vulnerability fosters an environment of trust, empathy, and understanding, the very foundation upon which authentic relationships are built.

Authenticity, in turn, is the catalyst that propels vulnerability forward. When we embrace our true selves and live in alignment with our values and beliefs, we naturally gravitate towards vulnerability. We no longer feel the need to hide behind masks or pretenses, as we find strength in the knowledge that our authentic selves are worthy of love and acceptance. Authenticity gives us the courage to be vulnerable, to share our stories, and to connect with others on a profound level.

The interconnection between vulnerability and authenticity is a powerful force that transforms relationships from superficial to meaningful. When we show up as our authentic selves and openly share our vulnerabilities, we create a space for others to do the same. This shared experience of vulnerability and authenticity forges deep, lasting connections that transcend the mundane and touch the very essence of what it means to be human.

Moreover, the symbiotic relationship between vulnerability and authenticity extends beyond interpersonal connections and into the realm of personal growth. When we embrace vulnerability and live authentically, we embark on a journey of self-discovery and self-acceptance. We learn to love ourselves, flaws and all, and to extend that same compassion and understanding to others. Through this process, we cultivate resilience, empathy, and a deeper appreciation for the rich tapestry of human experience.

In a world that often prizes perfection and self-protection, the interconnection between vulnerability and authenticity is a revolutionary force. It challenges us to strip away the layers of fear and pretense, to stand in our truth, and to connect with others from a place of raw, unfiltered humanity. By embracing these qualities, we open ourselves up to the transformative power of genuine connection, both with ourselves and with those around us.

Summary: Embracing the Transformative Power of Vulnerability and Authenticity

In this section, we have explored the profound significance of vulnerability and authenticity in fostering genuine connections and cultivating meaningful relationships. By delving into the core meanings of these two powerful concepts, we have discovered that vulnerability is the courageous act of allowing ourselves to be truly seen, while authenticity is the unapologetic expression of our true selves.

Through understanding the emotional and psychological components of vulnerability, we have recognized its potential to heal shame, build trust, and create spaces for deep, empathetic connections. Simultaneously, by examining the essence of authenticity, we have discovered its role in fostering self-acceptance, personal growth, and the development of relationships built on a foundation of trust and sincerity.

Perhaps most importantly, we have illuminated the intricate interconnection between vulnerability and authenticity, recognizing that these qualities are mutually reinforcing and essential for cultivating genuine, meaningful connections. By embracing vulnerability and living authentically, we open ourselves up to the transformative power of true human connection, both with ourselves and with those around us.

As we move forward in our exploration of relationships, let us carry with us the knowledge that vulnerability and authenticity are not weaknesses, but rather, they are the very strengths that enable us to build the deep, fulfilling connections we all yearn for. By courageously embracing these qualities and encouraging others to do the same, we have the power to transform our relationships and, ultimately, our lives.

In the next section, we will explore the common barriers that prevent us from fully embracing vulnerability and authenticity, and discover strategies for overcoming these obstacles on our path to more genuine, connected living.

Section 2: Overcoming Barriers to Vulnerability and Authenticity

In the pursuit of deeper, more meaningful connections, we often find ourselves confronted with internal obstacles that hinder our ability to embrace vulnerability and authenticity. These barriers, rooted in fear, past experiences, and societal expectations, can prevent us from fully expressing our true selves and forming genuine bonds with others. However, by identifying and understanding these common obstacles, we can develop strategies to overcome them and unlock the power of vulnerability and authenticity in our relationships.

Throughout this section, we will explore the various factors that contribute to our resistance to vulnerability and authenticity. From the fear of judgment and rejection to the influence of past traumas and the pressure to maintain a façade of perfection, we will delve into the complex web of emotions and beliefs that hold us back. By shining a light on these barriers, we can begin to dismantle them and create space for more open, honest, and fulfilling connections.

As we navigate this transformative journey, it is essential to approach the process with self-compassion and patience. Overcoming deeply ingrained patterns of behavior and thought takes time and practice, but the rewards are immeasurable. By equipping ourselves with practical strategies and tools, we can gradually build the confidence and resilience necessary to embrace vulnerability and authenticity in our daily lives.

Through relatable examples, expert insights, and actionable advice, this section will empower you to confront your fears, challenge limiting beliefs, and cultivate a more authentic way of being. Whether you are seeking to deepen your romantic partnership, strengthen family bonds, or forge more meaningful friendships, the insights and strategies presented here will serve as a valuable guide on your path to greater vulnerability and authenticity.

So, let us embark on this transformative journey together, armed with the knowledge and tools necessary to break down the barriers that stand between us and the profound connections we desire. By embracing vulnerability and authenticity, we open ourselves up to a world of possibilities, where our relationships can flourish, and our true selves can shine.

Subsection 2.1: Recognizing and Challenging Fear of Judgment

One of the most pervasive barriers to vulnerability and authenticity is the fear of judgment. This deeply rooted apprehension stems from our innate desire to be accepted, valued, and loved by others. The prospect of being judged, criticized, or rejected based on our true thoughts, feelings, and experiences can be paralyzing, leading us to hide behind a façade of perfection and conformity.

The fear of judgment often manifests in various forms, such as the fear of not being good enough, the fear of being misunderstood, or the fear of being perceived as weak or flawed. These fears can be traced back to early experiences, societal pressures, and cultural expectations that shape our beliefs about what is acceptable and desirable.

To overcome the fear of judgment and cultivate vulnerability and authenticity, it is essential to first recognize and acknowledge its presence in our lives. By bringing awareness to the thoughts and emotions that arise when we consider being vulnerable, we can begin to challenge the validity of these fears and reframe our perspective.

One powerful technique for overcoming the fear of judgment is to practice self-compassion. By treating ourselves with kindness, understanding, and acceptance, we can gradually build the resilience and confidence necessary to face potential criticism or rejection. Engaging in positive self-talk, such as reminding ourselves that our worth is not contingent upon others' opinions, can help us maintain a healthy sense of self in the face of judgment.

Another effective strategy is to surround ourselves with supportive, non-judgmental individuals who create a safe space for vulnerability and authenticity. By carefully selecting our confidants and building trust within these relationships, we can gradually expose our true selves and receive validation and encouragement, which can help diminish the fear of judgment over time.

Additionally, it is crucial to challenge the assumptions and beliefs that underlie our fear of judgment. Often, we overestimate the severity and likelihood of negative consequences, while underestimating our ability to cope with and learn from these experiences. By questioning the accuracy of these assumptions and reframing potential judgments as opportunities for growth and self-discovery, we can gradually chip away at the fear that holds us back.

Ultimately, overcoming the fear of judgment is a continuous process that requires patience, self-compassion, and a willingness to step outside our comfort zone. By recognizing the fear, challenging its validity, and embracing vulnerability and authenticity in the face of potential criticism, we can forge deeper, more meaningful connections with others and lead a more fulfilling life.

Subsection 2.2: Letting Go of Perfectionism

Perfectionism, the relentless pursuit of flawlessness, can be a significant barrier to vulnerability and authentic self-expression. When we are consumed by the need to present a perfect image to the world, we often sacrifice our true selves and hide behind a façade of invulnerability. This subsection explores how perfectionism can hinder genuine connections and provides strategies for embracing imperfection and vulnerability.

At its core, perfectionism is rooted in a deep-seated fear of judgment, rejection, and inadequacy. Perfectionists often hold themselves to impossibly high standards, believing that their worth is contingent upon achieving these unrealistic goals. This mindset can lead to a constant state of self-criticism, anxiety, and emotional exhaustion, as individuals strive to maintain an illusion of perfection in all aspects of their lives.

In the context of relationships, perfectionism can be particularly detrimental. When we are preoccupied with presenting a flawless image, we may struggle to be vulnerable and authentic with others. We might avoid sharing our fears, insecurities, and struggles, fearing that exposing our imperfections will lead to rejection or disappointment. This lack of vulnerability can create emotional distance and hinder the development of deep, meaningful connections.

To overcome perfectionism and embrace vulnerability, it is essential to challenge the underlying beliefs and assumptions that fuel this mindset. One powerful strategy is to practice self-compassion. By treating ourselves with kindness, understanding, and acceptance, we can begin to let go of the harsh self-criticism that often accompanies perfectionism. Acknowledging that imperfection is a natural and inevitable part of the human experience can help us develop a more balanced and forgiving perspective.

Another effective approach is to reframe our perception of vulnerability. Rather than viewing it as a weakness or liability, we can recognize vulnerability as a strength and a catalyst for personal growth and connection. By embracing our imperfections and sharing them with others, we create opportunities for empathy, understanding, and deeper emotional bonds. When we allow ourselves to be seen as we truly are, flaws and all, we invite others to do the same, fostering a culture of authenticity and acceptance.

Cultivating a growth mindset can also be instrumental in overcoming perfectionism. Instead of fixating on achieving a perfect outcome, we can focus on the process of learning, growth, and self-discovery. By embracing challenges and viewing mistakes as opportunities for improvement, we can gradually shift our perspective from one of self-judgment to one of self-compassion and resilience.

Ultimately, letting go of perfectionism and embracing vulnerability is a gradual and ongoing process. It requires a willingness to step outside our comfort zone, confront our fears, and accept ourselves as we are. By practicing self-compassion, reframing our perception of vulnerability, and cultivating a growth mindset, we can begin to dismantle the barriers that prevent us from expressing our authentic selves and forming genuine, meaningful connections with others.

Subsection 2.3: Healing from Past Experiences of Rejection or Betrayal

Past experiences of rejection or betrayal can leave deep emotional scars that hinder our ability to be vulnerable and authentic in future relationships. These painful memories can create a fear of opening up, as we strive to protect ourselves from further hurt. However, by acknowledging the impact of these experiences and actively working towards healing, we can break down the barriers that prevent us from forming genuine connections and cultivating vulnerability.

The first step in healing from past rejection or betrayal is to validate our own emotions. It is essential to recognize that the pain, anger, and fear we feel are normal and justified responses to the hurt we have endured. By allowing ourselves to fully experience and process these emotions, we can begin to release their hold on us and create space for healing.

Self-compassion plays a crucial role in the healing process. Instead of engaging in self-blame or criticism, we must treat ourselves with kindness, understanding, and forgiveness. Recognizing that our past experiences do not define our worth or future potential is a powerful step towards building resilience and embracing vulnerability.

Seeking support from trusted friends, family members, or mental health professionals can provide a safe space to process our emotions and gain new perspectives. Sharing our experiences with others who offer empathy and understanding can help us feel less alone and more validated in our journey towards healing.

As we work through the pain of past rejection or betrayal, it is important to challenge the negative beliefs and patterns that may have emerged as a result. This might involve questioning the assumption that vulnerability always leads to hurt, or recognizing that not all relationships will follow the same painful path. By consciously reframing our thoughts and beliefs, we can gradually rebuild trust in ourselves and others.

Engaging in self-care practices, such as mindfulness, journaling, or pursuing hobbies that bring joy and fulfillment, can support the healing process and promote emotional resilience. By prioritizing our own well-being and cultivating a strong sense of self, we become better equipped to face the challenges of vulnerability and authenticity in future relationships.

Healing from past experiences of rejection or betrayal is a gradual and ongoing process. It requires patience, self-compassion, and a willingness to confront and work through painful emotions. By acknowledging the impact of these experiences, seeking support, challenging negative beliefs, and engaging in self-care, we can gradually dismantle the barriers that prevent us from embracing vulnerability and authenticity in our relationships. As we heal and build resilience, we open ourselves up to the possibility of forming deeper, more meaningful connections with others, grounded in trust, empathy, and mutual understanding.

Summary: Embracing Vulnerability and Authenticity for Deeper Connections

Throughout this section, we have explored the common barriers that prevent individuals from embracing vulnerability and authenticity in their relationships. From the fear of judgment and the pressure of perfectionism to the lingering impact of past rejection and betrayal, these obstacles can seem daunting and insurmountable. However, by recognizing and addressing these challenges head-on, we can begin to dismantle the walls that keep us from forming deep, meaningful connections with others.

The journey towards vulnerability and authenticity is not always easy, but it is a path worth taking. By practicing self-compassion, challenging limiting beliefs, and seeking support from trusted loved ones, we can gradually build the resilience and confidence necessary to show up as our true selves in our relationships. As we learn to embrace our imperfections and share our authentic experiences, we open the door to greater empathy, understanding, and connection with those around us.

Remember, vulnerability and authenticity are not weaknesses, but rather powerful tools for personal growth and relationship building. By letting go of the need to present a perfect façade and allowing ourselves to be seen, flaws and all, we create space for genuine, heartfelt connections that can withstand the tests of time.

As you move forward on this journey, be patient and kind with yourself. Overcoming deeply ingrained patterns of behavior and thought takes time and practice, but each small step towards vulnerability and authenticity brings you closer to the fulfilling relationships you desire. Trust in the process, and know that by embracing your true self, you are not only improving your own life but also inspiring others to do the same.

So, take a deep breath, summon your courage, and step boldly into the realm of vulnerability and authenticity. The rewards – deeper love, stronger bonds, and a more genuine sense of belonging – are well worth the effort. As you continue to explore and implement the strategies and insights from this section, you will find yourself better equipped to navigate the complexities of human connection and forge the kind of relationships that nourish your soul.

Section 3: Cultivating Vulnerability and Authenticity in Relationships

In the journey of building meaningful connections, vulnerability and authenticity serve as the cornerstone of genuine, lasting relationships. When we allow ourselves to be seen, heard, and understood in our truest form, we create a foundation of trust and intimacy that can weather the storms of life. However, the path to cultivating these essential qualities is not always easy, as it requires courage, self-awareness, and a willingness to step outside of our comfort zones.

In this section, we will explore practical ways to foster vulnerability and authenticity in various types of relationships, from romantic partnerships to family dynamics, friendships, and even professional connections. By examining the unique challenges and opportunities present in each of these contexts, we will uncover strategies for creating a safe and supportive environment that encourages open communication, emotional honesty, and genuine self-expression.

Through relatable examples, expert insights, and actionable advice, you will gain the tools and confidence needed to cultivate deeper, more authentic connections with the people who matter most in your life. Whether you are seeking to strengthen your intimate bond with a partner, improve communication with family members, or build more meaningful friendships, the principles and techniques discussed in this section will serve as a guide on your journey towards more fulfilling relationships.

As we navigate the complexities of human connection, it is essential to remember that vulnerability and authenticity are not weaknesses, but rather the ultimate strengths that allow us to experience the richness and beauty of life's relationships. By embracing these qualities and integrating them into our daily interactions, we open ourselves up to a world of profound love, understanding, and personal growth. So, let us embark on this transformative journey together, as we explore the power of vulnerability and authenticity in creating the relationships we have always dreamed of.

Subsection 3.1: Vulnerability and Authenticity in Romantic Partnerships

In the realm of romantic partnerships, vulnerability and authenticity serve as the bedrock upon which genuine connection and lasting love are built. When we allow ourselves to be truly seen by our partners—flaws, fears, and all—we create a space for intimacy to flourish and trust to deepen. It is through this process of revealing our authentic selves that we foster a bond that can withstand the trials and tribulations of life.

However, the path to vulnerability and authenticity in romantic relationships is often fraught with fear and uncertainty. We may worry that exposing our true selves will lead to rejection, judgment, or even heartbreak. These fears are natural, but they can also prevent us from experiencing the profound love and connection we crave. By taking the courageous step to embrace vulnerability, we open ourselves up to the possibility of being fully accepted and loved for who we are.

Authenticity, too, plays a crucial role in creating a strong foundation for romantic partnerships. When we show up as our genuine selves, without pretense or facade, we allow our partners to know and love us deeply. This means being honest about our thoughts, feelings, and desires, even when it feels uncomfortable or scary. It also means being willing to have difficult conversations and work through challenges together, rather than hiding behind a mask of perfection.

Cultivating vulnerability and authenticity in romantic relationships requires a commitment to self-awareness, open communication, and emotional bravery. It means being willing to share our hopes, dreams, and fears with our partners, and creating a safe space for them to do the same. It also means being open to feedback, growth, and change, recognizing that true intimacy is a journey of continuous discovery and evolution.

When we embrace vulnerability and authenticity in our romantic partnerships, we create a bond that is rooted in trust, understanding, and unconditional love. We build a relationship that can weather the storms of life, and emerge stronger and more connected on the other side. By showing up as our true selves, we invite our partners to do the same, fostering a depth of intimacy and connection that is truly transformative.

Subsection 3.2: Vulnerability and Authenticity in Family Dynamics

Family relationships are often the most complex and emotionally charged connections we experience throughout our lives. These bonds are shaped by shared history, deeply ingrained patterns, and a sense of unconditional love that can be both comforting and challenging. In the context of family dynamics, vulnerability and authenticity play a crucial role in fostering open communication, trust, and resilience.

Vulnerability within family relationships involves the willingness to share one's true thoughts, feelings, and experiences, even when it feels uncomfortable or risky. It means being open and honest about our fears, insecurities, and dreams, trusting that our family members will respond with empathy and understanding. When we allow ourselves to be vulnerable with our loved ones, we create a space for genuine connection and growth.

However, vulnerability in family dynamics can be particularly challenging, as we may fear judgment, criticism, or even rejection from those closest to us. We may worry that exposing our true selves will disrupt the delicate balance of family roles and expectations. These fears are understandable, but they can also prevent us from experiencing the depth of love and support that family relationships have to offer.

Authenticity, too, is essential for building strong and healthy family bonds. Being authentic means showing up as our genuine selves, without pretense or facade. It involves being true to our values, beliefs, and desires, even when they may differ from those of our family members. When we embrace authenticity, we create a foundation of trust and respect that allows for open and honest communication.

Cultivating vulnerability and authenticity in family dynamics requires a commitment to self-awareness, compassion, and patience. It means being willing to have difficult conversations, to listen with an open heart, and to approach challenges with a spirit of collaboration and understanding. It also means being open to feedback and growth, recognizing that family relationships are a journey of continuous learning and evolution.

One powerful way to foster vulnerability and authenticity in family dynamics is through the practice of active listening. When we listen to our family members with undivided attention, without judgment or interruption, we create a safe space for them to share their thoughts and feelings. By validating their experiences and responding with empathy, we encourage them to be more open and authentic in return.

Another key strategy for building vulnerability and authenticity in family relationships is to lead by example. When we model these qualities in our own interactions, we inspire our loved ones to do the same. This may involve sharing our own struggles and triumphs, expressing gratitude and appreciation, and being willing to apologize when we fall short.

Ultimately, vulnerability and authenticity in family dynamics are about creating a culture of love, acceptance, and growth. When we embrace these qualities, we build relationships that are rooted in trust, understanding, and mutual respect. We foster a sense of belonging and connection that can withstand the challenges of life, and emerge stronger and more united on the other side.

Subsection 3.3: Vulnerability and Authenticity in Friendships

Friendships are the cornerstone of our social support system, providing us with a sense of belonging, shared experiences, and emotional connection. However, building and maintaining genuine friendships requires a willingness to be vulnerable and authentic. When we allow ourselves to be seen and understood by our friends, we create a foundation of trust and intimacy that can withstand the test of time.

Cultivating vulnerability in friendships means being open and honest about our thoughts, feelings, and experiences, even when it feels uncomfortable or risky. It involves sharing our hopes, dreams, fears, and insecurities with those we trust, knowing that they will respond with empathy and understanding. When we embrace vulnerability in our friendships, we create a space for genuine connection and growth.

However, being vulnerable in friendships can be challenging, as we may fear judgment, rejection, or even betrayal. We may worry that exposing our true selves will lead to a loss of respect or admiration from our friends. These fears are natural, but they can also prevent us from experiencing the depth of connection and support that friendships have to offer.

Authenticity, too, is essential for building strong and healthy friendships. Being authentic means showing up as our genuine selves, without pretense or facade. It involves being true to our values, beliefs, and desires, even when they may differ from those of our friends. When we embrace authenticity, we create a foundation of trust and respect that allows for open and honest communication.

Cultivating authenticity in friendships requires a commitment to self-awareness and self-acceptance. It means being willing to share our true thoughts and feelings, even when they may be unpopular or unconventional. It also means being open to feedback and growth, recognizing that friendships are a journey of continuous learning and evolution.

One powerful way to foster vulnerability and authenticity in friendships is through the practice of active listening. When we listen to our friends with undivided attention, without judgment or interruption, we create a safe space for them to share their experiences and emotions. By validating their feelings and responding with empathy, we encourage them to be more open and authentic in return.

Another key strategy for building vulnerability and authenticity in friendships is to lead by example. When we model these qualities in our own interactions, we inspire our friends to do the same. This may involve sharing our own struggles and triumphs, expressing gratitude and appreciation, and being willing to apologize when we fall short.

Ultimately, the benefits of cultivating vulnerability and authenticity in friendships are immeasurable. When we embrace these qualities, we create relationships that are rooted in trust, understanding, and mutual respect. We foster a sense of belonging and connection that can provide comfort and support during life's challenges, and celebrate with us during its joys.

Genuine friendships, built on a foundation of vulnerability and authenticity, have the power to transform our lives. They provide us with a safe haven to be ourselves, to grow and learn, and to experience the richness of human connection. By embracing these qualities and nurturing our friendships with intention and care, we open ourselves up to a world of love, laughter, and enduring support.

Subsection 3.4: Vulnerability and Authenticity in Professional Relationships

In the fast-paced, often competitive world of professional relationships, the concepts of vulnerability and authenticity may seem out of place or even counterproductive. However, these qualities are essential for building trust, fostering collaboration, and creating a positive work environment. When we allow ourselves to be vulnerable and authentic with our colleagues, we open the door to deeper connections, improved communication, and increased productivity.

Vulnerability in professional settings involves being open and honest about our challenges, uncertainties, and areas for growth. It means admitting when we need help, acknowledging our mistakes, and being receptive to feedback. While this may feel risky or uncomfortable, it demonstrates a level of self-awareness and humility that can earn the respect and trust of our coworkers. By showing vulnerability, we create a space for others to do the same, fostering a culture of openness and support.

Authenticity, too, plays a crucial role in building strong professional relationships. Being authentic means showing up as our genuine selves, aligning our actions with our values, and communicating with sincerity and transparency. When we are authentic, we build credibility and trust with our colleagues, as they can rely on us to be consistent and truthful in our interactions. Authenticity also allows for more meaningful connections, as we are able to relate to one another on a human level, beyond our professional roles.

Cultivating vulnerability and authenticity in professional relationships requires a delicate balance. While it is important to be open and genuine, it is equally crucial to maintain appropriate boundaries and professionalism. This means being mindful of the context and timing of our self-disclosure, ensuring that it is relevant and appropriate to the situation at hand. It also means being respectful of others' boundaries and preferences, recognizing that not everyone may be comfortable with the same level of vulnerability or authenticity.

One way to foster vulnerability and authenticity in professional relationships is through the practice of active listening. When we listen to our colleagues with undivided attention, without judgment or interruption, we create a safe space for them to share their thoughts and experiences. By validating their perspectives and responding with empathy, we encourage them to be more open and authentic in return. Active listening also helps us to better understand our coworkers' needs, challenges, and strengths, enabling us to collaborate more effectively.

Another key strategy for building vulnerability and authenticity in professional relationships is to lead by example. When we model these qualities in our own interactions, we set the tone for a more open and supportive work environment. This may involve sharing our own challenges and successes, expressing gratitude and appreciation for our colleagues' efforts, and being willing to admit when we have made a mistake or need assistance. By demonstrating vulnerability and authenticity ourselves, we create a culture that values these qualities and encourages others to embrace them as well.

Ultimately, the benefits of cultivating vulnerability and authenticity in professional relationships are far-reaching. When we embrace these qualities, we build a foundation of trust and collaboration that can lead to increased innovation, productivity, and job satisfaction. We foster a sense of belonging and connection that can make work feel more meaningful and fulfilling, even in the face of challenges or setbacks.

In a world that often prioritizes competition and self-promotion, vulnerability and authenticity in professional relationships may seem like a risk. However, by taking the courageous step to embrace these qualities, we open ourselves up to a more rewarding and impactful career, one built on genuine connections, mutual respect, and shared success.

Summary: Embracing Vulnerability and Authenticity for Stronger Connections

Throughout this section, we have explored the transformative power of vulnerability and authenticity in cultivating deeper, more meaningful relationships across various contexts, from romantic partnerships to family dynamics, friendships, and even professional connections. By embracing these qualities and integrating them into our interactions, we open ourselves up to a world of profound love, understanding, and personal growth.

The journey towards vulnerability and authenticity may not always be easy, as it requires courage, self-awareness, and a willingness to step outside of our comfort zones. However, the rewards of this journey are immeasurable. When we allow ourselves to be seen, heard, and understood in our truest form, we create a foundation of trust and intimacy that can weather life's challenges and celebrate its joys.

Whether you are seeking to strengthen your intimate bond with a partner, improve communication with family members, build more meaningful friendships, or foster collaboration in the workplace, the principles and strategies discussed in this section serve as a guide on your path towards more fulfilling relationships. By practicing active listening, leading by example, and maintaining a balance between openness and appropriate boundaries, you can create a safe and supportive environment that encourages genuine connection and growth.

As we conclude this section, we invite you to reflect on the relationships in your life and consider how you can begin to cultivate greater vulnerability and authenticity in your interactions. Remember that this is a continuous journey of self-discovery and evolution, and that each small step towards openness and genuineness has the power to transform your relationships in profound ways.

Embrace the power of vulnerability and authenticity, and watch as your connections deepen, your self-awareness expands, and your capacity for love and understanding grows. By showing up as your true self and inviting others to do the same, you are not only building stronger relationships but also contributing to a world that values empathy, compassion, and genuine human connection.

Section 4: The Benefits of Embracing Vulnerability and Authenticity

In a world that often celebrates strength, independence, and perfection, vulnerability and authenticity may seem like weaknesses. However, as you'll discover in this section, embracing these qualities can lead to profound personal growth and more meaningful connections with others.

When we allow ourselves to be vulnerable, we open the door to genuine self-expression and deeper emotional bonds. By sharing our fears, hopes, and struggles, we create opportunities for others to understand and connect with us on a more intimate level. Vulnerability fosters empathy, trust, and a sense of belonging, which are essential components of healthy relationships.

Moreover, authenticity is a powerful catalyst for personal growth and self-awareness. When we embrace our true selves, flaws and all, we liberate ourselves from the exhausting pursuit of perfection. We learn to accept and love ourselves as we are, which in turn enables us to extend that same compassion and understanding to others.

Throughout this section, we'll explore the transformative benefits of vulnerability and authenticity in various aspects of life. From building resilience in the face of challenges to cultivating more fulfilling relationships, you'll discover how these qualities can enrich your life and help you navigate the complexities of human connection.

So, let's dive in and uncover the hidden strengths that lie within vulnerability and authenticity. By the end of this section, you'll be equipped with the knowledge and tools to embrace these qualities and unlock their potential for personal growth and more meaningful relationships.

Subsection 4.1: Deeper Emotional Connections and Intimacy

Vulnerability and authenticity are the cornerstones of building deeper emotional connections and intimacy in relationships. When we allow ourselves to be vulnerable, we open the door to genuine self-expression and create a safe space for others to do the same. By sharing our fears, hopes, and dreams with those we care about, we foster a sense of trust and understanding that is essential for meaningful connections.

Authenticity goes hand in hand with vulnerability in creating intimate bonds. When we show up as our true selves, without pretense or façade, we invite others to connect with us on a more profound level. By being genuine and honest about our thoughts, feelings, and experiences, we create opportunities for others to see and appreciate the real us.

In romantic relationships, vulnerability and authenticity are the keys to building deep emotional intimacy. When partners are willing to share their innermost selves with each other, they create a foundation of trust and understanding that allows the relationship to thrive. This level of openness and honesty enables couples to navigate challenges, celebrate successes, and grow together in a meaningful way.

Vulnerability and authenticity are equally important in friendships and family relationships. By being open and genuine with our friends and loved ones, we create a sense of belonging and connection that is essential for our well-being. When we feel safe to be ourselves and share our true thoughts and feelings, we foster relationships that are built on mutual respect, empathy, and understanding.

Cultivating vulnerability and authenticity in relationships requires courage and a willingness to step outside of our comfort zones. It means being willing to take emotional risks and embrace the possibility of rejection or judgment. However, the rewards of deeper emotional connections and intimacy far outweigh the risks. By being vulnerable and authentic, we create relationships that are built on a foundation of trust, respect, and genuine connection, ultimately enriching our lives and the lives of those around us.

Subsection 4.2: Increased Self-Awareness and Personal Growth

Embracing vulnerability and authenticity can be a transformative journey that leads to greater self-awareness and personal growth. When we allow ourselves to be vulnerable, we open the door to a deeper understanding of our own emotions, thoughts, and behaviors. By confronting our fears, insecurities, and weaknesses, we gain valuable insights into our inner selves and the patterns that shape our lives.

Authenticity is a powerful tool for self-discovery and personal development. When we are true to ourselves, we create space for honest self-reflection and introspection. We begin to recognize our strengths, passions, and values, as well as the areas where we may need to grow and improve. This heightened self-awareness enables us to make more informed decisions, set meaningful goals, and align our actions with our true selves.

Embracing vulnerability and authenticity also requires courage and a willingness to step outside of our comfort zones. It means being open to feedback, both from ourselves and others, and using that feedback to fuel personal growth. When we are authentic, we create opportunities for genuine connections and meaningful conversations that can challenge our assumptions, broaden our perspectives, and inspire us to grow.

Moreover, vulnerability and authenticity can help us develop greater emotional intelligence and resilience. By acknowledging and expressing our emotions, we learn to navigate complex feelings and develop healthier coping mechanisms. We become more attuned to our own needs and the needs of others, fostering empathy and compassion. This emotional awareness and resilience can serve as a foundation for personal growth and help us navigate life's challenges with greater ease and grace.

Embracing vulnerability and authenticity is not always easy, but the rewards are immeasurable. As we become more self-aware and authentic, we unlock our potential for personal growth and transformation. We develop a deeper sense of purpose, self-acceptance, and fulfillment, which can positively impact all areas of our lives. By embracing our true selves, flaws and all, we create space for genuine happiness, meaningful connections, and a life that is rich with purpose and possibility.

Subsection 4.3: Enhanced Resilience and Adaptability

In an ever-changing world, the ability to bounce back from adversity and adapt to new circumstances is crucial for personal growth and well-being. Embracing vulnerability and authenticity can play a significant role in building resilience and adaptability, equipping individuals with the emotional tools necessary to navigate life's challenges and uncertainties.

Vulnerability, often perceived as a weakness, is actually a source of strength when it comes to building resilience. By acknowledging and accepting our fears, insecurities, and shortcomings, we develop a deeper understanding of ourselves and our emotional landscape. This self-awareness allows us to confront challenges head-on, armed with the knowledge of our own strengths and limitations. When we are vulnerable, we open ourselves up to the possibility of failure, rejection, or disappointment, but we also create opportunities for growth, learning, and personal development.

Authenticity, too, is a powerful ally in cultivating resilience and adaptability. When we are true to ourselves, we develop a strong sense of identity and purpose, which can serve as an anchor during times of change or uncertainty. By aligning our actions with our values and beliefs, we create a sense of integrity and coherence that can help us weather even the toughest storms. Authenticity allows us to trust our instincts, make decisions that are true to ourselves, and communicate our needs and boundaries effectively, all of which contribute to greater resilience and adaptability.

Moreover, vulnerability and authenticity can foster a sense of connection and support, which are essential for building resilience. When we are open and honest about our struggles, we create opportunities for others to offer empathy, encouragement, and guidance. By building genuine relationships based on trust and understanding, we develop a network of support that can help us navigate challenges and adapt to new circumstances. In times of adversity, knowing that we have people who accept and support us for who we are can provide the strength and motivation needed to persevere and grow.

Embracing vulnerability and authenticity also requires a willingness to learn from our experiences, both positive and negative. By reflecting on our successes and failures, we gain valuable insights into our own strengths, weaknesses, and areas for improvement. This self-reflection allows us to adapt our strategies, develop new skills, and approach challenges with a growth mindset. When we are authentic and vulnerable, we are more likely to seek out feedback, learn from our mistakes, and make necessary adjustments to our behavior or perspective, all of which contribute to greater resilience and adaptability over time.

In a world that is constantly evolving, the ability to embrace vulnerability and authenticity can be a powerful tool for building resilience and adaptability. By developing a deep understanding of ourselves, fostering genuine connections with others, and approaching challenges with a growth mindset, we can cultivate the emotional strength and flexibility needed to thrive in the face of change and uncertainty. As we navigate the complexities of relationships and personal growth, vulnerability and authenticity serve as essential guideposts, helping us to build the resilience and adaptability necessary to weather life's storms and emerge stronger, wiser, and more connected to ourselves and others.

Summary: Unlocking the Power of Vulnerability and Authenticity

Throughout this section, we've explored the transformative benefits of embracing vulnerability and authenticity in our relationships and personal lives. By opening ourselves up to genuine self-expression and emotional connection, we create opportunities for deeper intimacy, self-awareness, and personal growth.

Vulnerability and authenticity serve as the foundation for building trust, empathy, and understanding in our relationships. When we have the courage to share our true selves with others, we invite them to do the same, fostering a sense of belonging and connection that is essential for our well-being.

Moreover, by embracing these qualities, we embark on a journey of self-discovery and personal development. We learn to accept ourselves, flaws and all, and develop a greater sense of purpose and fulfillment. This heightened self-awareness enables us to make more informed decisions, set meaningful goals, and align our actions with our true values.

Vulnerability and authenticity also play a crucial role in building resilience and adaptability in the face of life's challenges. By acknowledging our fears, weaknesses, and struggles, we develop the emotional strength and flexibility needed to navigate change and uncertainty. We learn to lean on the support of others and approach challenges with a growth mindset, ultimately emerging stronger and more connected to ourselves and those around us.

As we move forward, remember that embracing vulnerability and authenticity is a continuous process, one that requires courage, self-compassion, and a willingness to step outside of our comfort zones. By committing to this journey, we open ourselves up to a world of profound personal growth, deeper connections, and more fulfilling relationships.

So, take a moment to reflect on how you can begin to incorporate vulnerability and authenticity into your own life. Start small, perhaps by sharing a personal story with a trusted friend or practicing self-compassion in moments of difficulty. As you continue to embrace these qualities, you'll discover the immense power they hold in transforming your relationships and your life as a whole.

Section 5: Practicing Vulnerability and Authenticity in Daily Life

In the previous sections, we explored the profound impact of vulnerability and authenticity on fostering deeper, more meaningful connections with others. We discovered how these powerful qualities can break down barriers, promote personal growth, and cultivate a greater sense of intimacy and trust in our relationships. But how can we integrate these concepts into our daily lives? How can we make vulnerability and authenticity a consistent part of our interactions and self-reflection?

In this section, we will delve into the practical application of vulnerability and authenticity, providing you with concrete strategies and exercises to help you embody these qualities in your everyday life. We will explore the art of self-reflection and authentic expression, offering guided exercises and journaling prompts to encourage you to dig deeper into your own thoughts, feelings, and experiences. By engaging in these practices, you will gain a clearer understanding of your authentic self and develop the confidence to share your truth with others.

Furthermore, we will discuss effective communication techniques and conversation starters that will enable you to express vulnerability and authenticity in your relationships. Whether you're interacting with a romantic partner, family member, friend, or colleague, these strategies will help you initiate meaningful dialogues and foster a sense of openness and trust.

However, it's important to recognize that vulnerability and authenticity do not mean oversharing or disregarding personal boundaries. In this section, we will also address the crucial balance between being vulnerable and maintaining healthy boundaries. You will learn how to navigate this delicate balance, ensuring that you can share your authentic self while still protecting your emotional well-being and respecting the boundaries of others.

By the end of this section, you will have a toolkit of practical exercises and strategies to help you cultivate vulnerability and authenticity in your daily life. You will be equipped with the knowledge and skills necessary to create more genuine, fulfilling connections with others and to live a life that is true to your authentic self. So, let's dive in and explore how you can make vulnerability and authenticity a consistent part of your journey towards deeper, more meaningful relationships.

Subsection 5.1: Exercises for Self-Reflection and Authentic Expression

Self-reflection and authentic expression are essential components of practicing vulnerability and authenticity in our daily lives. By taking the time to explore our innermost thoughts, feelings, and experiences, we can gain a deeper understanding of ourselves and develop the confidence to share our authentic selves with others. In this subsection, we will provide you with guided exercises and journaling prompts designed to encourage self-reflection and authentic self-expression.

One powerful exercise for self-reflection is the "Mirror Talk" technique. Stand in front of a mirror, look yourself in the eyes, and engage in a honest conversation with yourself. Ask yourself questions such as, "What are my deepest fears and insecurities?" or "What are my true desires and aspirations?" As you answer these questions, observe your body language and emotional responses. This exercise can help you develop a greater sense of self-awareness and authenticity by confronting your inner truths head-on.

Another effective tool for self-reflection is journaling. Set aside dedicated time each day to write freely about your thoughts, feelings, and experiences. Don't worry about perfect grammar or structure; instead, focus on allowing your authentic voice to flow onto the page. Some prompts to get you started include:

- "What are the masks I wear in different situations, and how do they differ from my authentic self?"

- "What are the moments in my life when I have felt most vulnerable, and what did I learn from those experiences?"

- "What are the things I am most passionate about, and how can I incorporate them into my daily life?"

By regularly engaging in these journaling exercises, you will develop a deeper understanding of your authentic self and become more comfortable with vulnerability.

In addition to self-reflection, it's important to practice authentic expression in your interactions with others. One way to do this is through the "Authentic Sharing" exercise. In a safe and supportive environment, such as with a trusted friend or family member, take turns sharing a personal story or experience that you have never shared before. As you share, focus on expressing your authentic emotions and thoughts, without holding back or censoring yourself. This exercise can help you build trust and intimacy in your relationships while also strengthening your ability to be vulnerable and authentic.

Remember, the key to authentic expression is to speak from your heart and to be true to yourself. It may feel uncomfortable or scary at first, but with practice, you will develop the confidence and resilience to express your authentic self in all areas of your life.

By incorporating these exercises for self-reflection and authentic expression into your daily routine, you will be well on your way to cultivating a deeper sense of vulnerability and authenticity in your life. In the next subsection, we will explore specific communication techniques and strategies for expressing vulnerability and authenticity in your relationships.

Subsection 5.2: Strategies for Communicating Vulnerably and Authentically

Effective communication is the cornerstone of any healthy relationship, and expressing vulnerability and authenticity is a crucial aspect of building deep, meaningful connections. However, many people struggle with how to communicate their innermost thoughts, feelings, and experiences in a way that feels safe and authentic. In this subsection, we will explore practical strategies and techniques for communicating vulnerably and authentically in your relationships.

One of the most important strategies for vulnerable communication is to create a safe and supportive environment. This means choosing a time and place where both you and the other person feel comfortable, free from distractions or interruptions. It also means approaching the conversation with an open, non-judgmental attitude, and a willingness to listen and understand each other's perspectives.

When expressing vulnerability, it's essential to use "I" statements that focus on your own thoughts, feelings, and experiences, rather than making accusations or assumptions about the other person. For example, instead of saying, "You never listen to me," try saying, "I feel unheard when I express my concerns." This approach takes ownership of your own emotions and experiences, and invites the other person to respond with empathy and understanding.

Another effective strategy for vulnerable communication is to ask open-ended questions that encourage deeper sharing and reflection. Instead of asking closed questions that can be answered with a simple "yes" or "no," try asking questions that invite the other person to elaborate on their thoughts and feelings. For example, "What was that experience like for you?" or "How did you feel when that happened?" These types of questions show genuine interest and curiosity, and can help create a more authentic and meaningful dialogue.

It's also important to practice active listening when engaging in vulnerable communication. This means giving the other person your full attention, without interrupting or planning your response. Use nonverbal cues, such as nodding and maintaining eye contact, to show that you are engaged and present. When the other person has finished speaking, reflect back on what you heard to ensure that you have understood their perspective accurately.

When it comes to starting vulnerable conversations, it can be helpful to have some prompts or conversation starters in mind. Some examples might include:

- "I've been feeling [emotion] lately, and I wanted to share that with you."

- "There's something that's been on my mind, and I trust you enough to talk about it."

- "I know we haven't talked about this before, but I feel like it's important for our relationship."

Remember, the goal of vulnerable communication is not to be perfect or to avoid discomfort, but rather to create a deeper sense of connection and understanding. It's normal to feel anxious or uncertain when expressing vulnerability, but with practice and patience, it can become a natural and rewarding part of your relationships.

By incorporating these strategies for communicating vulnerably and authentically into your interactions with others, you will be well on your way to building stronger, more meaningful connections. In the next subsection, we will explore the importance of maintaining healthy boundaries while practicing vulnerability and authenticity.

Subsection 5.3: Maintaining Boundaries While Being Vulnerable

As we explore the transformative power of vulnerability and authenticity in our relationships, it's crucial to recognize the importance of setting and maintaining healthy boundaries. While opening ourselves up to others can lead to deeper connections and personal growth, it's equally important to protect our emotional well-being and respect our own limits. In this subsection, we will discuss the delicate balance between vulnerability and boundaries, and provide strategies for navigating this essential aspect of healthy relationships.

Boundaries are the personal limits we set in our relationships to ensure that we feel safe, respected, and comfortable. They can encompass a wide range of aspects, including physical, emotional, time, and communication boundaries. When we practice vulnerability and share our authentic selves with others, it's essential to be mindful of these boundaries and communicate them clearly to those around us.

One of the key challenges in maintaining boundaries while being vulnerable is the fear of rejection or judgment. We may worry that setting boundaries will push others away or make us appear less authentic. However, it's important to recognize that true authenticity involves honoring our own needs and limits, even if it means having difficult conversations or facing potential discomfort.

To effectively maintain boundaries while practicing vulnerability, it's essential to develop a strong sense of self-awareness. Take time to reflect on your own needs, desires, and limits, and be honest with yourself about what you are and are not comfortable with. This self-awareness will serve as a foundation for communicating your boundaries to others in a clear and assertive manner.

When setting boundaries, it's important to use "I" statements that focus on your own feelings and needs, rather than placing blame or making demands on others. For example, instead of saying, "You always overstep my boundaries," try saying, "I feel overwhelmed when my personal space is not respected, and I need to set some limits to maintain my well-being." This approach allows for open, honest communication while minimizing defensiveness or conflict.

It's also crucial to be consistent in maintaining your boundaries over time. If you set a boundary but then allow it to be crossed repeatedly, others may become confused or disregard your limits altogether. By consistently enforcing your boundaries and following through with consequences when necessary, you communicate to others that your needs and well-being are a priority.

However, maintaining boundaries doesn't mean being rigid or inflexible. Healthy relationships involve a degree of give and take, and there may be times when it's appropriate to adjust your boundaries based on the situation or the needs of others. The key is to approach these moments with open communication, mutual respect, and a willingness to find solutions that work for everyone involved.

Ultimately, maintaining boundaries while being vulnerable is about striking a balance between openness and self-protection. By developing self-awareness, communicating clearly, and consistently enforcing our limits, we can create relationships that are built on trust, respect, and authentic connection. As we navigate this delicate balance, we foster a sense of safety and security that allows us to be fully present and engaged in our interactions with others.

Remember, vulnerability and authenticity are not about sacrificing our own well-being for the sake of others. By maintaining healthy boundaries, we create the space to be our true selves while also respecting and honoring the needs and limits of those around us. With practice and patience, we can cultivate relationships that are both deeply fulfilling and emotionally sustainable, allowing us to thrive in all areas of our lives.

Summary: Embracing Vulnerability and Authenticity in Everyday Life

Throughout this section, we have explored the transformative power of vulnerability and authenticity in our daily lives. By engaging in self-reflection, practicing authentic expression, and communicating openly and honestly with others, we can cultivate deeper, more meaningful connections and foster personal growth.

The exercises and strategies presented in this section, such as the "Mirror Talk" technique, journaling prompts, and the "Authentic Sharing" exercise, provide practical tools for developing self-awareness and building the confidence to express our authentic selves. By incorporating these practices into our daily routines, we can gradually break down the barriers that prevent us from being fully present and engaged in our relationships.

However, it's important to remember that vulnerability and authenticity must be balanced with healthy boundaries. By setting and maintaining clear limits, we protect our emotional well-being and create a safe space for genuine connection to flourish. This delicate balance requires self-awareness, clear communication, and a commitment to honoring our own needs while respecting the needs of others.

As we embrace vulnerability and authenticity in our everyday lives, we open ourselves up to a world of profound connection, personal growth, and emotional resilience. While the journey may be challenging at times, the rewards are immeasurable. By staying true to ourselves and nurturing authentic relationships, we can create a life filled with meaning, purpose, and deep, enduring love.

So, let us step forward with courage and compassion, ready to embrace the transformative power of vulnerability and authenticity in all aspects of our lives. As we do so, we will discover the true depth and richness of the human experience, and unlock the boundless potential for growth and connection that lies within each of us.

Chapter Summary: Embracing Your True Self for Deeper Connections

Vulnerability and authenticity are the cornerstones of building meaningful, genuine relationships. By understanding the essence of these qualities and their interconnectedness, we can begin to cultivate them in our daily lives and interactions with others. Overcoming barriers such as fear of judgment, perfectionism, and past experiences of rejection or betrayal is a crucial step in embracing our true selves and fostering deeper connections.

Practicing vulnerability and authenticity in various types of relationships, including romantic partnerships, family dynamics, friendships, and professional settings, can lead to increased intimacy, trust, and collaboration. By being open, honest, and genuine in our interactions, we create a safe space for others to do the same, fostering a culture of empathy, understanding, and mutual support.

Embracing vulnerability and authenticity not only benefits our relationships but also contributes to our personal growth and well-being. It allows us to develop greater self-awareness, resilience, and adaptability in the face of life's challenges. By engaging in self-reflection, authentic expression, and setting healthy boundaries, we can cultivate a strong sense of self and navigate relationships with confidence and integrity.

As we continue on our journey of building and maintaining fulfilling relationships, let us remember the transformative power of vulnerability and authenticity. By embracing our true selves and encouraging others to do the same, we create a world where genuine connections thrive, and the beauty of the human experience is celebrated in all its imperfect glory.

Chapter 8: Maintaining Healthy Boundaries

Boundaries are the invisible lines we draw around ourselves to protect our physical, emotional, and mental well-being. They define what we consider acceptable and unacceptable behavior from others, and they help us maintain a sense of autonomy and self-respect in our relationships. When we have clear, healthy boundaries, we feel more secure, empowered, and in control of our lives.

However, setting and maintaining boundaries can be challenging, especially in close relationships where emotions run deep and the fear of rejection or conflict looms large. We may struggle with feelings of guilt, anxiety, or self-doubt when asserting our needs and limits, or we may find ourselves constantly accommodating others at the expense of our own well-being.

The truth is, boundaries are not about being selfish or pushing others away. They are about practicing self-care, communicating our needs and values, and fostering mutual respect and understanding in our relationships. When we have healthy boundaries, we create a safe and supportive environment where both parties can thrive and grow together.

In this chapter, we will explore the importance of setting and maintaining healthy boundaries in various types of relationships, from romantic partnerships to family ties and friendships. We will delve into the common challenges and barriers to boundary-setting, such as people-pleasing tendencies, fear of rejection, and patterns of codependency, and provide practical strategies for overcoming these obstacles.

You will learn how to identify and communicate your personal boundaries assertively and respectfully, navigate boundary conflicts and negotiations, and establish specific boundaries in different relationship contexts. We will also discuss the role of self-care and emotional resilience in maintaining healthy boundaries over time.

By the end of this chapter, you will have a deeper understanding of the value of boundaries in relationships and the tools to create and sustain them in your own life. You will feel more empowered to prioritize your own needs and well-being while building stronger, more fulfilling connections with the people who matter most to you.

Section 1: Understanding the Importance of Boundaries in Relationships

Imagine a world where personal space is consistently invaded, where "no" is never taken for an answer, and where the lines between self and others are blurred beyond recognition. In such a world, relationships would be characterized by chaos, resentment, and a lack of respect for individual autonomy. This is the reality faced by those who struggle with setting and maintaining healthy boundaries in their relationships.

Boundaries, often misunderstood and overlooked, play a crucial role in fostering healthy, respectful, and fulfilling connections with others. They serve as invisible lines that define our personal limits, values, and expectations, allowing us to navigate the complexities of human interaction with clarity and confidence. When boundaries are clearly established and respected, relationships thrive on a foundation of trust, mutual understanding, and emotional well-being.

Throughout this section, we will embark on a journey to explore the concept of boundaries and their profound impact on the quality of our relationships. We will delve into the essence of personal boundaries, examining how they shape our interactions with others and contribute to our overall sense of self. By understanding the significance of boundaries, we can begin to cultivate healthier, more balanced connections with the people in our lives.

As we navigate the intricacies of boundary-setting, we will encounter the challenges that arise when boundaries are violated or disregarded. We will explore the consequences of weak or absent boundaries, such as emotional burnout, resentment, and unhealthy relationship dynamics. By recognizing these pitfalls, we can take proactive steps to assert our boundaries and protect our emotional well-being.

Through a combination of research-backed insights, real-life examples, and practical advice, this section aims to empower you with the knowledge and tools necessary to establish and maintain healthy boundaries in your relationships. Whether you struggle with saying "no," fear rejection, or find yourself consistently prioritizing others' needs over your own, the insights shared here will guide you towards a more balanced and self-assured approach to interpersonal connections.

As we embark on this transformative journey, it is essential to approach the topic of boundaries with an open mind and a willingness to engage in self-reflection. By exploring the importance of boundaries in relationships, we unlock the potential for personal growth, increased self-awareness, and more fulfilling connections with others. So, let us dive in and discover the power of setting and maintaining healthy boundaries in our lives.

Subsection 1.1: Defining Personal Boundaries

At the core of understanding the importance of boundaries in relationships lies the concept of personal boundaries. Personal boundaries are the invisible lines that define our individual limits, values, and expectations in various aspects of life. They encompass physical, emotional, mental, and spiritual dimensions, serving as a framework for how we interact with others and navigate the world around us.

Imagine personal boundaries as a protective bubble that surrounds each individual, defining their unique sense of self and separating them from others. This bubble is not rigid or impenetrable but rather a flexible, semi-permeable membrane that allows for healthy interaction and exchange with the outside world. It is through the establishment and maintenance of these boundaries that we are able to preserve our autonomy, maintain our emotional well-being, and foster respectful relationships.

Personal boundaries serve several crucial functions in our lives. Firstly, they act as a form of self-care, ensuring that we prioritize our own needs, desires, and values. By setting clear boundaries, we communicate to others what we are comfortable with and what we will not tolerate, thereby protecting ourselves from potential harm, exploitation, or violation of our personal space. Boundaries enable us to say "no" when necessary, to assert our rights, and to maintain a healthy sense of self-respect.

Moreover, personal boundaries play a vital role in maintaining our emotional well-being and preventing burnout. When we have well-defined boundaries, we are better equipped to manage the demands and expectations placed upon us by others. We can avoid overextending ourselves, taking on more than we can handle, or sacrificing our own needs in the process of pleasing others. By setting limits and respecting our own boundaries, we create a balanced and sustainable approach to our relationships and responsibilities.

In addition to protecting our own well-being, personal boundaries also serve as a foundation for healthy, mutually respectful relationships. When we clearly communicate our boundaries to others, we provide them with a roadmap for how to interact with us in a way that honors our individuality and autonomy. Boundaries help to prevent misunderstandings, conflicts, and resentment by ensuring that both parties are aware of each other's limits and expectations.

It is important to recognize that personal boundaries are not static or fixed entities. They can evolve and change over time as we grow, learn, and adapt to new circumstances. What may have been an acceptable boundary in the past may no longer serve us in the present, and it is our responsibility to continuously assess and adjust our boundaries as needed. This ongoing process of self-reflection and boundary-setting is an essential part of personal growth and self-discovery.

In summary, personal boundaries are the invisible lines that define our individual limits, values, and expectations. They serve as a form of self-care, protecting our emotional well-being and autonomy, while also providing a foundation for healthy, respectful relationships. By understanding and honoring our personal boundaries, we create a safe space for ourselves to thrive and navigate the complexities of human interaction with greater ease and confidence.

Subsection 1.2: The Impact of Healthy Boundaries on Relationships

The establishment and maintenance of healthy boundaries play a crucial role in fostering trust, respect, and mutual understanding in various types of relationships. When individuals clearly communicate their limits, expectations, and values, they create a solid foundation upon which meaningful connections can be built. By setting boundaries, we not only protect our own well-being but also demonstrate respect for the autonomy and needs of others.

One of the primary benefits of healthy boundaries in relationships is the promotion of trust. When we consistently enforce our boundaries and respect those of others, we send a clear message that we value honesty, integrity, and open communication. This, in turn, creates an atmosphere of reliability and dependability, where both parties feel secure in the knowledge that their needs and desires will be heard and respected. Trust is the bedrock of any strong relationship, and healthy boundaries help to foster and maintain this essential component.

Moreover, the presence of well-defined boundaries encourages mutual respect within relationships. By asserting our own limits and honoring those of others, we acknowledge the inherent worth and dignity of each individual. We recognize that every person has the right to make choices that align with their values and priorities, and we refrain from imposing our own expectations or desires upon them. This mutual respect allows for a more balanced and equitable dynamic, where both parties feel valued and heard.

Healthy boundaries also facilitate a deeper level of understanding and empathy in relationships. When we take the time to listen to and acknowledge the boundaries of others, we gain insight into their unique perspectives, experiences, and needs. This understanding enables us to approach interactions with greater compassion and sensitivity, as we recognize the complex factors that shape each individual's boundaries. By fostering this sense of understanding, healthy boundaries help to bridge gaps, resolve conflicts, and promote a more harmonious and supportive relational environment.

In addition to promoting trust, respect, and understanding, healthy boundaries also contribute to the overall well-being and longevity of relationships. When individuals feel secure in their ability to assert their limits and have those limits respected, they are less likely to experience feelings of resentment, burnout, or emotional depletion. This emotional equilibrium allows for more positive and fulfilling interactions, as both parties are able to engage from a place of wholeness and authenticity. By prioritizing self-care and self-respect through healthy boundaries, individuals are better equipped to show up fully and consistently in their relationships.

It is important to note that the impact of healthy boundaries extends across various types of relationships, including romantic partnerships, friendships, family bonds, and professional connections. While the specific boundaries may vary depending on the nature and context of the relationship, the fundamental principles of trust, respect, and mutual understanding remain constant. By adapting our boundary-setting approach to the unique dynamics of each relationship, we can cultivate a network of supportive, empowering, and growth-oriented connections.

In conclusion, the impact of healthy boundaries on relationships cannot be overstated. By promoting trust, respect, and mutual understanding, well-defined boundaries create a solid foundation for meaningful and fulfilling connections. They foster an atmosphere of emotional safety, empathy, and authenticity, allowing individuals to show up fully and consistently in their interactions with others. As we navigate the complexities of human relationships, the establishment and maintenance of healthy boundaries serve as a guiding light, illuminating the path towards more positive, supportive, and growth-oriented connections.

Subsection 1.3: The Consequences of Weak or Absent Boundaries

The absence or weakness of personal boundaries can have far-reaching and detrimental effects on an individual's well-being and the health of their relationships. When boundaries are not clearly defined or consistently enforced, a person becomes vulnerable to a range of negative outcomes that can erode their sense of self, compromise their emotional resilience, and strain their connections with others.

One of the most common consequences of weak or absent boundaries is the development of resentment. When an individual consistently prioritizes the needs and desires of others over their own, they may begin to feel taken for granted, unappreciated, and even exploited. This can lead to a simmering resentment that gradually poisons their relationships and diminishes their overall life satisfaction. Without the protective buffer of healthy boundaries, the individual may find themselves repeatedly sacrificing their own well-being for the sake of others, leading to a deep-seated bitterness that can be difficult to overcome.

Another significant risk associated with weak boundaries is the increased likelihood of experiencing burnout. When personal limits are not clearly defined, an individual may find themselves overextending their time, energy, and resources in an attempt to meet the expectations and demands of others. This chronic overexertion can lead to physical, mental, and emotional exhaustion, leaving the individual depleted and unable to effectively manage their own responsibilities and self-care needs. Burnout can have serious implications for personal health, work performance, and the quality of relationships, highlighting the importance of setting and maintaining appropriate boundaries.

In addition to resentment and burnout, weak or absent boundaries can contribute to the development of unhealthy relationship dynamics. Without clear limits and expectations, individuals may find themselves enmeshed in patterns of codependency, enabling, or even abuse. They may struggle to assert their own needs and desires, feeling powerless to stand up for themselves in the face of others' demands or manipulations. This can lead to a loss of autonomy and self-respect, as the individual becomes increasingly dependent on others for validation and direction. In extreme cases, the absence of boundaries can make a person more vulnerable to exploitation, mistreatment, and even physical or emotional harm.

The consequences of weak or absent boundaries extend beyond the realm of personal relationships and can also impact an individual's professional life. In the workplace, a lack of boundaries can lead to overcommitment, difficulty delegating tasks, and an inability to say "no" to unreasonable requests. This can result in decreased productivity, increased stress levels, and a higher risk of job burnout. Moreover, weak boundaries in professional settings can make an individual more susceptible to workplace bullying, harassment, or exploitation, as they may struggle to assert their rights and maintain appropriate distance from problematic colleagues or superiors.

It is important to recognize that the consequences of weak or absent boundaries are not limited to the individual experiencing them. The ripple effects of these negative outcomes can extend to family members, friends, and colleagues, straining relationships and creating a climate of tension and discord. Children who grow up in households where boundaries are not consistently modeled or enforced may struggle to develop healthy boundary-setting skills themselves, perpetuating a cycle of dysfunction and emotional distress.

Acknowledging the potential consequences of weak or absent boundaries is a crucial step in motivating individuals to prioritize the development and maintenance of healthy personal limits. By understanding the risks associated with a lack of boundaries, people can begin to take proactive steps to assert their needs, protect their well-being, and cultivate more balanced, respectful, and fulfilling relationships. Through self-reflection, education, and the support of trusted others, individuals can learn to establish and enforce boundaries that promote their own resilience, autonomy, and overall life satisfaction.

Summary: Embracing Boundaries for Healthier, More Fulfilling Relationships

Throughout this section, we have explored the crucial role that boundaries play in fostering healthy, respectful, and fulfilling relationships. By understanding the concept of personal boundaries and recognizing their impact on our emotional well-being and interpersonal connections, we can begin to cultivate a more balanced and self-assured approach to navigating the complexities of human interaction.

We have seen how well-defined boundaries serve as a foundation for trust, respect, and mutual understanding in our relationships. By clearly communicating our limits and expectations, we create a safe space for both ourselves and others to thrive, promoting a more harmonious and supportive relational environment. Moreover, we have acknowledged the potential consequences of weak or absent boundaries, such as resentment, burnout, and unhealthy relationship dynamics, emphasizing the importance of setting and maintaining appropriate personal limits.

As we move forward, it is essential to remember that embracing boundaries is an ongoing process of self-reflection, growth, and adaptation. By consistently prioritizing our own well-being and asserting our needs and values, we not only protect ourselves from potential harm but also model healthy boundary-setting for those around us. In doing so, we contribute to a ripple effect of positive change, fostering a culture of respect, empathy, and mutual understanding in our relationships and communities.

Armed with the knowledge and insights gained from this section, you are now better equipped to embark on a transformative journey of boundary-setting and self-discovery. As you continue to explore the various aspects of maintaining healthy boundaries in your relationships, remember to approach the process with compassion, patience, and a willingness to learn and grow. By embracing the power of boundaries, you are taking a significant step towards cultivating more authentic, fulfilling, and resilient connections with yourself and others.

Section 2: Identifying and Communicating Personal Boundaries

Boundaries serve as the foundation for healthy, respectful relationships, allowing individuals to maintain their autonomy, emotional well-being, and sense of self. However, many people struggle with recognizing and effectively communicating their personal boundaries, leading to potential conflicts, resentment, and unhealthy relationship dynamics. In this section, we will explore the importance of identifying and expressing your boundaries in a clear, assertive, and respectful manner.

Imagine a world where everyone is aware of their own limits and communicates them effectively to others. A world where relationships thrive on mutual understanding, respect, and trust. By learning to identify and communicate your personal boundaries, you can take a significant step towards creating such a reality in your own life.

We will begin by guiding you through the process of assessing your own boundaries, helping you reflect on your values, needs, and limits in various aspects of your relationships. Through practical exercises and prompts, you will gain a deeper understanding of what you are comfortable with and what you are not, empowering you to set clear boundaries that align with your authentic self.

Next, we will delve into the art of communicating boundaries assertively and respectfully. You will learn effective techniques for expressing your needs and limits to others, ensuring that your message is heard and understood. We will also explore strategies for navigating boundary conflicts and negotiations, equipping you with the tools to address and resolve any challenges that may arise when setting and maintaining boundaries in your relationships.

Throughout this section, we will emphasize the importance of self-awareness, self-respect, and open communication in fostering healthy, balanced relationships. By the end of this section, you will have a solid foundation for identifying and communicating your personal boundaries, enabling you to create more fulfilling, respectful, and mutually supportive connections with others.

Subsection 2.1: Assessing Your Own Boundaries

Understanding and setting personal boundaries is a crucial step in building healthy, respectful relationships. However, many individuals struggle with identifying their own limits and communicating them effectively to others. This subsection aims to guide you through the process of assessing your personal boundaries, empowering you to create relationships that align with your values, needs, and desires.

To begin, take a moment to reflect on your past experiences in relationships. Consider instances where you felt uncomfortable, overwhelmed, or resentful. These feelings often serve as indicators that your boundaries have been crossed or that you have not effectively communicated your needs. By examining these experiences, you can gain valuable insights into the areas where you need to establish or strengthen your boundaries.

One effective exercise for assessing your boundaries is to create a "boundary inventory." Start by dividing your life into various categories, such as physical, emotional, time, and material boundaries. For each category, ask yourself questions that help you identify your limits and preferences. For example, in the physical boundary category, you might ask, "How comfortable am I with physical touch in different relationships?" or "What level of personal space do I need to feel safe and respected?"

As you explore your emotional boundaries, consider questions like, "How much emotional support am I willing to provide to others?" and "What are my limits when it comes to sharing personal information?" These questions will help you understand your emotional needs and the extent to which you are comfortable opening up to others.

Time boundaries are another essential aspect to consider. Reflect on how you prioritize your time and energy, and ask yourself, "How much time am I willing to dedicate to others?" and "What are my non-negotiable self-care practices?" By identifying your time boundaries, you can ensure that you have the space and energy to nurture your own well-being while still being present for your loved ones.

Material boundaries involve your possessions, finances, and personal space. Ask yourself, "Am I comfortable lending my belongings to others?" and "What are my expectations when it comes to financial matters in relationships?" Clarifying your material boundaries can help you navigate sharing resources and maintain a sense of autonomy.

As you work through your boundary inventory, be honest with yourself and listen to your intuition. Your boundaries are unique to you and may differ from those of others. It's essential to recognize that your needs and limits are valid and deserving of respect.

Once you have a clearer understanding of your personal boundaries, it's time to practice communicating them assertively and respectfully. In the next subsection, we will explore effective strategies for expressing your boundaries to others and navigating potential conflicts that may arise.

Remember, assessing your boundaries is an ongoing process. As you grow and evolve, your needs and limits may change, and that's okay. By regularly checking in with yourself and adjusting your boundaries as needed, you can cultivate relationships that support your personal growth and well-being.

Subsection 2.2: Communicating Boundaries Assertively and Respectfully

Effective communication is the cornerstone of healthy relationships, and this holds true when it comes to expressing and maintaining personal boundaries. Once you have identified your boundaries, the next crucial step is to communicate them assertively and respectfully to others. This subsection will provide you with practical techniques and strategies to express your limits and needs clearly, ensuring that your boundaries are understood and respected by those around you.

One of the most important aspects of communicating boundaries is to be direct and specific. Avoid using vague or ambiguous language that leaves room for interpretation. Instead, express your boundaries in a clear, concise manner that leaves no doubt about your intentions. For example, instead of saying, "I don't feel comfortable with that," try saying, "I am not okay with you borrowing my car without asking me first." By being specific, you eliminate confusion and minimize the chances of your boundaries being unintentionally violated.

When communicating your boundaries, it's essential to use "I" statements. This means focusing on your own feelings, needs, and experiences, rather than placing blame or making accusations. For instance, instead of saying, "You always invade my privacy," try saying, "I feel uncomfortable when my personal space is not respected." By using "I" statements, you take ownership of your emotions and experiences, making it easier for others to understand and empathize with your perspective.

It's also crucial to communicate your boundaries in a calm and assertive manner. Speak in a firm, confident tone, while maintaining a respectful and non-confrontational demeanor. Avoid using aggressive or passive-aggressive language, as this can lead to defensiveness and hinder productive communication. Remember, the goal is to express your boundaries in a way that invites understanding and cooperation, rather than conflict or resentment.

Active listening is another key component of effective boundary communication. When discussing your boundaries with others, make sure to create a safe and open space for dialogue. Encourage the other person to express their thoughts and feelings, and listen attentively to their perspective. By engaging in active listening, you demonstrate respect for their point of view and create an opportunity for mutual understanding and compromise.

It's important to remember that communicating boundaries is an ongoing process. As your relationships evolve and new situations arise, you may need to reaffirm or adjust your boundaries. Be prepared to engage in ongoing conversations and negotiations, always maintaining a respectful and assertive approach. If you encounter resistance or pushback, remain calm and firm in your stance, while being open to finding mutually beneficial solutions.

In some cases, you may find yourself in situations where your boundaries are repeatedly violated, despite your best efforts to communicate them clearly. In such instances, it's essential to be prepared to enforce your boundaries and set consequences for non-compliance. This may involve limiting contact, ending a relationship, or seeking outside support from a trusted friend, family member, or mental health professional.

Remember, communicating your boundaries assertively and respectfully is a skill that can be developed and strengthened over time. By practicing these techniques and remaining committed to your personal limits and needs, you can foster healthier, more fulfilling relationships built on a foundation of mutual respect and understanding.

Subsection 2.3: Navigating Boundary Conflicts and Negotiations

Despite our best efforts to communicate our boundaries clearly and respectfully, conflicts and disagreements may still arise in our relationships. When our boundaries are crossed or challenged, it's essential to have effective strategies in place to address and resolve these issues in a healthy, constructive manner. This subsection will explore various approaches to navigating boundary conflicts and negotiations, empowering you to maintain your personal limits while fostering understanding and compromise in your relationships.

One of the first steps in addressing boundary conflicts is to remain calm and composed. When emotions run high, it can be tempting to react impulsively or defensively, but this often exacerbates the situation. Instead, take a moment to breathe deeply, collect your thoughts, and approach the conversation with a clear, level-headed perspective. By maintaining a calm demeanor, you create a more conducive environment for productive dialogue and problem-solving.

Active listening is a crucial skill when navigating boundary conflicts. Before engaging in a discussion, make a conscious effort to set aside your own assumptions and biases, and truly listen to the other person's perspective. Ask open-ended questions to gain a deeper understanding of their thoughts, feelings, and motivations. By demonstrating a genuine interest in their point of view, you lay the foundation for a more empathetic and collaborative approach to resolving the conflict.

As you express your own boundaries and needs, it's important to use "I" statements and focus on your own experiences and emotions. For example, instead of saying, "You always disrespect my boundaries," try saying, "I feel frustrated when my boundaries are not respected." By owning your feelings and experiences, you avoid placing blame or making accusations, which can lead to defensiveness and hinder progress.

When negotiating boundaries, be open to finding mutually beneficial solutions. Recognize that compromise is often necessary to maintain healthy, balanced relationships. Consider the other person's needs and desires alongside your own, and work together to identify areas where you can both make concessions. By approaching boundary negotiations with a spirit of collaboration and flexibility, you increase the likelihood of reaching an agreement that satisfies both parties.

In some cases, boundary conflicts may stem from a lack of understanding or awareness. Take the time to educate others about the importance of boundaries and why they matter to you. Share resources, such as articles or books, that explain the concept of personal limits and the role they play in fostering healthy relationships. By increasing understanding and awareness, you create a more supportive and respectful environment for discussing and maintaining boundaries.

If, despite your best efforts, boundary conflicts persist or escalate, it may be necessary to seek outside support. Consider involving a neutral third party, such as a mediator or therapist, who can facilitate a constructive dialogue and help both parties work towards a resolution. In more severe cases, where boundaries are consistently violated, and the relationship becomes toxic or abusive, it may be necessary to establish firmer consequences or even consider ending the relationship altogether.

Remember, navigating boundary conflicts and negotiations is a skill that develops over time. Be patient with yourself and others as you learn and grow. Celebrate the small victories and the progress you make in asserting your boundaries and finding mutually respectful solutions. With practice, you'll become more confident and adept at addressing boundary issues, fostering healthier, more fulfilling relationships built on a foundation of trust, understanding, and respect.

Summary: Embracing Your Boundaries for Healthier Relationships

Throughout this section, we have explored the crucial role of personal boundaries in fostering healthy, respectful relationships. By taking the time to assess your own limits and needs, you have laid the foundation for creating connections that align with your authentic self. Remember, your boundaries are unique to you and deserve to be honored and respected.

Communicating your boundaries assertively and respectfully is a skill that can be developed and strengthened over time. By using clear, specific language and focusing on your own experiences and emotions, you can express your needs in a way that invites understanding and cooperation. Active listening and a willingness to engage in ongoing dialogue are key to navigating boundary conflicts and finding mutually beneficial solutions.

As you continue on your journey of self-discovery and boundary-setting, be patient with yourself and others. Embracing your boundaries is an ongoing process that requires commitment, courage, and self-compassion. Remember, by honoring your own limits and needs, you create the space for more authentic, fulfilling relationships built on a foundation of mutual respect and understanding.

Take a moment to reflect on the insights and strategies you have learned in this section. How can you apply these tools to your own relationships? What boundaries do you need to communicate more clearly? What steps can you take to create a more supportive, respectful environment for yourself and others?

As you move forward, carry these lessons with you and trust in your ability to create relationships that nurture your growth and well-being. In the next section, we will explore how to establish and maintain healthy boundaries in various types of relationships, from romantic partnerships to family dynamics and professional interactions. With the knowledge and skills you have gained, you are well-equipped to navigate the complexities of human connection with grace, empathy, and self-assurance.

Section 3: Establishing Boundaries in Different Types of Relationships

Navigating the complex world of relationships can be a challenging task, especially when it comes to setting and maintaining healthy boundaries. Every relationship, whether it's romantic, familial, platonic, or professional, requires a unique set of boundaries to ensure the well-being and respect of all parties involved. In this section, we will delve into the specific boundary considerations and challenges that arise in various relationship contexts.

Understanding the nuances of boundary-setting in different types of relationships is crucial for fostering positive, fulfilling connections with others. From the intimate bonds of romantic partnerships to the dynamics of family interactions, friendships, and workplace relationships, each context presents its own set of challenges and opportunities for growth.

As we explore the intricacies of establishing boundaries in these diverse relationship landscapes, we will uncover valuable insights and practical strategies for creating and maintaining healthy, respectful connections. By examining real-life examples and drawing upon expert advice, we will equip you with the tools and knowledge necessary to navigate the complexities of boundary-setting with confidence and grace.

Whether you're seeking to strengthen your romantic relationship, improve family dynamics, cultivate meaningful friendships, or establish professional boundaries, this section will provide you with a comprehensive guide to understanding and implementing effective boundary-setting techniques. Together, we will embark on a journey of self-discovery, empowerment, and relationship transformation, as we learn to create the healthy, fulfilling connections we all deserve.

Subsection 3.1: Boundaries in Romantic Relationships

Romantic relationships are built on a foundation of love, trust, and intimacy, but they also require a delicate balance of personal boundaries to thrive. Setting and maintaining healthy boundaries in romantic partnerships is essential for fostering mutual respect, preventing resentment, and ensuring that both partners feel valued and supported.

One of the most crucial aspects of boundaries in romantic relationships is intimacy. Intimacy encompasses physical, emotional, and sexual closeness, and it is important for partners to openly communicate their comfort levels and desires. This includes discussing consent, expressing personal preferences, and respecting each other's limits. By establishing clear boundaries around intimacy, couples can create a safe and trusting environment that allows their connection to flourish.

Another key area where boundaries play a significant role in romantic relationships is personal space. While it is natural for partners to spend a great deal of time together, it is equally important for each individual to have their own space and time for self-care, hobbies, and personal growth. Setting boundaries around personal space can involve communicating the need for alone time, respecting each other's privacy, and encouraging individual pursuits. By striking a balance between togetherness and independence, couples can maintain a healthy sense of self while nurturing their relationship.

Emotional needs are another critical aspect of boundaries in romantic partnerships. Each person in a relationship has unique emotional requirements, and it is essential for partners to express and understand these needs. Setting emotional boundaries involves communicating openly about feelings, expectations, and triggers. It also means taking responsibility for one's own emotional well-being and not relying solely on a partner for happiness or validation. By establishing clear emotional boundaries, couples can create a supportive and empathetic environment that promotes personal growth and relationship satisfaction.

Navigating boundaries in romantic relationships can be challenging, as it requires ongoing communication, compromise, and adaptability. However, by prioritizing open and honest conversations about intimacy, personal space, and emotional needs, couples can lay the groundwork for a strong, healthy, and fulfilling partnership. Remember, boundaries are not about creating walls or limitations; rather, they are about fostering mutual respect, understanding, and love in a romantic relationship.

Subsection 3.2: Boundaries in Family Relationships

Family relationships are among the most complex and emotionally charged connections we experience throughout our lives. The dynamics between parents, siblings, and extended family members can greatly influence our personal growth, self-esteem, and overall well-being. However, navigating the unique challenges that arise within family relationships requires a delicate balance of love, respect, and healthy boundaries.

One of the primary challenges in maintaining boundaries with family members is the deep-rooted history and emotional ties that exist. Unlike friendships or romantic partnerships, family relationships are not chosen, and they often come with a set of expectations, obligations, and patterns of behavior that have developed over many years. These ingrained dynamics can make it difficult for individuals to assert their boundaries and establish a sense of autonomy within the family structure.

When it comes to setting boundaries with parents, many adults struggle with the transition from the parent-child relationship to a more equal, adult-to-adult dynamic. Parents may continue to treat their adult children as if they were still young, offering unsolicited advice, making demands on their time, or invading their privacy. In these situations, it is essential for individuals to communicate their boundaries clearly and respectfully, emphasizing their need for independence and the right to make their own decisions.

Sibling relationships also present unique boundary challenges, as the competitive nature and long-standing rivalries that often exist between brothers and sisters can create tension and conflict. Siblings may struggle with issues of comparison, jealousy, or resentment, leading to the violation of personal boundaries. To maintain healthy sibling relationships, it is crucial to establish clear boundaries around communication, personal space, and emotional support. This may involve setting limits on teasing or criticism, respecting each other's privacy, and learning to appreciate and celebrate individual differences.

Extended family members, such as grandparents, aunts, uncles, and cousins, can also pose boundary challenges, particularly when it comes to family gatherings, holidays, and shared family resources. Boundary issues may arise when extended family members offer unsolicited opinions on personal matters, make demands on time and energy, or expect conformity to family traditions or beliefs. In these situations, it is important to communicate boundaries assertively and consistently, while also being mindful of the larger family dynamics at play.

Strategies for maintaining healthy boundaries with family members include open and honest communication, active listening, and a willingness to compromise when appropriate. It is essential to approach boundary-setting conversations with empathy and understanding, recognizing that family members may have different perspectives and needs. By engaging in respectful dialogue and seeking common ground, individuals can work towards creating a family environment that respects and supports the personal boundaries of all members.

In some cases, maintaining healthy boundaries with family members may require professional support, such as therapy or counseling. This can be particularly helpful when dealing with toxic or abusive family dynamics, where boundaries have been consistently violated, and individuals struggle to assert their own needs and well-being. Seeking the guidance of a trained professional can provide valuable tools and strategies for navigating complex family relationships and establishing healthy boundaries.

Ultimately, the key to maintaining healthy boundaries in family relationships lies in striking a balance between honoring the love and connection that exists within the family while also prioritizing personal well-being and autonomy. By approaching boundary-setting with compassion, clarity, and consistency, individuals can foster more positive, supportive, and respectful family dynamics that allow all members to thrive.

Subsection 3.3: Boundaries in Friendships and Social Interactions

Friendships and social interactions form the fabric of our daily lives, providing us with a sense of connection, support, and belonging. However, just like any other type of relationship, friendships and social situations require the establishment and maintenance of healthy boundaries to ensure the well-being and respect of all parties involved.

One of the key areas where boundaries play a crucial role in friendships is time management. In today's fast-paced world, it is common for individuals to feel overwhelmed by the demands of their social lives, leading to feelings of stress and burnout. Setting clear boundaries around the amount of time and energy invested in friendships is essential for maintaining a healthy balance between personal and social commitments. This may involve communicating availability, being honest about limitations, and learning to say "no" when necessary.

Another important aspect of boundaries in friendships is emotional support. While friends are often a source of comfort and understanding during challenging times, it is essential to recognize that each person has their own emotional capacity and limitations. Setting boundaries around emotional support involves being clear about what one is willing and able to offer, as well as being respectful of a friend's emotional boundaries. This may include establishing limits on the frequency and intensity of emotional conversations, encouraging friends to seek professional help when needed, and being mindful of one's own emotional well-being.

Personal information sharing is another area where boundaries are crucial in friendships and social interactions. In an age where social media and digital communication have blurred the lines between public and private life, it is essential to be mindful of the information shared with friends and acquaintances. Setting boundaries around personal information involves being selective about what is disclosed, respecting others' privacy, and being cautious about sharing sensitive or confidential details. It is also important to communicate expectations around the sharing of personal information, such as requesting that friends refrain from posting certain content online or sharing private conversations with others.

Navigating boundaries in friendships and social situations can be challenging, as it requires a delicate balance between openness and self-protection. It is essential to approach boundary-setting conversations with honesty, empathy, and respect, recognizing that each individual has their own unique needs and preferences. By engaging in open and respectful communication, friends can work together to establish and maintain healthy boundaries that foster mutual trust, support, and understanding.

In some cases, maintaining boundaries in friendships may require difficult decisions, such as distancing oneself from toxic or draining relationships. While it can be painful to let go of long-standing friendships, it is important to prioritize one's own well-being and surround oneself with supportive, positive influences. Seeking the guidance of a trusted friend, family member, or mental health professional can provide valuable perspective and support when navigating complex friendship dynamics.

Ultimately, the key to maintaining healthy boundaries in friendships and social interactions lies in self-awareness, communication, and mutual respect. By taking the time to reflect on one's own needs and limitations, expressing boundaries clearly and kindly, and being open to feedback and compromise, individuals can cultivate meaningful, fulfilling friendships that enrich their lives and contribute to their overall well-being.

Subsection 3.4: Boundaries in Professional Relationships

The workplace is a unique environment where individuals from diverse backgrounds come together to achieve common goals. While professional relationships are built on collaboration, trust, and mutual respect, they also require the establishment and maintenance of appropriate boundaries to ensure a healthy, productive, and inclusive work environment. Examining the significance of maintaining proper boundaries in the workplace, including relationships with colleagues, supervisors, and clients, is crucial for fostering a positive and successful professional life.

One of the primary reasons for setting clear boundaries in professional relationships is to maintain a sense of professionalism and respect. When colleagues understand and adhere to appropriate boundaries, they create an atmosphere of trust and mutual regard, which is essential for effective teamwork and collaboration. This includes respecting each other's time, personal space, and expertise, as well as refraining from engaging in gossip, favoritism, or inappropriate behavior that could undermine the integrity of the workplace.

Another critical aspect of boundaries in professional relationships is the power dynamics that exist between employees and their supervisors or managers. It is essential for both parties to recognize and respect the inherent power imbalance in these relationships and to establish clear boundaries that prevent any abuse of authority or inappropriate behavior. Supervisors should maintain a professional demeanor, provide constructive feedback, and support their team members' growth and development without blurring the lines between personal and professional relationships.

When it comes to client relationships, maintaining appropriate boundaries is paramount for providing high-quality service and protecting the interests of both the client and the organization. This includes setting clear expectations regarding communication, deliverables, and professional conduct. It is essential to establish a rapport with clients based on trust, respect, and professionalism while avoiding any behavior that could be perceived as unprofessional or unethical, such as discussing personal matters or engaging in activities that could compromise the client's confidence in the organization.

Maintaining proper boundaries in professional relationships also involves being mindful of the impact of personal beliefs, values, and biases on work-related interactions. It is essential to create an inclusive work environment that respects diversity and promotes equality, regardless of individual differences. This requires setting aside personal prejudices and treating all colleagues, supervisors, and clients with the same level of respect and professionalism, regardless of their background, gender, age, or cultural identity.

In today's digital age, the boundaries between personal and professional life have become increasingly blurred, making it even more crucial to establish clear guidelines for appropriate online behavior. This includes being mindful of the content shared on social media platforms, ensuring that personal opinions and activities do not reflect negatively on the organization, and refraining from engaging in online harassment or discrimination. It is also essential to respect the privacy and confidentiality of colleagues, supervisors, and clients, both online and offline.

Establishing and maintaining appropriate boundaries in professional relationships requires ongoing communication, self-awareness, and a commitment to ethical behavior. Organizations can support their employees in navigating these boundaries by providing clear policies, training, and resources that promote a healthy and respectful work environment. By fostering a culture of open communication, mutual respect, and professionalism, individuals can build strong, positive relationships with their colleagues, supervisors, and clients while maintaining the necessary boundaries that ensure the success and well-being of all parties involved.

Summary: Nurturing Healthy Relationships Through Effective Boundary-Setting

Throughout this section, we have explored the intricacies of establishing and maintaining healthy boundaries in various types of relationships. From the intimate bonds of romantic partnerships to the complex dynamics of family, friendships, and professional relationships, we have seen how effective boundary-setting is essential for fostering mutual respect, trust, and personal well-being.

By examining the specific challenges and considerations that arise in each relationship context, we have gained valuable insights into the art of creating and sustaining positive, fulfilling connections with others. We have learned that open communication, self-awareness, and a commitment to personal growth are key components in navigating the complexities of boundary-setting.

As we reflect on the knowledge and strategies presented in this section, we are empowered to take a proactive approach to nurturing our relationships. By implementing the practical advice and actionable tips provided, we can cultivate a greater sense of self-respect, emotional resilience, and relationship satisfaction.

Remember, the journey of establishing healthy boundaries is an ongoing process, requiring patience, compassion, and a willingness to adapt and grow. As you continue to apply these insights to your own relationships, you will develop a deeper understanding of your own needs and values, as well as a greater appreciation for the importance of setting and respecting boundaries in all aspects of life.

Embrace the power of effective boundary-setting, and watch as your relationships flourish, built on a foundation of mutual respect, trust, and understanding. By prioritizing your own well-being and honoring the boundaries of others, you will create a ripple effect of positive change, not only in your own life but in the lives of those around you.

As we move forward, let us carry these valuable lessons with us, armed with the knowledge and tools necessary to cultivate strong, healthy relationships that stand the test of time. In the next section, we will delve into the complexities of overcoming common relationship challenges, exploring strategies for navigating the ups and downs of our connections with others.

Section 4: Overcoming Barriers to Setting and Maintaining Boundaries

Picture this: You've read about the importance of setting boundaries, and you're convinced that it's time to make a change. You're ready to take control of your life and relationships, but as you start to put your plans into action, you find yourself facing a series of unexpected obstacles. Perhaps you struggle with feelings of guilt or fear of rejection, or maybe you find yourself slipping back into old patterns of people-pleasing and codependency.

If this sounds familiar, you're not alone. Setting and maintaining healthy boundaries is a crucial skill, but it's one that many of us struggle with. The truth is, there are numerous barriers that can stand in the way of our best intentions, from deep-seated emotional challenges to ingrained social conditioning.

In this section, we'll take a closer look at some of the most common obstacles that individuals face when trying to set and uphold healthy boundaries. We'll explore the roots of these challenges and provide practical, actionable strategies for overcoming them. Whether you're dealing with a fear of confrontation, a history of toxic relationships, or simply a lack of confidence in your own abilities, we'll provide you with the tools and insights you need to break through these barriers and assert your boundaries with clarity and conviction.

By the end of this section, you'll have a deeper understanding of the psychological and emotional factors that can hold us back from setting healthy boundaries, as well as a toolbox of proven techniques for overcoming these obstacles. You'll be equipped with the knowledge and skills you need to navigate even the most challenging relationships with grace and resilience, while staying true to your own needs and values.

So if you're ready to break free from the patterns that have been holding you back and start setting boundaries that stick, let's dive in and explore the transformative power of boundary-setting together.

Subsection 4.1: Recognizing and Challenging People-Pleasing Tendencies

People-pleasing is a common behavior that many individuals struggle with, often without even realizing it. At its core, people-pleasing stems from a desire to be liked, accepted, and appreciated by others. While the intention behind this behavior may be positive, it can have detrimental effects on one's personal boundaries and overall well-being.

When we engage in people-pleasing, we prioritize the needs and wants of others over our own. We may find ourselves saying "yes" to requests or invitations that we don't truly want to accept, or we may go out of our way to avoid conflict or confrontation. This behavior can lead to feelings of resentment, burnout, and a loss of self-identity.

One of the key reasons why people-pleasing undermines personal boundaries is that it sends a message to others that our own needs and desires are not important. When we consistently put others first, we teach them that it's acceptable to ignore or override our boundaries. This can lead to a cycle of increasingly demanding requests and a gradual erosion of our own sense of self.

To break free from people-pleasing tendencies, it's essential to start by recognizing the behavior in ourselves. Some common signs of people-pleasing include:

- Difficulty saying "no" to requests, even when they are unreasonable or inconvenient

- Apologizing excessively, even for things that are not our fault

- Feeling responsible for the emotions and reactions of others

- Avoiding conflict or confrontation at all costs

- Seeking validation and approval from others to feel worthy or valued

Once we become aware of these tendencies, we can begin to challenge them and prioritize our own needs and well-being. This process may feel uncomfortable at first, especially if we are used to putting others first, but it is a crucial step in establishing and maintaining healthy boundaries.

One effective technique for overcoming people-pleasing is to practice self-compassion. When we treat ourselves with kindness and understanding, we are more likely to recognize and honor our own needs. This may involve setting aside time for self-care activities, such as exercise, meditation, or hobbies that bring us joy.

Another important strategy is to learn how to communicate our boundaries assertively and respectfully. This means being clear and direct about what we are and are not willing to do, without apologizing or making excuses. It can be helpful to practice saying "no" in low-stakes situations, such as declining a social invitation or setting limits on our time and energy.

Ultimately, overcoming people-pleasing tendencies requires a shift in mindset. We must learn to value ourselves and our own needs as much as we value the needs of others. By doing so, we can create healthier, more balanced relationships that allow us to thrive both personally and professionally.

Subsection 4.2: Dealing with Guilt and Fear of Rejection

Setting boundaries is an essential aspect of maintaining healthy relationships, but it can also be an emotionally challenging process. Many individuals struggle with feelings of guilt and fear of rejection when asserting their boundaries, which can make it difficult to prioritize their own needs and well-being.

Guilt often arises when we feel that we are letting others down or not meeting their expectations. We may worry that by setting boundaries, we are being selfish or uncaring. This guilt can be particularly intense in close relationships, such as those with family members or long-term partners, where there may be a history of self-sacrifice and putting others' needs first.

Fear of rejection is another common emotional obstacle to setting boundaries. We may worry that by asserting our limits, we will be met with anger, disapproval, or even abandonment. This fear can be rooted in past experiences of rejection or in a lack of self-worth and self-esteem.

To cope with these challenging emotions, it is important to first acknowledge and validate them. Recognize that feeling guilty or afraid is a normal response to setting boundaries, particularly if it is a new or unfamiliar practice. However, it is crucial to remember that these emotions do not negate the importance or legitimacy of your boundaries.

One effective strategy for dealing with guilt is to reframe boundary-setting as an act of self-care and self-respect. By prioritizing your own needs and well-being, you are not being selfish; rather, you are ensuring that you have the emotional resources to be present and supportive in your relationships. It can be helpful to remind yourself that setting boundaries is not about rejecting others, but about creating a healthy and sustainable dynamic that benefits everyone involved.

To overcome fear of rejection, it is important to cultivate a strong sense of self-worth and self-validation. This means learning to value and trust your own feelings, needs, and desires, even if they differ from those of others. It can be helpful to surround yourself with supportive people who respect and encourage your boundaries, and to seek therapy or counseling if fear of rejection is a persistent or overwhelming issue.

Another useful technique for coping with guilt and fear is to practice self-compassion. Treat yourself with the same kindness, understanding, and forgiveness that you would extend to a beloved friend. Acknowledge that setting boundaries is a learning process, and that it is okay to make mistakes or experience discomfort along the way.

Finally, it is important to communicate your boundaries clearly and assertively, while also being open to negotiation and compromise when appropriate. Use "I" statements to express your needs and feelings, and avoid blaming or attacking others. Be prepared to listen to their perspective and find mutually acceptable solutions, but also be willing to stand firm in your boundaries when necessary.

Remember, setting boundaries is not about creating rigid, inflexible rules, but about establishing a foundation of respect, trust, and open communication in your relationships. By learning to cope with guilt and fear of rejection, you can assert your boundaries with greater confidence and clarity, leading to healthier, more fulfilling connections with others.

Subsection 4.3: Breaking Patterns of Codependency and Enmeshment

Codependency and enmeshment are two closely related patterns of behavior that can significantly undermine the health and autonomy of relationships. These patterns are characterized by an excessive emotional, psychological, and sometimes physical reliance on another person, often to the detriment of one's own well-being and personal growth.

In codependent relationships, individuals often prioritize the needs and desires of their partner above their own, leading to a loss of self-identity and personal boundaries. Codependent individuals may feel responsible for their partner's happiness, and they may go to great lengths to avoid conflict or abandonment, even if it means sacrificing their own needs and values.

Enmeshment, on the other hand, refers to a blurring of boundaries between individuals, often within family systems. In enmeshed relationships, there is little differentiation between the thoughts, feelings, and experiences of each person, leading to a lack of autonomy and independence. Enmeshed individuals may struggle to make decisions or form opinions without the input or approval of others, and they may feel guilty or anxious when attempting to assert their own needs or desires.

Breaking free from patterns of codependency and enmeshment requires a concerted effort to establish healthier, more autonomous relationship dynamics. This process begins with self-awareness and a willingness to take responsibility for one's own thoughts, feelings, and behaviors. It is essential to recognize that you are not responsible for the happiness or well-being of others, and that it is okay to prioritize your own needs and desires.

One key strategy for overcoming codependency and enmeshment is to work on developing a strong sense of self. This may involve exploring your own values, interests, and goals, and learning to trust your own judgment and instincts. It can be helpful to engage in activities that promote self-discovery and personal growth, such as therapy, journaling, or mindfulness practices.

Another important step is to learn how to set and maintain healthy boundaries in your relationships. This means being clear and assertive about what you are and are not willing to do, and learning to say "no" when necessary. It can be challenging to break long-standing patterns of people-pleasing or self-sacrifice, but it is crucial for establishing a sense of autonomy and self-respect.

In addition to setting boundaries, it is important to work on developing healthy communication skills. This means learning to express your thoughts and feelings openly and honestly, while also being willing to listen and consider the perspectives of others. It can be helpful to practice active listening, which involves giving your full attention to the person speaking and seeking to understand their point of view before responding.

Finally, it is essential to cultivate a support system of healthy, independent relationships outside of the codependent or enmeshed dynamic. This may involve reaching out to friends, family members, or a therapist who can offer guidance and encouragement as you work to establish greater autonomy and self-reliance.

Breaking free from patterns of codependency and enmeshment is a gradual process that requires patience, self-compassion, and a willingness to step outside of your comfort zone. By learning to prioritize your own needs and desires, set healthy boundaries, and communicate effectively, you can begin to establish more balanced, fulfilling relationships that allow you to thrive both personally and interpersonally.

Summary: Embracing the Journey of Boundary-Setting

Throughout this section, we've explored some of the most common barriers that can hinder individuals from setting and maintaining healthy boundaries in their relationships. From the deep-seated emotional challenges of guilt and fear of rejection to the ingrained patterns of people-pleasing, codependency, and enmeshment, these obstacles can feel daunting and overwhelming at times.

However, it's important to remember that overcoming these barriers is a journey, not a destination. It's a process of self-discovery, growth, and empowerment that requires patience, self-compassion, and a willingness to step outside of your comfort zone. By developing a strong sense of self, cultivating healthy communication skills, and surrounding yourself with supportive, autonomous relationships, you can begin to break free from the patterns that have held you back and establish boundaries that honor your own needs and desires.

As you continue on this path, remember to be kind and forgiving with yourself. Setting and maintaining boundaries is a learning process, and it's okay to make mistakes or experience setbacks along the way. What matters most is that you remain committed to your own growth and well-being, and that you continue to prioritize your own needs and values in your relationships.

By embracing the journey of boundary-setting, you open yourself up to a world of healthier, more fulfilling connections – both with others and with yourself. You learn to trust your own instincts, to communicate your needs with clarity and conviction, and to create relationships that are built on a foundation of mutual respect, trust, and autonomy.

So as you move forward from this section, take the insights and strategies you've learned and apply them to your own life with curiosity, compassion, and courage. Remember that you are worthy of healthy, thriving relationships, and that by setting and maintaining boundaries, you are not only honoring yourself – you are also creating the space for deeper, more authentic connections with others.

Section 5: Practicing Self-Care and Resilience in Boundary Setting

As we navigate the complexities of relationships and the challenges that come with setting and maintaining healthy boundaries, it's essential to recognize the vital role that self-care and resilience play in this process. Many of us may find ourselves struggling to assert our needs and limits, often prioritizing the comfort and happiness of others over our own well-being. However, neglecting our own self-care can lead to burnout, resentment, and a diminished capacity to cultivate meaningful, balanced connections with others.

In this section, we will delve into the profound connection between self-care, resilience, and the ability to establish and uphold healthy boundaries in our relationships. We'll explore how dedicating time and energy to nurturing ourselves can fortify our emotional reserves, enabling us to approach boundary-setting with greater clarity, confidence, and compassion. By developing a strong foundation of self-care and resilience, we can more effectively communicate our needs, navigate difficult conversations, and maintain the boundaries necessary for our personal growth and relationship success.

Through a combination of practical strategies, real-life examples, and expert insights, this section will empower you to prioritize your own well-being while fostering healthier, more fulfilling connections with others. We'll examine the various facets of self-care, from physical and emotional to spiritual and intellectual, and discover how each contributes to our overall resilience and boundary-setting abilities. You'll gain valuable tools for managing stress, coping with the discomfort that often accompanies boundary-setting, and cultivating a deeper sense of self-awareness and self-compassion.

Whether you're seeking to establish boundaries in a romantic partnership, family dynamic, friendship, or professional setting, the insights and strategies presented in this section will equip you with the knowledge and skills necessary to prioritize your well-being and build resilient, balanced relationships. By embracing the power of self-care and developing a strong foundation of resilience, you'll be better prepared to navigate the inevitable challenges of boundary-setting and create a life filled with healthy, nurturing connections.

Subsection 5.1: The Role of Self-Care in Boundary Maintenance

Self-care is a crucial aspect of maintaining healthy boundaries in relationships. When we neglect our own needs and well-being, we become more susceptible to compromising our boundaries and allowing others to overstep them. Regular self-care practices can provide us with the emotional resilience and clarity needed to assert and uphold our personal limits effectively.

One of the primary benefits of self-care is that it helps us develop a strong sense of self-worth and self-respect. When we prioritize our own needs and engage in activities that nurture our physical, emotional, and mental well-being, we send a powerful message to ourselves and others that our boundaries are important and deserving of respect. This increased self-awareness and self-esteem can make it easier to communicate our boundaries clearly and confidently, even in challenging situations.

Moreover, self-care practices can help reduce stress and prevent burnout, which are common obstacles to maintaining healthy boundaries. When we are overwhelmed, exhausted, or emotionally depleted, we may find it more difficult to assert ourselves and stand firm in our boundaries. By engaging in regular self-care activities, such as exercise, meditation, hobbies, or spending time in nature, we can recharge our emotional batteries and cultivate a greater sense of inner peace and resilience. This, in turn, can enhance our ability to navigate boundary-related challenges with greater ease and effectiveness.

Another key aspect of self-care in relation to boundary maintenance is learning to listen to and trust our own instincts and feelings. When we are attuned to our emotions and physical sensations, we are better equipped to recognize when a boundary has been crossed or when we are feeling uncomfortable in a situation. By cultivating this self-awareness through practices like journaling, therapy, or mindfulness, we can develop a keener sense of our own limits and be more proactive in communicating and enforcing our boundaries.

Ultimately, self-care is about taking responsibility for our own well-being and recognizing that we cannot effectively care for others or maintain healthy relationships if we neglect ourselves. By making self-care a priority and integrating it into our daily lives, we can develop the emotional strength, clarity, and resilience needed to set and maintain healthy boundaries in all our relationships. This, in turn, can lead to more fulfilling, balanced, and mutually respectful connections with others.

Subsection 5.2: Building Resilience and Emotional

Strength

Developing emotional resilience and inner strength is crucial for navigating the challenges that come with setting and maintaining healthy boundaries in relationships. Resilience refers to our ability to bounce back from adversity, adapt to change, and cope with stress in a healthy manner. When we cultivate resilience and emotional strength, we are better equipped to handle the discomfort and potential pushback that may arise when asserting our boundaries.

One key strategy for building resilience is to develop a growth mindset. This involves viewing challenges and setbacks as opportunities for learning and personal development, rather than as insurmountable obstacles. By embracing a growth mindset, we can approach boundary-setting with a sense of curiosity and openness, rather than fear or avoidance. We can learn to reframe negative experiences as valuable lessons that help us refine our boundary-setting skills and strengthen our emotional resilience.

Another important aspect of building resilience is practicing self-compassion. Self-compassion involves treating ourselves with kindness, understanding, and forgiveness, particularly in moments of difficulty or perceived failure. When we encounter resistance or pushback while setting boundaries, it's easy to fall into patterns of self-criticism or self-blame. However, by extending compassion to ourselves, we can maintain a sense of emotional equilibrium and stay committed to our boundaries, even in the face of challenges.

Cultivating mindfulness is another powerful tool for developing emotional resilience. Mindfulness involves bringing our attention to the present moment, without judgment or reactivity. By practicing mindfulness regularly, we can develop a greater awareness of our thoughts, feelings, and bodily sensations, which can help us respond to boundary-related challenges with greater clarity and intentionality. Mindfulness practices such as meditation, deep breathing, or body scans can help us stay grounded and centered, even in emotionally charged situations.

Building a strong support system is also essential for developing resilience and emotional strength. Surrounding ourselves with supportive, understanding individuals who respect our boundaries can provide a sense of validation and encouragement. Whether it's trusted friends, family members, or a therapist, having people in our lives who can offer guidance, empathy, and a listening ear can make a significant difference in our ability to navigate boundary-setting challenges with resilience.

Finally, engaging in regular self-care practices can help us build and maintain emotional resilience. Self-care encompasses a wide range of activities that nurture our physical, emotional, and mental well-being, such as exercise, healthy eating, sufficient sleep, and engaging in hobbies or creative pursuits. By prioritizing self-care, we send a message to ourselves and others that our well-being matters and that we are committed to maintaining healthy boundaries. When we feel emotionally strong and resilient, we are better prepared to handle the challenges that come with boundary-setting and maintain a sense of inner peace and stability.

Subsection 5.3: Seeking Support and Professional Help

Setting and maintaining healthy boundaries in relationships can be a challenging process, and there may be times when we feel overwhelmed, stuck, or unsure of how to proceed. In these moments, it's crucial to remember that seeking support from trusted friends, family members, or mental health professionals is a sign of strength and self-awareness, not weakness.

One of the first steps in seeking support is to identify the people in our lives who we feel safe and comfortable confiding in. These may be close friends, family members, or even colleagues who have demonstrated empathy, trustworthiness, and respect for our boundaries in the past.

Sharing our struggles and concerns with these individuals can provide a sense of validation, relief, and perspective. They may offer valuable insights, share their own experiences, or simply lend a listening ear, which can help us feel less alone and more supported in our boundary-setting efforts.

However, it's important to recognize that not all friends or family members may be equipped to provide the level of support or guidance we need. In some cases, our loved ones may be too close to the situation, have their own biases or limitations, or lack the necessary skills to help us navigate complex boundary-related issues. In these instances, seeking the help of a qualified mental health professional, such as a therapist or counselor, can be invaluable.

Mental health professionals are trained to provide a safe, non-judgmental space for individuals to explore their thoughts, feelings, and experiences related to boundaries and relationships. They can help us gain a deeper understanding of our own patterns, motivations, and challenges, as well as provide evidence-based strategies and tools for setting and maintaining healthy boundaries. Through therapy or counseling, we can learn to communicate our needs more effectively, develop greater self-awareness and self-compassion, and build the emotional resilience needed to navigate difficult boundary-related situations.

In addition to individual therapy, support groups can be another valuable resource for those struggling with boundary-related issues. These groups bring together individuals who are facing similar challenges, providing a sense of community, shared understanding, and mutual support. Participating in a support group can help us feel less isolated, gain new perspectives and insights, and learn from the experiences of others who have successfully navigated boundary-setting in their own relationships.

It's important to remember that seeking support and professional help is not a one-time event, but rather an ongoing process. As we continue to grow, change, and face new challenges in our relationships, we may need to revisit our support systems and resources to ensure that we have the guidance and tools we need to maintain healthy boundaries. By staying open to seeking help and prioritizing our own well-being, we can cultivate the resilience and self-awareness needed to build and sustain fulfilling, mutually respectful relationships.

Summary: Nurturing Yourself for Stronger Boundaries and Relationships

Throughout this section, we've explored the vital role that self-care and resilience play in setting and maintaining healthy boundaries in relationships. By prioritizing our own well-being and developing emotional strength, we can more effectively communicate our needs, navigate challenges, and cultivate fulfilling connections with others.

We've seen how regular self-care practices can enhance our self-awareness, self-respect, and ability to assert our boundaries with clarity and confidence. By reducing stress, preventing burnout, and nurturing our physical, emotional, and mental health, we create a solid foundation for boundary-setting and relationship success.

Moreover, we've discovered the power of resilience in navigating the challenges that come with establishing and upholding personal limits. By embracing a growth mindset, practicing self-compassion, cultivating mindfulness, and building a supportive network, we can develop the inner strength needed to weather the ups and downs of boundary-setting and maintain our commitment to our own well-being.

Lastly, we've recognized the importance of seeking support and professional help when needed. Whether it's confiding in trusted friends and family or working with a mental health professional, reaching out for guidance and support is a sign of strength and self-awareness. By leveraging these resources, we can gain valuable insights, tools, and strategies for navigating boundary-related challenges and building healthier, more balanced relationships.

As we move forward, remember that practicing self-care and building resilience is an ongoing journey. By making these practices a priority and staying committed to your own growth and well-being, you can cultivate the inner strength, clarity, and compassion needed to set and maintain healthy boundaries in all your relationships. Embrace the power of self-care and resilience, and watch as your connections with others flourish, grounded in mutual respect, understanding, and love.

Chapter Summary: Embracing Boundaries for Healthier, Happier Relationships

Throughout this chapter, we have explored the crucial role that maintaining healthy boundaries plays in fostering personal well-being and mutual respect within relationships. By understanding the importance of boundaries, learning to identify and communicate them effectively, and navigating the challenges that may arise, individuals can create a solid foundation for more fulfilling and harmonious connections with others.

Setting and upholding boundaries is not always easy, as it requires a deep understanding of one's own needs, values, and limits. It also demands the courage to communicate these boundaries assertively and respectfully, even in the face of potential conflict or resistance. However, the benefits of establishing healthy boundaries far outweigh the challenges.

When we maintain clear boundaries, we create a sense of safety, trust, and respect within our relationships. We protect our emotional well-being, prevent burnout, and foster a greater sense of autonomy and self-respect. By teaching others how to treat us and respecting their boundaries in return, we cultivate more balanced, reciprocal, and supportive connections.

Embracing the importance of boundaries is a journey of self-discovery and growth. It requires ongoing self-reflection, communication, and a willingness to adapt as our relationships and circumstances evolve. By committing to this process and prioritizing our own well-being, we can build more resilient, authentic, and deeply satisfying relationships that stand the test of time.

As you continue on your path to creating and maintaining healthy boundaries, remember to be patient, compassionate, and kind to yourself. Seek support when needed, whether from trusted loved ones or professional help, and celebrate the progress you make along the way. By embracing the power of boundaries, you are taking a significant step towards cultivating the loving, respectful, and fulfilling relationships you deserve.

Chapter 9: Nurturing Intimacy and Connection

Intimacy and connection lie at the heart of every fulfilling relationship, be it a romantic partnership, a cherished friendship, or the unbreakable bonds of family. These essential elements provide the foundation upon which trust, understanding, and love can flourish. In a world that often prioritizes superficial connections and fleeting encounters, the pursuit of genuine intimacy has become increasingly vital for our emotional well-being and overall happiness.

Intimacy is a multifaceted concept that encompasses emotional, physical, and spiritual closeness. It is the feeling of being deeply understood, accepted, and cherished by another person. When we cultivate intimacy in our relationships, we create a safe space where we can be vulnerable, share our deepest thoughts and feelings, and experience a profound sense of belonging.

However, building and maintaining intimacy is not always an easy journey. It requires intentional effort, open communication, and a willingness to confront our own fears and insecurities. We must learn to let down our guard, express our authentic selves, and embrace the beautiful imperfections that make us human.

Throughout this chapter, we will explore the various ways in which we can nurture intimacy and connection in our most precious relationships. From the passionate embrace of romantic love to the unbreakable ties that bind families together, we will delve into the strategies and techniques that can help us foster deeper, more meaningful connections with the people who matter most to us.

Whether you are seeking to reignite the spark in your romantic partnership, strengthen the bonds with your family members, or cultivate more authentic friendships, the insights and guidance provided in this chapter will empower you to create relationships that are built on a foundation of genuine intimacy and unwavering connection.

So, let us embark on this transformative journey together, as we discover the power of vulnerability, the beauty of emotional attunement, and the immeasurable rewards of nurturing intimacy and connection in every aspect of our lives.

Section 1: Understanding the Foundations of Intimacy

Intimacy is the heart of every meaningful relationship, serving as the foundation upon which deep connections are built. It is the closeness, familiarity, and vulnerability that we share with others, allowing us to feel seen, heard, and understood. Whether in romantic partnerships, family bonds, or close friendships, intimacy plays a crucial role in fostering a sense of belonging, trust, and emotional fulfillment.

But what exactly is intimacy, and how does it manifest in different types of relationships? This section will delve into the various forms of intimacy, exploring the key components and building blocks that contribute to the development of close, authentic connections. By understanding the foundations of intimacy, we can cultivate the skills and awareness necessary to nurture and sustain the relationships that matter most to us.

Through relatable examples, research-backed insights, and practical wisdom, we will examine the role of trust, vulnerability, and self-awareness in creating intimate bonds. We will also explore the challenges that can arise when building intimacy and offer guidance on navigating these obstacles with compassion and resilience.

As we embark on this journey of understanding intimacy, it is essential to approach the topic with an open mind and an open heart. By embracing the complexities and joys of human connection, we can deepen our capacity for love, empathy, and personal growth. So let us dive in and discover the transformative power of intimacy in our lives.

Subsection 1.1: Defining Intimacy and Its Different Forms

Intimacy is a deep, close, and familiar connection that we share with another person, characterized by a sense of openness, vulnerability, and mutual understanding. It is a bond that allows us to feel seen, heard, and accepted for who we truly are, without fear of judgment or rejection. Intimacy is a fundamental human need, essential for our emotional well-being and the health of our relationships.

While intimacy is often associated with romantic partnerships, it is not limited to this context. Intimacy can manifest in various forms and across different types of relationships, including friendships, family bonds, and even the connection we have with ourselves. Understanding these different forms of intimacy can help us cultivate more meaningful and fulfilling connections in all areas of our lives.

One of the most well-known forms of intimacy is emotional intimacy. This type of intimacy involves the sharing of our innermost thoughts, feelings, and experiences with another person. It requires a level of trust and vulnerability that allows us to open up and express ourselves authentically, without fear of criticism or rejection. Emotional intimacy is the foundation upon which deep, lasting connections are built, as it fosters a sense of closeness, empathy, and mutual support.

Physical intimacy is another important form of intimacy, particularly in romantic relationships. This type of intimacy encompasses physical expressions of affection, such as touching, hugging, kissing, and sexual activity. Physical intimacy helps to strengthen the emotional bond between partners, promoting feelings of closeness, desire, and attachment. However, it is important to note that physical intimacy is not just about sexual contact; it also includes non-sexual forms of physical affection that contribute to a sense of comfort, security, and connection.

In addition to emotional and physical intimacy, there is also spiritual intimacy. This form of intimacy involves a deep, shared connection to something greater than oneself, such as a higher power, a sense of purpose, or a set of shared values and beliefs. Spiritual intimacy can be experienced in the context of a religious or spiritual practice, but it can also manifest in a more general sense of unity, oneness, or interconnectedness with the world around us. When we share this sense of spiritual connection with another person, it can create a profound bond that transcends the boundaries of the physical world.

It is important to recognize that these different forms of intimacy are not mutually exclusive; rather, they often overlap and intersect in the context of our relationships. A truly intimate connection is one that encompasses emotional, physical, and spiritual elements, creating a multifaceted and deeply satisfying bond. By understanding and nurturing these different forms of intimacy, we can create more authentic, meaningful, and fulfilling relationships in all areas of our lives.

Subsection 1.2: The Role of Trust and Vulnerability in Intimacy

Trust and vulnerability are the cornerstones of intimacy, serving as the essential foundations upon which deep, meaningful connections are built. Without trust and the willingness to be vulnerable, it is impossible to create and maintain the close, authentic bonds that characterize truly intimate relationships.

At its core, trust is the firm belief in the reliability, truth, and strength of another person. It is the confidence that allows us to open up, share our innermost thoughts and feelings, and rely on our loved ones for support and understanding. When we trust someone, we feel safe in their presence, knowing that they will hold our confidences, respect our boundaries, and act with our best interests at heart.

Vulnerability, on the other hand, is the courage to be authentic, to let ourselves be seen and known, even in the face of uncertainty or potential rejection. It is the willingness to remove our masks, to share our fears, insecurities, and dreams, and to allow others to witness our true selves. Vulnerability is a profound act of bravery, as it requires us to step outside of our comfort zones and risk emotional exposure for the sake of deeper connection.

Together, trust and vulnerability create a powerful synergy that enables intimacy to flourish. When we trust someone, we feel more comfortable being vulnerable with them, sharing the parts of ourselves that we might otherwise keep hidden. And when we are vulnerable with someone, we demonstrate our trust in them, inviting them to reciprocate and deepen the connection between us.

However, building trust and embracing vulnerability is not always easy. It requires a leap of faith, a willingness to take emotional risks, and a deep sense of self-awareness and self-acceptance. We must be willing to confront our own fears, insecurities, and past wounds, and to communicate openly and honestly with our loved ones about our needs, boundaries, and expectations.

Moreover, trust and vulnerability are not one-time achievements, but rather ongoing practices that require consistent effort and attention. They must be nurtured and sustained through open communication, active listening, and a commitment to growth and healing. When conflicts or misunderstandings arise, it is essential to approach them with empathy, patience, and a willingness to work through the challenges together.

Ultimately, the role of trust and vulnerability in intimacy cannot be overstated. They are the very fabric of deep, meaningful connections, enabling us to love and be loved in the most authentic, fulfilling ways possible. By cultivating these essential qualities in our relationships, we open ourselves up to a world of profound intimacy, connection, and personal growth.

Subsection 1.3: The Importance of Self-Awareness and Personal Growth

The journey towards building and maintaining intimate relationships begins with a deep understanding of oneself. Self-awareness, the conscious knowledge of one's own character, feelings, motives, and desires, plays a crucial role in fostering meaningful connections with others. When we take the time to explore our inner world, we gain valuable insights into our strengths, weaknesses, and emotional patterns, enabling us to show up more authentically and compassionately in our relationships.

Self-awareness is not a destination but rather an ongoing process of self-discovery and personal growth. It requires a willingness to honestly examine our thoughts, beliefs, and behaviors, even when it feels uncomfortable or challenging. By developing a curious and non-judgmental attitude towards ourselves, we can begin to identify the ways in which our past experiences, fears, and insecurities may be influencing our current relationships.

This heightened sense of self-awareness allows us to take responsibility for our own emotional well-being and communicate our needs and boundaries more effectively. When we are in touch with our own feelings and desires, we are better equipped to express them clearly and compassionately to our loved ones. This open and honest communication is the foundation of healthy, intimate relationships, as it fosters trust, understanding, and mutual respect.

Moreover, self-awareness is closely linked to personal growth and the ongoing process of becoming the best version of ourselves. As we gain a deeper understanding of our own strengths and limitations, we can actively work on developing the skills and qualities that will enhance our relationships. This may involve learning new communication techniques, practicing empathy and active listening, or working through past traumas and emotional barriers.

By committing to personal growth, we not only improve our own emotional well-being but also create a ripple effect that positively impacts our relationships. When we are actively engaged in our own self-improvement, we inspire and encourage our loved ones to do the same. This shared commitment to growth and self-discovery can create a powerful bond, as partners support and challenge each other to become their best selves.

It is important to recognize that the journey of self-awareness and personal growth is not always easy. It requires courage, vulnerability, and a willingness to confront uncomfortable truths about ourselves. However, the rewards of this inner work are immeasurable. As we develop a deeper understanding of ourselves and actively work on personal growth, we create a solid foundation for building and maintaining intimate, fulfilling relationships that stand the test of time.

In conclusion, self-awareness and personal growth are essential components of fostering intimate connections with others. By taking the time to explore our inner world, communicate openly and honestly, and actively work on becoming our best selves, we create the conditions for deep, meaningful relationships to thrive. As we embrace the ongoing journey of self-discovery and growth, we open ourselves up to a world of profound connection, love, and personal transformation.

Summary: Building the Foundations of Intimacy

Throughout this section, we have explored the fundamental components and building blocks of intimacy in various types of relationships. By understanding the different forms of intimacy, the role of trust and vulnerability, and the importance of self-awareness and personal growth, we lay the groundwork for creating and maintaining deep, meaningful connections with others.

Intimacy is a multifaceted concept that encompasses emotional, physical, and spiritual elements, each contributing to the depth and richness of our relationships. By recognizing and nurturing these different forms of intimacy, we can create more authentic and fulfilling bonds with our loved ones.

At the heart of intimacy lies trust and vulnerability, two essential qualities that enable us to open up, share our true selves, and forge deep connections with others. By cultivating trust and embracing vulnerability, we create a safe space for love, understanding, and personal growth to flourish.

Moreover, the journey towards building intimate relationships begins with a commitment to self-awareness and personal growth. By exploring our inner world, communicating openly and honestly, and actively working on becoming our best selves, we create a solid foundation for attracting and maintaining healthy, intimate connections.

As we move forward in our exploration of intimacy, remember that building and nurturing these foundations is an ongoing process that requires patience, dedication, and a willingness to embrace the challenges and joys of human connection. By committing to this journey of self-discovery and growth, we open ourselves up to a world of profound love, understanding, and personal transformation.

Section 2: Cultivating Intimacy in Romantic Relationships

Intimacy is the heart and soul of any romantic relationship. It is the deep, personal connection that allows partners to share their innermost thoughts, feelings, and desires with each other. When intimacy thrives, it creates a strong foundation of love, trust, and understanding that can weather the storms of life. However, building and maintaining intimacy is not always easy. It requires effort, dedication, and a willingness to be vulnerable with your partner.

In this section, we will explore the various strategies and techniques for cultivating intimacy in romantic relationships. From prioritizing quality time together to enhancing emotional and physical intimacy, we will delve into the practical steps couples can take to deepen their connection and strengthen their bond. We will also discuss how to navigate the challenges that can arise along the way, such as busy schedules, communication breakdowns, and the inevitable changes that come with time.

Whether you are in a new relationship or have been with your partner for many years, this section will provide you with valuable insights and tools for nurturing the intimacy that is so essential to a fulfilling and lasting romantic partnership. By the end of this section, you will have a clearer understanding of what intimacy truly means and how to create a deeper, more meaningful connection with your loved one. So, let us embark on this journey together and discover the secrets to cultivating intimacy in your romantic relationship.

Subsection 2.1: Prioritizing Quality Time and Shared Experiences

In the hustle and bustle of modern life, it's easy to let the demands of work, family, and other obligations take precedence over nurturing our romantic relationships. However, prioritizing quality time and shared experiences with our partners is crucial for maintaining a strong, intimate connection. When we carve out dedicated time to be fully present with each other, we create opportunities for deeper understanding, emotional bonding, and the creation of cherished memories.

Quality time goes beyond merely being in the same room together or engaging in routine activities. It involves giving our undivided attention to our partner, setting aside distractions, and actively participating in meaningful interactions. This could mean engaging in heartfelt conversations, trying new hobbies or adventures together, or simply savoring moments of quiet companionship. By prioritizing quality time, we send a clear message to our partner that they are valued, appreciated, and worthy of our focused attention.

Shared experiences play a vital role in strengthening the intimate bonds between partners. When we embark on new adventures, face challenges together, or create special moments of joy and laughter, we foster a sense of teamwork, trust, and shared history. These experiences become the threads that weave the tapestry of our relationship, providing a foundation of mutual understanding and a well of positive memories to draw upon during times of stress or difficulty.

To make quality time and shared experiences a priority, it's essential to be intentional and proactive in our approach. This may involve setting aside dedicated date nights, planning weekend getaways, or carving out daily rituals of connection, such as enjoying morning coffee together or taking evening walks. It's also important to be fully present during these times, letting go of the distractions of technology or outside concerns and focusing on the person in front of us.

In addition to grand gestures and planned outings, it's equally important to appreciate the small, everyday moments of connection. A lingering kiss before leaving for work, a heartfelt compliment, or a spontaneous dance in the kitchen can all contribute to the intimate bond between partners. By consistently prioritizing quality time and seeking out opportunities for shared experiences, we create a strong foundation of love, trust, and intimacy that can withstand the tests of time and the challenges of life.

Subsection 2.2: Enhancing Emotional and Physical Intimacy

Emotional and physical intimacy are two essential pillars of a strong and fulfilling romantic relationship. When partners feel emotionally connected and comfortable with physical closeness, it creates a deep sense of bonding, trust, and satisfaction. However, maintaining and enhancing intimacy requires ongoing effort and intentionality from both partners.

One of the key components of emotional intimacy is open and honest communication. When partners feel safe to express their thoughts, feelings, and desires without fear of judgment or rejection, it fosters a sense of closeness and understanding. This means being willing to share both the joys and the challenges, the hopes and the fears, and everything in between. It also means being an active and empathetic listener, creating a space where your partner feels heard, validated, and supported.

Another important aspect of emotional intimacy is vulnerability. When we allow ourselves to be vulnerable with our partner, we create opportunities for deeper connection and trust. This could mean sharing our insecurities, admitting our mistakes, or expressing our deepest longings and dreams. By letting down our guard and allowing our partner to see our authentic selves, we invite them to do the same, creating a profound sense of intimacy and acceptance.

Physical intimacy, on the other hand, encompasses a wide range of expressions, from affectionate touch and cuddling to sexual connection. The key to enhancing physical intimacy is to approach it with openness, curiosity, and a willingness to explore and communicate. This means taking the time to discover each other's preferences, desires, and boundaries, and being attentive to both verbal and nonverbal cues.

One simple yet powerful way to nurture physical intimacy is through affectionate touch. This could be as simple as holding hands, giving a loving hug, or offering a gentle massage. These small gestures of physical connection can help to build a sense of comfort, security, and bonding between partners. They also serve as a reminder that intimacy is not just about sexual activity, but about the ongoing physical expression of love and affection.

When it comes to sexual intimacy, communication is key. Partners should feel comfortable discussing their desires, fantasies, and boundaries, and be willing to listen and respect each other's needs. This means creating a safe, non-judgmental space for exploration and experimentation, while also being mindful of each other's comfort levels and consent. It also means being open to trying new things, whether that's exploring different positions, incorporating toys or props, or simply setting aside dedicated time for intimate connection.

Ultimately, enhancing emotional and physical intimacy requires a combination of openness, vulnerability, communication, and a willingness to prioritize connection. By approaching intimacy as an ongoing journey of discovery and growth, partners can create a deep sense of closeness, trust, and satisfaction that will strengthen their bond and enrich their relationship over time.

Subsection 2.3: Maintaining Intimacy Through Life Transitions and Challenges

Throughout the course of a romantic relationship, couples inevitably face various life transitions and challenges that can put a strain on their intimate connection. From the joys and responsibilities of parenthood to the demands of career changes and the difficulties of navigating health issues, these experiences can test the strength and resilience of even the most committed partnerships. However, by approaching these transitions and challenges with a spirit of unity, open communication, and adaptability, couples can not only maintain but even deepen their intimacy during these transformative times.

One of the most significant transitions many couples face is the journey into parenthood. The arrival of a child brings immense joy and love, but it can also fundamentally alter the dynamics of a relationship. As new parents focus their energy and attention on caring for their little one, it's common for the intimate connection between partners to take a backseat. To maintain intimacy during this time, it's crucial for couples to prioritize their relationship and carve out dedicated moments for connection, even amidst the demands of parenting. This could mean setting aside regular date nights, sharing the responsibilities of childcare, or finding small, daily gestures of affection and appreciation.

Another common challenge couples may encounter is navigating career changes or professional upheavals. Whether it's one partner pursuing a new job opportunity, facing a layoff, or deciding to return to school, these transitions can create stress, uncertainty, and shifts in the relationship dynamic. To sustain intimacy during these times, it's essential for couples to approach the situation as a team, offering each other support, understanding, and a willingness to adapt. This may involve open discussions about how the career change will impact the relationship, finding ways to redistribute household responsibilities, or simply being a listening ear and a source of encouragement for each other.

When health issues arise, whether it's a chronic condition, a serious illness, or an unexpected injury, couples may find their intimate connection tested in new ways. The physical and emotional toll of these challenges can create distance, frustration, and a sense of helplessness. To maintain intimacy in the face of health struggles, it's crucial for partners to approach the situation with empathy, patience, and a commitment to being there for each other. This may mean adapting to new limitations, finding alternative ways to express affection and connection, or seeking outside support through therapy or support groups.

Ultimately, the key to maintaining intimacy through life transitions and challenges is to approach them as opportunities for growth, rather than obstacles to connection. By embracing open communication, flexibility, and a willingness to adapt, couples can weather these storms together and emerge with a deeper sense of love, trust, and understanding. It's important to remember that intimacy is not a static state, but rather an ongoing journey that requires effort, intention, and a commitment to growing together, no matter what life may bring.

Summary: Nurturing the Bonds of Love and Connection

Cultivating intimacy in romantic relationships is an ongoing journey that requires dedication, effort, and a willingness to be vulnerable with your partner. By prioritizing quality time, enhancing emotional and physical intimacy, and navigating life's transitions and challenges together, couples can create a strong foundation of love, trust, and understanding that will stand the test of time.

Throughout this section, we have explored the various strategies and techniques for deepening the intimate connection between partners. From carving out meaningful moments of togetherness to fostering open communication and vulnerability, these practices serve to strengthen the bonds of love and create a safe space for both partners to be their authentic selves.

As you reflect on the insights and advice shared in this section, consider how you can apply these principles to your own romantic relationship. Whether it's setting aside dedicated date nights, expressing your feelings and desires more openly, or finding new ways to show affection and appreciation, every small step towards greater intimacy can have a profound impact on the health and happiness of your partnership.

Remember, intimacy is not a destination, but rather a lifelong journey of discovery, growth, and connection. By committing to nurturing your intimate bond with your partner, you are investing in the future of your relationship and creating a love that can weather any storm. So cherish the moments of closeness, embrace the challenges as opportunities for growth, and never stop exploring the depths of your connection. With patience, understanding, and an open heart, you and your partner can build a relationship that is truly intimate, fulfilling, and enduring.

Section 3: Building Strong and Intimate Family Bonds

Family relationships form the foundation of our lives, shaping our experiences, values, and emotional well-being. The bonds we share with our parents, siblings, and extended family members have a profound impact on our personal growth and the quality of our relationships outside the family unit. Building strong and intimate family connections requires intentional effort, open communication, and a willingness to nurture these relationships through the ups and downs of life.

In this section, we will explore the various ways to foster intimacy and connection within family relationships. We will delve into the unique dynamics of parent-child relationships, sibling bonds, and extended family connections, offering insights and strategies to strengthen these ties. By understanding the importance of trust, empathy, and shared experiences, we can cultivate a family environment that promotes love, support, and personal growth.

Whether you are a parent seeking to create a closer bond with your children, a sibling looking to improve your relationship with your brothers or sisters, or an individual hoping to reconnect with extended family members, this section will provide you with valuable tools and insights. Through real-life examples, research-backed strategies, and practical advice, you will learn how to navigate the complexities of family relationships and build a strong, intimate family unit that can weather any storm.

As we explore the various aspects of building strong and intimate family bonds, it is essential to approach this topic with an open mind and heart. Every family is unique, with its own history, challenges, and strengths. By embracing empathy, understanding, and a willingness to grow, we can create a family environment that fosters love, trust, and support for one another. So, let us embark on this journey together, discovering the keys to unlocking the full potential of our family relationships and creating a legacy of love that will endure for generations to come.

Subsection 3.1: Nurturing Strong Parent-Child Bonds

The relationship between parents and children is one of the most significant and influential in our lives. From the moment a child is born, they rely on their parents for love, support, and guidance as they navigate the complexities of growing up. As parents, it is our responsibility to nurture and cultivate a strong, supportive connection with our children that will serve as a foundation for their emotional well-being and future relationships.

Building and maintaining strong, supportive relationships with our children requires intentional effort and adaptability. As our children grow and develop, their needs and the dynamics of our relationship will evolve. It is essential to recognize and respond to these changes, tailoring our approach to fostering connection and attachment at each developmental stage.

In the early years, physical affection, responsive caregiving, and consistent, loving communication are crucial for establishing a secure attachment between parents and children. By creating a safe, nurturing environment where our children feel loved, valued, and understood, we lay the groundwork for a lifetime of trust and emotional closeness.

As children enter adolescence, the nature of our connection may shift, but its importance remains paramount. During this time, it is essential to create an open, non-judgmental space for communication, where our children feel comfortable sharing their thoughts, feelings, and experiences. By actively listening, validating their emotions, and offering support and guidance, we can maintain a strong, supportive bond that will help them navigate the challenges of adolescence.

Nurturing strong parent-child bonds also involves being present and engaged in our children's lives. By showing genuine interest in their passions, hobbies, and experiences, we demonstrate that we value and prioritize our relationship with them. Sharing quality time together, whether through family meals, outdoor activities, or heartfelt conversations, helps strengthen the emotional connection between parents and children.

It is important to recognize that building and maintaining strong parent-child relationships is not always easy. There will be moments of conflict, misunderstanding, and frustration. However, by approaching these challenges with empathy, patience, and a willingness to learn and grow, we can use these experiences as opportunities to deepen our connection and understanding of one another.

Ultimately, nurturing strong parent-child bonds is a lifelong journey that requires commitment, adaptability, and unconditional love. By prioritizing our relationship with our children and consistently working to foster a strong, supportive connection, we can create a bond that will weather the storms of life and provide a source of comfort, guidance, and joy for years to come.

Subsection 3.2: Strengthening Sibling Connections

Siblings share a unique bond that is shaped by a lifetime of shared experiences, memories, and family dynamics. While sibling relationships can be incredibly rewarding and supportive, they can also be complex, with rivalries, disagreements, and personality differences creating challenges. Strengthening sibling connections requires effort, understanding, and a willingness to prioritize these relationships throughout life's journey.

One of the key elements in fostering close, supportive relationships among siblings is open and honest communication. Encouraging siblings to express their thoughts, feelings, and concerns in a safe, non-judgmental environment can help build trust and understanding. By actively listening to one another and validating each other's experiences, siblings can develop a deeper appreciation for their unique perspectives and strengths.

Shared interests and experiences can also play a significant role in strengthening sibling bonds. Encouraging siblings to engage in activities they enjoy together, such as hobbies, sports, or creative pursuits, can create opportunities for bonding and positive interactions. These shared experiences can serve as a foundation for inside jokes, cherished memories, and a sense of camaraderie that can last a lifetime.

Navigating conflicts and disagreements in a constructive manner is another essential aspect of maintaining strong sibling relationships.

Teaching siblings to approach conflicts with empathy, respect, and a willingness to compromise can help prevent minor disagreements from escalating into lasting resentments. Encouraging siblings to apologize, forgive, and learn from their mistakes can foster resilience and strengthen their ability to weather challenges together.

As siblings grow older and their lives take different paths, it is crucial to make an effort to stay connected and involved in each other's lives. Regular check-ins, whether through phone calls, video chats, or in-person visits, can help maintain the emotional connection and provide ongoing support. Celebrating each other's milestones, offering encouragement during difficult times, and being present for important moments can reinforce the significance of the sibling bond.

It is also important to recognize and respect the individual differences and needs of each sibling. While some siblings may naturally gravitate towards a close, emotionally expressive relationship, others may have a more reserved or independent nature. By honoring these differences and finding ways to connect that feel comfortable and authentic for each sibling, families can create an environment that nurtures strong, supportive sibling relationships.

Ultimately, strengthening sibling connections is an ongoing process that requires intentional effort, patience, and love. By prioritizing open communication, shared experiences, and a commitment to understanding and supporting one another, siblings can cultivate a lifelong bond that serves as a source of comfort, joy, and resilience throughout their lives.

Subsection 3.3: Cultivating Intimacy in Extended Family Relationships

Extended family relationships, including those with grandparents, aunts, uncles, and cousins, play a significant role in our lives and contribute to our sense of belonging and identity. These relationships offer unique opportunities for love, support, and the sharing of family history and traditions. Cultivating intimacy in extended family relationships requires effort, intentionality, and a genuine desire to connect with one another on a deeper level.

One of the key aspects of nurturing intimate connections with extended family members is regular communication. In today's fast-paced world, it's easy to let these relationships fall by the wayside, especially when geographical distance is a factor. Making a conscious effort to stay in touch through phone calls, video chats, or even old-fashioned letter writing can help maintain the emotional bond and keep family members informed about each other's lives. Sharing updates, stories, and experiences helps foster a sense of closeness and involvement, even when physically apart.

Another essential element in cultivating intimacy with extended family is creating shared experiences and memories. Family gatherings, such as reunions, holidays, or milestone celebrations, provide invaluable opportunities to strengthen connections and create lasting memories. Engaging in activities together, whether it's cooking a family recipe, playing games, or exploring a new place, helps build a sense of camaraderie and shared history. These experiences serve as touchstones that family members can reflect on and cherish, reinforcing the emotional bonds that tie them together.

Showing genuine interest and empathy is also crucial in nurturing intimate extended family relationships. Taking the time to listen attentively to family members' stories, challenges, and aspirations demonstrates that you value their experiences and care about their well-being. Offering support, advice, or simply a sympathetic ear during difficult times can deepen the emotional connection and foster a sense of trust and reliance. By being present and engaged, we show our extended family members that they matter to us and that we are invested in their lives.

It's important to recognize and respect the unique dynamics and histories that exist within extended family relationships. Some family members may have closer bonds than others, while some relationships may be strained due to past conflicts or misunderstandings. Approaching these relationships with sensitivity, patience, and an open heart can help bridge gaps and heal old wounds. Acknowledging and addressing past hurts, offering forgiveness, and expressing gratitude for the positive aspects of the relationship can pave the way for greater intimacy and understanding.

Cultivating intimacy in extended family relationships also involves embracing the diversity and individuality of each family member. Recognizing and celebrating the unique qualities, talents, and perspectives that each person brings to the family can foster a sense of appreciation and respect. Encouraging open-mindedness and inclusivity, especially when family members have different lifestyles, beliefs, or cultural backgrounds, helps create a safe and welcoming environment where everyone feels valued and accepted.

Ultimately, nurturing intimate connections with grandparents, aunts, uncles, and other extended family members is a lifelong process that requires ongoing effort and dedication. By prioritizing communication, creating shared experiences, showing empathy and interest, and embracing the unique qualities of each family member, we can cultivate deep, meaningful relationships that span generations and enrich our lives in countless ways. These intimate extended family bonds serve as a source of love, support, and belonging, reminding us of the importance of family and the enduring power of connection.

Summary: Nurturing the Bonds That Shape Our Lives

Building strong and intimate family connections is a lifelong journey that requires dedication, empathy, and a willingness to grow alongside our loved ones. By nurturing the bonds we share with our parents, siblings, and extended family members, we create a solid foundation of love, trust, and support that can withstand the challenges and changes life inevitably brings.

Throughout this section, we have explored the various strategies and approaches to fostering intimacy and connection within our family relationships. From the tender, nurturing bond between parents and children to the complex, yet deeply rewarding relationships between siblings and the rich tapestry of extended family connections, each of these relationships plays a unique and significant role in shaping our lives and our sense of belonging.

By prioritizing open communication, shared experiences, and a commitment to understanding and supporting one another, we can cultivate family bonds that are resilient, adaptable, and deeply fulfilling. Whether it's through heartfelt conversations, cherished traditions, or the simple act of being present and engaged in each other's lives, the effort we put into nurturing our family relationships pays dividends that extend far beyond the present moment.

As we navigate the joys and challenges of family life, it is essential to remember that building strong and intimate family connections is not about perfection, but rather about the willingness to show up, to listen, and to love unconditionally. By approaching our relationships with patience, empathy, and an open heart, we create a family environment that fosters growth, healing, and a deep sense of belonging.

So let us cherish the bonds we share with our family members, recognizing the profound impact they have on our lives and the lives of those around us. By nurturing these connections with intentionality, love, and a commitment to growth, we create a legacy of love and support that will endure for generations to come, serving as a source of strength, comfort, and joy throughout our lives.

Section 4: Deepening Intimacy in Friendships

Friendship is one of life's most precious gifts, offering us a source of support, joy, and connection. While we often focus on romantic relationships when discussing intimacy, the bonds we share with our friends are equally important and deserving of nurturing. In this section, we will explore the art of cultivating intimacy in platonic friendships, delving into the strategies and practices that can help us create deeper, more meaningful connections with the people who enrich our lives.

Intimacy in friendships goes beyond surface-level interactions and casual acquaintances. It involves a level of trust, vulnerability, and emotional closeness that allows us to share our innermost thoughts, feelings, and experiences with those we hold dear. By fostering intimacy in our friendships, we create a safe space where we can be our authentic selves, find understanding and acceptance, and navigate life's challenges and triumphs together.

Throughout this section, we will examine the building blocks of intimate friendships, such as establishing trust, practicing open and honest communication, and creating shared experiences that strengthen our bonds. We will also explore the challenges that can arise in friendships, such as navigating conflicts, maintaining connections through life transitions, and balancing intimacy with personal boundaries.

By the end of this section, you will have a deeper understanding of the value and importance of intimate friendships, as well as practical tools and strategies for nurturing these precious relationships. Whether you are seeking to deepen existing friendships or build new ones, the insights and advice in this section will guide you on a journey of connection, growth, and cherished memories. So, let us embark on this exploration of the beautiful world of intimate friendships, and discover the transformative power of these special bonds.

Subsection 4.1: Building Trust and Emotional Safety in Friendships

Trust and emotional safety form the bedrock of any intimate friendship. Without these essential elements, it becomes challenging to foster the vulnerability and openness necessary for deep, meaningful connections. Building trust and creating an emotionally safe environment requires intentional effort and a commitment to nurturing the friendship over time.

One of the key ways to establish trust in a friendship is through consistent reliability and dependability. When we follow through on our commitments, show up for our friends during both good times and bad, and maintain confidentiality when entrusted with sensitive information, we demonstrate our trustworthiness. This reliability helps our friends feel secure in the knowledge that we will be there for them, no matter what.

Open and honest communication is another crucial aspect of building trust and emotional safety. By expressing our thoughts, feelings, and needs clearly and directly, we create a foundation of transparency that allows for genuine understanding and connection. Encouraging our friends to do the same, and actively listening without judgment, fosters an atmosphere of acceptance and validation.

Vulnerability is often the key that unlocks the door to intimate friendships. When we have the courage to share our fears, insecurities, and dreams with our friends, we invite them to do the same. This mutual vulnerability creates a bond of trust and understanding that deepens over time. It is essential to honor and respect the vulnerability of our friends, treating their shared experiences with care and compassion.

Creating an emotionally safe environment also involves setting and respecting boundaries. By communicating our own boundaries clearly and respecting those of our friends, we establish a sense of mutual trust and understanding. This includes being mindful of each other's emotional triggers, respecting privacy, and knowing when to give space or offer support.

Cultivating empathy and practicing forgiveness are also essential in building trust and emotional safety. When conflicts or misunderstandings arise, approaching the situation with empathy and a willingness to understand our friend's perspective can help maintain trust. Forgiveness, when warranted, demonstrates our commitment to the friendship and our ability to work through challenges together.

Ultimately, building trust and emotional safety in friendships is an ongoing process that requires patience, effort, and genuine care. By consistently showing up for our friends, communicating openly and honestly, honoring vulnerability, respecting boundaries, and practicing empathy and forgiveness, we create the foundation for intimate, lasting friendships that weather the tests of time and life's ups and downs.

Subsection 4.2: Nurturing Meaningful Connections Through Shared Interests and Experiences

Shared interests and experiences have the power to transform casual friendships into deep, meaningful connections that stand the test of time. When we engage in activities that we both enjoy, we create a common ground that fosters a sense of unity and understanding. These shared experiences provide a foundation for building trust, creating lasting memories, and strengthening the bonds of friendship.

One of the most effective ways to nurture meaningful connections through shared interests is to actively seek out opportunities to explore and engage in hobbies and activities together. This could involve joining a sports team, attending a cooking class, or participating in a book club. By dedicating time and effort to pursue common passions, friends create a space where they can connect on a deeper level, share their thoughts and feelings, and support each other's growth and development.

Engaging in shared experiences also provides a platform for friends to challenge themselves, step out of their comfort zones, and discover new aspects of their personalities. Whether it's embarking on a hiking adventure, learning a new skill, or volunteering for a cause they both believe in, these experiences offer opportunities for friends to witness each other's strengths, vulnerabilities, and personal growth. Through these shared challenges and triumphs, friends forge a deeper understanding and appreciation for one another, strengthening the foundation of their relationship.

Meaningful connections can also be nurtured through the simple act of sharing and celebrating life's milestones and special moments together. Attending weddings, graduations, or birthdays, and being there to support each other during both joyous and difficult times, creates a sense of shared history and emotional investment in the friendship. These shared experiences become the threads that weave the tapestry of a rich, intimate friendship, filled with cherished memories and a deep sense of connection.

In today's fast-paced, digital world, it's easy to fall into the trap of maintaining friendships solely through social media or virtual interactions. While these platforms have their place, it's crucial to prioritize face-to-face interactions and shared experiences to truly nurture meaningful connections. Making the effort to regularly spend quality time together, whether it's through a weekly coffee date, a monthly movie night, or an annual weekend getaway, demonstrates a commitment to the friendship and creates opportunities for deeper bonding and conversation.

Nurturing meaningful connections through shared interests and experiences requires intentionality, effort, and a willingness to invest time and energy into the friendship. It involves actively seeking out opportunities to create shared memories, being present and engaged during these experiences, and reflecting on the lessons learned and bonds formed. By prioritizing these shared moments and making them a regular part of the friendship, friends can cultivate a deep, lasting connection that enriches their lives and provides a source of joy, support, and personal growth.

Subsection 4.3: Navigating Challenges and Changes in Intimate Friendships

Intimate friendships, like all relationships, are not immune to the challenges and changes that life inevitably brings. As we navigate the ebbs and flows of our personal journeys, our friendships may encounter obstacles, conflicts, and transformations that test the strength and resilience of our bonds. In this subsection, we will explore strategies for maintaining intimacy and connection in friendships during these trying times, offering guidance on how to weather the storms and emerge with even stronger, more meaningful relationships.

One of the most common challenges that intimate friendships face is the impact of major life transitions. Whether it's a cross-country move, a career change, the birth of a child, or a significant shift in personal circumstances, these transitions can strain even the most solid friendships. The key to maintaining intimacy during these times is open, honest communication and a willingness to adapt. By sharing our experiences, fears, and hopes with our friends, we create a space for mutual understanding and support. It's essential to be patient and empathetic with each other, recognizing that life transitions often require time and energy to navigate.

Conflict is another inevitable aspect of intimate friendships. While disagreements and misunderstandings can be uncomfortable, they also present opportunities for growth and deepening connection. When conflicts arise, it's crucial to approach them with a spirit of compassion, respect, and a genuine desire to understand each other's perspectives. Active listening, taking responsibility for our own actions, and being open to compromise are all essential skills for navigating conflicts in a healthy, constructive manner. By working through challenges together, friends can strengthen their bond and develop a deeper appreciation for each other's unique qualities and needs.

As friendships evolve over time, it's natural for the dynamics and circumstances to shift. Friends may develop new interests, form romantic partnerships, or experience personal growth that leads them in different directions. While these changes can be unsettling, they don't necessarily spell the end of an intimate friendship. The key is to remain open, flexible, and supportive of each other's individual journeys. By celebrating each other's successes, offering encouragement during struggles, and finding new ways to connect and share experiences, friends can maintain intimacy and relevance in each other's lives, even as their paths diverge.

Maintaining intimacy in friendships during challenging times also requires a commitment to self-awareness and personal growth. By taking responsibility for our own emotional well-being, setting healthy boundaries, and practicing self-care, we become better equipped to show up fully and authentically in our friendships. When we approach challenges and changes with resilience, self-compassion, and a growth mindset, we inspire our friends to do the same, fostering an environment of mutual support and empowerment.

Ultimately, navigating challenges and changes in intimate friendships is a testament to the power of vulnerability, trust, and unconditional love. By embracing the ups and downs, communicating openly and honestly, and remaining committed to each other's growth and well-being, friends can weather any storm and emerge with a deeper, more unbreakable bond. In the face of life's uncertainties, the strength and resilience of intimate friendships serve as a reminder of the immeasurable value of these precious connections, and the incredible capacity we have to support, inspire, and uplift one another through even the most trying of times.

Summary: Nurturing the Bonds of Friendship

Throughout this section, we have explored the beautiful world of intimate friendships and the strategies for cultivating deep, meaningful connections with the people who enrich our lives. We have seen how trust, vulnerability, and emotional safety form the bedrock of these special bonds, and how open communication, shared experiences, and mutual support can help us navigate the challenges and changes that life inevitably brings.

As we reflect on the insights and advice covered in this section, let us remember that nurturing intimate friendships is an ongoing journey that requires effort, patience, and a willingness to invest in the relationships that matter most to us. By consistently showing up for our friends, honoring their vulnerabilities, and celebrating their successes, we create a foundation of love, trust, and understanding that can weather any storm.

Whether you are seeking to deepen existing friendships or build new ones, the strategies and practices outlined in this section can serve as a guide and inspiration on your path to more fulfilling, intimate connections. By embracing vulnerability, practicing empathy, and maintaining a commitment to personal growth, you can cultivate friendships that not only enrich your life but also help you become the best version of yourself.

As we move forward, let us carry the lessons of this section with us, and approach our friendships with an open heart, a compassionate spirit, and a deep appreciation for the transformative power of these precious bonds. In a world that can often feel uncertain and challenging, the strength, resilience, and joy we find in our intimate friendships serve as a reminder of the incredible capacity we have to support, inspire, and uplift one another. So, let us cherish these connections, nurture them with care, and watch as they blossom into a beautiful tapestry of love, laughter, and shared memories that will last a lifetime.

Section 5: Overcoming Barriers to Intimacy

Intimacy is the foundation of any strong, healthy relationship, yet many people struggle to cultivate and maintain it. Fear, past traumas, and personal insecurities can create seemingly insurmountable obstacles on the path to deep, meaningful connections. However, with self-awareness, compassion, and a willingness to grow, it is possible to break down these barriers and experience the transformative power of true intimacy.

In this section, we will explore some of the most common obstacles that hinder intimacy and provide practical strategies for overcoming them. We will delve into the roots of fear and vulnerability, examining how past experiences and societal conditioning can make it difficult to open up and trust others. Through relatable examples and expert insights, we will offer guidance on how to gradually dismantle these fears and cultivate the courage to be authentically yourself in your relationships.

We will also address the impact of past relationship traumas and betrayals, acknowledging the pain and challenges they can create in future connections. With empathy and understanding, we will provide tools and techniques for healing these wounds and developing the resilience needed to love again. You will learn how to set healthy boundaries, communicate your needs, and create an environment of emotional safety in your relationships.

Furthermore, we will explore the delicate balance between intimacy and autonomy, recognizing that true closeness requires a strong sense of self. You will discover strategies for maintaining your individuality while fostering deep, meaningful connections with others. By the end of this section, you will be equipped with the knowledge and skills needed to break through the barriers holding you back from the intimacy you desire and deserve.

Remember, overcoming obstacles to intimacy is a journey, not a destination. With patience, self-compassion, and a commitment to personal growth, you can cultivate the kind of authentic, fulfilling relationships that nourish your soul and enrich your life. Let us embark on this transformative path together, one step at a time.

Subsection 5.1: Addressing Fear of Intimacy and Vulnerability

Fear of intimacy and vulnerability is a common barrier that prevents many individuals from forming deep, meaningful connections with others. This fear often stems from past experiences, such as childhood trauma, emotional neglect, or painful relationships, which can leave lasting scars and make it difficult to trust and open up to others. Additionally, societal pressures and cultural norms that emphasize independence and self-sufficiency can further reinforce the belief that vulnerability is a weakness to be avoided.

However, it is crucial to recognize that vulnerability is not a weakness, but rather a strength that allows us to connect with others on a profound level. When we have the courage to be authentic and share our true selves, we create opportunities for genuine intimacy and understanding. By gradually confronting and overcoming our fears, we can cultivate the kind of deep, fulfilling relationships that we all crave.

One effective technique for addressing fear of intimacy is to start small and take incremental steps towards vulnerability. This might involve sharing a personal story with a trusted friend, expressing a genuine emotion, or asking for help when needed. As we practice these small acts of vulnerability and receive positive responses from others, we begin to build trust in ourselves and in the process of opening up.

Another key strategy is to work on developing a strong sense of self-worth and self-compassion. When we have a healthy relationship with ourselves, we are less likely to fear rejection or abandonment from others. We can cultivate self-compassion by treating ourselves with kindness, understanding, and forgiveness, just as we would a dear friend. This inner foundation of self-love and acceptance can provide the stability and resilience needed to navigate the challenges of intimacy.

In addition to these personal strategies, seeking the guidance of a skilled therapist or counselor can be incredibly beneficial in addressing deep-seated fears of intimacy. A professional can help us explore the roots of our fears, develop healthy coping mechanisms, and build the skills needed to form secure, intimate attachments.

Ultimately, overcoming fear of intimacy and vulnerability is a process that requires patience, self-awareness, and a willingness to step outside of our comfort zones. By embracing the discomfort and uncertainty that comes with opening up to others, we create space for the kind of authentic, nurturing connections that can transform our lives. With practice and perseverance, we can gradually dismantle the barriers that hold us back and experience the joy and fulfillment of true intimacy.

Subsection 5.2: Healing from Past Relationship Traumas and Betrayals

The wounds of past relationship traumas and betrayals can run deep, leaving scars that may feel impossible to heal. These painful experiences can shape our beliefs about love, trust, and intimacy, making it difficult to open our hearts to new connections. However, with self-compassion, patience, and a willingness to confront the hurt, it is possible to break free from the shadows of the past and cultivate the capacity for healthy, fulfilling relationships.

One of the first steps in healing from relationship traumas is to acknowledge and validate your pain. It is essential to recognize that your feelings are valid and that you have every right to grieve the loss of trust and security you experienced. By giving yourself permission to feel and express your emotions, you create space for processing and releasing the hurt, rather than allowing it to fester and control your life.

As you navigate the healing process, it can be helpful to seek the support of a skilled therapist or counselor who specializes in relationship issues. A professional can provide a safe, non-judgmental space for you to explore your experiences, identify unhealthy patterns, and develop coping strategies. They can also help you challenge negative beliefs about yourself and relationships that may have taken root as a result of your past traumas.

In addition to seeking professional support, cultivating self-compassion is a powerful tool for healing. Treat yourself with the same kindness, understanding, and forgiveness that you would extend to a beloved friend who has been through a difficult experience. Recognize that your worth and lovability are not diminished by the actions of others, and that you deserve to be treated with respect and care.

As you work through your past wounds, it is also important to set healthy boundaries in your current and future relationships. Learn to communicate your needs clearly and assertively, and be willing to walk away from situations or people that compromise your emotional well-being. By honoring your own boundaries and values, you send a message to yourself and others that you are worthy of love and respect.

Rebuilding trust after betrayal can be a gradual process, but it is possible with patience and intentionality. Start by taking small risks in your relationships, such as sharing a vulnerable thought or feeling with a trusted friend. As you experience positive, supportive responses, you can begin to challenge your fears and gradually open yourself up to deeper levels of intimacy.

It is also crucial to practice forgiveness, both for others and for yourself. Forgiveness does not mean condoning hurtful actions or forgetting the pain you experienced. Rather, it is a conscious choice to release the burden of resentment and anger, allowing yourself to move forward with greater peace and freedom. Remember that forgiveness is a gift you give yourself, not a pardon for the offender.

Ultimately, healing from past relationship traumas and betrayals is a journey of self-discovery and growth. By confronting your wounds, developing self-compassion, setting healthy boundaries, and gradually rebuilding trust, you can reclaim your capacity for intimacy and create the kind of loving, supportive relationships you deserve. Remember that healing is not a linear process, and there may be setbacks and challenges along the way. However, with perseverance and a commitment to your own well-being, you can emerge from the shadows of your past, stronger, wiser, and more open to the possibilities of love.

Subsection 5.3: Balancing Intimacy and Autonomy in Relationships

In the pursuit of deep, meaningful connections, it is easy to lose sight of the importance of maintaining a strong sense of self. Many people believe that intimacy requires sacrificing their individuality, but in reality, the healthiest relationships are those that strike a delicate balance between closeness and autonomy. When we nurture our own identities and interests while also cultivating intimate bonds, we create a solid foundation for lasting, fulfilling partnerships.

Autonomy, or the ability to make decisions and take actions independently, is a crucial component of personal growth and self-actualization. It allows us to explore our passions, set boundaries, and develop a robust sense of self-worth. In the context of relationships, autonomy enables us to maintain our individuality while still being emotionally connected to our partners. When we have a strong sense of self, we are better equipped to communicate our needs, set healthy boundaries, and engage in mutual respect and understanding.

However, balancing intimacy and autonomy is not always easy. It requires ongoing communication, self-awareness, and a willingness to navigate the complexities of human connection. One effective strategy for achieving this balance is to prioritize open, honest dialogue with your partner. Regularly discuss your individual needs, desires, and boundaries, and work together to find ways to honor both your connection and your autonomy. This might involve setting aside dedicated time for personal pursuits, while also making a conscious effort to nurture your intimate bond through shared experiences and emotional vulnerability.

Another key aspect of balancing intimacy and autonomy is learning to support your partner's individuality without feeling threatened by it. Encourage each other to pursue personal goals, maintain friendships outside of the relationship, and engage in activities that bring joy and fulfillment. When we celebrate our partner's growth and independence, we create a dynamic of mutual respect and admiration that strengthens the intimate connection between us.

It is also important to recognize that the balance between intimacy and autonomy may shift over time as the relationship evolves and life circumstances change. What works in the early stages of a partnership may need to be renegotiated as you navigate new challenges, such as parenthood, career transitions, or health issues. By remaining open, flexible, and committed to ongoing communication, you can continually adapt and find new ways to honor both your connection and your individuality.

Ultimately, balancing intimacy and autonomy is about creating a relationship that allows both partners to thrive as individuals while also building a deep, unbreakable bond. It requires trust, respect, and a willingness to embrace the inherent tensions that arise when two unique souls come together. By nurturing your own sense of self while also cultivating a profound connection with your partner, you can experience the transformative power of love without losing yourself in the process. With patience, self-awareness, and a commitment to growth, you can create a relationship that honors both the "me" and the "we," and stand the test of time.

Summary: Embracing the Journey of Overcoming Barriers to Intimacy

Throughout this section, we have explored the common obstacles that hinder intimacy in relationships, from fear of vulnerability to the lingering impact of past traumas and the challenge of balancing closeness with autonomy. By examining these barriers with honesty, compassion, and a willingness to grow, we have discovered that overcoming them is not only possible but also essential for cultivating the deep, meaningful connections we all crave.

The journey of overcoming barriers to intimacy is one of self-discovery and transformation. It requires us to confront our deepest fears, heal our most painful wounds, and embrace the discomfort of change. Along the way, we may stumble, fall, and question our progress, but it is through these challenges that we develop the resilience, self-awareness, and emotional intelligence necessary to build authentic, lasting relationships.

As we have learned, the key to overcoming these barriers lies in developing a strong sense of self-worth, setting healthy boundaries, and cultivating open, honest communication with our partners. By treating ourselves with kindness and respect, we create a solid foundation for intimacy that is grounded in self-love and self-acceptance. And by expressing our needs, desires, and vulnerabilities with clarity and compassion, we invite our partners to meet us in a space of mutual understanding and support.

Ultimately, the journey of overcoming barriers to intimacy is one that we must walk with patience, perseverance, and an open heart. It is a journey that requires us to let go of our past hurts, embrace our present selves, and trust in the possibilities of the future. And while the path may be difficult at times, the rewards – the joy, connection, and love that await us on the other side – are truly immeasurable.

As you reflect on the insights and strategies shared in this section, remember that you are not alone in your struggles, and that every step you take towards greater intimacy is a step towards a more fulfilling, authentic life. With courage, compassion, and a commitment to growth, you have the power to break free from the barriers that hold you back and create the kind of deep, nurturing relationships your heart longs for. So take a deep breath, trust in your own strength, and embrace the journey ahead – for it is through the challenges that we find the greatest rewards.

Chapter Summary: Cultivating Intimacy for Stronger Bonds

Throughout this chapter, we have explored the various facets of intimacy and the ways in which it can be nurtured and strengthened in romantic relationships, friendships, and family bonds. By understanding the foundations of intimacy, such as trust, vulnerability, and self-awareness, we can create a solid base upon which to build deeper connections with those we care about.

In romantic relationships, prioritizing quality time, enhancing emotional and physical intimacy, and maintaining closeness through life's transitions and challenges are key to fostering a strong and lasting bond. Family relationships can be strengthened by nurturing parent-child intimacy, fostering sibling connections, and cultivating closeness with extended family members. Friendships, too, can be deepened through building trust, sharing meaningful experiences, and navigating the ups and downs of life together.

However, we must also acknowledge and address the barriers that can hinder intimacy, such as fear of vulnerability, past relationship traumas, and the delicate balance between intimacy and autonomy. By working through these challenges with empathy, understanding, and a willingness to grow, we can create a safe and supportive environment that allows intimacy to thrive.

Ultimately, nurturing intimacy is an ongoing process that requires effort, patience, and a deep commitment to the relationships that matter most to us. By embracing the strategies and insights shared in this chapter, we can cultivate the intimacy and closeness that will enrich our lives and strengthen the bonds we share with others. As we continue on this journey of love, connection, and personal growth, let us cherish the intimate moments and the profound impact they have on our happiness and well-being.

Chapter 10: Overcoming Relationship Challenges

Relationships, like any other aspect of life, are not always smooth sailing. Even the strongest and most loving partnerships can encounter obstacles and challenges that put their bond to the test. These challenges can range from trust issues and jealousy to the feeling of growing apart and losing the spark that once brought you together.

When faced with such difficulties, it's essential to remember that every relationship goes through ups and downs. What matters most is how you and your partner navigate these challenges together. By approaching these issues with open communication, empathy, and a willingness to work through them as a team, you can not only overcome the obstacles but also strengthen your relationship in the process.

In this chapter, we will delve into some of the most common relationship challenges and explore practical strategies for overcoming them. We'll discuss the importance of building and maintaining trust, managing jealousy and insecurity, and rekindling the connection when you feel like you're growing apart.

Through a combination of real-life examples, research-backed insights, and actionable advice, you'll gain the tools and knowledge needed to face these challenges head-on and emerge with a stronger, more resilient relationship. Whether you're currently facing a specific issue or simply looking to fortify your bond against future challenges, this chapter will provide you with the guidance and support you need to overcome any obstacle and build a lasting, fulfilling partnership.

So, let's dive in and explore how you can navigate the ups and downs of your relationship with grace, compassion, and a deep commitment to growing together.

Section 1: Identifying and Addressing Trust

Issues

Trust forms the bedrock of any healthy relationship, be it romantic, familial, or platonic. When trust is present, it fosters a sense of security, comfort, and intimacy that allows the relationship to thrive. However, trust is a fragile entity that can be easily shattered by various factors, such as dishonesty, betrayal, or inconsistency in words and actions. Once trust is broken, it can be challenging to rebuild, leading to a host of emotional and interpersonal difficulties.

In this section, we will delve into the complex world of trust issues in relationships. We will explore the common signs and symptoms of broken trust, such as increased suspicion, emotional distance, and communication breakdowns. By understanding these indicators, you can better identify when trust has been compromised in your own relationships and take steps to address the issue head-on.

Rebuilding trust is a gradual process that requires patience, commitment, and a willingness to confront uncomfortable truths. We will provide you with practical strategies and tools to help you navigate this challenging journey. From learning how to communicate effectively about trust concerns to demonstrating consistency and reliability in your actions, you will gain valuable insights into the process of restoring trust and fostering a renewed sense of security in your relationships.

Throughout this section, we will also highlight the importance of self-reflection and personal growth in the trust-building process. By examining your own behaviors, attitudes, and patterns, you can identify areas where you may be contributing to trust issues and take proactive steps to make positive changes.

Whether you are currently dealing with trust issues in your relationships or seeking to prevent them from arising in the future, this section will provide you with the knowledge, skills, and support you need to cultivate strong, trusting bonds with the people who matter most to you. So, let's embark on this transformative journey together and unlock the power of trust in your relationships.

Subsection 1.1: Recognizing Signs of Broken Trust

Trust is the foundation upon which all healthy relationships are built. It is the confidence that your partner, friend, or family member will act in your best interest, be honest with you, and keep their promises. However, when trust is broken, it can lead to a range of emotional and behavioral changes that can erode the very fabric of the relationship.

One of the most common signs of broken trust is dishonesty. When someone lies to you, whether it's a small white lie or a significant deception, it can cause you to question their integrity and wonder what else they might be hiding. Dishonesty can manifest in various forms, such as lying about whereabouts, finances, or personal history. It can also involve lying by omission, where someone deliberately withholds important information that they know would upset or concern you.

Another indicator of broken trust is secretiveness. When someone becomes evasive or defensive when asked simple questions, or when they start hiding their phone, email, or social media accounts, it can be a sign that they have something to hide. Secretiveness can also involve making plans without informing you or failing to share important details about their life or activities.

Inconsistent behavior is another red flag that trust has been compromised. When someone's actions don't align with their words, or when they make promises they don't keep, it can cause you to doubt their reliability and commitment to the relationship. Inconsistent behavior can also involve sudden changes in attitude or demeanor, such as becoming distant, irritable, or dismissive without explanation.

Other signs of broken trust may include a lack of accountability, blaming others for their mistakes, or refusing to apologize or make amends when they have done something wrong. They may also become defensive or angry when confronted about their behavior, rather than being open to honest communication and problem-solving.

It's important to remember that these signs of broken trust can occur in any type of relationship, whether it's with a romantic partner, a friend, or a family member. By being aware of these indicators and addressing them early on, you can take steps to rebuild trust and prevent further damage to the relationship. In the following subsections, we will explore strategies for communicating effectively about trust concerns and rebuilding trust through consistent actions and transparency.

Subsection 1.2: Communicating Effectively About Trust Concerns

When trust issues arise in a relationship, it can be challenging to know how to approach the subject with your partner, friend, or family member. The fear of confrontation, rejection, or further damaging the relationship may cause you to avoid the conversation altogether. However, addressing trust concerns in a timely and constructive manner is crucial for the health and longevity of the relationship.

The first step in communicating effectively about trust issues is to choose the right time and place for the conversation. Avoid bringing up the topic during heated arguments or when emotions are running high. Instead, set aside a specific time to discuss your concerns in a calm, private setting where both parties feel comfortable and free from distractions.

Before initiating the conversation, take some time to reflect on your feelings and the specific incidents or behaviors that have led to your trust concerns. Identify concrete examples that illustrate your points and consider how these issues have impacted you and the relationship. By having a clear understanding of your own thoughts and emotions, you'll be better equipped to express yourself in a clear and concise manner.

When expressing your trust concerns, it's essential to use "I" statements that focus on your own feelings and experiences, rather than making accusations or placing blame. For example, instead of saying, "You always lie to me," try saying, "I feel hurt and confused when I discover that you haven't been completely honest with me." This approach helps to minimize defensiveness and creates a more open, non-confrontational dialogue.

Active listening is another crucial component of effective communication when addressing trust issues. Give your partner the opportunity to express their thoughts and feelings without interruption, and make an effort to understand their perspective. Ask clarifying questions and reflect on what they've said to ensure that you've understood their point of view. By demonstrating genuine interest and empathy, you create a safe space for honest, productive dialogue.

As you work through trust concerns together, focus on finding solutions and rebuilding trust, rather than dwelling on past mistakes or assigning blame. Brainstorm concrete actions that both parties can take to restore trust and create a more transparent, reliable dynamic in the relationship. This may involve setting boundaries, establishing check-ins, or seeking the support of a therapist or counselor.

Remember that rebuilding trust is a gradual process that requires patience, commitment, and consistency from both parties. By approaching conversations about trust concerns with openness, empathy, and a solution-oriented mindset, you lay the foundation for a stronger, more resilient relationship built on a bedrock of mutual trust and understanding.

Subsection 1.3: Rebuilding Trust Through Consistent Actions and Transparency

Rebuilding trust in a relationship is a gradual process that requires consistent effort, patience, and commitment from both parties involved. It is not enough to simply apologize or make promises; actions must align with words to demonstrate a genuine desire to restore trust and create a more transparent, reliable dynamic in the relationship.

One of the most critical aspects of rebuilding trust is consistency. When you make a promise or commitment, it is essential to follow through and deliver on that promise consistently. This means being reliable in your actions, showing up on time, and doing what you say you will do. Consistency in behavior helps to establish a sense of predictability and stability in the relationship, which is crucial for fostering trust.

Transparency is another key component of rebuilding trust. Being open and honest about your thoughts, feelings, and actions creates a sense of safety and security in the relationship. This means being willing to share information, even when it may be difficult or uncomfortable, and being receptive to your partner's questions and concerns. Transparency also involves admitting when you have made a mistake or fallen short of your commitments and taking responsibility for your actions.

Effective communication is also essential for rebuilding trust. This involves being clear and direct in your communication, actively listening to your partner's perspective, and expressing your own thoughts and feelings in a non-defensive manner. Regular check-ins and open discussions about the state of the relationship can help to identify and address any lingering trust issues and create a more collaborative, supportive dynamic.

It is also important to be patient and understanding throughout the trust-rebuilding process. Recognize that it may take time for your partner to fully trust you again, and be willing to put in the consistent effort required to demonstrate your trustworthiness. Celebrate small victories and progress along the way, and remain committed to the process even when faced with setbacks or challenges.

In some cases, seeking the support of a therapist or counselor can be beneficial for rebuilding trust in a relationship. A trained professional can provide valuable insights, tools, and guidance for navigating the complex emotions and challenges associated with trust issues and help both partners develop the skills and strategies needed for long-term success.

Ultimately, rebuilding trust requires a willingness to be vulnerable, transparent, and consistent in your actions and communication. By demonstrating a genuine commitment to the relationship and a desire to create a more trusting, reliable dynamic, you can gradually restore a sense of safety, security, and connection with your partner, laying the foundation for a stronger, more resilient bond.

Subsection 1.4: Seeking Professional Help for Severe Trust Breaches

When trust issues in a relationship become severe and seem insurmountable, it may be necessary to seek the guidance of a qualified therapist or counselor. While many couples can work through minor trust breaches on their own, some situations require professional intervention to prevent further damage and facilitate healing.

One of the most common scenarios that may warrant professional help is infidelity. When one partner has engaged in an affair or other form of betrayal, the emotional fallout can be devastating. The betrayed partner may experience intense feelings of hurt, anger, and betrayal, while the offending partner may grapple with guilt, shame, and a desire to make amends. In such cases, a therapist can provide a safe, neutral space for both partners to express their emotions, work through the underlying issues that led to the betrayal, and develop a plan for rebuilding trust.

Another situation that may necessitate professional intervention is when trust issues stem from a history of trauma or abuse. If one or both partners have experienced physical, emotional, or sexual abuse in the past, it can have a profound impact on their ability to trust others, including their current partner. A therapist who specializes in trauma-informed care can help individuals process their past experiences, develop coping strategies, and learn how to build healthy, trusting relationships.

In some cases, severe trust breaches may be linked to underlying mental health issues, such as anxiety, depression, or personality disorders. When one partner's mental health struggles contribute to a pattern of dishonesty, instability, or emotional volatility, it can erode trust and strain the relationship. A mental health professional can provide a comprehensive assessment, develop a personalized treatment plan, and offer guidance on how to manage the impact of mental health issues on the relationship.

It is important to note that seeking professional help for trust issues is not a sign of weakness or failure. Rather, it is a proactive step towards healing, growth, and a stronger, more resilient relationship. A skilled therapist can provide valuable insights, tools, and support to help couples navigate the complex emotions and challenges associated with rebuilding trust.

When selecting a therapist or counselor, it is essential to choose someone who has experience working with couples and specializes in relationship issues. Look for a licensed professional who employs evidence-based approaches, such as Emotionally Focused Therapy (EFT) or Cognitive-Behavioral Therapy (CBT), and has a track record of success in helping couples overcome trust issues.

Ultimately, seeking professional help for severe trust breaches is a courageous and necessary step towards healing and growth. By investing in the support and guidance of a qualified therapist or counselor, couples can work through even the most challenging trust issues and emerge stronger, more connected, and better equipped to build a foundation of lasting trust and intimacy.

Summary: Nurturing Trust for Stronger, More Fulfilling Relationships

In this section, we have explored the critical role that trust plays in the health and longevity of relationships. By understanding the common signs of broken trust, such as dishonesty, secretiveness, and inconsistent behavior, we can more readily identify when trust has been compromised and take proactive steps to address the issue.

Rebuilding trust requires open, honest communication and a willingness to be vulnerable. By approaching conversations about trust concerns with empathy, active listening, and a focus on finding solutions, we create a safe space for healing and growth. Consistency in our actions and transparency in our interactions are key to demonstrating our commitment to restoring trust and fostering a more reliable, supportive relationship dynamic.

Remember, rebuilding trust is a gradual process that requires patience, understanding, and a dedication to personal growth. By consistently aligning our actions with our words and maintaining open, transparent communication, we can gradually restore a sense of security and lay the foundation for a stronger, more resilient bond.

In cases where trust has been severely breached, seeking the guidance of a qualified therapist or counselor can provide invaluable support and tools for navigating the complex emotions and challenges involved in the healing process.

As we move forward, let us embrace the power of trust in our relationships. By nurturing trust through our words, actions, and commitment to growth, we open the door to deeper intimacy, understanding, and fulfillment in all of our connections. With trust as our guide, we can build the kind of relationships that weather life's storms and stand the test of time.

Section 2: Managing Jealousy and Insecurity

Jealousy and insecurity are common emotions that can arise in even the healthiest of relationships. These feelings, if left unchecked, have the potential to erode trust, create conflict, and ultimately undermine the very foundation of a partnership. In this section, we will delve into the complex roots of jealousy and insecurity, exploring how they manifest in relationships and the impact they can have on both individuals and the bond they share.

Through a combination of research-backed insights, real-life examples, and practical advice, we will equip you with the tools and strategies needed to effectively manage these challenging emotions. By gaining a deeper understanding of the psychological and emotional factors that contribute to jealousy and insecurity, you will be better prepared to recognize and address these issues when they arise in your own relationships.

Throughout this section, we will emphasize the importance of self-awareness, open communication, and mutual trust in fostering a secure and supportive relationship dynamic. You will learn how to cultivate self-confidence, establish healthy boundaries, and create an environment where both partners feel valued, respected, and emotionally safe.

Whether you are currently struggling with jealousy and insecurity or simply seeking to build a more resilient and emotionally intelligent partnership, the insights and techniques shared in this section will provide you with a roadmap for navigating these complex emotions. By the end of this section, you will be empowered with the knowledge and skills necessary to transform jealousy and insecurity from potential roadblocks into opportunities for growth, connection, and lasting love.

Subsection 2.1: Understanding the Origins of Jealousy and Insecurity

Jealousy and insecurity are complex emotions that can have a profound impact on the dynamics of a relationship. To effectively manage these feelings, it is crucial to first understand their psychological and emotional roots. By exploring the various factors that contribute to the development of jealousy and insecurity, individuals can gain valuable insights into their own experiences and those of their partners.

One of the primary psychological factors that can give rise to jealousy and insecurity is a lack of self-esteem. When individuals struggle with low self-worth, they may be more prone to doubting their own value and questioning their partner's commitment to the relationship. This internal struggle can manifest as a constant need for reassurance, a fear of abandonment, or a tendency to interpret innocent situations as threats to the relationship.

Attachment styles, which are shaped by early childhood experiences, also play a significant role in the development of jealousy and insecurity. Individuals with anxious or insecure attachment styles may be more susceptible to these emotions, as they often struggle with a deep-seated fear of rejection and a strong desire for closeness and validation from their partners. On the other hand, those with secure attachment styles tend to have a more stable sense of self and are better equipped to manage feelings of jealousy and insecurity when they arise.

Past relationship experiences can also contribute to the emergence of jealousy and insecurity in current partnerships. Individuals who have experienced infidelity, betrayal, or abandonment in previous relationships may carry emotional baggage that makes them more vulnerable to these feelings. The pain and trauma of past hurts can create a heightened sensitivity to perceived threats, leading to a cycle of doubt and mistrust in new relationships.

In some cases, jealousy and insecurity may be fueled by external factors, such as societal pressures or cultural expectations. The constant bombardment of idealized images of relationships in media and social networks can create unrealistic standards and comparisons that feed into feelings of inadequacy and insecurity. Additionally, certain cultural norms or gender roles may contribute to the development of jealousy, such as the belief that possessiveness is a sign of love or that one partner should have control over the other's social interactions.

It is important to recognize that while jealousy and insecurity are often rooted in deeply ingrained psychological and emotional patterns, they are not unchangeable. By developing a greater understanding of the origins of these feelings, individuals can begin to challenge and reframe their thoughts, beliefs, and behaviors. Through self-reflection, open communication with partners, and a commitment to personal growth, it is possible to break free from the grip of jealousy and insecurity and cultivate healthier, more trusting relationships.

Subsection 2.2: Developing Self-Awareness and Self-Confidence

Cultivating self-awareness and self-confidence is a crucial step in managing jealousy and insecurity in relationships. When individuals have a strong sense of self and a healthy level of self-esteem, they are better equipped to navigate the challenges and uncertainties that can arise in intimate partnerships.

Self-awareness involves developing a deep understanding of one's own thoughts, feelings, and behaviors. By engaging in introspection and self-reflection, individuals can gain valuable insights into the underlying beliefs and experiences that contribute to their feelings of jealousy and insecurity. This process may involve exploring past relationships, childhood experiences, and personal insecurities that have shaped their emotional landscape.

One effective strategy for building self-awareness is mindfulness meditation. By practicing mindfulness, individuals can learn to observe their thoughts and emotions without judgment, gaining a clearer perspective on the patterns and triggers that fuel their jealousy and insecurity. Regular meditation can also help cultivate a sense of inner calm and emotional resilience, reducing the intensity and frequency of negative emotions.

Journaling is another powerful tool for developing self-awareness. By writing down their thoughts, feelings, and experiences, individuals can gain a deeper understanding of their emotional world and identify the root causes of their jealousy and insecurity. This practice can also serve as a means of self-expression and emotional release, helping to reduce the burden of pent-up feelings and promote a greater sense of clarity and self-understanding.

In addition to self-awareness, building self-confidence is essential for managing jealousy and insecurity in relationships. Self-confidence refers to a strong belief in one's own abilities, worth, and value as an individual. When people have a healthy level of self-confidence, they are less likely to feel threatened by their partner's independence or success, and more likely to trust in the strength and resilience of their relationship.

One key strategy for building self-confidence is to focus on personal growth and self-improvement. By setting and pursuing meaningful goals, individuals can develop a sense of purpose and accomplishment that boosts their self-esteem and self-worth. This may involve pursuing educational or career aspirations, engaging in creative hobbies or passions, or working on personal development through therapy or self-help resources.

Another important aspect of building self-confidence is learning to practice self-compassion. Many people who struggle with jealousy and insecurity are often their own harshest critics, holding themselves to unrealistic standards of perfection and beating themselves up for perceived failings or shortcomings. By learning to treat oneself with kindness, understanding, and forgiveness, individuals can develop a more balanced and accepting relationship with themselves, reducing the impact of negative self-talk and self-doubt.

Ultimately, developing self-awareness and self-confidence is an ongoing process that requires patience, commitment, and a willingness to confront one's own fears and insecurities. By investing in personal growth and self-discovery, individuals can cultivate a stronger, more resilient sense of self that allows them to navigate the challenges of relationships with greater ease and confidence. Through this process, they can learn to trust in their own worth and value, and build partnerships based on mutual respect, trust, and emotional security.

Subsection 2.3: Establishing Trust and Open Communication

Trust and open communication are the cornerstones of a secure and supportive relationship dynamic. When partners feel safe to express their thoughts, feelings, and vulnerabilities without fear of judgment or rejection, they create an environment that fosters emotional intimacy and connection. Establishing trust and open communication requires a conscious effort from both individuals, as well as a commitment to honesty, transparency, and active listening.

At the heart of trust lies the belief that one's partner has their best interests in mind and will act in ways that prioritize the well-being of the relationship. This belief is built over time through consistent actions, reliability, and follow-through on commitments. When partners demonstrate that they are true to their word and can be counted on to support each other through both good times and bad, they lay the foundation for a deep and abiding sense of trust.

Open communication, in turn, is essential for maintaining trust and preventing misunderstandings that can erode the bond between partners. When individuals feel safe to express their thoughts and feelings openly, they create opportunities for growth, problem-solving, and deeper understanding. This requires a willingness to be vulnerable, to share one's fears, insecurities, and dreams without fear of rejection or criticism.

Active listening is a crucial component of open communication. When partners truly listen to each other, they demonstrate respect, empathy, and a genuine desire to understand each other's perspectives. This involves not only hearing the words being spoken but also paying attention to nonverbal cues, such as tone of voice, facial expressions, and body language. By creating a safe and non-judgmental space for open communication, partners can work together to navigate challenges, resolve conflicts, and strengthen their bond.

Establishing trust and open communication is particularly important when dealing with jealousy and insecurity in relationships. When individuals feel secure in their partner's love and commitment, they are less likely to interpret innocent situations as threats or to react with possessiveness or suspicion. By openly discussing their fears and insecurities, partners can work together to find ways to reassure each other and build a stronger, more resilient bond.

It is important to note that building trust and open communication is an ongoing process that requires continued effort and attention. Even in the strongest of relationships, there may be moments of doubt, misunderstanding, or conflict. The key is to approach these challenges with a spirit of empathy, patience, and a willingness to work together towards a resolution.

Ultimately, establishing trust and open communication creates a solid foundation for a healthy, secure, and emotionally intimate relationship. By prioritizing honesty, transparency, and active listening, partners can create a safe haven in which they can be their true selves, share their deepest hopes and fears, and face life's challenges hand in hand. Through this process, they can build a love that is resilient, enduring, and deeply satisfying.

Subsection 2.4: Setting Healthy Boundaries and Expectations

Establishing clear, reasonable boundaries and expectations is a critical step in minimizing jealousy and insecurity in relationships. When partners have a shared understanding of what is and is not acceptable within the context of their partnership, they create a sense of safety, trust, and mutual respect that forms the foundation for a healthy, secure relationship.

Boundaries are the personal limits we set to protect our physical, emotional, and mental well-being. In a relationship, boundaries help define where one partner's needs and desires end and the other's begin.

They serve as a guide for navigating the complex landscape of intimacy, ensuring that both individuals feel respected, valued, and heard.

When setting boundaries, it is essential to be clear, specific, and consistent. This may involve openly discussing one's comfort levels with various aspects of the relationship, such as personal space, time spent together or apart, communication styles, and physical intimacy. By clearly articulating these boundaries, partners can avoid misunderstandings and prevent unintentional violations that can fuel feelings of jealousy or insecurity.

Expectations, on the other hand, refer to the standards and assumptions we hold about how our partners should behave and how the relationship should function. These expectations are often shaped by our individual experiences, beliefs, and values, as well as societal norms and cultural influences.

In order to minimize jealousy and insecurity, it is crucial that partners openly discuss and align their expectations for the relationship. This may involve exploring topics such as fidelity, honesty, communication, and emotional support. By ensuring that both individuals are on the same page about what they want and need from the partnership, couples can reduce the likelihood of disappointment, resentment, and mistrust.

It is important to recognize that setting boundaries and expectations is not a one-time event, but rather an ongoing process that requires regular communication and adjustment. As individuals grow and change over time, so too may their needs and desires within the relationship. By fostering an environment of open dialogue and flexibility, partners can continually adapt and refine their boundaries and expectations to maintain a strong, healthy bond.

When boundaries and expectations are clearly established and consistently respected, partners create a sense of predictability and security within the relationship. This, in turn, reduces the likelihood of jealousy and insecurity taking root, as both individuals feel confident in their understanding of what is and is not acceptable within the partnership.

However, it is equally important to ensure that the boundaries and expectations set are reasonable and healthy. Overly rigid or controlling boundaries, or unrealistic expectations, can be just as damaging to a relationship as a lack of boundaries altogether. Partners must strike a balance between protecting their individual needs and desires and being open to compromise and flexibility in service of the relationship as a whole.

Ultimately, setting healthy boundaries and expectations is about creating a relationship dynamic built on trust, respect, and open communication. By taking the time to clearly define and consistently honor these limits and standards, partners lay the groundwork for a strong, secure, and emotionally satisfying partnership that can weather the challenges of jealousy and insecurity.

Summary: Conquering Jealousy and Insecurity for Stronger, Healthier Relationships

Throughout this section, we have explored the complex nature of jealousy and insecurity, delving into the psychological and emotional factors that contribute to these challenging emotions. By gaining a deeper understanding of the roots of jealousy and insecurity, we can begin to develop the self-awareness and emotional intelligence necessary to effectively manage these feelings in our relationships.

The journey towards conquering jealousy and insecurity begins with a commitment to personal growth and self-discovery. By cultivating self-awareness through practices such as mindfulness, journaling, and self-reflection, we can gain valuable insights into our own thoughts, feelings, and behaviors. This increased self-understanding allows us to recognize and challenge the negative patterns and beliefs that fuel our insecurities, empowering us to make positive changes in our emotional landscape.

Equally important is the development of self-confidence and self-worth. By focusing on personal growth, pursuing meaningful goals, and practicing self-compassion, we can build a strong, resilient sense of self that is less susceptible to the influence of jealousy and insecurity. When we learn to trust in our own value and worth, we create a solid foundation for healthy, secure relationships built on mutual respect and trust.

Open communication and the establishment of clear boundaries and expectations are also essential tools in managing jealousy and insecurity. By fostering an environment of honesty, transparency, and active listening, we create opportunities for growth, problem-solving, and deeper understanding within our relationships. When we feel safe to express our fears, insecurities, and desires, we can work together with our partners to find ways to reassure and support one another, strengthening the bond between us.

Ultimately, conquering jealousy and insecurity is an ongoing process that requires patience, commitment, and a willingness to confront our own fears and vulnerabilities. By embracing the insights and strategies shared in this section, we can begin to transform these challenging emotions from sources of conflict and distress into opportunities for growth, connection, and lasting love. As we continue on this path of self-discovery and emotional mastery, we empower ourselves to build relationships that are resilient, fulfilling, and deeply satisfying, both for ourselves and our loved ones.

Section 3: Navigating Growing Apart and Changing Priorities

As relationships evolve and individuals grow, it's not uncommon for partners to find themselves on different paths or with shifting priorities. The once-shared vision of the future may begin to diverge, leaving couples feeling disconnected and uncertain about the direction of their relationship. In this section, we'll explore the challenges that arise when partners grow apart or experience changes in their goals and aspirations.

Growing apart doesn't necessarily mean the end of a relationship, but it does require a willingness to confront the issues head-on and work together to find a new path forward. We'll delve into the signs that indicate partners may be growing apart, such as decreased intimacy, communication breakdowns, and diverging interests. By recognizing these red flags early on, couples can take proactive steps to address the underlying issues and prevent further distancing.

Open and honest communication is crucial when navigating this challenging terrain. We'll discuss strategies for maintaining a dialogue that allows both partners to express their feelings, concerns, and desires without fear of judgment or retribution. Through transparent conversations, couples can gain a deeper understanding of each other's evolving needs and work together to find compromises and solutions.

Finding common ground and shared experiences is another key aspect of bridging the gap when partners grow apart. We'll explore ways to identify and nurture mutual interests, hobbies, and goals that can help rekindle a sense of togetherness and connection. By focusing on the things that bring them closer, couples can counterbalance the forces that may be pulling them in different directions.

At the same time, it's essential to recognize and support each other's personal growth and individual journeys. We'll discuss how partners can encourage one another to pursue their passions and aspirations while still maintaining a strong, supportive relationship. By embracing change and celebrating each other's successes, couples can foster a dynamic and resilient partnership that adapts to life's inevitable transformations.

Throughout this section, we'll provide practical advice, real-life examples, and expert insights to help couples navigate the challenges of growing apart and changing priorities. By approaching these issues with empathy, understanding, and a commitment to growth, partners can emerge stronger, more connected, and better equipped to face the future together.

Subsection 3.1: Recognizing Signs of Growing Apart

In the journey of a relationship, it's not uncommon for partners to experience periods of emotional distance or disconnection. Growing apart is a gradual process that can be difficult to detect, as the signs may be subtle and easily overlooked. However, recognizing these indicators early on is crucial for addressing the underlying issues and preventing further distancing between partners.

One of the most telling signs of growing apart is decreased intimacy, both physical and emotional. Couples who once shared a deep connection may find themselves less inclined to engage in affectionate gestures, such as holding hands, hugging, or kissing. The frequency and quality of sexual intimacy may also decline, leading to a sense of emotional detachment. When partners feel more like roommates than lovers, it's a clear indication that the relationship has veered off course.

Communication breakdowns are another common sign of growing apart. Partners who once enjoyed open and honest conversations may find themselves struggling to connect on a deeper level. Discussions may become superficial, focusing on mundane topics rather than the thoughts, feelings, and aspirations that truly matter. Misunderstandings and unresolved conflicts may become more frequent, as partners fail to effectively express their needs and concerns.

Diverging interests and priorities can also contribute to a sense of growing apart. As individuals evolve and change over time, their goals, values, and passions may shift. When partners no longer share the same vision for the future or find themselves pursuing separate paths, the connection between them can begin to fray. One partner may become increasingly focused on career advancement, while the other prioritizes family and personal growth, leading to a misalignment of priorities.

Other signs of growing apart include spending less quality time together, engaging in separate social circles, and a lack of shared experiences. When partners stop making an effort to create meaningful moments and memories together, the bond between them can weaken. They may find themselves leading parallel lives, with few points of intersection or shared interests.

It's important to note that growing apart doesn't necessarily mean the end of a relationship. By recognizing these signs early on and taking proactive steps to address the underlying issues, couples can work together to bridge the gap and rediscover the connection that brought them together in the first place. Open communication, a willingness to compromise, and a commitment to personal and relational growth are key to navigating this challenging terrain.

Subsection 3.2: Maintaining Open and Honest Dialogue

When navigating the challenges of growing apart and changing priorities, maintaining open and honest communication is paramount. It is through ongoing, transparent dialogue that couples can address concerns, share their feelings, and work together to find solutions. Without effective communication, misunderstandings can fester, resentment can build, and the connection between partners can erode.

One of the key aspects of maintaining open and honest dialogue is creating a safe and non-judgmental space for both partners to express themselves. This means actively listening to each other without interruption, criticism, or defensiveness. It involves approaching the conversation with empathy, seeking to understand rather than to be understood. By fostering an environment of trust and respect, couples can feel more comfortable sharing their thoughts, fears, and aspirations.

Effective communication also requires vulnerability and a willingness to be honest about one's own needs, desires, and concerns. This can be challenging, as it involves exposing oneself to potential discomfort or rejection. However, by being transparent about their feelings, partners can gain a deeper understanding of each other's perspectives and work together to find mutually satisfying solutions.

When having difficult conversations, it's essential to focus on using "I" statements rather than "you" statements. For example, instead of saying, "You never make time for me anymore," try, "I feel lonely and disconnected when we don't spend quality time together." By taking ownership of one's own emotions and experiences, partners can avoid placing blame or making accusations, which can lead to defensiveness and further disconnection.

Another crucial aspect of maintaining open and honest dialogue is being willing to listen and validate each other's feelings. Even if one partner doesn't fully understand or agree with the other's perspective, acknowledging and validating their emotions can go a long way in fostering a sense of connection and understanding. Statements like, "I hear you, and I can see how that would be frustrating," can help partners feel seen, heard, and supported.

It's also important to approach communication with a spirit of curiosity and a desire to learn. Asking open-ended questions, such as, "Can you tell me more about what you're feeling?" or "What do you need from me in this situation?" can help partners gain a deeper understanding of each other's experiences and needs. By approaching the conversation with genuine interest and a willingness to learn, couples can foster a sense of collaboration and teamwork.

Maintaining open and honest dialogue is an ongoing process that requires commitment, patience, and practice. It may not always be easy, especially when emotions are running high or when partners have differing opinions. However, by prioritizing transparent communication and approaching conversations with empathy, respect, and a desire to understand, couples can navigate the challenges of growing apart and changing priorities with greater ease and resilience.

Subsection 3.3: Finding Common Ground and Shared

Experiences

When partners find themselves growing apart or experiencing shifts in their priorities, it's essential to actively seek out common ground and shared experiences to maintain a sense of togetherness and connection. By focusing on the things that bring them closer together, couples can counterbalance the forces that may be pulling them in different directions.

One effective strategy for finding common ground is to explore new hobbies and interests together. This can involve taking a class, joining a club, or simply trying out a new activity that both partners find intriguing. By stepping out of their comfort zones and experiencing something novel as a team, couples can create fresh memories, spark engaging conversations, and rediscover the joy of learning and growing together.

Another way to nurture shared experiences is to make a conscious effort to prioritize quality time together. In the midst of busy schedules and competing demands, it's easy for couples to neglect the importance of carving out dedicated time for one another. By setting aside regular date nights, planning weekend getaways, or even establishing daily rituals like sharing a meal or taking a walk together, partners can create a sense of continuity and connection that helps bridge the gap when they feel themselves drifting apart.

Revisiting shared passions and values is another powerful way to find common ground. By reflecting on the things that initially brought them together, such as a love for travel, a commitment to social justice, or a desire to build a loving family, couples can rekindle the spark that ignited their relationship in the first place. Engaging in activities that align with these shared passions, such as volunteering together, attending events that reflect their values, or simply having heartfelt conversations about the things that matter most to them, can help partners feel more connected and aligned.

It's also important to cultivate a sense of curiosity and openness toward each other's individual interests and experiences. While it may not be possible for partners to share every passion or hobby, showing genuine interest in and support for one another's pursuits can foster a sense of appreciation and understanding. By asking questions, offering encouragement, and celebrating each other's successes, couples can demonstrate that they value and respect the things that bring their partner joy, even if they don't necessarily share those same interests.

Ultimately, finding common ground and shared experiences requires a willingness to prioritize the relationship and invest time and energy into nurturing the connection between partners. It involves being proactive, creative, and open to new possibilities, while also cherishing the foundation of shared history and values that brought the couple together in the first place. By making a conscious effort to seek out and cultivate these points of connection, couples can weather the challenges of growing apart and changing priorities, emerging stronger, more united, and more deeply committed to one another.

Subsection 3.4: Embracing Personal Growth and Supporting Each Other's Journey

In any long-term relationship, it's natural for individuals to grow, evolve, and pursue their own personal development. While this growth is essential for a fulfilling life, it can sometimes create challenges within the partnership. Partners may fear that their individual journeys will lead them away from each other or that their personal growth will be stifled by the demands of the relationship. However, by embracing personal growth and finding ways to support each other's individual journeys, couples can foster a stronger, more resilient bond that allows both partners to thrive.

One of the keys to successfully navigating personal growth within a relationship is open and honest communication. It's essential for partners to share their aspirations, goals, and desires with each other, even if they don't always align perfectly. By having candid conversations about their individual needs and dreams, couples can work together to find ways to support and encourage each other's growth while still maintaining a strong connection.

Another crucial aspect of embracing personal growth is cultivating a mindset of curiosity and openness. Rather than viewing a partner's growth as a threat to the relationship, couples can choose to approach it with a sense of excitement and possibility. By asking questions, showing genuine interest, and celebrating each other's successes, partners can foster a sense of teamwork and collaboration in the pursuit of personal development.

It's also important for couples to find practical ways to support each other's individual journeys. This may involve making compromises, adjusting schedules, or finding creative solutions to accommodate each other's needs. For example, if one partner decides to pursue a new career path that requires additional training or education, the other partner may need to take on more household responsibilities or provide emotional support during challenging times. By being willing to make sacrifices and find ways to accommodate each other's growth, couples can demonstrate their commitment to the relationship and to each other's happiness.

In addition to providing practical support, partners can also play a crucial role in each other's personal growth by serving as a source of encouragement and inspiration. By expressing belief in each other's abilities, offering words of affirmation, and celebrating milestones and achievements, couples can create a positive and uplifting environment that nurtures growth and self-discovery.

Ultimately, embracing personal growth within a relationship requires a willingness to adapt, compromise, and support each other through the inevitable changes and challenges that come with individual development. By approaching growth with a spirit of curiosity, openness, and collaboration, couples can not only weather the storms of change but also emerge stronger, more connected, and more deeply committed to each other's happiness and fulfillment.

Summary: Embracing Change and Growing Together

Navigating the challenges of growing apart and changing priorities in a relationship can be a daunting task, but it is also an opportunity for couples to deepen their connection and build a more resilient partnership. By recognizing the signs of growing apart, maintaining open and honest communication, finding common ground, and supporting each other's personal growth, partners can overcome the obstacles that arise when their paths diverge.

It is essential to remember that change is a natural and inevitable part of any long-term relationship. As individuals evolve and their needs and desires shift, it is crucial for couples to adapt and find new ways to connect and support one another. This requires a willingness to be vulnerable, to listen with empathy, and to approach challenges with a spirit of collaboration and understanding.

Through the process of navigating growing apart and changing priorities, couples have the opportunity to rediscover the strength of their bond and to build a relationship that is more flexible, more resilient, and more deeply satisfying. By embracing change and committing to growing together, partners can create a love that endures, a connection that deepens, and a partnership that thrives in the face of life's many transformations.

Section 4: Dealing with External Stressors and Challenges

Relationships do not exist in a vacuum; they are inevitably influenced by the world around us. Throughout our lives, we encounter a myriad of external stressors and challenges that can put a strain on even the strongest of partnerships. From the demands of work and financial pressures to family conflicts and unexpected life events, these external factors have the power to create tension, discord, and emotional distance between partners.

In this section, we will explore how these external stressors can impact the dynamics of a relationship, and more importantly, we will provide you with practical strategies and tools to help you navigate these challenges together. By understanding the potential effects of external factors on your relationship, you and your partner can develop a united front, fostering resilience and maintaining a strong, supportive partnership in the face of adversity.

We will delve into the importance of recognizing and acknowledging the external stressors that may be influencing your relationship, as well as the value of open, honest communication in addressing these challenges. You will learn how to create a shared support system, prioritize your relationship amidst competing demands, and set healthy boundaries to protect your partnership from the negative impact of external pressures.

Moreover, we will discuss the role of adaptability and flexibility in navigating life's unexpected twists and turns, emphasizing the significance of working together as a team to overcome obstacles and emerge stronger. By the end of this section, you will be equipped with the knowledge and skills necessary to not only weather the storms of external stressors but to use these challenges as opportunities for growth, deepening your connection, and strengthening the foundation of your relationship.

Subsection 4.1: Identifying and Acknowledging External Stressors

In the midst of navigating the complexities of a relationship, it's easy to overlook the significant impact that external stressors can have on the dynamic between partners. These stressors, which can range from demanding work schedules and financial pressures to family conflicts and health concerns, have the power to create tension, breed resentment, and erode the foundation of even the most solid partnerships. However, by learning to identify and acknowledge these external factors, couples can take the first crucial step towards effectively managing their influence on the relationship.

One of the most common external stressors that couples face is work-related stress. In today's fast-paced, competitive work environment, it's not uncommon for individuals to bring home the pressures and frustrations of their professional lives. Long hours, tight deadlines, and workplace conflicts can leave partners feeling exhausted, irritable, and emotionally distant. When these stressors go unrecognized or unacknowledged, they can quickly lead to misunderstandings, arguments, and a breakdown in communication.

Financial strain is another significant external stressor that can put immense pressure on a relationship. Whether it's the burden of debt, the struggle to make ends meet, or the stress of managing shared finances, money-related issues can create a great deal of anxiety and conflict between partners. Couples who fail to openly discuss and validate the impact of financial stressors on their relationship may find themselves engaging in blame-shifting, resentment-fueled arguments, or even financial infidelity.

Family dynamics and conflicts can also serve as powerful external stressors, influencing the health and stability of a relationship. Unresolved childhood traumas, strained relationships with in-laws, or the challenges of blending families can all contribute to increased tension and emotional turmoil. When partners fail to recognize and validate the role that family-related stressors play in their relationship, they may inadvertently allow these issues to fester, leading to feelings of isolation, frustration, and disconnection.

To effectively identify and acknowledge external stressors, couples must cultivate a culture of open, honest communication within their relationship. This involves creating a safe, non-judgmental space where both partners feel comfortable sharing their thoughts, feelings, and concerns about the external factors impacting their lives. By actively listening to one another and validating each other's experiences, couples can foster a deeper sense of understanding, empathy, and unity in the face of adversity.

Moreover, acknowledging the presence of external stressors is not about making excuses or shirking responsibility for one's actions within the relationship. Rather, it's about recognizing that these factors can place additional strain on the partnership and that both individuals may require extra support, patience, and understanding during challenging times. By working together to identify and address external stressors, couples can develop a shared sense of resilience and strengthen their ability to weather life's storms as a united front.

Subsection 4.2: Developing a United Front and Support System

When external stressors threaten to disrupt the harmony of a relationship, it is essential for couples to come together and form a united front. By creating a strong support system built on a foundation of mutual understanding, empathy, and collaboration, partners can weather the storms of life's challenges and emerge with a more resilient, deeply connected bond.

One of the key strategies for developing a united front is to foster open, honest communication. When couples make a conscious effort to share their thoughts, feelings, and concerns about external stressors, they create a safe space for vulnerability and validation. This open dialogue allows partners to gain a deeper understanding of each other's perspectives and experiences, promoting a sense of unity and shared purpose in the face of adversity.

Another crucial aspect of creating a united front is to approach challenges as a team. Instead of allowing external stressors to drive a wedge between them, couples who work together to brainstorm solutions, devise coping strategies, and provide emotional support to one another can cultivate a powerful sense of partnership. By focusing on their shared goals and values, couples can maintain a strong connection and navigate difficult times with grace and resilience.

Developing a support system extends beyond the confines of the relationship itself. Encouraging each other to seek support from trusted friends, family members, or mental health professionals can provide an additional layer of strength and stability during trying times. By fostering a network of supportive individuals who can offer guidance, encouragement, and a listening ear, couples can alleviate the burden of facing external stressors alone and maintain a healthier, more balanced perspective.

Moreover, creating a united front involves setting clear boundaries and priorities. When external stressors threaten to consume a couple's time, energy, and emotional resources, it is crucial to have open discussions about what matters most to the relationship. By establishing clear boundaries around work, family obligations, and personal time, couples can ensure that their relationship remains a top priority and that they have the necessary space to nurture their connection, even amidst life's demands.

Developing a united front and support system is an ongoing process that requires intentional effort and commitment from both partners. By consistently practicing open communication, teamwork, and boundary-setting, couples can cultivate a deep sense of unity and resilience in the face of external challenges. Through this unwavering support and collaboration, partners can not only survive the trials of life but also thrive, strengthening their bond and creating a love that endures.

Subsection 4.3: Maintaining Boundaries and Prioritizing the Relationship

In the face of external stressors and demands, it is all too easy for the lines between our personal lives and the outside world to blur. When work pressures, family obligations, and social commitments begin to encroach upon the sacred space of our romantic partnerships, it is crucial that we learn to set and maintain healthy boundaries. By establishing clear limits and prioritizing our relationships amidst the chaos of everyday life, we can foster a sense of stability, intimacy, and mutual respect that will allow our love to thrive.

Setting boundaries is not always an easy task, particularly when we find ourselves pulled in multiple directions by the competing demands of our lives. However, it is essential to recognize that without these protective barriers in place, our relationships can quickly become strained, leading to feelings of resentment, neglect, and disconnection. To begin the process of boundary-setting, couples must first engage in open, honest communication about their individual needs, desires, and limitations. This requires a willingness to be vulnerable, to listen with empathy, and to approach the conversation with a spirit of collaboration and compromise.

Once these needs have been clearly articulated, it is important to work together to establish specific, actionable boundaries that honor the integrity of the relationship. This may involve setting limits on work hours, carving out dedicated time for one another, or learning to say "no" to external commitments that threaten to undermine the health of the partnership. By creating a shared understanding of what is and is not acceptable, couples can develop a united front against the external pressures that might otherwise drive them apart.

Of course, maintaining boundaries is an ongoing process that requires consistent effort and vigilance. In the heat of the moment, it can be tempting to let our guard down and allow outside influences to seep into the sanctuary of our relationships. This is why it is so important to regularly check in with one another, to assess the effectiveness of our boundaries, and to make adjustments as needed. By approaching boundary-setting as a dynamic, collaborative process, we can ensure that our relationships remain a top priority, even in the face of life's most pressing demands.

Ultimately, the act of maintaining boundaries and prioritizing our relationships is a powerful expression of love and commitment. It sends a clear message to our partners that they matter, that their needs and desires are valid, and that we are willing to do whatever it takes to protect the sacred bond we share. In a world that often seems to pull us in a thousand different directions, this kind of devotion is a rare and precious gift. By learning to set healthy limits and keep our love at the center of our lives, we can weather any storm, overcome any obstacle, and build a partnership that will stand the test of time.

Subsection 4.4: Seeking Outside Support and Resources

When faced with significant external stressors, it is essential to recognize that seeking support from others can be a powerful tool in maintaining the health and well-being of a relationship. While it is crucial for partners to develop a strong, united front in the face of adversity, there are times when the challenges they face may be too overwhelming to tackle alone. In these instances, reaching out to trusted friends, family members, or even professionals can provide invaluable support, guidance, and perspective.

One of the primary benefits of seeking outside support is the opportunity to gain fresh insights and advice from those who are not directly involved in the relationship. Friends and family members who have navigated similar challenges can offer valuable wisdom and practical tips based on their own experiences. They can provide a listening ear, a shoulder to lean on, and a safe space to express feelings and concerns without fear of judgment or reprisal. By sharing their burdens with trusted confidants, couples can alleviate some of the emotional weight they carry and feel less alone in their struggles.

In some cases, the external stressors a couple faces may be too complex or deeply rooted to address without professional intervention. Seeking the guidance of a qualified therapist or counselor can be an incredibly effective way to navigate these challenges and strengthen the relationship in the process. These trained professionals can help couples identify unhealthy patterns of communication, develop coping strategies for managing stress, and work through unresolved conflicts or traumas that may be impacting their partnership.

Moreover, therapy can provide a neutral, objective space for couples to explore their thoughts and feelings, free from the distractions and pressures of everyday life. By engaging in this process together, partners can gain a deeper understanding of one another's needs, fears, and desires, and develop a shared language for addressing the challenges they face. Through this work, couples can cultivate greater empathy, resilience, and intimacy, laying the foundation for a stronger, more enduring relationship.

It is important to note that seeking outside support is not a sign of weakness or failure, but rather a testament to the strength and commitment of the partnership. By recognizing their limitations and reaching out for help when needed, couples demonstrate a willingness to do whatever it takes to protect and nurture their bond. This openness to growth and change can be a powerful catalyst for transformation, both individually and as a couple.

Ultimately, the decision to seek outside support will depend on the unique needs and circumstances of each relationship. Some couples may find that they are able to navigate external stressors on their own, while others may require the guidance and expertise of professionals. What is most important is that partners approach this decision with honesty, compassion, and a shared commitment to the health and happiness of their relationship. By working together to identify the resources and support they need, couples can weather any storm and emerge stronger, more connected, and more deeply in love than ever before.

Summary: Navigating Life's Challenges Together

Throughout this section, we have explored the profound impact that external stressors can have on the health and well-being of our relationships. From the demands of work and the strain of financial pressures to the complexities of family dynamics and unexpected life events, these challenges can test even the strongest of bonds. However, by approaching these stressors with intention, compassion, and a commitment to unity, we can not only survive but thrive in the face of adversity.

The key to navigating these challenges lies in our ability to recognize and acknowledge the external factors that shape our relationships. By cultivating a culture of open, honest communication and creating a safe space for vulnerability and validation, we can develop a deeper understanding of one another's experiences and work together to find solutions. Through the power of collaboration, boundary-setting, and a shared sense of purpose, we can build a united front that allows us to weather any storm.

Moreover, we have seen the value of reaching out for support when the burdens we face become too heavy to bear alone. By seeking the guidance and wisdom of trusted friends, family members, or professionals, we can gain new perspectives, develop coping strategies, and find the strength to persevere. This willingness to be open and vulnerable, to admit when we need help, is not a weakness but a testament to the depth of our commitment to our relationships and our own personal growth.

As we move forward, let us remember that the challenges we face are not obstacles to be overcome but opportunities to deepen our love, strengthen our resilience, and reaffirm our dedication to one another. By embracing the inevitable ups and downs of life with an open heart, a curious mind, and an unwavering commitment to our partnerships, we can create a love that endures, a bond that stands the test of time. So let us face the world hand in hand, secure in the knowledge that together, we can conquer anything.

Section 5: Knowing When to Seek Professional Help

Navigating the complexities of relationships can be a challenging and emotionally taxing experience. While many couples strive to resolve their issues independently, there may come a time when seeking professional help becomes necessary. Recognizing when your relationship has reached a point where the assistance of a therapist or counselor is crucial can be a daunting task, especially if you are unsure of what signs to look for or fear the stigma associated with seeking outside support.

In this section, we will explore the various indicators that suggest it may be time to consider professional intervention for your relationship challenges. By understanding these signs and acknowledging the potential benefits of therapy, you can take a proactive step towards improving the health and longevity of your partnership.

It is essential to remember that seeking professional help is not a sign of weakness or failure; rather, it is a courageous and responsible decision that demonstrates your commitment to your relationship and your willingness to invest in its future. Whether you are facing persistent trust issues, struggling with communication breakdowns, or grappling with the impact of external stressors, a qualified therapist or counselor can provide the guidance, tools, and support needed to navigate these challenges effectively.

Throughout this section, we will discuss the common barriers that prevent couples from seeking therapy and offer strategies for overcoming these obstacles. We will also provide guidance on how to choose the right therapist or counselor who can best support your unique needs and goals as a couple.

By the end of this section, you will be equipped with the knowledge and confidence to recognize when professional help may be necessary for your relationship, and you will have a clear understanding of the steps you can take to find the support you need to build a stronger, more resilient partnership.

Subsection 5.1: Identifying Persistent or Unresolvable Issues

In any relationship, conflicts and challenges are inevitable. However, there may come a point when certain issues persist despite repeated attempts to resolve them, or when the complexity of the problem seems insurmountable. Recognizing these signs is crucial in determining whether professional intervention is necessary to help the couple navigate their difficulties and find a path forward.

One of the most prominent indicators that a relationship challenge may require outside help is the presence of recurring arguments or conflicts that seem to follow a predictable pattern. If couples find themselves constantly revisiting the same issues without making progress or finding a resolution, it may be a sign that the root of the problem is deeper than they initially believed. These persistent conflicts can lead to feelings of frustration, resentment, and emotional exhaustion, ultimately eroding the foundation of the relationship.

Another red flag is the inability to communicate effectively about the issues at hand. When couples struggle to express their thoughts, feelings, and needs in a constructive manner, misunderstandings and miscommunications can quickly escalate into heated arguments or emotional shut-downs. If attempts to improve communication skills through self-help resources or open discussions prove ineffective, seeking the guidance of a professional who can facilitate healthy dialogue and provide tools for better understanding may be necessary.

In some cases, the presence of unresolved trauma, deep-seated trust issues, or significant mental health concerns can contribute to the persistence of relationship challenges. These complex factors often require specialized knowledge and expertise to address effectively. If one or both partners are grappling with the aftermath of past experiences or struggling with conditions such as depression, anxiety, or addiction, the support of a qualified therapist or counselor can be invaluable in helping the couple navigate these challenges while maintaining the health of their relationship.

It is also important to consider the emotional toll that persistent or unresolvable issues can take on both partners. When couples find themselves constantly drained, emotionally distant, or questioning the viability of their relationship due to ongoing conflicts, it may be a sign that professional help is needed to break the cycle and restore a sense of hope and connection. A therapist can provide a safe, neutral space for couples to process their emotions, gain new perspectives, and develop strategies for moving forward together.

Recognizing the signs that a relationship challenge may be too complex or entrenched to address without professional intervention is a critical step in seeking the support needed to overcome these difficulties. By acknowledging the persistence of certain issues, the inability to communicate effectively, the presence of unresolved trauma or mental health concerns, and the emotional toll on the relationship, couples can make an informed decision to seek the guidance of a qualified therapist or counselor. With the right support and tools, even the most challenging relationship issues can be navigated, allowing couples to build a stronger, more resilient bond.

Subsection 5.2: Overcoming Stigma and Resistance to Therapy

Despite the numerous benefits of seeking professional help for relationship challenges, many couples find themselves hesitant to take this crucial step. The stigma surrounding therapy and the misconceptions about what it entails can create significant barriers that prevent partners from reaching out for the support they need. These fears and reservations often stem from a lack of understanding about the therapeutic process, as well as deeply ingrained societal beliefs about the meaning of seeking help.

One of the most common misconceptions about couples therapy is that it is only meant for relationships that are on the brink of collapse. Many individuals believe that seeking professional help is an admission of failure or a sign that their partnership is doomed. However, this could not be further from the truth. In reality, couples therapy is a proactive and responsible choice that demonstrates a commitment to the relationship and a willingness to invest in its future. By addressing challenges early on and learning effective communication and problem-solving skills, couples can strengthen their bond and build a more resilient partnership.

Another barrier that may prevent couples from seeking therapy is the fear of being judged or misunderstood. Opening up about personal struggles and vulnerabilities can be a daunting prospect, especially in the presence of a stranger. However, it is essential to remember that therapists and counselors are trained professionals who provide a safe, non-judgmental space for couples to explore their issues. They are there to offer guidance, support, and tools for navigating challenges, not to criticize or assign blame. By embracing vulnerability and trusting in the therapeutic process, couples can break down the walls that hinder their progress and forge a path towards healing and growth.

In some cases, resistance to therapy may stem from cultural or societal norms that place a high value on self-reliance and emotional stoicism. Couples may feel pressure to handle their problems on their own, viewing seeking outside help as a sign of weakness or inadequacy. However, it is crucial to recognize that asking for support is a sign of strength and self-awareness. Just as we seek medical attention for physical ailments, addressing emotional and relational health is an equally valid and necessary step in maintaining overall well-being.

To overcome the stigma and resistance surrounding couples therapy, it is essential to engage in open and honest conversations about the benefits of seeking professional help. Couples can start by exploring their individual beliefs and attitudes towards therapy, as well as any fears or reservations they may have. By creating a safe space to discuss these concerns and educating themselves about the therapeutic process, partners can begin to break down the barriers that prevent them from taking action.

It can also be helpful to seek out success stories from couples who have benefited from therapy, as well as recommendations from trusted friends, family members, or healthcare providers. Hearing firsthand accounts of how therapy has positively impacted other relationships can provide inspiration and encouragement for couples who are on the fence about seeking help.

Ultimately, overcoming the stigma and resistance to couples therapy requires a willingness to prioritize the health and well-being of the relationship above all else. By recognizing the value of professional support and embracing the opportunity for growth and healing, couples can take a courageous step towards building a stronger, more resilient partnership. With the right mindset and a commitment to the therapeutic process, even the most challenging obstacles can be overcome, paving the way for a brighter, more fulfilling future together.

Subsection 5.3: Choosing the Right Therapist or Counselor

Once a couple has made the decision to seek professional help for their relationship challenges, the next crucial step is to find a qualified, compatible therapist or counselor who can effectively support them in addressing their specific needs. Choosing the right mental health professional is a highly personal process that requires careful consideration and research. The therapeutic relationship is built on trust, rapport, and a shared understanding of the couple's goals, making it essential to select a therapist who aligns with their values, communication style, and approach to treatment.

When beginning the search for a therapist or counselor, couples should start by considering their specific needs and preferences. This may include factors such as the therapist's area of expertise, cultural background, gender, or therapeutic approach. For example, if a couple is struggling with issues related to infidelity or trust, they may benefit from working with a therapist who specializes in these areas and has extensive experience in helping couples navigate the complex emotions and challenges involved.

In addition to considering their specific needs, couples should also take into account practical factors such as the therapist's location, availability, and cost. While it may be tempting to prioritize convenience or affordability, it is important to remember that investing in the right therapeutic relationship can have a profound impact on the success of treatment and the long-term health of the relationship.

One effective way to find potential therapists or counselors is to seek referrals from trusted sources, such as primary care physicians, friends, or family members who have had positive experiences with mental health professionals. Online directories and therapy networks can also be valuable resources, as they often provide detailed information about a therapist's background, qualifications, and areas of specialty.

When evaluating potential therapists, couples should take the time to review their credentials, training, and experience. Look for professionals who are licensed in their state and have received specialized training in couples therapy or related fields. Many therapists also have websites or online profiles that provide information about their therapeutic approach, philosophy, and treatment methods, which can help couples determine if they are a good fit.

Once a couple has identified a few potential therapists, it is important to schedule initial consultations to gauge compatibility and comfort level. These consultations provide an opportunity to ask questions, discuss goals and expectations, and get a sense of the therapist's communication style and approach to treatment. Couples should pay attention to how they feel during these interactions, noting any feelings of unease, judgment, or discomfort that may indicate a poor fit.

Ultimately, choosing the right therapist or counselor is a deeply personal decision that requires open communication, trust, and a willingness to invest in the therapeutic process. By taking the time to carefully consider their needs, research potential providers, and prioritize compatibility and comfort, couples can lay the foundation for a successful therapeutic relationship that supports their journey towards healing, growth, and a stronger, more resilient partnership.

Summary: Prioritizing Your Relationship's Well-being

Recognizing when professional help is necessary for your relationship is a crucial step in prioritizing the health and well-being of your partnership. By understanding the signs that indicate a need for outside support, such as persistent and unresolvable issues, communication breakdowns, and the presence of unresolved trauma or mental health concerns, you can make an informed decision to seek the guidance of a qualified therapist or counselor.

Overcoming the stigma and resistance surrounding couples therapy is essential in order to break down the barriers that prevent many partners from reaching out for the help they need. By engaging in open and honest conversations about the benefits of professional support, exploring individual beliefs and attitudes towards therapy, and seeking out success stories from others who have benefited from the process, couples can begin to challenge the misconceptions and fears that hold them back.

Choosing the right therapist or counselor is a deeply personal process that requires careful consideration of your specific needs, preferences, and goals as a couple. By taking the time to research potential providers, evaluating their credentials and experience, and prioritizing compatibility and comfort, you can lay the foundation for a successful therapeutic relationship that supports your journey towards healing, growth, and a stronger, more resilient partnership.

Ultimately, seeking professional help for your relationship challenges is a courageous and proactive step that demonstrates your commitment to your partnership and your willingness to invest in its future. By embracing the support and guidance of a qualified therapist or counselor, you can navigate even the most complex and challenging issues, developing the tools and insights necessary to build a thriving, fulfilling relationship that stands the test of time. Remember, the decision to prioritize your relationship's well-being is a powerful testament to the love, dedication, and resilience that you and your partner share.

Chapter Summary: Navigating the Path to Stronger, More Resilient Relationships

Throughout this chapter, we have explored some of the most common challenges that relationships face, including trust issues, jealousy, growing apart, and external stressors. By recognizing these challenges and understanding their origins, we can take proactive steps to address them and build stronger, more resilient partnerships.

The key to overcoming relationship challenges lies in fostering open, honest communication and creating a safe, supportive environment where both partners feel heard and valued. By developing self-awareness, setting healthy boundaries, and embracing personal growth, we can navigate the ups and downs of relationships with greater ease and grace.

It is important to remember that every relationship is unique, and there is no one-size-fits-all solution to the challenges that arise. However, by cultivating empathy, patience, and a willingness to work through difficult times together, we can deepen our connections and build relationships that stand the test of time.

In some cases, seeking the guidance of a qualified therapist or counselor may be necessary to address persistent or complex issues. By overcoming the stigma surrounding therapy and recognizing the value of professional support, couples can gain the tools and insights needed to overcome even the most challenging obstacles.

Ultimately, the journey of building strong, healthy relationships is an ongoing process that requires commitment, effort, and a willingness to learn and grow. By embracing the strategies and insights outlined in this chapter, readers can take meaningful steps towards creating the kind of relationships they truly desire – ones built on trust, respect, and enduring love.

Chapter 11: The Impact of Technology on Modern Relationships

In the digital age, technology has become an integral part of our lives, transforming the way we communicate, connect, and interact with one another. From the rise of smartphones and social media to the proliferation of dating apps and virtual communication tools, technology has reshaped the landscape of modern relationships in profound ways. As we navigate this ever-evolving digital world, it is crucial to understand the multifaceted impact of technology on our relationships and learn how to harness its power while mitigating its potential drawbacks.

Technology has undeniably brought about numerous benefits for our relationships, offering unprecedented opportunities for connection, communication, and shared experiences. With just a few taps on a screen, we can instantly reach out to loved ones across the globe, share our thoughts and feelings, and maintain a sense of closeness despite physical distance. The convenience and accessibility provided by technology have made it easier than ever to stay connected with our partners, friends, and family members, fostering a sense of constant presence and support.

However, the pervasive nature of technology in our lives has also given rise to a unique set of challenges and concerns. The constant connectivity and the blurring of boundaries between our online and offline lives can sometimes lead to a paradoxical sense of disconnection and distraction. The temptation to constantly check our devices, engage in virtual interactions, and compare our relationships to the curated images we see on social media can strain our real-life connections and erode the quality of our face-to-face interactions.

Moreover, the digital world has introduced new complexities and gray areas in relationships, such as the definition and boundaries of online infidelity, the risks of digital miscommunication and misinterpretation, and the potential for technology addiction and relationship neglect. As we grapple with these challenges, it becomes increasingly important to develop strategies for navigating technology in a way that supports and enhances our relationships rather than undermining them.

In this chapter, we will delve into the multifaceted impact of technology on modern relationships, exploring both its benefits and its challenges. We will examine how technology has transformed the way we form, maintain, and experience relationships, and discuss practical strategies for cultivating a healthy balance between our digital and real-life connections. By understanding the role of technology in our relationships and learning how to harness its power mindfully, we can build stronger, more resilient, and more fulfilling connections in the modern world.

Section 1: The Prevalence of Technology in Modern Relationships

In today's fast-paced, digitally connected world, technology has become an integral part of our daily lives, and its influence extends far beyond mere convenience and entertainment. As we navigate the complexities of modern relationships, it is crucial to understand the pervasive role that technology plays in shaping the way we communicate, connect, and maintain intimacy with our loved ones.

From the initial stages of relationship formation to the ongoing maintenance of long-term partnerships, technology has revolutionized the landscape of human interaction. Online dating platforms have transformed the way people seek and find potential partners, offering a vast pool of possibilities and unique challenges. In established relationships, digital communication tools like instant messaging, video calls, and social media have become essential for staying connected, especially in the face of geographical distance or busy schedules.

However, the omnipresence of technology in our relationships is not without its drawbacks. The constant buzz of notifications, the pressure to maintain an online presence, and the blurring of boundaries between the virtual and the real can strain even the strongest of bonds. As we explore the multifaceted impact of technology on modern relationships, we will delve into the benefits, challenges, and strategies for navigating this digital landscape while nurturing genuine, meaningful connections with those we hold dear.

In this section, we will embark on a thought-provoking journey to uncover the ways in which technology has reshaped the fabric of human relationships. By examining the latest research, real-life anecdotes, and expert insights, we will gain a deeper understanding of how to harness the power of technology for the betterment of our relationships while mitigating its potential pitfalls. Together, we will explore the delicate balance between the virtual and the tangible, the convenience and the chaos, and the opportunities and the obstacles that technology presents in the realm of love, friendship, and family bonds.

Subsection 1.1: The Rise of Online Dating and Relationship Formation

In the past two decades, online dating has transformed from a niche activity to a mainstream phenomenon, revolutionizing the way people seek and form romantic connections. The proliferation of dating websites and apps has created a vast digital landscape where individuals can explore potential partnerships from the comfort of their own devices. This shift in relationship formation has been driven by a combination of factors, including the increasing ubiquity of internet access, the fast-paced nature of modern life, and the desire for more efficient and targeted ways of finding compatible partners.

The appeal of online dating lies in its ability to transcend geographical boundaries and connect people based on shared interests, values, and preferences. With the click of a button, users can access a diverse pool of potential matches from around the world, exponentially expanding their chances of finding someone who aligns with their desires and expectations. Online dating platforms employ sophisticated algorithms and detailed questionnaires to suggest compatible matches, taking into account factors such as personality traits, lifestyle choices, and relationship goals. This targeted approach to matchmaking has proven to be an attractive alternative to traditional methods of meeting partners, such as through friends, family, or chance encounters.

Moreover, online dating offers a level of convenience and flexibility that is particularly appealing to younger generations who have grown up in a digital world. The ability to connect with potential partners at any time, from anywhere, has made online dating an integral part of modern romance. The rise of mobile dating apps has further enhanced this convenience, allowing users to swipe, match, and chat with potential partners on the go. This instant gratification and the gamification of dating have contributed to the growing popularity of online dating, particularly among millennials and Gen Z.

However, the rise of online dating has also brought with it a unique set of challenges and concerns. The anonymity and distance afforded by digital communication can sometimes lead to deceptive behavior, such as misrepresentation of one's appearance, age, or intentions. The abundance of choice and the ease of rejection can also create a sense of disposability in relationships, leading some to engage in more casual or short-term connections. Additionally, the emphasis on visual presentation and the potential for superficial judgments based on profile pictures and brief bios have raised questions about the authenticity and depth of connections formed online.

Despite these challenges, the influence of online dating on relationship formation cannot be understated. As more people turn to digital platforms to find love and companionship, it is clear that online dating has become a central feature of the modern romantic landscape. The success stories of countless couples who have met and formed lasting relationships through online dating are a testament to its potential to create meaningful connections. As technology continues to evolve and shape the way we interact, it is likely that online dating will remain a powerful force in shaping the future of relationships.

Subsection 1.2: The Integration of Technology in Established Relationships

In the modern era, technology has become deeply interwoven into the fabric of our daily lives, and its influence extends far beyond the realm of forming new relationships. As couples navigate the complexities of maintaining and nurturing their established partnerships, digital communication tools and platforms have emerged as essential components in the relationship landscape. From instant messaging and video calls to social media and shared online experiences, technology is reshaping the way couples interact, communicate, and sustain their emotional bonds.

One of the most significant ways in which technology has transformed established relationships is by enabling constant connectivity. With the ubiquity of smartphones and high-speed internet access, partners can now stay in touch throughout the day, regardless of their physical location. This perpetual connection has the potential to strengthen emotional intimacy and foster a sense of closeness, particularly for couples who are separated by geographical distance or demanding schedules. The ability to share thoughts, feelings, and experiences in real-time through text messages, voice notes, or photos can help bridge the gap between partners and maintain a strong sense of presence in each other's lives.

Moreover, technology has opened up new avenues for shared experiences and quality time, even when couples are not physically together. Virtual date nights, where partners simultaneously watch a movie, enjoy a meal, or engage in an activity over a video call, have become increasingly popular. These shared digital experiences can help maintain a sense of connection and create cherished memories, despite the physical distance. Similarly, online gaming and virtual reality platforms offer couples the opportunity to engage in immersive, interactive experiences that can foster teamwork, communication, and playfulness within the relationship.

However, the integration of technology in established relationships is not without its challenges. The constant availability and the pressure to respond quickly to messages can sometimes lead to feelings of anxiety, obligation, or even resentment. The blurring of boundaries between personal and shared digital spaces can also create tensions, particularly when it comes to privacy, trust, and the need for individual autonomy. Couples may struggle to find the right balance between staying connected and allowing for healthy solitude and self-care.

Another potential pitfall of technology in established relationships is the risk of digital distractions and the erosion of quality face-to-face interactions. When partners are constantly tethered to their devices, they may miss out on the nuances of body language, eye contact, and the full emotional presence that comes with undivided attention. The allure of social media, notifications, and the endless stream of digital content can also compete with the time and energy that could be invested in nurturing the relationship. Couples must be mindful of these challenges and work together to establish healthy boundaries and priorities around technology use.

To harness the benefits of technology while mitigating its potential drawbacks, couples in established relationships can adopt various strategies. Setting clear expectations and boundaries around digital communication, such as agreeing on response times or device-free zones, can help maintain a sense of balance and respect. Regularly scheduling tech-free quality time, where partners fully engage with each other without the interference of screens, can strengthen emotional intimacy and reinforce the value of face-to-face connection. Additionally, couples can explore ways to use technology collaboratively, such as creating shared digital spaces for organizing their lives, expressing affection, or pursuing common goals.

As technology continues to evolve and shape the landscape of human interaction, its impact on established relationships will undoubtedly grow. By approaching the integration of technology with intention, openness, and a commitment to nurturing authentic connection, couples can navigate this digital terrain and build relationships that thrive in the modern world. Through honest communication, shared boundaries, and a willingness to adapt, partners can harness the power of technology to enhance their emotional bonds while preserving the essence of what makes their relationship unique and meaningful.

Subsection 1.3: The Role of Social Media in Relationship Dynamics

In the digital age, social media has become an inextricable part of our daily lives, and its influence on relationship dynamics cannot be overlooked. From the way we present ourselves online to the way we interact with our partners and perceive their digital presence, social media has added a new layer of complexity to modern relationships. This subsection will delve into the multifaceted impact of social media on relationship dynamics, exploring issues of privacy, trust, and comparison.

One of the most significant ways in which social media affects relationships is through the blurring of boundaries between the public and the private. Couples must navigate the challenges of determining what aspects of their relationship to share online and what to keep intimate and personal. The pressure to present a curated, idealized version of one's relationship on social media can lead to feelings of inauthenticity and strain, as partners may feel compelled to maintain a certain image for their digital audience. Moreover, the constant accessibility of a partner's social media presence can create tensions around privacy and autonomy, as individuals may struggle to find a balance between their online and offline lives.

Trust is another crucial aspect of relationship dynamics that can be heavily influenced by social media. The ease with which people can connect and communicate with others online can sometimes lead to feelings of insecurity, jealousy, or suspicion within a relationship. The ambiguity of online interactions, such as likes, comments, or private messages, can fuel misunderstandings and doubts, particularly if there is a lack of open communication between partners. The temptation to engage in online flirtation or to seek validation from others through social media can also erode trust and create conflicts within a relationship.

Furthermore, social media can exacerbate the human tendency to compare oneself and one's relationship to others. The highlight reel nature of social media, where people typically share only the most positive and enviable aspects of their lives, can create a distorted perception of reality. Couples may find themselves measuring their own relationship against the carefully curated images and narratives presented by others online, leading to feelings of inadequacy, dissatisfaction, or even resentment. The constant exposure to seemingly perfect relationships and lifestyles can put undue pressure on couples to live up to unrealistic standards, potentially straining their emotional connection and sense of contentment.

To navigate the impact of social media on relationship dynamics, couples must approach this digital landscape with intention, communication, and mutual understanding. Setting clear boundaries and expectations around social media use, such as agreeing on what is appropriate to share online and what should remain private, can help mitigate potential conflicts and maintain a sense of trust and respect. Regularly engaging in honest, open conversations about the role of social media in the relationship can foster a deeper understanding of each other's perspectives and needs. Additionally, cultivating a strong sense of self-worth and self-acceptance, independent of social media validation, can help individuals maintain a healthy perspective on their relationship and resist the temptation to compare themselves to others.

Ultimately, the key to managing the impact of social media on relationship dynamics lies in prioritizing the authentic, face-to-face connection between partners. By focusing on nurturing the emotional intimacy and shared experiences that exist beyond the digital realm, couples can build resilience against the potential pitfalls of social media and create a relationship that thrives in the modern world. Through mindfulness, communication, and a commitment to each other's well-being, partners can harness the benefits of social media while minimizing its negative influence on their relationship dynamics.

Summary: Navigating the Digital Landscape of Modern Relationships

In this section, we have explored the pervasive role of technology in contemporary relationships and its profound impact on communication, connection, and intimacy. From the rise of online dating and the integration of digital tools in established partnerships to the influence of social media on relationship dynamics, it is clear that technology has become an inextricable part of the modern romantic landscape.

As we navigate this digital terrain, it is essential to approach technology with intention, mindfulness, and a commitment to nurturing authentic human connections. By setting clear boundaries, engaging in open communication, and prioritizing face-to-face interactions, couples can harness the benefits of technology while mitigating its potential pitfalls. The key lies in finding a healthy balance between the virtual and the tangible, the convenience and the chaos, and the opportunities and the obstacles that technology presents.

As we move forward in this ever-evolving digital age, it is crucial to remember that technology is ultimately a tool – one that can either enhance or hinder our relationships, depending on how we choose to use it. By staying attuned to our own needs and the needs of our partners, and by approaching technology with wisdom, empathy, and a genuine desire for connection, we can cultivate relationships that thrive in the face of the digital revolution. With this foundation, we can navigate the complexities of modern love and build bonds that are resilient, meaningful, and deeply fulfilling.

Section 2: The Benefits of Technology in Relationships

In today's fast-paced, digitally connected world, technology has become an integral part of our lives, and its influence on our relationships cannot be overlooked. While some may view technology as a barrier to genuine human connection, it is important to recognize the many ways in which it can enhance, support, and strengthen our relationships. In this section, we will explore the positive aspects of technology and how it can be harnessed to improve communication, foster deeper connections, and provide invaluable support in our relationships.

As we navigate the complexities of modern relationships, it is essential to acknowledge the role that technology plays in bringing people closer together, even when physical distance separates them. From instant messaging and video calls to social media and online communities, technology has opened up new avenues for individuals to connect, share, and support one another in ways that were once unimaginable.

Throughout this section, we will delve into the various benefits that technology can bring to our relationships, examining how it can enhance communication, facilitate shared experiences, and provide access to valuable resources and support networks. By understanding and embracing the positive aspects of technology, we can learn to use it as a tool to strengthen our bonds, build trust, and cultivate more fulfilling relationships in the digital age.

Subsection 2.1: Increased Accessibility and Convenience

In the fast-paced world of modern relationships, technology has emerged as a powerful tool for enhancing communication and maintaining connections, particularly in situations where physical distance separates loved ones. One of the most significant benefits of technology in this context is the increased accessibility and convenience it offers, enabling more frequent and efficient communication between partners, friends, and family members.

Gone are the days when long-distance relationships were characterized by sporadic phone calls, handwritten letters, and the occasional visit. With the advent of instant messaging, video calls, and social media platforms, staying connected with loved ones has become easier than ever before. Couples can now engage in real-time conversations, share their daily experiences, and maintain a sense of intimacy, regardless of the miles that separate them.

The convenience of technology has also made it possible for individuals to communicate on their own terms, at times that suit their schedules and preferences. Whether it's a quick text message during a lunch break, a late-night video call, or a heartfelt email composed during a moment of reflection, technology has provided us with a multitude of ways to express our thoughts, feelings, and support for one another.

Moreover, the accessibility of technology has opened up new avenues for relationship formation and maintenance. Online dating platforms have revolutionized the way people connect and find compatible partners, transcending geographical boundaries and traditional social circles. Social media has also played a significant role in helping individuals stay connected with friends and family members, allowing them to share updates, photos, and milestones, fostering a sense of belonging and togetherness.

However, it is important to recognize that while technology can greatly enhance communication and convenience in relationships, it should not be relied upon as a complete substitute for face-to-face interaction. Striking a balance between the use of technology and in-person connection is crucial for maintaining the depth and authenticity of our relationships.

In conclusion, the increased accessibility and convenience brought about by technology have transformed the landscape of modern relationships, providing new opportunities for connection, communication, and support. By embracing these benefits while also prioritizing the value of direct, personal interaction, we can harness the power of technology to strengthen our bonds and build more resilient, fulfilling relationships in the digital age.

Subsection 2.2: Expanded Opportunities for Shared Experiences

In the realm of modern relationships, technology has not only enhanced communication and convenience but has also opened up a world of possibilities for couples to engage in shared experiences, even when they are physically apart. From virtual date nights and online gaming to watching movies together remotely, technology has transformed the way we connect and create meaningful moments with our loved ones.

One of the most significant advantages of technology in this context is its ability to bridge the gap between partners who are separated by distance. With the help of video conferencing platforms and streaming services, couples can now enjoy virtual date nights, recreating the intimacy and excitement of a traditional date from the comfort of their own homes. Whether it's cooking a meal together over a video call, playing an online game, or watching a movie in sync, technology has made it possible for partners to share experiences and create lasting memories, regardless of their physical location.

Moreover, technology has also paved the way for couples to explore new interests and hobbies together, even when they are apart. Online gaming, for instance, has emerged as a popular activity for couples, allowing them to collaborate, compete, and bond over a shared passion. From casual puzzle games to immersive role-playing adventures, gaming has become a platform for couples to strengthen their connection, foster teamwork, and enjoy quality time together.

Similarly, streaming services have revolutionized the way couples consume and discuss entertainment. With the ability to watch movies and TV shows together remotely, partners can now engage in shared viewing experiences, creating opportunities for meaningful conversations and emotional bonding. Platforms that offer synchronized viewing and built-in chat features have further enhanced this experience, enabling couples to react, discuss, and connect in real-time, as if they were sitting side by side.

Technology has also made it easier for couples to explore and appreciate each other's interests and passions. Through online learning platforms and virtual workshops, partners can now engage in shared learning experiences, attending courses or seminars together, even when they are physically apart. This not only promotes personal growth and development but also fosters a deeper understanding and appreciation of each other's aspirations and goals.

However, it is important to recognize that while technology can facilitate shared experiences, it should not be relied upon as a complete substitute for in-person interaction. Striking a balance between virtual and physical shared experiences is crucial for maintaining the depth and authenticity of a relationship. Couples should strive to use technology as a tool to complement and enhance their connection, rather than as a replacement for face-to-face interaction.

In conclusion, technology has expanded the opportunities for couples to engage in shared experiences, transcending the limitations of physical distance. From virtual date nights and online gaming to remote movie viewing and shared learning, technology has provided new avenues for partners to connect, bond, and create meaningful memories together. By embracing these opportunities while also prioritizing the value of in-person experiences, couples can harness the power of technology to strengthen their relationship and build a deeper, more resilient connection in the digital age.

Subsection 2.3: Enhanced Support and Resources

In the face of relationship challenges, it is not uncommon for individuals to feel overwhelmed, isolated, and unsure of where to turn for support. However, in the digital age, technology has emerged as a powerful tool for providing access to a wealth of resources, online communities, and support groups that can help individuals navigate even the most difficult of relationship hurdles.

One of the most significant benefits of technology in this context is its ability to connect individuals with others who are facing similar challenges. Through online forums, social media groups, and dedicated support websites, people can find solace, guidance, and encouragement from a community of peers who understand their struggles. These digital spaces offer a safe and non-judgmental environment where individuals can share their experiences, seek advice, and learn from the wisdom of others who have faced and overcome similar obstacles.

Moreover, technology has made it easier than ever before to access professional support and resources for relationship issues. From online therapy platforms and virtual counseling sessions to self-help resources and educational materials, individuals can now access a wide range of tools and expertise from the comfort of their own homes. This increased accessibility is particularly valuable for those who may face barriers to traditional in-person support, such as geographical distance, time constraints, or financial limitations.

In addition to providing emotional support and practical guidance, technology has also played a crucial role in raising awareness about relationship issues and promoting healthy relationship practices. Through online campaigns, educational initiatives, and digital content, individuals can now access a wealth of information and resources that can help them build stronger, more resilient relationships. From articles and blog posts that offer insights and advice to podcasts and webinars that delve into the complexities of modern relationships, technology has created a rich tapestry of resources that can empower individuals to take charge of their relationship health.

However, it is important to approach online support and resources with a critical eye and to exercise caution when seeking guidance from digital sources. While the internet can be a valuable tool for accessing support and information, it is crucial to verify the credibility and reliability of the sources one engages with. Seeking recommendations from trusted professionals, such as therapists or relationship experts, can help individuals navigate the digital landscape more effectively and ensure that they are accessing high-quality, evidence-based resources.

In conclusion, technology has greatly enhanced the availability and accessibility of support and resources for individuals facing relationship challenges. From online communities and support groups to professional guidance and educational materials, technology has created a multitude of avenues for individuals to find the help and encouragement they need to navigate the complexities of modern relationships. By harnessing the power of these digital resources while also exercising discernment and seeking professional guidance when needed, individuals can leverage technology to build stronger, more resilient relationships in the face of even the most daunting challenges.

Summary: Embracing Technology for Stronger, More Connected Relationships

In this section, we have explored the numerous benefits that technology can bring to modern relationships, highlighting its potential to enhance communication, foster deeper connections, and provide invaluable support. From increasing accessibility and convenience to expanding opportunities for shared experiences and offering a wealth of resources and support, technology has transformed the way we connect and maintain our relationships in the digital age.

However, it is crucial to recognize that technology is not a panacea for all relationship challenges, and it should be used as a tool to complement and enhance, rather than replace, face-to-face interaction. By striking a balance between the use of technology and in-person connection, we can harness its power to build stronger, more resilient relationships while still maintaining the depth and authenticity that come from direct, personal interaction.

As we move forward in our exploration of the impact of technology on modern relationships, it is essential to approach its use with mindfulness, intentionality, and a commitment to prioritizing the well-being of our connections. By embracing the benefits of technology while also setting healthy boundaries and nurturing our relationships through face-to-face interaction, we can navigate the complexities of the digital age and build meaningful, lasting connections that thrive both online and offline.

Section 3: The Challenges and Pitfalls of Technology in Relationships

In today's digital age, technology has become an integral part of our lives, transforming the way we communicate, connect, and maintain relationships. While technology has undoubtedly brought numerous benefits, it is crucial to acknowledge and address the potential negative consequences it can have on our relationships. This section delves into the challenges and pitfalls that arise when technology becomes a dominant force in our personal connections.

As we navigate the complexities of modern relationships, it is essential to understand how the constant presence of screens, the allure of social media, and the instant gratification of digital communication can strain the bonds we share with others. From the paradox of feeling disconnected despite being constantly connected to the risks of misinterpretation and digital infidelity, technology presents a unique set of obstacles that can hinder the growth and well-being of our relationships.

By exploring these challenges head-on, we can develop a deeper awareness of the impact technology has on our connections with loved ones, friends, and partners. Through this awareness, we can learn to strike a healthy balance between embracing the advantages of technology and preserving the authenticity and intimacy of our relationships. In the following subsections, we will examine the specific challenges that arise when technology infiltrates our personal lives and discuss strategies for navigating these hurdles to build and maintain strong, meaningful connections in the digital era.

Subsection 3.1: The Paradox of Constant Connectivity

In the digital age, we find ourselves perpetually tethered to our devices, constantly connected to a vast network of information and people. While this constant connectivity has undeniably brought convenience and opportunities for communication, it has also given rise to a paradoxical phenomenon: the more connected we are, the more disconnected we may feel.

The incessant buzz of notifications, the allure of social media feeds, and the pressure to respond instantly to messages can create a sense of being always "on," leaving little room for genuine, uninterrupted human interaction. This constant digital presence can lead to a fragmented attention span, as we find ourselves continually distracted by the pings and vibrations of our devices, even when in the company of loved ones.

As we prioritize virtual connections over face-to-face interactions, we risk losing the depth and richness of in-person communication. The nuances of body language, the warmth of a smile, and the comfort of a gentle touch cannot be fully replicated through a screen. When we rely too heavily on digital communication, we may find ourselves feeling isolated and disconnected, yearning for the authentic human connection that technology cannot provide.

Moreover, the pressure to curate a perfect online persona can further contribute to feelings of disconnection and loneliness. As we scroll through the highlight reels of others' lives on social media, we may begin to compare ourselves unfavorably, leading to a sense of inadequacy and alienation. The constant exposure to carefully crafted images and messages can create a distorted perception of reality, making it harder to form genuine, vulnerable connections with others.

To combat the paradox of constant connectivity, it is crucial to establish boundaries and create intentional spaces for face-to-face interaction. By setting aside dedicated time to unplug from our devices and engage in meaningful conversations, shared experiences, and physical presence, we can cultivate a deeper sense of connection and fulfillment in our relationships. It is through these moments of undivided attention and authentic engagement that we can truly nurture the bonds that matter most.

Subsection 3.2: The Risks of Digital Miscommunication and Misinterpretation

In the realm of digital communication, the absence of nonverbal cues such as facial expressions, tone of voice, and body language can create a breeding ground for misunderstandings and misinterpretations. When we rely solely on written words to convey our thoughts and emotions, we lose the rich tapestry of context that face-to-face interactions provide. This lack of nonverbal information can lead to a breakdown in effective communication, potentially causing conflict and strain in our relationships.

One of the primary risks of digital miscommunication lies in the ambiguity of text-based messages. Without the benefit of hearing the speaker's tone or seeing their facial expressions, the intended meaning behind the words can easily be lost or misinterpreted. A seemingly harmless comment or joke may be perceived as sarcastic, insensitive, or even offensive when stripped of its nonverbal context. This ambiguity can give rise to misunderstandings, as the receiver of the message may draw conclusions based on their own emotional state, past experiences, or personal biases.

Moreover, the instant nature of digital communication can exacerbate the potential for misinterpretation. In the heat of the moment, it is all too easy to fire off a hastily composed message without fully considering its impact or clarity. The lack of a "pause button" in digital interactions can lead to impulsive responses, further fueling misunderstandings and conflict. Without the opportunity to clarify intentions or read the other person's reaction in real-time, minor miscommunications can quickly escalate into full-blown arguments.

The absence of nonverbal cues in digital communication can also create challenges in conveying empathy, support, and understanding. In face-to-face interactions, a comforting touch, a sympathetic smile, or a reassuring tone of voice can go a long way in communicating care and concern. However, in the digital realm, these subtle yet powerful gestures are lost, making it harder to provide emotional support and connection. As a result, individuals may feel less understood, validated, or emotionally fulfilled in their digital interactions, leading to a sense of disconnection and dissatisfaction in their relationships.

To mitigate the risks of digital miscommunication and misinterpretation, it is crucial to approach online interactions with mindfulness and clarity. Taking the time to carefully compose messages, asking for clarification when needed, and using emojis or other visual cues to convey tone and emotion can help bridge the gap left by the absence of nonverbal communication. Additionally, cultivating a habit of assuming positive intent and giving others the benefit of the doubt can prevent minor misunderstandings from escalating into larger conflicts.

Ultimately, while digital communication has revolutionized the way we connect with others, it is essential to recognize its limitations and potential pitfalls. By being aware of the risks of miscommunication and misinterpretation, we can take proactive steps to ensure that our digital interactions are as clear, empathetic, and constructive as possible. Through a combination of mindfulness, openness, and a willingness to clarify and communicate effectively, we can harness the power of technology to build and maintain strong, healthy relationships in the digital age.

Subsection 3.3: The Temptation of Digital Infidelity and Secrecy

In the digital age, the boundaries of fidelity and infidelity have become increasingly blurred. With the proliferation of social media, dating apps, and instant messaging platforms, individuals now have unprecedented access to a vast network of potential romantic interests and opportunities for clandestine communication. This new landscape has given rise to the complex and often murky world of digital infidelity, where the lines between innocent online interactions and betrayal can be difficult to define.

At its core, digital infidelity refers to the engagement in emotionally or sexually charged online behavior that violates the trust and commitment of a primary relationship. This can take many forms, from flirtatious messages and intimate online conversations to the exchange of explicit photos and videos. While some may argue that these virtual interactions lack the physical component of traditional infidelity, the emotional and psychological impact on the betrayed partner can be just as devastating.

One of the primary challenges in navigating digital infidelity lies in the ambiguity of what constitutes cheating in the online realm. For some couples, engaging in online flirtation or maintaining secret social media accounts may be considered a breach of trust, while others may view these behaviors as harmless or even acceptable. The lack of clear, universally agreed-upon boundaries can create confusion and conflict within relationships, as partners struggle to align their expectations and values surrounding online conduct.

Moreover, the ease and accessibility of digital communication can make it all too tempting to engage in secretive online behavior. The anonymity and distance provided by the internet can create a false sense of security, leading individuals to say and do things they might not otherwise consider in face-to-face interactions. This illusion of privacy can fuel the temptation to seek out emotional or sexual fulfillment outside of the primary relationship, without fully considering the consequences.

The impact of digital infidelity on trust and intimacy within a relationship cannot be overstated. When one partner discovers that their significant other has been engaging in secret online behavior, it can shatter the foundation of trust and create deep wounds that are difficult to heal. The betrayal of secrecy and the violation of agreed-upon boundaries can lead to feelings of hurt, anger, and a profound sense of disconnection. Rebuilding trust in the aftermath of digital infidelity often requires a commitment to transparency, open communication, and a willingness to work through the underlying issues that may have contributed to the breach.

To navigate the challenges of digital infidelity and secrecy, couples must engage in honest and ongoing conversations about their expectations and boundaries surrounding online behavior. By openly discussing what constitutes infidelity in the digital age, partners can create a shared understanding and establish clear guidelines for their relationship. This may involve setting parameters around social media use, agreeing to share passwords, or committing to transparency in online interactions.

It is also crucial for individuals to cultivate self-awareness and integrity in their online conduct. By recognizing the temptations and potential pitfalls of digital communication, individuals can make conscious choices to prioritize their primary relationship and avoid engaging in behavior that could jeopardize trust and intimacy. This may involve setting personal boundaries, such as limiting contact with former partners or refraining from seeking validation through online flirtation.

Ultimately, the key to navigating digital infidelity and secrecy lies in fostering a culture of honesty, transparency, and open communication within the relationship. By creating a safe space to discuss fears, insecurities, and temptations, couples can work together to build resilience and maintain a strong, trusting bond in the face of the challenges posed by the digital age. Through a commitment to mutual respect, empathy, and accountability, partners can navigate the complexities of online infidelity and emerge with a deeper understanding of themselves and their relationship.

Subsection 3.4: The Potential for Technology Addiction and Relationship Neglect

In the digital age, the pervasive presence of technology has given rise to a new set of challenges that can have a profound impact on our relationships and personal well-being. One of the most significant and often overlooked risks is the potential for technology addiction and the subsequent neglect of real-life connections. As we become increasingly tethered to our devices, the allure of constant stimulation and instant gratification can lead to a dangerous cycle of compulsive technology use, ultimately eroding the quality of our relationships and overall sense of fulfillment.

Technology addiction, also known as digital addiction or internet addiction disorder, is characterized by an unhealthy dependence on digital devices and online activities. This addiction can manifest in various forms, such as compulsive social media use, excessive gaming, or a constant need to check emails and messages. When individuals become consumed by their digital lives, they may find themselves unable to resist the pull of their devices, even when it comes at the expense of face-to-face interactions and meaningful connections with loved ones.

The consequences of technology addiction on relationships can be severe and far-reaching. As individuals prioritize their online activities over real-life interactions, they may begin to neglect the needs and feelings of their partners, family members, and friends. This neglect can take many forms, from failing to engage in meaningful conversations and shared experiences to being physically present but emotionally absent due to constant digital distractions. Over time, this lack of attention and connection can erode trust, intimacy, and the overall quality of the relationship, leading to feelings of isolation, resentment, and disconnection.

Moreover, the impact of technology addiction extends beyond the realm of interpersonal relationships, affecting an individual's overall well-being and personal growth. When excessive screen time becomes a primary source of stimulation and validation, individuals may begin to neglect other essential aspects of their lives, such as self-care, physical health, and personal development. The constant bombardment of digital stimuli can lead to increased stress levels, sleep disturbances, and a diminished ability to engage in deep, focused thinking and reflection. As a result, individuals may find themselves stuck in a cycle of technology dependence, unable to cultivate the inner resources and resilience necessary for personal growth and fulfillment.

To combat the potential for technology addiction and relationship neglect, it is crucial to develop a mindful and intentional approach to technology use. This begins with recognizing the signs of problematic technology habits, such as feeling anxious or irritable when separated from devices, neglecting responsibilities in favor of online activities, or experiencing a sense of guilt or shame around technology use. By cultivating self-awareness and honesty about the impact of technology on their lives, individuals can take proactive steps to establish healthy boundaries and prioritize real-life connections.

One effective strategy for maintaining a balanced relationship with technology is to set aside dedicated "unplugged" time, both individually and as a couple or family. This may involve establishing device-free zones in the home, such as the dinner table or bedroom, or planning regular technology-free activities and outings. By creating intentional spaces for face-to-face interaction and shared experiences, individuals can nurture the bonds that matter most and rediscover the joy and fulfillment that comes from authentic human connection.

Additionally, seeking support and guidance from friends, family members, or mental health professionals can be invaluable in addressing technology addiction and its impact on relationships. By opening up about their struggles and working collaboratively to develop strategies for change, individuals can break free from the grip of compulsive technology use and cultivate a more balanced, fulfilling life.

Ultimately, the key to navigating the potential for technology addiction and relationship neglect lies in recognizing the power and limitations of digital tools. While technology has undoubtedly brought countless benefits to our lives, it is essential to remember that it is no substitute for the depth, richness, and transformative potential of real-life human connection. By approaching technology with mindfulness, intentionality, and a commitment to nurturing the relationships that matter most, we can harness its power while ensuring that it remains a tool for growth and connection, rather than a source of isolation and neglect.

Summary: Navigating the Digital Landscape for Stronger Connections

The rapid advancement and ubiquitous presence of technology have undeniably reshaped the landscape of modern relationships. While digital tools have brought countless benefits and opportunities for connection, it is crucial to acknowledge and address the potential challenges and pitfalls that arise when technology becomes a dominant force in our personal lives. From the paradox of constant connectivity leading to feelings of disconnection, to the risks of misinterpretation in digital communication, to the temptations of online infidelity and the dangers of technology addiction, the digital age presents a complex array of obstacles that can strain the bonds we share with others.

However, by cultivating awareness, establishing clear boundaries, and prioritizing authentic human connection, we can navigate these challenges and harness the power of technology to enhance, rather than hinder, our relationships. It is through open and honest communication, a commitment to presence and mindfulness, and a willingness to seek support when needed that we can build the resilience and skills necessary to thrive in the digital age.

As we move forward, it is essential to approach technology with intention and purpose, recognizing its immense potential as a tool for growth and connection, while also acknowledging its limitations. By striking a healthy balance between our online and offline lives, we can create a strong foundation for nurturing the relationships that matter most. Through this mindful and empowered approach, we can embrace the opportunities of the digital age while safeguarding the depth, richness, and transformative power of authentic human connection.

Section 4: Strategies for Navigating Technology in Relationships

In today's digital age, technology has become an integral part of our lives, and its impact on our relationships cannot be understated. From the way we communicate to how we connect with our loved ones, technology has transformed the landscape of modern relationships. While it has brought numerous benefits, such as increased accessibility and convenience, it has also introduced new challenges and potential pitfalls that can strain even the strongest of bonds.

As we navigate this ever-evolving digital world, it is crucial to develop strategies that allow us to harness the power of technology in a way that supports and nurtures our relationships, rather than hinders them. In this section, we will explore practical approaches and techniques that individuals and couples can employ to strike a healthy balance between technology use and building meaningful connections with one another.

By setting clear boundaries, prioritizing face-to-face communication, and being mindful of our digital habits, we can create a solid foundation for our relationships to thrive in the modern era. Whether you are in a long-distance relationship, navigating the world of online dating, or simply trying to maintain a strong connection with your partner amidst the distractions of screens and notifications, the strategies discussed in this section will provide you with the tools and insights needed to build and sustain a healthy, fulfilling relationship in the digital age.

So, let us embark on this journey together, as we explore the art of navigating technology in relationships and discover how we can use it to enhance, rather than detract from, the bonds we share with those we love.

Subsection 4.1: Establishing Boundaries and Agreements

In any relationship, setting clear boundaries and agreements is essential for maintaining a healthy and respectful dynamic. This is especially true when it comes to technology use, as the constant presence of digital devices can easily intrude upon quality time spent together and create feelings of neglect or disconnection. To minimize the negative impact of technology on your relationship, it is crucial to have open and honest conversations with your partner about your expectations and needs surrounding technology use.

One effective approach is to establish designated "tech-free" times, such as during meals, date nights, or intimate moments. By mutually agreeing to put away your phones, tablets, or laptops during these specific periods, you create opportunities for uninterrupted, face-to-face communication and connection. This not only helps to foster a sense of presence and attentiveness but also demonstrates respect for your partner and the time you spend together.

Another important aspect of setting boundaries around technology use is discussing the appropriate use of devices in shared spaces, such as the bedroom. Research has shown that the presence of digital devices in the bedroom can interfere with sleep quality and intimacy. By agreeing to keep the bedroom a technology-free zone or establishing a cutoff time for device use before bed, you can create a sacred space that prioritizes rest, relaxation, and connection with your partner.

It is also essential to establish boundaries around the use of technology for work-related purposes outside of designated work hours. In today's fast-paced, always-connected world, it can be tempting to respond to emails or take work calls at all hours of the day. However, this constant availability can strain relationships and lead to feelings of neglect or resentment. By setting clear boundaries around when and how you will attend to work-related matters, you can ensure that your relationship remains a top priority and that you have adequate time to nurture your connection with your partner.

When establishing boundaries and agreements around technology use, it is important to approach the conversation with empathy, understanding, and a willingness to compromise. Recognize that you and your partner may have different needs and preferences when it comes to technology use, and be open to finding solutions that work for both of you. Regularly check in with one another to ensure that the boundaries you have set are effective and make adjustments as needed.

By proactively establishing clear boundaries and agreements around technology use, you can minimize its negative impact on your relationship and create a solid foundation for a healthy, connected partnership in the digital age.

Subsection 4.2: Prioritizing Face-to-Face Communication and Quality Time

In the digital age, it is all too easy to fall into the trap of relying heavily on technology for communication and connection with our loved ones. While text messages, social media interactions, and video calls have their place in maintaining relationships, nothing can replace the value of face-to-face communication and quality time spent together.

When we prioritize in-person interactions, we create opportunities for deeper, more meaningful connections with our partners. Face-to-face communication allows us to pick up on subtle nonverbal cues, such as facial expressions, body language, and tone of voice, which are essential for understanding and empathizing with one another. These cues are often lost or misinterpreted in digital communication, leading to misunderstandings and potential conflicts.

Moreover, the act of being physically present with your partner, without the distractions of screens and notifications, demonstrates your commitment to the relationship and your willingness to invest time and energy into nurturing your bond. It sends a powerful message that you value your partner and the connection you share.

Quality time spent together, whether it's engaging in a shared hobby, trying a new activity, or simply enjoying each other's company, is crucial for maintaining a strong emotional connection. These shared experiences create lasting memories, foster a sense of teamwork, and provide opportunities for laughter, joy, and intimacy. They help to strengthen the foundation of your relationship and provide a solid base from which to weather any challenges that may arise.

To prioritize face-to-face communication and quality time in your relationship, consider setting aside dedicated "date nights" or "unplugged" times where you both agree to put away your digital devices and focus solely on each other. Use this time to engage in meaningful conversations, share your thoughts and feelings, and actively listen to your partner. Plan activities that allow you to connect and enjoy each other's company, such as cooking a meal together, going for a hike, or exploring a new part of your city.

It is also important to be mindful of the quality of your in-person interactions. Make an effort to be fully present and engaged when spending time with your partner, avoiding the temptation to check your phone or let your mind wander to other tasks or concerns. Show genuine interest in your partner's thoughts, feelings, and experiences, and express your appreciation and affection through both words and actions.

By making face-to-face communication and quality time a priority in your relationship, you can foster a deeper, more meaningful connection with your partner. You will create a strong foundation of trust, understanding, and intimacy that will help your relationship thrive, even in the face of the challenges and distractions of the digital world.

Subsection 4.3: Practicing Mindfulness and Presence

In a world filled with constant digital distractions, practicing mindfulness and presence has become more important than ever for nurturing healthy relationships. When we are fully present and engaged in the moment, we create opportunities for deeper, more meaningful connections with our partners. Mindfulness allows us to set aside the noise and clutter of our digital lives and focus on the person in front of us, fostering a sense of intimacy, understanding, and appreciation.

Mindfulness is the practice of bringing our attention to the present moment, without judgment or distraction. When applied to relationships, it means being fully attuned to your partner's thoughts, feelings, and needs, and responding with empathy and compassion. By cultivating mindfulness, we become more aware of our own emotions and reactions, enabling us to communicate more effectively and navigate challenges with greater ease.

One of the key aspects of practicing mindfulness in relationships is minimizing digital distractions. When we are constantly checking our phones, responding to notifications, or multitasking with various devices, we send a message to our partner that they are not our top priority. This can lead to feelings of neglect, resentment, and disconnection, eroding the foundation of trust and intimacy in the relationship.

To practice mindfulness and minimize digital distractions, start by setting aside dedicated time each day to be fully present with your partner. This could be during meals, conversations, or shared activities. Make a conscious effort to put away your devices and give your partner your undivided attention. Listen actively, maintain eye contact, and show genuine interest in what they have to say. By being fully engaged in the moment, you demonstrate your commitment to the relationship and your desire to strengthen your bond.

Another effective way to cultivate mindfulness in your relationship is to practice mindful communication. This involves speaking with intention, clarity, and compassion, and listening with an open heart and mind. When discussing sensitive topics or navigating conflicts, take a moment to pause and reflect before responding. This allows you to choose your words carefully and avoid reacting impulsively or defensively. By approaching communication with mindfulness, you create a safe, supportive space for both partners to express themselves and work towards a deeper understanding.

Incorporating mindfulness practices, such as meditation or deep breathing exercises, into your daily routine can also have a positive impact on your relationship. These practices help to reduce stress, increase emotional regulation, and promote a greater sense of inner peace and clarity. By taking time to nurture your own well-being, you become better equipped to show up fully and compassionately in your relationship.

Ultimately, practicing mindfulness and presence in your relationship is about prioritizing connection and understanding over the constant pull of digital distractions. It requires a conscious effort to set aside the noise and focus on the person in front of you, but the rewards are immeasurable. By being fully present and attuned to your partner, you create a strong foundation of trust, intimacy, and love that can weather any challenge and deepen over time.

Subsection 4.4: Harnessing Technology for Relationship Enhancement

While technology can sometimes pose challenges in relationships, it also offers a wealth of opportunities to strengthen and enhance the bonds we share with our loved ones. By harnessing the power of digital tools and platforms in creative and thoughtful ways, we can foster deeper connections, express our love and appreciation, and keep the spark alive in our relationships, even amidst the demands of modern life.

One simple yet effective way to use technology to strengthen your relationship is by sending thoughtful messages to your partner throughout the day. A heartfelt text message, a loving email, or a sweet voice note can go a long way in making your partner feel loved, appreciated, and connected to you, even when you're physically apart. Take a moment to express your gratitude for your partner's presence in your life, remind them of a cherished memory you share, or simply let them know that you're thinking of them. These small gestures, facilitated by technology, can have a profound impact on the emotional intimacy and resilience of your relationship.

Technology can also be a powerful tool for planning surprises and creating memorable experiences for your partner. Use online resources and apps to research and plan special dates, getaways, or adventures that cater to your partner's interests and preferences. You can create a digital scavenger hunt, leading your partner to various locations or clues that hold special meaning for your relationship. Or, you can use technology to coordinate with friends and family to organize a surprise party or celebration for your partner's birthday or other milestones. By leveraging the convenience and connectivity offered by technology, you can create unique and thoughtful experiences that strengthen your bond and create lasting memories.

Another way to harness technology for relationship enhancement is by engaging in virtual acts of love and appreciation. Create a digital photo album or video montage showcasing your favorite moments together, set to a meaningful soundtrack. Write a heartfelt blog post or social media update expressing your love and gratitude for your partner, and tag them so they can share in the joy. Use video chat platforms to have virtual date nights, where you can cook the same meal together, watch a movie in sync, or engage in a fun online game or quiz. These virtual experiences can help bridge the gap when you're physically separated and provide opportunities for shared laughter, connection, and intimacy.

Technology can also be a valuable resource for learning and growing together as a couple. Engage in online courses, webinars, or workshops that focus on relationship skills, communication techniques, or personal growth. Read and discuss articles, books, or podcasts that offer insights and advice on building strong, healthy relationships. By using technology to access valuable information and resources, you can work together to continuously strengthen and evolve your relationship, fostering a deeper sense of understanding, empathy, and mutual support.

When harnessing technology for relationship enhancement, it's essential to approach it with intention, mindfulness, and a focus on your partner's unique needs and preferences. Use technology as a tool to supplement and enhance your in-person interactions, rather than replacing them entirely. Be attentive to your partner's comfort level with different forms of digital communication and respect their boundaries and privacy. By using technology thoughtfully and in service of your relationship goals, you can create a more connected, appreciative, and resilient bond that thrives in the digital age.

Summary: Embracing Technology for Stronger, More Connected Relationships

In this section, we have explored a range of strategies for navigating technology in relationships, focusing on how individuals and couples can harness the power of digital tools to foster deeper connections, express love and appreciation, and maintain a healthy balance in the modern world. By establishing clear boundaries and agreements, prioritizing face-to-face communication and quality time, practicing mindfulness and presence, and using technology creatively to enhance the relationship, couples can build a strong foundation of trust, intimacy, and mutual understanding.

As we navigate the ever-evolving landscape of technology and its impact on our relationships, it is essential to remember that the key to success lies in our intentional, mindful approach. By consistently communicating with our partners, setting shared goals and expectations, and remaining open to adapting our strategies as needed, we can ensure that technology serves as a powerful ally in our quest for stronger, more fulfilling connections.

Ultimately, the strategies outlined in this section empower us to take control of our digital lives and shape our relationships in a way that aligns with our deepest values and aspirations. By embracing technology as a tool for growth, connection, and love, we can create a new paradigm for relationships in the digital age – one that celebrates the best of what both human connection and technological innovation have to offer. As we move forward on this journey together, let us remain committed to nurturing the bonds that matter most, and to harnessing the power of technology to build a brighter, more connected future for ourselves and those we love.

Section 5: Maintaining a Healthy Balance in the Digital Age

In today's fast-paced, technology-driven world, it's easy to get caught up in the constant buzz of notifications, messages, and social media updates. While technology has undoubtedly brought us closer together in many ways, it has also created new challenges and complexities in our relationships. As we navigate this digital landscape, it's crucial to strike a healthy balance between our online and offline lives, ensuring that our use of technology enhances, rather than detracts from, our connections with others.

In this section, we'll explore the importance of maintaining a healthy balance between technology and relationships in the modern world. We'll delve into the potential pitfalls of excessive screen time and the impact it can have on our ability to be present and engaged with our loved ones. By examining the role of technology in our daily lives and relationships, we can develop strategies to ensure that we're using it in a way that supports, rather than hinders, our connections with others.

Through a combination of research-backed insights, practical tips, and real-life examples, this section will provide you with the tools and knowledge you need to navigate the digital age with confidence and intention. Whether you're looking to strengthen your romantic partnership, deepen your friendships, or simply create more meaningful connections in your life, the insights and advice in this section will help you find the right balance between technology and human connection.

So, let's dive in and explore how we can harness the power of technology to enhance our relationships, while also knowing when to unplug and focus on the people and experiences that matter most. By being mindful and intentional in our use of technology, we can cultivate stronger, more resilient relationships that thrive in the face of the unique challenges and opportunities of the digital age.

Subsection 5.1: Regularly Assessing Technology's Impact on the Relationship

In the fast-paced digital age, it's easy for technology to gradually and unknowingly infiltrate our relationships, influencing the way we communicate, connect, and spend time together. To maintain a healthy balance, it's crucial for couples to regularly assess the impact of technology on their relationship and make necessary adjustments.

One effective way to do this is by setting aside dedicated time to have an open and honest conversation about technology use. During this discussion, partners can share their observations, concerns, and feelings about how technology is affecting their relationship. This conversation should be approached with a non-judgmental and empathetic attitude, focusing on understanding each other's perspectives and finding common ground.

Some key questions to consider during this assessment include: Are we spending more time on our devices than engaging with each other? Do we feel distracted or disconnected during face-to-face interactions due to technology? Are we using technology to avoid difficult conversations or emotional intimacy? By honestly answering these questions, couples can gain valuable insights into the role technology plays in their relationship.

Based on the insights gained from this assessment, couples can work together to make necessary adjustments to their technology habits. This may involve setting boundaries around screen time, establishing "tech-free" zones or activities, or finding ways to use technology to enhance their connection, such as sending loving messages or planning virtual date nights.

It's important to remember that every relationship is unique, and there is no one-size-fits-all approach to managing technology. What works for one couple may not work for another. The key is to find a balance that feels authentic and sustainable for both partners, and to be willing to adapt and adjust as needed.

By regularly assessing technology's impact on the relationship and making conscious efforts to maintain a healthy balance, couples can ensure that their connection remains strong and vibrant in the digital age. This ongoing process of evaluation and adjustment not only safeguards the relationship from the potential pitfalls of excessive technology use but also creates opportunities for deeper understanding, growth, and intimacy.

Subsection 5.2: Cultivating Shared Tech-Free Experiences

In a world where technology has become an integral part of our daily lives, it's easy to fall into the trap of constant digital connection. While technology has its benefits, it's crucial for couples to recognize the value of cultivating shared experiences that don't involve screens or digital devices. By intentionally creating tech-free moments, partners can foster a deeper sense of connection, presence, and intimacy in their relationship.

One of the most effective ways to cultivate shared tech-free experiences is to engage in outdoor adventures together. Whether it's hiking a scenic trail, exploring a nearby park, or simply taking a leisurely walk around the neighborhood, being in nature provides a refreshing break from the constant buzz of technology. Outdoor activities not only promote physical well-being but also encourage meaningful conversations and create opportunities for bonding and shared memories.

Another way to nurture tech-free connections is by pursuing hobbies and interests together. Engaging in activities such as cooking, gardening, or creating art can be incredibly rewarding and fulfilling for couples. These shared pursuits provide a sense of accomplishment and allow partners to learn and grow together, strengthening their bond and fostering a deeper appreciation for each other's unique talents and passions.

Regular tech-free date nights are also an excellent way to prioritize quality time and maintain a strong emotional connection. By setting aside dedicated time to focus solely on each other, without the distractions of phones, laptops, or televisions, couples can rediscover the joy of engaging in meaningful conversations, active listening, and physical affection. Whether it's a candlelit dinner at home, a picnic in the park, or a night of stargazing, tech-free date nights create sacred spaces for couples to reconnect and nurture their relationship.

It's important to note that cultivating shared tech-free experiences doesn't mean completely abandoning technology or viewing it as inherently negative. Instead, it's about being intentional and mindful in our use of technology, recognizing when it's time to unplug and focus on the people and experiences that matter most. By finding a healthy balance and regularly incorporating tech-free moments into their relationship, couples can build a strong foundation of connection, intimacy, and shared joy that will sustain them in the face of the challenges and distractions of the digital age.

Subsection 5.3: Modeling Healthy Technology Habits for Future Generations

As parents, caregivers, and role models, we have a significant influence on the way future generations approach technology and its role in their relationships. In today's digital age, children are growing up surrounded by screens and devices, making it more important than ever to model healthy technology habits and foster a balanced approach to relationships in the digital age.

One of the most effective ways to teach children about healthy technology use is by setting a positive example ourselves. When we prioritize face-to-face interactions, engage in active listening, and demonstrate the value of unplugging and being present, we send a powerful message to the young people in our lives. By showing them that it's possible to maintain strong, meaningful connections without constantly relying on technology, we help them develop the skills and mindset needed to navigate the digital world with confidence and intention.

It's also crucial to have open, honest conversations with children about the benefits and challenges of technology in relationships. By discussing the potential pitfalls of excessive screen time, such as distraction, disconnection, and the pressure to constantly compare oneself to others online, we can help them develop a more critical and self-aware approach to technology use. At the same time, we should also acknowledge the positive aspects of technology, such as its ability to facilitate long-distance connections and provide access to valuable resources and support networks.

Another key aspect of modeling healthy technology habits is setting clear boundaries and expectations around screen time and device use. This may involve establishing designated tech-free zones in the home, such as the dinner table or bedrooms, or setting limits on the amount of time spent on devices each day. By creating structure and consistency around technology use, we help children develop a sense of balance and self-regulation, which will serve them well in their future relationships.

It's important to remember that modeling healthy technology habits is an ongoing process, not a one-time event. As technology continues to evolve and new challenges arise, we must remain adaptable and open to adjusting our approach as needed. By engaging in regular conversations, staying informed about the latest research and best practices, and being willing to model flexibility and resilience in the face of change, we can help future generations develop the skills and mindset needed to thrive in the digital age.

Ultimately, by modeling healthy technology habits and fostering a balanced approach to relationships, we not only set the stage for our children's future success but also contribute to a broader cultural shift toward more mindful and intentional technology use. As we work to create a world in which digital tools enhance, rather than detract from, our ability to connect with others, we lay the foundation for a future in which strong, resilient relationships can thrive, both online and off.

Summary: Embracing Mindful Technology Use for Thriving Relationships

In this digital age, maintaining a healthy balance between technology and relationships is more important than ever. By regularly assessing the impact of technology on our connections, cultivating shared tech-free experiences, and modeling healthy habits for future generations, we can harness the power of digital tools to enhance, rather than detract from, our most meaningful relationships.

Throughout this section, we've explored practical strategies and insights for navigating the challenges and opportunities of technology in modern relationships. From setting boundaries and prioritizing face-to-face communication to pursuing shared hobbies and creating tech-free moments, the key is to approach technology with intention and mindfulness.

As we move forward in this ever-evolving digital landscape, it's crucial to remember that the most fulfilling relationships are built on a foundation of presence, empathy, and genuine connection. By finding a healthy balance between our online and offline lives, we not only strengthen our own relationships but also set a positive example for the generations to come.

So, let us embrace the power of technology to bring us closer together, while also cherishing the irreplaceable value of face-to-face interactions and shared experiences. By doing so, we can cultivate relationships that thrive in the digital age – relationships built on trust, understanding, and a deep appreciation for the people and moments that matter most.

Chapter Summary: Embracing Technology for Stronger Connections

In today's digital age, technology has become an integral part of our lives, and its impact on modern relationships is undeniable. From the way we form new connections to how we maintain existing ones, technology has transformed the landscape of relationships. While it brings numerous benefits, such as increased accessibility, convenience, and opportunities for shared experiences, it also presents challenges and potential pitfalls that must be navigated with care and intention.

To harness the power of technology for stronger, healthier relationships, it is essential to establish clear boundaries and agreements, prioritize face-to-face communication and quality time, and practice mindfulness and presence in our interactions. By using technology as a tool to enhance rather than replace meaningful connections, we can cultivate deeper intimacy, understanding, and support in our relationships.

As we move forward in the digital age, it is crucial to maintain a healthy balance between our online and offline lives. Regularly assessing technology's impact on our relationships, cultivating shared tech-free experiences, and modeling healthy technology habits for future generations will help us foster a more balanced and fulfilling approach to relationships in the modern world.

Ultimately, the key to navigating the impact of technology on our relationships lies in our ability to embrace its benefits while being mindful of its challenges. By approaching technology with intention, compassion, and a commitment to nurturing authentic connections, we can build stronger, more resilient relationships that thrive in the face of the ever-evolving digital landscape.

Chapter 12: Cultivating Lasting Love and Commitment

In the realm of relationships, one of the most sought-after and cherished goals is to build a love that endures the test of time. A love that not only weathers the storms of life but also grows stronger and deeper with each passing year. While falling in love may seem effortless, maintaining that love and commitment requires dedication, effort, and a willingness to continually nurture the bond between partners.

Throughout this chapter, we will embark on a journey to uncover the secrets behind cultivating lasting love and commitment. We will explore the essential ingredients that form the foundation of an enduring relationship, delving into the importance of shared values, emotional intimacy, and unwavering trust. By understanding these core elements, couples can create a solid bedrock upon which their love can flourish.

However, building a long-lasting relationship is not solely about laying a strong foundation; it also involves actively nurturing and maintaining the connection over time. We will discuss practical strategies for keeping the spark alive, from prioritizing quality time together to expressing love and appreciation in meaningful ways. Through these efforts, couples can reignite the passion and excitement that first brought them together, ensuring that their love remains vibrant and fulfilling.

Of course, no relationship is without its challenges, and the ability to navigate conflicts and disagreements constructively is crucial for long-term success. We will explore effective communication techniques, emphasizing the importance of open, honest, and respectful dialogue. By developing strong listening skills and practicing empathy, partners can foster a deeper understanding of each other's perspectives and work together to find mutually satisfying solutions.

As individuals grow and evolve throughout their lives, so too must their relationships adapt and change. We will delve into the concept of balancing individuality and togetherness, recognizing the importance of supporting each other's personal growth while maintaining a strong sense of partnership. By embracing change and continuously learning together, couples can ensure that their love remains dynamic and resilient.

Through the pages of this chapter, we will explore these themes and more, providing you with the insights, tools, and inspiration needed to cultivate a love that lasts a lifetime. Whether you are in the early stages of a relationship or have been with your partner for decades, the wisdom shared here will help you strengthen your bond, deepen your connection, and create a love story that stands the test of time. So, let us embark on this journey together, unlocking the secrets to enduring love and commitment.

Section 1: The Foundations of Enduring Love

Love is a beautiful, complex, and ever-evolving emotion that lies at the heart of every meaningful relationship. While falling in love may seem effortless, building and maintaining a lasting, committed partnership requires a solid foundation of essential elements and qualities. In this section, we will explore the bedrock upon which enduring love is built, delving into the key ingredients that enable couples to weather the storms of life and emerge stronger, more connected, and deeply in love.

As we embark on this journey, it is crucial to recognize that every relationship is unique, shaped by the individual experiences, personalities, and aspirations of the people involved. However, amidst the diversity of human connections, there exist universal threads that weave together the fabric of lasting love. By understanding and cultivating these fundamental qualities, couples can create a resilient bond that not only endures but thrives over time.

Throughout this section, we will examine the role of shared values, emotional intimacy, mutual respect, and adaptability in fostering an unbreakable partnership. We will explore how aligning your life goals, communicating openly and honestly, and supporting each other's growth can create a deep sense of unity and purpose. Moreover, we will discuss the importance of trust, loyalty, and forgiveness in overcoming challenges and strengthening your bond.

As you read on, remember that building a lasting, loving relationship is not a destination but a lifelong journey of discovery, growth, and commitment. By laying a strong foundation rooted in the essential elements of enduring love, you and your partner can create a beautiful, fulfilling partnership that stands the test of time. So, let us dive in and uncover the secrets to cultivating a love that lasts a lifetime.

Subsection 1.1: Shared Values and Life Goals

At the core of every enduring partnership lies a foundation of shared values and compatible life goals. When two individuals come together with a common vision for their future, they create a powerful bond that can withstand the tests of time. Shared values serve as the guiding principles that shape a couple's decisions, actions, and interactions, providing a sense of unity and purpose.

Imagine a couple, Sarah and Michael, who have been together for over a decade. From the early days of their relationship, they discovered a deep connection rooted in their mutual respect for honesty, kindness, and personal growth. As they navigated the ups and downs of life together, their shared values acted as a compass, helping them make choices that aligned with their beliefs and strengthened their bond.

Compatible life goals are equally crucial in building a strong, lasting partnership. When couples have similar aspirations and dreams, they can work together towards a common purpose, supporting and encouraging each other along the way. This sense of shared direction fosters a deep sense of intimacy and commitment, as both partners feel invested in each other's happiness and success.

Consider another couple, Alex and Emma, who met in college and bonded over their passion for environmental conservation. As they grew together, they discovered a shared desire to build a life centered around sustainability and making a positive impact on the world. Their compatible life goals became the foundation for a fulfilling partnership, as they pursued careers in eco-friendly industries and volunteered for environmental causes side by side.

When shared values and life goals align, couples create a synergy that propels them forward, even in the face of challenges. They find strength in their common beliefs and aspirations, which serve as a source of motivation and resilience. By consistently prioritizing their shared values and working towards their mutual goals, couples can cultivate a deep sense of trust, respect, and understanding that endures through the years.

It is important to note that having shared values and compatible life goals does not mean that couples must agree on everything. Healthy partnerships allow for individual differences and perspectives, as long as there is a fundamental alignment on the core principles that guide their lives together. Open communication, compromise, and a willingness to grow together are key to maintaining this balance.

In essence, shared values and compatible life goals form the bedrock of enduring love. They provide a solid foundation upon which couples can build a life of meaning, purpose, and fulfillment. By consistently nurturing and honoring these shared elements, partners can create an unbreakable bond that withstands the test of time and grows stronger with each passing year.

Subsection 1.2: Deep Emotional Connection and Intimacy

At the heart of every enduring relationship lies a profound emotional connection and a sense of intimacy that binds two souls together. This deep, intangible bond serves as the lifeblood of love, nourishing and sustaining the commitment between partners through the joys and challenges of life. In this subsection, we will explore the crucial role that emotional connection and intimacy play in fostering and maintaining long-lasting love.

Emotional connection refers to the profound sense of understanding, empathy, and unity that exists between two individuals. It is the feeling of being seen, heard, and accepted for who you are, flaws and all. When partners cultivate a strong emotional connection, they create a safe haven where they can be vulnerable, authentic, and wholly themselves. This connection allows couples to navigate life's ups and downs together, providing a steadfast source of support, comfort, and resilience.

Intimacy, on the other hand, is the closeness and familiarity that emerges from this emotional connection. It encompasses not only physical affection but also the sharing of thoughts, feelings, dreams, and fears. Intimacy is the foundation upon which trust, respect, and understanding are built, enabling couples to grow together and deepen their love over time.

To illustrate the power of emotional connection and intimacy, consider the story of Lila and Ethan, a couple who have been married for over three decades. From the early days of their relationship, they made a conscious effort to prioritize emotional intimacy, setting aside time each day to share their thoughts and feelings without judgment or interruption. As they navigated the challenges of parenthood, career changes, and personal growth, their emotional connection served as an unwavering anchor, providing strength and stability amidst life's storms.

Cultivating and maintaining a deep emotional connection requires intentional effort and commitment from both partners. It involves open, honest communication, active listening, and a willingness to be vulnerable. Couples must create a safe space where they can express their needs, fears, and aspirations without fear of rejection or criticism. By consistently nurturing this emotional bond, partners can foster a sense of closeness and understanding that endures through the years.

Intimacy, too, requires ongoing attention and care. It thrives on small, daily gestures of affection, appreciation, and support, such as a heartfelt compliment, a tender touch, or a thoughtful act of kindness. By consistently prioritizing intimacy, couples can keep the spark of love alive and maintain a deep sense of connection, even as the nature of their relationship evolves over time.

It is important to recognize that emotional connection and intimacy are not static states but rather dynamic processes that require ongoing effort and investment. Life's challenges, such as stress, illness, or personal growth, can sometimes strain these bonds, causing partners to feel disconnected or distant. In these moments, it is crucial for couples to recommit to nurturing their emotional connection, seeking professional help if needed to navigate difficult emotions or communication barriers.

Ultimately, a deep emotional connection and a strong sense of intimacy form the bedrock of enduring love. They provide the resilience, comfort, and joy that enable couples to weather life's storms and emerge stronger, more united, and deeply committed to one another. By consistently prioritizing and nurturing these essential elements, partners can cultivate a love that not only endures but thrives, growing richer and more profound with each passing year.

Subsection 1.3: Mutual Respect, Trust, and Loyalty

In the tapestry of enduring love, mutual respect, trust, and loyalty are the golden threads that weave a strong and resilient bond between partners. These essential qualities form the cornerstone of a healthy, long-lasting relationship, providing a solid foundation upon which love can flourish and withstand the test of time. When couples cultivate and maintain these vital elements, they create a safe haven of emotional security, enabling them to navigate life's challenges hand in hand, with unwavering support and devotion.

Mutual respect is the bedrock of any strong partnership. It is the deep admiration and appreciation for each other's individuality, beliefs, and boundaries. When partners treat each other with respect, they create an atmosphere of emotional safety, where both individuals feel valued, heard, and understood. This respect extends beyond mere courtesy; it is a profound acknowledgment of each other's inherent worth and dignity. By consistently demonstrating respect through their words, actions, and decisions, couples foster a sense of equality and partnership that strengthens their bond and allows their love to thrive.

Trust, another essential pillar of lasting love, is the unshakable belief in each other's reliability, honesty, and integrity. It is the confidence that your partner will be there for you, no matter what life throws your way. When trust is present, couples can be vulnerable, sharing their deepest fears, dreams, and aspirations without fear of judgment or betrayal. This emotional openness allows for a profound level of intimacy and connection, as partners become each other's safe haven in a world of uncertainty. Trust is not inherent; it is earned through consistent actions, kept promises, and a steadfast commitment to honesty and transparency.

Loyalty, the third cornerstone of enduring love, is the unwavering dedication and commitment to one's partner and the relationship. It is the choice to stand by each other's side, through the highs and lows, the triumphs and the challenges. Loyalty is not blind allegiance; rather, it is a conscious decision to prioritize the well-being and happiness of the relationship, even when faced with temptation or adversity. When partners are loyal to each other, they create a sense of security and stability that allows their love to weather any storm. They become each other's anchor, providing a steadfast source of support, encouragement, and comfort.

Cultivating mutual respect, trust, and loyalty requires intentional effort and commitment from both partners. It involves open, honest communication, active listening, and a willingness to be accountable for one's actions. Couples must consistently demonstrate these qualities through their daily interactions, from the smallest gestures of kindness to the most significant decisions that impact their shared life. By prioritizing respect, trust, and loyalty, partners create a positive feedback loop, where each action reinforces and strengthens the bond between them.

It is important to recognize that these cornerstones of lasting love are not impervious to damage. Disrespectful behavior, broken promises, or breaches of trust can erode the foundation of a relationship, causing pain and disconnection. In these moments, it is crucial for couples to address the issue head-on, engaging in open, honest dialogue and working together to rebuild the damaged trust and respect. This process requires patience, empathy, and a shared commitment to healing and growth.

Ultimately, mutual respect, trust, and loyalty are the essential nutrients that nourish the roots of enduring love. They provide the stability, security, and emotional sustenance that enable couples to grow together, weather life's challenges, and emerge stronger and more united. By consistently nurturing and honoring these vital qualities, partners can cultivate a love that not only endures but thrives, becoming a testament to the power of a relationship built on a foundation of unwavering respect, trust, and devotion.

Subsection 1.4: Resilience and Adaptability

In the journey of lasting love, resilience and adaptability are the essential tools that enable couples to navigate the inevitable challenges and changes that life presents. These qualities are the foundation of a strong, enduring partnership, allowing lovers to weather the storms of adversity and emerge stronger, more united, and deeply committed to one another. In this subsection, we will explore the crucial role that resilience and adaptability play in building and maintaining a love that stands the test of time.

Resilience, the ability to bounce back from setbacks and hardships, is a vital component of any healthy relationship. It is the inner strength that allows couples to face difficulties head-on, learning from their experiences and growing together in the process. When partners cultivate resilience, they develop a shared sense of perseverance and determination, knowing that they can overcome any obstacle as long as they have each other's support and love.

Consider the story of Olivia and James, a couple who faced numerous challenges throughout their decades-long marriage. From financial hardships to health scares, they encountered many situations that tested their resilience. However, instead of allowing these difficulties to tear them apart, Olivia and James chose to lean on each other, finding strength in their shared commitment and unwavering love. They approached each challenge as an opportunity to grow, adapt, and deepen their bond, emerging from each trial with renewed appreciation for one another and the life they had built together.

Adaptability, the capacity to adjust and evolve in response to changing circumstances, is equally essential for the longevity of love. In a world that is constantly shifting, couples must be willing to adapt and grow together, embracing new experiences and learning from one another. When partners approach change with an open mind and a flexible spirit, they create a dynamic, evolving relationship that can withstand the test of time.

To illustrate the power of adaptability, let us consider the journey of Sofia and Michael, a couple who fell in love in their early twenties. As they navigated the various stages of their lives together – from college graduation to career changes, parenthood, and beyond – they encountered numerous moments that required them to adapt and redefine their relationship. By embracing change and approaching each new chapter with curiosity and a willingness to learn, Sofia and Michael were able to grow together, discovering new facets of their love and strengthening their bond with every shared experience.

Cultivating resilience and adaptability in a relationship requires intentional effort and commitment from both partners. It involves fostering open, honest communication, practicing empathy and understanding, and maintaining a positive, growth-oriented mindset. Couples must create a safe space where they can express their fears, vulnerabilities, and aspirations, working together to find solutions and support one another through life's challenges.

Moreover, building resilience and adaptability requires a foundation of trust, respect, and emotional intimacy. When partners feel secure in their connection and confident in each other's love and support, they are better equipped to face adversity and embrace change. By consistently nurturing these essential elements of their relationship, couples can cultivate the resilience and adaptability needed to weather any storm and emerge stronger, more united, and deeply in love.

Ultimately, resilience and adaptability are the keys to unlocking the full potential of enduring love. They enable couples to navigate the ups and downs of life with grace, compassion, and a shared sense of purpose, creating a bond that is unbreakable and eternally fulfilling. By embracing these qualities and consistently working to strengthen them, partners can build a love that not only endures but thrives, growing richer and more profound with each passing year.

Summary: Building a Love That Lasts

As we conclude this exploration of the foundations of enduring love, it becomes clear that crafting a long-lasting, committed relationship requires a combination of essential elements and qualities. By nurturing shared values, cultivating deep emotional connections, fostering mutual respect and trust, and embracing resilience and adaptability, couples can create a love that withstands the test of time.

The journey of enduring love is not always easy, but it is infinitely rewarding. It demands intentional effort, open communication, and a willingness to grow together. By consistently prioritizing the fundamental building blocks of a strong partnership, couples can weather any storm and emerge stronger, more united, and deeply in love.

As you reflect on the insights and wisdom shared in this section, consider how you can apply these principles to your own relationship. Take the time to discuss your shared values and life goals with your partner, and work together to create a vision for your future. Nurture your emotional intimacy through open, honest communication and small gestures of affection. Consistently demonstrate respect, trust, and loyalty, and be willing to adapt and grow together as you navigate life's challenges hand in hand.

Remember, building a love that lasts is not a destination but a lifelong journey of discovery, growth, and commitment. By laying a strong foundation rooted in the essential elements of enduring love, you and your partner can create a beautiful, fulfilling partnership that stands the test of time. So, cherish each moment, celebrate your shared triumphs, and never stop working to strengthen the bond that brings you together. With dedication, compassion, and an unwavering commitment to one another, your love will endure, now and forever.

Section 2: Nurturing and Maintaining the Spark

In the journey of cultivating lasting love and commitment, one of the most significant challenges couples face is keeping the spark alive. As time passes and the novelty of a new relationship fades, it's all too easy to fall into a routine that slowly erodes the sense of excitement and passion that once brought you together. However, with intentional effort and a willingness to nurture your connection, it is possible to maintain and even reignite the spark in your long-term relationship.

Picture this: you and your partner, years into your relationship, still looking at each other with the same adoring eyes and feeling the same flutter of anticipation when you're together. It's a beautiful vision, isn't it? But how do you make it a reality? The answer lies in the small, daily choices you make to prioritize your relationship and keep the love alive.

In this section, we'll explore a range of strategies and ideas for nurturing and maintaining the spark in your long-term relationship. From prioritizing quality time together to expressing love and appreciation in meaningful ways, we'll delve into the practical steps you can take to keep your connection strong and vibrant. We'll also discuss the importance of keeping the romance and excitement alive, and how embracing a mindset of continuous learning and growth can help you and your partner evolve together over time.

Whether you're in the early stages of a committed relationship or have been with your partner for decades, the insights and advice in this section will empower you to take an active role in nurturing the love and passion that brought you together. By the end of this section, you'll have a toolkit of strategies and ideas for keeping the spark alive, ensuring that your relationship remains a source of joy, fulfillment, and deep connection for years to come. So, let's dive in and explore how you can create a love that lasts a lifetime.

Subsection 2.1: Prioritizing Quality Time and Shared Experiences

In the hustle and bustle of daily life, it's all too easy to let quality time with your partner fall by the wayside. Between work commitments, family obligations, and the endless distractions of modern life, finding moments to truly connect can feel like an uphill battle. However, prioritizing quality time and shared experiences is essential for maintaining a strong, intimate connection with your partner.

When we talk about quality time, we're not just referring to the quantity of time spent together, but rather the intentionality and presence brought to that time. It's about setting aside distractions, being fully engaged, and creating a space where you can focus solely on each other. This might mean putting away your phones during dinner, turning off the TV for an evening of conversation, or carving out a few hours each week for a shared hobby or activity.

The benefits of prioritizing quality time are numerous. For one, it allows you to continue learning about each other, even years into your relationship. As individuals, we are constantly growing and evolving, and taking the time to share our thoughts, dreams, and experiences with our partner helps us stay connected to who they are and who they are becoming. Additionally, quality time fosters a sense of intimacy and closeness that is essential for maintaining a strong emotional bond. When we feel truly seen, heard, and understood by our partner, it deepens our sense of connection and strengthens our commitment to the relationship.

Beyond simply spending time together, creating meaningful shared experiences is another key aspect of nurturing the spark in your relationship. Shared experiences provide opportunities for bonding, growth, and the creation of lasting memories. They can be as simple as trying a new restaurant together, taking a weekend getaway, or learning a new skill as a couple. The key is to step outside of your comfort zone and embrace novelty and adventure together.

Shared experiences also play a crucial role in building a sense of partnership and teamwork within your relationship. When you navigate new situations or challenges together, you learn to rely on each other, communicate effectively, and work towards a common goal. This sense of partnership and collaboration can then translate into other areas of your relationship, strengthening your bond and deepening your commitment to one another.

Of course, prioritizing quality time and shared experiences requires effort and intentionality. It means being proactive in carving out space in your schedule, saying no to other commitments when necessary, and being willing to invest time and energy into your relationship. However, the payoff is well worth it. By making your connection a priority and consistently nurturing it through quality time and shared experiences, you lay the foundation for a love that can weather any storm and stand the test of time.

Subsection 2.2: Expressing Love and Appreciation

In the tapestry of a long-lasting, loving relationship, the threads of expressed love and appreciation are woven throughout, creating a strong, resilient bond that can withstand the test of time. Regularly expressing your love, gratitude, and appreciation for your partner is a powerful way to sustain a positive, supportive relationship dynamic that nourishes both individuals and strengthens the connection between them.

One of the most fundamental ways to express love and appreciation is through verbal affirmations. Taking the time to tell your partner how much you love them, what you admire about them, and how grateful you are for their presence in your life can have a profound impact on your relationship. These heartfelt expressions don't need to be grandiose or elaborate; often, the most meaningful affirmations are the simple, genuine ones that come from a place of deep love and respect. Whether it's a whispered "I love you" before drifting off to sleep or a heartfelt compliment over your morning coffee, regularly verbalizing your love and appreciation can help your partner feel seen, valued, and cherished.

Another powerful way to express love and gratitude is through thoughtful gestures and acts of kindness. These gestures can be small, everyday acts that show your partner you're thinking of them and want to make their life a little easier or brighter. Perhaps it's surprising them with their favorite meal after a long day at work, leaving a sweet note in their pocket, or taking on a chore they typically handle to give them a break. These seemingly small actions speak volumes about your love and appreciation, demonstrating that you're attuned to your partner's needs and wants and are willing to go out of your way to show them you care.

In addition to daily gestures, expressing love and appreciation can also involve more elaborate, planned expressions of affection. This might include planning a surprise date night, writing a heartfelt letter detailing your love and gratitude, or creating a thoughtful gift that reflects your deep understanding and appreciation of your partner. These larger expressions of love serve as powerful reminders of your commitment to the relationship and your desire to continually nurture and strengthen your bond.

It's important to note that expressing love and appreciation is not a one-size-fits-all endeavor. We all give and receive love in different ways, and understanding your partner's love language can help you tailor your expressions of affection to their unique needs and preferences. Whether your partner feels most loved through words of affirmation, quality time, physical touch, acts of service, or receiving gifts, making an effort to express your love in a way that resonates with them can deepen your connection and make your partner feel truly cherished.

Ultimately, the key to expressing love and appreciation in a long-term relationship is consistency and authenticity. It's not about grand, sporadic gestures, but rather a steady, genuine outpouring of love and gratitude that becomes a fundamental part of your relationship dynamic. By making the conscious choice to regularly express your love and appreciation, you create a positive feedback loop that reinforces your bond, fosters a sense of security and belonging, and helps your relationship thrive. So, never underestimate the power of a heartfelt "I love you," a gentle touch, or a thoughtful gesture – these small expressions of love and gratitude are the building blocks of a relationship that can stand the test of time.

Subsection 2.3: Keeping the Romance and Excitement Alive

In the journey of a long-term relationship, it's natural for the initial excitement and passion to ebb and flow. As the years go by and the demands of daily life take precedence, couples may find themselves settling into a comfortable routine, inadvertently allowing the romance and spontaneity that once defined their relationship to take a backseat. However, keeping the spark alive is not only possible but essential for maintaining a vibrant, fulfilling partnership that stands the test of time.

The key to keeping romance and excitement alive lies in a willingness to break free from the mundane and embrace creativity, playfulness, and a sense of adventure. It's about making a conscious effort to prioritize your connection and infuse your relationship with novel experiences, heartfelt gestures, and moments of surprise that remind you of the love and passion that brought you together in the first place.

One way to reignite the spark is by planning surprise date nights or weekend getaways. These don't have to be elaborate or expensive; the focus should be on creating opportunities for quality time, undivided attention, and shared experiences that allow you to reconnect and rediscover each other. Whether it's a picnic in the park, a cooking class, or a spontaneous road trip to a nearby town, the act of breaking your usual routine and embarking on a new adventure together can work wonders for rekindling romance and excitement.

Another essential aspect of keeping the spark alive is maintaining a sense of physical and emotional intimacy. Over time, it's easy for couples to fall into a pattern of taking each other's affection for granted or neglecting the importance of physical touch and emotional connection. Make a conscious effort to prioritize intimacy, whether through regular date nights, heartfelt conversations, or simply taking a moment to hold hands or exchange a loving embrace. By nurturing your physical and emotional bond, you create a foundation of closeness and trust that allows romance and passion to thrive.

Keeping the romance alive also involves a willingness to be playful, spontaneous, and open to trying new things together. This might mean surprising your partner with a thoughtful gift, leaving love notes in unexpected places, or initiating a flirtatious text exchange in the middle of the day. It could also involve exploring new hobbies or interests as a couple, whether it's taking a dance class, learning a new language, or embarking on a fitness challenge together. By stepping outside your comfort zone and embracing a sense of curiosity and adventure, you create opportunities for growth, bonding, and the creation of new, exciting memories together.

Ultimately, keeping romance and excitement alive in a long-term relationship requires a commitment to prioritizing your connection and making a conscious effort to nurture your bond. It's about recognizing that love and passion are not static entities but rather dynamic forces that require ongoing attention, effort, and creativity to flourish. By embracing a spirit of playfulness, spontaneity, and a willingness to continually explore and rediscover each other, you can create a relationship that remains vibrant, exciting, and deeply fulfilling, no matter how many years pass. So, take the time to surprise your partner, plan new adventures, and infuse your relationship with moments of romance and excitement – your love story deserves nothing less.

Subsection 2.4: Continuously Learning and Growing Together

In the journey of nurturing a lasting, loving relationship, embracing a mindset of continuous learning and personal growth is essential for fostering a dynamic, evolving connection that stands the test of time. When couples commit to growing together, they create a partnership that is resilient, adaptable, and forever young at heart.

At the core of this mindset is a shared belief that love is not a static destination but rather an ongoing adventure of discovery and development. It's a recognition that, as individuals, we are constantly evolving – our interests, passions, and aspirations shifting and expanding over time. By actively choosing to learn and grow alongside each other, couples create a relationship that is vibrant, engaging, and deeply fulfilling.

One of the most powerful ways to cultivate a growth-oriented relationship is to approach life with a sense of curiosity and openness. This means being willing to step outside of your comfort zone, try new things, and explore uncharted territory together. Whether it's taking a cooking class, learning a new language, or embarking on a travel adventure, engaging in novel experiences as a couple can reignite a sense of excitement and shared purpose.

Moreover, a commitment to continuous learning and growth involves being open to each other's ideas, perspectives, and feedback. It's about creating a safe, supportive space where both partners feel encouraged to share their thoughts, dreams, and challenges, knowing that they will be met with empathy, understanding, and a willingness to grow together.

By actively listening to each other and engaging in honest, constructive dialogue, couples can deepen their connection and foster a sense of intimacy that transcends the passage of time.

Another key aspect of growing together is supporting each other's individual growth and development. This means encouraging your partner to pursue their passions, chase their dreams, and become the best version of themselves. It's about celebrating each other's successes, offering guidance and support during challenges, and being a constant source of inspiration and motivation. When both partners are committed to their own personal growth, they bring fresh energy, insights, and experiences back into the relationship, enriching their bond and keeping the spark alive.

Of course, embracing a mindset of continuous learning and growth is not always easy. It requires vulnerability, courage, and a willingness to step into the unknown. There may be times when you stumble, face setbacks, or encounter growing pains as you navigate new territory together. However, it is in these moments of challenge and uncertainty that the true strength of your bond is forged. By leaning on each other, communicating openly, and maintaining a shared commitment to growth, you can weather any storm and emerge stronger, wiser, and more deeply connected.

Ultimately, when couples embrace a mindset of continuous learning and personal growth, they create a relationship that is not only built to last but one that thrives and evolves over time. They become not just partners but fellow adventurers, explorers, and lifelong learners, forever seeking new ways to expand their horizons and deepen their love. So, hand in hand, heart to heart, let us embark on this beautiful journey of growth and discovery, knowing that the best is yet to come.

Summary: Keeping the Flame of Love Burning Bright

In the journey of nurturing and maintaining the spark in a long-term relationship, the key lies in a commitment to prioritizing your connection, infusing your bond with intentional acts of love and appreciation, and embracing a mindset of continuous growth and discovery. By making quality time a non-negotiable priority, regularly expressing your love and gratitude, and seeking out new experiences and adventures together, you create a relationship that is vibrant, passionate, and built to stand the test of time.

Remember, the spark in your relationship is not a static entity but rather a dynamic flame that requires ongoing attention, effort, and creativity to keep burning bright. It's about making the conscious choice, day after day, to show up for your partner, to cherish the love you share, and to approach your relationship with a sense of curiosity, playfulness, and a willingness to step outside of your comfort zone.

As you navigate the ups and downs of life together, hold fast to the conviction that your love story is worth fighting for, worth nurturing, and worth celebrating. Embrace the power of small, daily acts of love and devotion, and trust in the resilience of a bond that is rooted in mutual respect, unwavering support, and a shared commitment to growth.

So, as you embark on this beautiful journey of love, keep the spark alive by choosing each other every day, by finding joy in the ordinary moments, and by never losing sight of the magic that brought you together in the first place. With an open heart, a curious mind, and a willingness to grow together, you have all the tools you need to create a love that lasts a lifetime.

Section 3: Effective Communication and Conflict Resolution

Picture this: you're in a relationship, and things are going well. You feel connected, understood, and appreciated by your partner. But then, a disagreement arises, and suddenly, the air is thick with tension. Words are exchanged, emotions run high, and before you know it, you're caught in a cycle of misunderstandings and hurt feelings. Sound familiar?

Effective communication and conflict resolution skills are the lifeblood of any healthy, long-lasting relationship. When we can express ourselves clearly, listen actively, and navigate disagreements with empathy and respect, we create a strong foundation of trust and understanding. On the other hand, when communication breaks down and conflicts are left unresolved, resentment and distance can creep in, eroding the very fabric of our connection.

In this section, we'll dive deep into the art of healthy communication and explore practical strategies for resolving conflicts constructively. We'll examine the common pitfalls that can derail conversations and learn how to avoid them. We'll discover the power of active listening, empathy, and vulnerability in fostering deeper understanding and connection with our partners. And we'll equip you with a toolkit of proven techniques for navigating even the most challenging disagreements with grace and resilience.

Whether you're in a new relationship or have been with your partner for decades, the skills you'll learn in this section will be invaluable. By mastering the art of effective communication and conflict resolution, you'll not only strengthen your bond with your loved one but also cultivate a more harmonious, fulfilling relationship that can weather any storm. So, let's roll up our sleeves and dive in – your relationship will thank you for it.

Subsection 3.1: Open, Honest, and Respectful Communication

At the heart of every healthy, long-lasting relationship lies a foundation of open, honest, and respectful communication. When we express ourselves with transparency and sincerity, we create an environment of trust and understanding that allows our connections to thrive. Honest communication involves sharing our thoughts, feelings, and needs with our partners, even when it feels vulnerable or challenging. It means being willing to have difficult conversations and addressing issues head-on, rather than sweeping them under the rug or allowing resentment to fester.

Openness in communication goes hand in hand with honesty. It requires us to be receptive to our partner's perspectives and experiences, even when they differ from our own. By cultivating an atmosphere of openness, we create space for genuine dialogue and mutual understanding. This means listening actively, without judgment or interruption, and striving to see things from our partner's point of view. When we approach communication with an open mind and heart, we foster a deeper sense of connection and intimacy.

Respect is equally crucial in maintaining healthy communication. It involves treating our partners with kindness, consideration, and empathy, even in the midst of disagreements or conflicts. Respectful communication means avoiding personal attacks, name-calling, or dismissive language. Instead, we focus on expressing our own thoughts and feelings, while acknowledging and validating our partner's perspective. By communicating with respect, we create a safe and supportive environment where both partners feel heard, valued, and understood.

Maintaining open, honest, and respectful communication is an ongoing process that requires commitment and effort from both partners. It involves being mindful of our words and tone, taking responsibility for our own emotions, and being willing to apologize when we fall short. By making communication a priority and consistently practicing these principles, we lay the groundwork for a relationship built on trust, understanding, and mutual growth. As we navigate the ups and downs of life together, the power of open, honest, and respectful communication will serve as a guiding light, strengthening our bond and helping us weather any storm.

Subsection 3.2: Active Listening and Empathy

In the dance of effective communication, active listening and empathy are the essential steps that keep partners moving in harmony. These powerful tools allow us to truly hear and understand our loved ones, fostering a deeper sense of connection and mutual understanding. When we practice active listening, we go beyond simply hearing the words our partner speaks; we tune in to their emotions, their body language, and the unspoken messages between the lines. We create a safe space for them to express themselves fully, without fear of judgment or interruption.

Empathy, the ability to put ourselves in our partner's shoes and see the world through their eyes, is the companion to active listening. It allows us to connect with our partner's experiences on a profound level, to feel their joys and sorrows as if they were our own. When we approach conversations with empathy, we demonstrate that we value and respect our partner's perspective, even if it differs from our own. We show them that they are heard, understood, and supported, which is the foundation of any strong, healthy relationship.

So, how can we cultivate active listening and empathy in our relationships? One key strategy is to give our full attention to our partner when they are speaking. This means putting aside distractions, such as phones or televisions, and focusing solely on the conversation at hand. We can show our engagement through eye contact, nodding, and other nonverbal cues that demonstrate our interest and understanding. When our partner pauses, we can reflect back what we've heard, using phrases like "What I'm hearing is..." or "It sounds like you're feeling..." This not only confirms that we've been listening attentively but also allows our partner to clarify or elaborate on their thoughts.

Another powerful technique for practicing empathy is to ask open-ended questions that encourage our partner to share their feelings and experiences more deeply. Instead of making assumptions or offering immediate advice, we can ask questions like "How did that make you feel?" or "What was that experience like for you?" By creating space for our partner to explore their emotions, we show that we value their inner world and are committed to understanding them on a profound level.

Of course, active listening and empathy are skills that require practice and patience. There will be times when we fall short, when we find ourselves distracted or struggling to connect with our partner's perspective. In these moments, it's essential to approach ourselves with kindness and self-compassion, recognizing that building these skills is a lifelong journey. We can also communicate openly with our partner about our challenges, asking for their support and feedback as we work to strengthen our listening and empathy muscles.

Ultimately, the rewards of active listening and empathy are immeasurable. By creating a relationship culture where both partners feel heard, understood, and valued, we lay the foundation for a love that can weather any storm. We build trust, intimacy, and a deep sense of partnership that allows us to grow and thrive together. So let us embrace the power of active listening and empathy, and watch as our relationships blossom into something truly extraordinary.

Subsection 3.3: Addressing Conflicts and Disagreements Constructively

Conflicts and disagreements are an inevitable part of any relationship, but how we navigate these challenges can make all the difference in the health and longevity of our partnerships. When handled constructively, conflicts can actually serve as opportunities for growth, deepening understanding, and strengthening the bond between partners. However, when approached with a destructive or avoidant mindset, disagreements can quickly escalate into painful, damaging cycles that erode trust and intimacy.

The key to addressing conflicts and disagreements constructively lies in adopting a solution-oriented approach that prioritizes mutual understanding, respect, and collaboration. This means setting aside the urge to "win" the argument or prove our partner wrong, and instead focusing on finding a resolution that meets both partners' needs and concerns. It requires a willingness to listen actively, express ourselves honestly and respectfully, and remain open to compromise and creative problem-solving.

One powerful technique for navigating conflicts constructively is to use "I" statements when expressing our thoughts and feelings. Instead of making accusations or generalizations, such as "You always..." or "You never...," we can frame our concerns in terms of our own experiences and emotions. For example, "I feel hurt and disconnected when we go days without spending quality time together." This approach helps to minimize defensiveness and blame, and instead promotes empathy and understanding.

Another key strategy is to approach disagreements with a spirit of curiosity and openness, rather than judgment or rigidity. This means asking questions to better understand our partner's perspective, even if we don't agree with it. It means being willing to consider alternative viewpoints and solutions, and remaining flexible in our thinking. By creating a safe, non-judgmental space for open dialogue, we encourage our partner to share their thoughts and feelings more freely, leading to deeper insight and more effective problem-solving.

When conflicts arise, it's also essential to take breaks as needed to prevent escalation and allow for emotional processing. If tensions are running high and productive communication becomes difficult, it's okay to suggest a temporary pause in the discussion. During this time, both partners can engage in self-care activities, such as deep breathing, meditation, or physical exercise, to regulate their emotions and gain clarity. The key is to agree on a specific time to revisit the issue, ensuring that it's not simply swept under the rug.

As we navigate disagreements, it's crucial to maintain a focus on the present issue at hand, rather than bringing up past grievances or unrelated concerns. This helps to keep the conversation focused and productive, and prevents the conflict from spiraling out of control. If other issues arise during the discussion, it's best to make a note of them and agree to address them separately at a later time.

Ultimately, the goal of constructive conflict resolution is to find a mutually satisfying solution that takes both partners' needs and concerns into account. This may involve compromise, creative brainstorming, or seeking the guidance of a neutral third party, such as a couples therapist or mediator. By approaching disagreements with a spirit of collaboration and a commitment to finding a resolution that works for both partners, we build trust, resilience, and a deeper sense of partnership.

Of course, mastering the art of constructive conflict resolution is an ongoing process that requires patience, practice, and a willingness to learn and grow. There will be moments when we stumble, when our emotions get the best of us, or when finding a solution feels daunting. In these moments, it's essential to extend compassion and forgiveness to ourselves and our partner, recognizing that building a strong, healthy relationship is a journey, not a destination.

By embracing the challenges of conflict as opportunities for growth and connection, and by equipping ourselves with the tools and strategies for constructive resolution, we lay the foundation for a relationship that can weather any storm. We create a partnership built on trust, respect, and mutual understanding – a love that is resilient, enduring, and truly extraordinary.

Subsection 3.4: Forgiveness and Letting Go of Resentment

In the tapestry of long-term relationships, forgiveness and the ability to let go of resentment are the threads that bind two hearts together, even in the face of challenges and hurt. These powerful acts of emotional healing are not always easy, but they are essential for nurturing the resilience and longevity of any partnership. When we hold onto resentment and bitterness, we create a toxic environment that slowly erodes the foundation of love and trust we have built with our partner. Forgiveness, on the other hand, is the balm that soothes the wounds of the past and allows us to move forward with a renewed sense of connection and understanding.

Forgiveness is not about condoning hurtful actions or forgetting the pain they caused. Rather, it is a conscious choice to release the grip of anger and resentment, and to extend compassion and understanding to our partner and ourselves. It is a process of acknowledging the hurt, expressing our feelings honestly and respectfully, and making a commitment to work through the issues together. Forgiveness requires vulnerability, humility, and a willingness to see beyond the surface of the conflict to the deeper needs and fears that may be driving our partner's actions.

One of the most powerful tools for cultivating forgiveness is empathy. When we take the time to truly listen to our partner's perspective and experiences, we begin to understand the underlying emotions and motivations behind their behavior. We may discover that their hurtful actions were not intentional, but rather a result of their own unresolved pain, fear, or insecurity. By approaching conflicts with a spirit of curiosity and compassion, we create a safe space for our partner to express themselves fully and for us to respond with understanding and support.

Another key aspect of forgiveness is taking responsibility for our own role in the conflict. It is easy to focus on our partner's mistakes and shortcomings, but true healing requires us to look inward and acknowledge the ways in which we may have contributed to the problem. This may involve recognizing patterns of behavior or communication that are unhealthy, or admitting to our own hurtful actions and taking steps to make amends. By owning our part in the conflict and expressing genuine remorse, we demonstrate our commitment to growth and change, and invite our partner to do the same.

Letting go of resentment is a crucial companion to forgiveness. Resentment is like a poison that slowly contaminates the well of our relationship, tainting even the most loving interactions with bitterness and mistrust. When we hold onto resentment, we become trapped in a cycle of negativity and blame, unable to fully engage in the present moment or appreciate the good in our partner. Letting go of resentment requires a conscious effort to release the past and focus on the present and future of our relationship.

One powerful technique for letting go of resentment is the practice of gratitude. By actively focusing on the positive aspects of our partner and our relationship, we shift our attention away from the hurts of the past and cultivate a sense of appreciation and joy. We can make a habit of expressing gratitude for the small, everyday gestures of love and kindness that our partner offers, and for the ways in which our relationship enriches our life. By consistently choosing to focus on the good, we create a positive feedback loop that strengthens our bond and makes it easier to let go of resentment when conflicts arise.

Another effective strategy for releasing resentment is the use of mindfulness and self-reflection. By taking time each day to sit quietly and observe our thoughts and emotions without judgment, we gain insight into the patterns of negativity and blame that may be fueling our resentment. We can practice acknowledging these feelings with compassion and then consciously choosing to let them go, focusing instead on the present moment and the opportunities for connection and growth that lie ahead.

Ultimately, forgiveness and letting go of resentment are ongoing processes that require commitment, patience, and self-compassion. There will be times when the hurt feels too deep, or the resentment too entrenched, to release easily. In these moments, it is essential to reach out for support, whether from a trusted friend, family member, or mental health professional. By surrounding ourselves with a network of love and understanding, we gain the strength and perspective needed to continue the work of forgiveness and healing.

As we practice forgiveness and letting go of resentment, we create a relationship culture of resilience, empathy, and growth. We learn to weather the storms of conflict and emerge stronger, more connected, and more deeply in love. We discover that the challenges we face together are not obstacles to our happiness, but rather opportunities to deepen our understanding, strengthen our bond, and create a love that endures. By embracing forgiveness and releasing resentment, we open our hearts to the limitless possibilities of a truly extraordinary relationship.

Summary: Mastering the Art of Loving Communication and Conflict Resolution

Effective communication and conflict resolution are the cornerstones of any healthy, long-lasting relationship. By cultivating the skills of open, honest, and respectful communication, active listening, empathy, and constructive problem-solving, we create a solid foundation of trust, understanding, and intimacy that can weather any storm. Forgiveness and letting go of resentment are equally crucial in maintaining the resilience and vitality of our partnerships, allowing us to heal from past hurts and move forward with renewed connection and love.

As we navigate the inevitable challenges and disagreements that arise in any relationship, it is essential to approach these moments as opportunities for growth, learning, and deepening our bond. By embracing the tools and strategies outlined in this section, we empower ourselves to communicate with clarity, compassion, and respect, and to find mutually satisfying solutions that honor the needs and desires of both partners.

Remember, mastering the art of loving communication and conflict resolution is an ongoing journey, one that requires patience, practice, and a willingness to learn and grow. There will be moments of struggle and setback, but by remaining committed to the process and to each other, we can cultivate a love that is truly extraordinary – a love that is built on a bedrock of trust, understanding, and unwavering support.

So let us embrace the challenges and the joys of this journey together, armed with the knowledge and tools to create a relationship that is a source of strength, comfort, and inspiration for a lifetime. With open hearts, curious minds, and a commitment to loving communication and compassionate conflict resolution, there is no limit to the depths of intimacy, growth, and fulfillment we can achieve together.

Section 4: Balancing Individuality and Togetherness

In the journey of cultivating lasting love and commitment, one of the most crucial aspects is finding harmony between your individuality and your identity as a couple. While it's essential to nurture your relationship and build a strong partnership, it's equally important to maintain a sense of self and continue pursuing personal growth. Striking this delicate balance can be challenging, but it is a fundamental component of healthy, enduring relationships.

When two individuals come together to form a partnership, they bring with them their unique personalities, dreams, and aspirations. The beauty of a thriving relationship lies in celebrating and supporting each other's individuality while simultaneously creating a shared vision for the future. By encouraging personal growth and self-discovery, couples can foster an environment of mutual respect, admiration, and inspiration.

However, the quest for personal fulfillment should not come at the cost of neglecting the relationship. Maintaining a strong connection requires intentional effort, open communication, and a willingness to prioritize the needs of the partnership. Couples who successfully navigate this balance understand the importance of carving out quality time together, engaging in shared interests, and supporting each other's goals and aspirations.

In this section, we will delve into the art of balancing individuality and togetherness, exploring practical strategies for nurturing personal growth while strengthening the bond between partners. We'll discuss the value of maintaining individual interests and friendships, setting healthy boundaries, and creating a shared vision that encompasses both individual and collective dreams. By embracing the unique qualities that each person brings to the relationship and working together to build a strong foundation of love and support, couples can achieve a harmonious balance that allows their love to thrive and endure the test of time.

Subsection 4.1: Encouraging Personal Growth and Self-Discovery

In a loving, committed relationship, one of the most valuable gifts partners can give each other is the support and encouragement to pursue personal growth and self-discovery. When individuals feel secure and supported in their relationship, they are more likely to take risks, explore new interests, and work towards becoming the best version of themselves. This process of continuous self-improvement not only benefits the individual but also strengthens the bond between partners, as it fosters a sense of admiration, respect, and inspiration.

Encouraging personal growth and self-discovery starts with creating a safe, non-judgmental space within the relationship where both partners feel comfortable sharing their dreams, aspirations, and fears. By actively listening to each other's goals and desires, couples can offer support and encouragement tailored to their partner's unique needs. This may involve providing emotional support during challenging times, offering practical assistance in pursuing new endeavors, or simply being a sounding board for ideas and concerns.

Moreover, couples who actively encourage each other's personal growth demonstrate a deep level of trust and belief in their partner's potential. This unwavering support can be a powerful motivator, inspiring individuals to push past their comfort zones and strive for greater heights. When partners celebrate each other's successes and provide comfort during setbacks, they create a strong foundation of love and support that can weather any storm.

To foster an environment of personal growth and self-discovery, couples can engage in activities that promote self-reflection and introspection.

This may include attending workshops or seminars together, engaging in meaningful conversations about personal values and life goals, or setting aside dedicated time for individual pursuits. By prioritizing personal development and supporting each other's journey of self-discovery, couples can maintain a vibrant, fulfilling relationship that continues to evolve and thrive over time.

Ultimately, encouraging personal growth and self-discovery within a relationship is about recognizing that true love is not about possession or control, but rather about empowering each other to become the best possible version of themselves. When partners wholeheartedly support each other's personal growth, they create a relationship built on mutual respect, admiration, and a shared commitment to lifelong learning and self-improvement.

Subsection 4.2: Maintaining Individual Interests and Friendships

In the pursuit of a strong, healthy relationship, it's essential to remember that both partners are unique individuals with their own interests, passions, and social connections. While it's natural for couples to spend a significant amount of time together and develop shared experiences, maintaining individual interests and friendships is crucial for personal growth and overall relationship satisfaction.

When partners nurture their own interests and friendships outside of the relationship, they bring a sense of vitality and fresh perspectives back into the partnership. Engaging in activities that fuel personal passions and hobbies allows individuals to maintain a strong sense of self and continue to grow as unique beings. Whether it's pursuing a beloved hobby, attending classes to learn a new skill, or dedicating time to a fulfilling volunteer opportunity, these individual pursuits provide a source of joy, fulfillment, and self-expression that can enrich the relationship as a whole.

Moreover, preserving friendships outside of the romantic partnership is equally important. Close friendships offer a different type of emotional support, camaraderie, and shared experiences that complement the bond between partners. These friendships serve as a reminder that both individuals have lives and connections beyond the relationship, fostering a sense of independence and preventing partners from becoming overly reliant on each other for all their social and emotional needs.

However, it's crucial to strike a healthy balance between individual pursuits and the needs of the relationship. Open communication and mutual understanding are key to ensuring that both partners feel supported and valued while maintaining their individual interests and friendships. This may involve setting aside dedicated time for personal pursuits, establishing clear boundaries, and being transparent about plans and commitments.

Couples who successfully navigate this balance often find that their individual growth and external connections ultimately strengthen their bond as a couple. By bringing new ideas, experiences, and a renewed sense of self into the relationship, partners can continually inspire and challenge each other to grow together. Additionally, having a strong support system outside of the relationship can provide a valuable source of advice, perspective, and encouragement during challenging times.

Ultimately, nurturing individual interests and friendships while prioritizing the relationship is a delicate dance that requires ongoing communication, trust, and mutual respect. By recognizing and celebrating each other's unique identities and supporting personal growth, couples can build a strong, resilient partnership that allows both individuals to thrive within the context of a loving, committed relationship.

Subsection 4.3: Creating a Shared Vision and Sense of Partnership

In the journey of cultivating a lasting, loving relationship, creating a shared vision and fostering a strong sense of partnership are essential elements. When couples work together to develop a common understanding of their future and align their goals, they lay the foundation for a relationship that can withstand the test of time.

A shared vision is a powerful force that unites partners and provides a roadmap for their life together. It encompasses the dreams, aspirations, and values that both individuals hold dear, and it serves as a guiding light through the ups and downs of the relationship. By taking the time to openly discuss their hopes and desires, couples can create a vision that reflects their unique bond and the life they want to build together.

To develop a shared vision, partners must engage in honest, heartfelt conversations about their long-term goals, priorities, and expectations. This process requires vulnerability, active listening, and a willingness to compromise. By sharing their innermost thoughts and feelings, couples can gain a deeper understanding of each other's needs and desires, and work together to find common ground.

Once a shared vision is established, it's crucial to cultivate a strong sense of partnership and collaboration to bring that vision to life. This involves treating the relationship as a team effort, where both partners are equally invested in each other's happiness and success. By supporting one another, celebrating achievements, and facing challenges together, couples can foster a deep sense of unity and solidarity.

One effective strategy for nurturing a sense of partnership is to regularly engage in shared experiences and activities that promote bonding and teamwork. This can include pursuing common interests, working on projects together, or simply carving out quality time to connect and enjoy each other's company. By creating opportunities for collaboration and shared joy, couples can strengthen their emotional connection and reinforce their commitment to their shared vision.

Another key aspect of maintaining a strong partnership is open, respectful communication. When partners feel safe to express their thoughts, feelings, and concerns without fear of judgment or criticism, they can work together to navigate challenges and find solutions that benefit the relationship as a whole. By practicing active listening, empathy, and constructive problem-solving, couples can build a resilient partnership that can weather any storm.

Ultimately, creating a shared vision and cultivating a sense of partnership requires ongoing effort, dedication, and a willingness to grow together. By consistently prioritizing their relationship and working towards their common goals, couples can build a love that endures, inspires, and enriches their lives in countless ways. Through the power of a shared vision and a steadfast commitment to each other, they can create a partnership that is greater than the sum of its parts – a love that stands the test of time.

Summary: Finding Harmony in Love: Balancing Me, You, and Us

Cultivating a lasting, loving relationship requires a delicate balance between nurturing your individuality and fostering a strong sense of togetherness. It's a continuous dance of supporting each other's personal growth, maintaining cherished friendships and interests, and creating a shared vision that encompasses your dreams as individuals and as a couple.

By encouraging self-discovery and celebrating the unique qualities that each partner brings to the relationship, you create a foundation of mutual respect, admiration, and inspiration. This support for personal development strengthens your bond, as you witness each other's growth and cheer on every milestone achieved.

At the same time, building a thriving partnership involves prioritizing your connection and dedicating effort to your shared journey. Engaging in activities that promote bonding, collaborating on projects, and consistently making time for each other reinforces your commitment to your relationship and your shared vision for the future.

Remember, a healthy relationship is not about losing yourself or sacrificing your identity. Instead, it's about finding harmony between your individual needs and the needs of your partnership. It's about open communication, mutual understanding, and a willingness to support each other's growth while growing together as a couple.

As you navigate the path of love, cherish your individuality and nurture your shared bond. Embrace the beautiful balance of me, you, and us, and watch as your love flourishes and stands the test of time. With a commitment to personal growth, a dedication to your partnership, and a shared vision for your future, you can create a love that is truly extraordinary – a love that empowers you both to be the best versions of yourselves while building a life together filled with joy, inspiration, and endless possibilities.

Section 5: Overcoming Challenges and Evolving Together

Every relationship, no matter how strong and loving, will inevitably face challenges and obstacles along the way. These challenges can range from minor disagreements to major life transitions that test the resilience and adaptability of the partnership. However, it is through these challenges that couples have the opportunity to grow, learn, and evolve together, ultimately strengthening their bond and deepening their commitment to one another.

In this section, we will explore some of the most common challenges that relationships face and provide practical guidance on how to navigate these challenges with grace, compassion, and a growth mindset. From learning how to support each other through difficult times to reigniting the spark after periods of disconnection, we will delve into the strategies and tools that can help couples overcome adversity and emerge stronger than ever.

We will also discuss the importance of maintaining emotional connection and intimacy throughout the various stages of a relationship, including major life transitions such as career changes, parenthood, and retirement. By learning how to adapt and evolve together, couples can build a love that not only withstands the test of time but also continues to flourish and grow.

Whether you are currently facing a challenge in your relationship or simply looking to build a stronger, more resilient partnership, this section will provide you with the insights, advice, and inspiration you need to overcome obstacles and create a love that lasts a lifetime. So, let's dive in and explore the transformative power of facing challenges together and evolving as a couple.

Subsection 5.1: Navigating Major Life Transitions

Throughout the course of a long-term relationship, couples inevitably face significant life transitions that can either strengthen or strain their bond. These major milestones, such as career changes, becoming parents, or entering retirement, require a great deal of adaptation, flexibility, and mutual support. Navigating these transitions successfully can lead to personal and relational growth, while failing to adapt can result in increased stress, disconnection, and even the erosion of the relationship.

One of the most crucial aspects of navigating major life transitions is maintaining open, honest communication. Couples must be willing to share their fears, hopes, and expectations surrounding the change, creating a safe space for vulnerability and emotional intimacy. By actively listening to each other's concerns and validating one another's experiences, partners can foster a sense of unity and collaboration in the face of uncertainty.

Another key strategy for supporting each other through major life transitions is to approach the change as a team. This means working together to develop a shared vision for the future, setting realistic goals, and creating a plan of action that takes both partners' needs and desires into account. By viewing the transition as a joint venture rather than an individual challenge, couples can cultivate a sense of partnership and shared purpose that can help them weather even the toughest of times.

Adaptability and flexibility are also essential qualities for couples navigating major life transitions. As circumstances change, partners must be willing to adjust their expectations, roles, and routines to accommodate the new reality. This may involve compromising, finding creative solutions, or even redefining what success and happiness look like within the relationship. By embracing change and remaining open to new possibilities, couples can build resilience and strengthen their ability to cope with future challenges.

It is also important for couples to prioritize self-care and maintain a strong support system during major life transitions. Engaging in activities that promote physical, emotional, and mental well-being, such as exercise, meditation, or therapy, can help partners manage stress and maintain a positive outlook. Additionally, seeking support from friends, family, or professional counselors can provide a valuable outlet for processing emotions and gaining new perspectives.

Ultimately, navigating major life transitions requires a foundation of love, commitment, and mutual respect. By approaching these changes with empathy, patience, and a willingness to grow together, couples can not only survive but thrive in the face of life's greatest challenges. Through the process of adaptation and evolution, partners can deepen their connection, strengthen their resilience, and build a love that endures through every season of life.

Subsection 5.2: Maintaining Connection Through Difficult Times

In every relationship, there will be periods of stress, loss, and hardship that can strain even the strongest of bonds. Whether facing a personal crisis, a family tragedy, or a global pandemic, couples must learn to navigate these challenging times together, providing emotional support and maintaining a deep sense of connection despite the adversity.

One of the most essential aspects of maintaining connection during difficult times is prioritizing open, honest communication. When stress levels are high and emotions are running wild, it can be tempting to shut down or lash out at one's partner. However, it is precisely during these moments that couples must make a conscious effort to express their feelings, fears, and needs in a calm, respectful manner. By creating a safe space for vulnerability and emotional intimacy, partners can lean on each other for comfort, understanding, and support.

Active listening also plays a crucial role in maintaining connection through hardship. When one partner is struggling, the other must be fully present, offering their undivided attention and empathy. This means putting aside distractions, refraining from judgment or unsolicited advice, and focusing on understanding and validating their partner's experiences. By showing genuine interest and concern, couples can foster a sense of unity and shared resilience in the face of adversity.

Another key strategy for maintaining emotional connection during difficult times is to prioritize physical touch and affection. Even simple gestures, such as holding hands, hugging, or cuddling, can provide a powerful sense of comfort, security, and love. Physical touch releases oxytocin, the "cuddle hormone," which helps to reduce stress, lower blood pressure, and promote feelings of bonding and attachment. By making a conscious effort to engage in physical affection, couples can maintain a deep sense of intimacy and connection, even in the midst of chaos.

In addition to communication and physical touch, couples must also make time for shared activities and experiences that promote joy, relaxation, and togetherness. This can be as simple as watching a favorite movie, cooking a meal together, or taking a walk in nature. By carving out moments of respite and pleasure, partners can create a sense of normalcy and stability amidst the turmoil, reminding each other of the love and happiness that exists beyond the current hardship.

It is also essential for couples to maintain a sense of perspective and gratitude during difficult times. While it is natural to focus on the challenges and pain, partners must also make a conscious effort to acknowledge the blessings and silver linings in their lives. This can involve expressing appreciation for each other's support, celebrating small victories, or finding meaning and purpose in the face of adversity. By cultivating a positive, resilient mindset, couples can weather even the toughest of storms together.

Ultimately, maintaining emotional connection through difficult times requires a deep commitment to love, empathy, and mutual support. By prioritizing open communication, active listening, physical affection, shared experiences, and a grateful perspective, couples can build the resilience and strength needed to overcome any obstacle. Through the power of their connection, partners can emerge from hardship stronger, wiser, and more deeply bonded than ever before.

Subsection 5.3: Reigniting the Spark After Periods of Disconnection

Even the most loving and committed relationships can experience periods of emotional distance or disconnection. Whether caused by external stressors, personal struggles, or a gradual erosion of intimacy over time, these moments of disconnect can leave couples feeling lost, lonely, and uncertain about the future of their relationship. However, it is possible to reignite the spark and rekindle the love and passion that once brought two hearts together.

The first step in rekindling love and intimacy after a period of disconnection is to acknowledge and validate the emotional distance that has grown between partners. This requires a willingness to have open, honest conversations about the state of the relationship, the factors that have contributed to the disconnect, and the feelings and needs of both individuals. By creating a safe, non-judgmental space for dialogue, couples can begin to rebuild trust, understanding, and emotional intimacy.

One powerful way to reignite the spark is to prioritize quality time together, free from distractions and focused solely on nurturing the relationship. This can involve setting aside regular date nights, planning special outings or adventures, or simply carving out moments each day to connect and engage in meaningful conversation. By making a conscious effort to create shared experiences and memories, couples can rediscover the joy, laughter, and affection that initially drew them together.

Another key strategy for rekindling love and intimacy is to express appreciation, gratitude, and admiration for one another. When relationships fall into a state of disconnection, it is easy to focus on the negative aspects or take each other for granted. However, by actively seeking out and acknowledging the positive qualities, actions, and contributions of one's partner, couples can reignite feelings of love, respect, and desire. This can involve leaving love notes, offering compliments, or simply expressing heartfelt thanks for the small, everyday gestures that make a relationship special.

Physical intimacy also plays a crucial role in reigniting the spark after periods of disconnection. While sexual desire may have waned due to emotional distance, couples can gradually rebuild physical closeness through non-sexual touch, such as holding hands, cuddling, or giving massages. As emotional intimacy deepens, partners can explore new ways to rekindle sexual passion, such as trying new techniques, fantasies, or romantic gestures. The key is to approach physical intimacy with patience, sensitivity, and a willingness to communicate openly about desires, boundaries, and concerns.

Ultimately, reigniting the spark after periods of disconnection requires a commitment to personal growth, both as individuals and as a couple. This may involve seeking the guidance of a therapist or relationship coach, attending workshops or retreats, or engaging in self-reflection and self-improvement practices. By taking responsibility for one's own emotional well-being and actively working to become the best version of oneself, partners can bring renewed energy, passion, and love into the relationship.

Rekindling love and intimacy after emotional distance is a journey that requires patience, effort, and a deep commitment to the relationship. By prioritizing open communication, quality time, expressions of appreciation, physical closeness, and personal growth, couples can overcome periods of disconnection and reignite the spark that once brought them together. Through the power of resilience, forgiveness, and an unwavering belief in the transformative nature of love, partners can emerge from the darkness of disconnection into the light of renewed passion and intimacy.

Subsection 5.4: Growing Old Together Gracefully

As couples navigate the later stages of life, they face a unique set of challenges and opportunities that can test the strength and resilience of their relationship. Growing old together gracefully requires a deep commitment to love, understanding, and mutual support, as well as a willingness to adapt to the changing circumstances and needs of both partners.

One of the most significant challenges that couples may face as they age is the decline in physical health and mobility. Chronic illnesses, disabilities, and the natural effects of aging can place a strain on the relationship, as partners must learn to cope with new limitations and dependencies. However, by approaching these challenges with empathy, patience, and a spirit of teamwork, couples can deepen their bond and find new ways to express their love and devotion.

Effective communication becomes increasingly important as couples age, particularly when it comes to discussing sensitive topics such as health concerns, end-of-life decisions, and financial planning. By maintaining open, honest dialogue and actively listening to each other's needs and fears, partners can navigate these difficult conversations with grace and compassion, ensuring that both individuals feel heard, respected, and supported.

Another key aspect of growing old together gracefully is finding joy and purpose in the present moment. While it is natural to reflect on the past with nostalgia or to worry about the future with uncertainty, couples who cultivate a sense of gratitude and mindfulness can find deep fulfillment in the simple pleasures of daily life. This may involve pursuing shared hobbies and interests, volunteering in the community, or simply savoring quiet moments of connection and laughter together.

As the dynamics of the relationship shift with age, it is also essential for couples to maintain a sense of independence and individuality. By encouraging each other to pursue personal goals, maintain social connections, and engage in self-care activities, partners can prevent feelings of resentment or suffocation that can arise from an over-reliance on the relationship. At the same time, it is important to recognize the value of interdependence and to be willing to ask for and receive support when needed.

Ultimately, growing old together gracefully is a testament to the enduring power of love and commitment. By approaching the challenges of aging with a spirit of acceptance, adaptability, and mutual respect, couples can create a legacy of love that inspires and uplifts all those around them. Through the tender moments of holding hands, sharing memories, and facing the unknown together, partners can find a profound sense of meaning and purpose in the final chapters of their love story.

Summary: Embracing the Journey of Love and Growth

Throughout this section, we have explored the various challenges and opportunities that couples face as they navigate the ever-changing landscape of their relationship. From major life transitions to periods of emotional disconnection, every partnership will inevitably encounter obstacles that test the strength and resilience of their bond. However, it is through these challenges that couples have the greatest potential for growth, both as individuals and as a united team.

By approaching each challenge with a spirit of empathy, patience, and open communication, partners can cultivate a deep sense of understanding and support that will carry them through even the toughest of times. Whether it's navigating the joys and struggles of parenthood, supporting each other through career changes, or finding new ways to reignite the spark of passion, the key to overcoming adversity lies in a willingness to adapt, evolve, and grow together.

As couples enter the later stages of life, they may face unique challenges related to aging, health, and shifting relationship dynamics. However, by maintaining a commitment to love, respect, and mutual care, partners can continue to find joy, purpose, and fulfillment in their shared journey. Growing old together gracefully requires a willingness to embrace change, to find beauty in the simple moments, and to cherish the profound connection that has stood the test of time.

Ultimately, the path to lasting love is not always smooth or straightforward. It is a winding road filled with unexpected detours, obstacles, and opportunities for growth. By approaching each challenge as an invitation to deepen their bond, to learn more about themselves and each other, and to evolve as individuals and as a couple, partners can build a love that not only survives but thrives in the face of adversity. So let us embrace the journey of love and growth, knowing that with each step, we are creating a legacy of resilience, compassion, and unwavering commitment that will inspire and uplift us for a lifetime.

Chapter Summary: Nurturing Enduring Love and Commitment

Cultivating a lasting, loving, and committed relationship requires dedication, effort, and a deep understanding of the essential elements that form the foundation of enduring love. By prioritizing shared values, emotional connection, mutual respect, and resilience, couples can weather the challenges and changes that life inevitably brings.

Maintaining the spark in a long-term relationship involves making time for each other, expressing love and appreciation, and continuously learning and growing together. Effective communication, active listening, and constructive conflict resolution skills are crucial for navigating disagreements and fostering a deeper understanding between partners.

Balancing individuality and togetherness is another key aspect of nurturing a healthy, long-lasting relationship. Encouraging personal growth, maintaining individual interests, and creating a shared vision can help couples thrive both as individuals and as a united team.

Throughout the journey of a committed relationship, couples may face various challenges, such as major life transitions, periods of disconnection, and the unique obstacles that come with growing old together. By staying connected, supportive, and adaptable, partners can overcome these hurdles and emerge stronger, with a love that endures the test of time.

Ultimately, cultivating lasting love and commitment is an ongoing process that requires intentional effort, patience, and a willingness to grow and evolve together. By embracing the principles and strategies outlined in this chapter, couples can build a solid foundation for a fulfilling, lifelong partnership characterized by deep love, unwavering commitment, and cherished memories that will last a lifetime.

Chapter 13: The Importance of Forgiveness and Letting Go

Forgiveness is a powerful tool that can transform your life and relationships in profound ways. It is the key to unlocking the shackles of resentment, anger, and bitterness that can weigh heavily on your heart and mind. When you hold onto grudges and past hurts, you create a prison for yourself, limiting your ability to experience joy, love, and inner peace. However, by embracing the act of forgiveness and learning to let go, you embark on a journey of personal growth, healing, and liberation.

Throughout our lives, we encounter various situations where we may feel wronged, betrayed, or hurt by others. These experiences can range from minor misunderstandings to deep, emotional wounds that leave lasting scars. It is natural to feel anger, disappointment, and even a desire for revenge in the face of such pain. However, holding onto these negative emotions can have detrimental effects on your mental, emotional, and physical well-being, as well as your relationships with others.

Forgiveness is not about condoning or excusing the hurtful actions of others. It does not mean forgetting the past or pretending that the pain never existed. Instead, forgiveness is a conscious choice to release the burden of resentment and to extend compassion and understanding towards those who have wronged you. It is an act of empowerment, allowing you to take control of your own emotions and to break free from the cycle of negativity that can consume your thoughts and energy.

The journey of forgiveness is not always easy, and it may require time, patience, and a willingness to confront difficult emotions. It involves acknowledging the hurt you have experienced, validating your feelings, and making a deliberate decision to let go of the anger and resentment that have been holding you back. By engaging in this process, you create space for healing, growth, and the opportunity to rebuild relationships on a foundation of trust, empathy, and mutual understanding.

In this chapter, we will explore the transformative power of forgiveness and the importance of letting go. We will delve into the personal benefits of forgiveness, including emotional healing, reduced stress, and increased self-awareness. We will also examine the role of forgiveness in various types of relationships, such as romantic partnerships, family dynamics, and friendships. Through relatable examples, practical advice, and evidence-based insights, you will gain the tools and understanding necessary to cultivate a forgiving mindset and to incorporate forgiveness into your daily life.

As you embark on this journey of forgiveness and letting go, remember that it is a process of self-discovery and personal growth. By releasing the burdens of the past and embracing a more compassionate and understanding perspective, you open yourself up to a world of possibilities, deeper connections, and a greater sense of inner peace. So, let us explore the transformative power of forgiveness together and unlock the path to a more fulfilling and harmonious life.

Section 1: Understanding the Nature of Forgiveness

Forgiveness is a powerful, transformative force that has the ability to heal wounds, mend broken relationships, and liberate individuals from the shackles of resentment and bitterness. In a world where conflicts, misunderstandings, and hurtful actions are an inevitable part of the human experience, the act of forgiveness stands as a beacon of hope, offering a path towards personal growth, emotional well-being, and the restoration of harmony in our connections with others.

But what exactly is forgiveness, and why is it so crucial in the context of our relationships and personal journeys? This section delves into the very nature of forgiveness, exploring its various forms, its profound significance, and the ways in which it can reshape our lives and the bonds we share with those around us.

As we embark on this exploration, it is essential to recognize that forgiveness is not a simple, one-dimensional concept. It is a complex, multi-faceted process that involves a deep understanding of our own emotions, the perspectives of others, and the intricate dynamics that shape our relationships. By gaining a clearer understanding of what forgiveness truly entails, we can begin to harness its transformative potential and cultivate a more compassionate, resilient, and fulfilling approach to life and love.

Through the pages of this section, we will examine the key components of forgiveness, distinguishing it from mere condoning or forgetting, and highlighting the vital role that empathy and understanding play in the forgiveness process. We will also explore the various forms that forgiveness can take, from the profound act of self-forgiveness to the challenging yet liberating experience of forgiving others who have caused us pain.

As we unravel the intricacies of forgiveness, it becomes clear that this powerful act is not only essential for the health and longevity of our relationships but also for our own personal growth and emotional well-being. By embracing forgiveness, we open ourselves up to a world of possibilities, where the wounds of the past no longer define us, and where we can forge ahead with renewed strength, resilience, and hope.

So, let us embark on this transformative journey together, as we explore the depths of forgiveness and discover the profound impact it can have on our lives, our relationships, and our ability to navigate the complexities of the human experience with grace, compassion, and understanding.

Subsection 1.1: Defining Forgiveness and Its Key Components

Forgiveness is a complex and multifaceted concept that lies at the heart of personal growth and relationship healing. At its core, forgiveness is the conscious decision to release feelings of resentment, anger, or vengeance toward someone who has caused harm or wrongdoing. It is a deliberate choice to let go of negative emotions and thoughts, replacing them with understanding, empathy, and compassion.

One of the key components of forgiveness is acknowledging the hurt that has been experienced. This involves recognizing and validating the pain, disappointment, or betrayal that has occurred, rather than denying or minimizing its impact. By openly acknowledging the hurt, individuals can begin to process their emotions and take steps toward healing.

Another essential element of forgiveness is releasing resentment. Resentment is a toxic emotion that can fester over time, causing bitterness, anger, and emotional distress. When we hold onto resentment, we allow the past to control our present and future, preventing us from moving forward and experiencing the freedom that comes with letting go. Forgiveness requires consciously releasing these negative feelings and choosing to focus on the present moment.

Choosing compassion is another fundamental aspect of forgiveness. Compassion involves understanding and empathizing with the other person's perspective, even if we do not condone their actions. It means recognizing that everyone makes mistakes and has flaws, and that holding onto anger or bitterness only perpetuates a cycle of negativity. By choosing compassion, we open ourselves up to the possibility of healing, growth, and positive change in our relationships.

It is important to note that forgiveness does not necessarily mean forgetting the harm that has been done or excusing the behavior of the offender. Rather, it is a personal choice to release the emotional burden of the past and move forward with a renewed sense of peace and understanding. Forgiveness is not about condoning wrongdoing or allowing others to continue hurtful behavior; it is about reclaiming our own emotional well-being and creating space for positive growth and change.

Ultimately, forgiveness is a powerful tool for personal transformation and relationship healing. By acknowledging the hurt, releasing resentment, and choosing compassion, we can break free from the shackles of the past and cultivate a more positive, fulfilling, and resilient approach to life and love. As we explore the nature of forgiveness and its key components, we begin to understand its profound significance in our personal journeys and the relationships that shape our lives.

Subsection 1.2: Distinguishing Forgiveness from Condoning or Forgetting

One of the most common misconceptions about forgiveness is that it implies condoning or forgetting the hurtful behavior. This misunderstanding often leads people to resist the idea of forgiveness, believing that it means excusing the offender's actions or minimizing the impact of the offense. However, it is crucial to recognize that forgiveness is not synonymous with condoning or forgetting, and that it is possible to forgive while still acknowledging the severity of the transgression.

Condoning involves accepting or approving of the hurtful behavior, essentially sending the message that the offense was acceptable or justified. When we condone someone's actions, we may inadvertently encourage them to repeat the behavior in the future, as they may perceive our lack of objection as tacit approval. Forgiveness, on the other hand, does not require us to accept or approve of the hurtful behavior. Instead, it involves acknowledging the pain caused by the offense while choosing to release the negative emotions associated with it.

Similarly, forgiveness does not necessitate forgetting the hurtful event or pretending that it never occurred. In fact, attempting to forget or suppress the memory of the offense can be counterproductive, as it may hinder the healing process and prevent us from learning valuable lessons from the experience. Forgiveness allows us to remember the event without being consumed by the negative emotions it evokes, enabling us to move forward with greater wisdom and resilience.

It is important to emphasize that forgiveness is not about minimizing the severity of the offense or the pain it has caused. Acknowledging the gravity of the hurtful behavior is an essential step in the forgiveness process, as it validates the victim's experience and feelings. By recognizing the full extent of the harm done, we can better understand the challenges involved in forgiving and appreciate the strength and compassion required to embark on this transformative journey.

Ultimately, forgiveness is a deeply personal choice that involves prioritizing one's own emotional well-being and growth. It is a conscious decision to release the burden of resentment and anger, not for the benefit of the offender, but for the sake of our own peace and healing. By distinguishing forgiveness from condoning or forgetting, we can approach the process with greater clarity and purpose, understanding that it is possible to forgive while still holding the offender accountable and maintaining healthy boundaries in our relationships.

Subsection 1.3: The Role of Empathy and Understanding in Forgiveness

Empathy and understanding play a crucial role in facilitating the forgiveness process, as they enable individuals to see the situation from the other person's perspective. When we empathize with others, we attempt to put ourselves in their shoes, to understand their thoughts, feelings, and motivations. This act of perspective-taking is essential in the context of forgiveness, as it allows us to move beyond our own pain and anger and consider the complex factors that may have contributed to the hurtful behavior.

Empathy involves recognizing that every individual has a unique set of experiences, beliefs, and circumstances that shape their actions and reactions. By seeking to understand the context in which the offense occurred, we can begin to see the other person as a flawed human being, rather than a one-dimensional villain. This shift in perspective can be transformative, as it opens the door to compassion, understanding, and, ultimately, forgiveness.

When we approach the forgiveness process with empathy, we acknowledge that the offender may have been acting out of their own pain, fear, or ignorance, rather than a deliberate desire to cause harm. This recognition does not excuse the hurtful behavior, but it can help us to see the offender in a more nuanced light, as someone who is also struggling and in need of understanding and growth.

Moreover, empathy and understanding can help us to recognize our own role in the conflict or hurt. By examining the situation from multiple angles, we may come to realize that we, too, have contributed to the problem through our own actions, reactions, or communication style. This self-awareness is essential for personal growth and can facilitate a more balanced, compassionate approach to forgiveness.

It is important to note that empathy and understanding do not require us to agree with or approve of the offender's actions. Rather, they involve a willingness to see the humanity in the other person and to acknowledge the complex web of factors that may have contributed to their behavior. By cultivating empathy and understanding, we create a space for genuine dialogue, healing, and reconciliation.

Ultimately, empathy and understanding are powerful tools in the forgiveness process, as they enable us to move beyond our own pain and anger and connect with the other person on a deeper, more compassionate level. By seeking to understand the other person's perspective, we open ourselves up to the possibility of forgiveness, personal growth, and the restoration of damaged relationships. As we navigate the complex terrain of forgiveness, empathy and understanding serve as essential guides, lighting the way toward healing, reconciliation, and a more compassionate, connected way of being in the world.

Summary: Embracing the Transformative Power of Forgiveness

As we conclude this exploration of the nature of forgiveness, it becomes clear that this powerful act is a catalyst for personal growth, emotional healing, and the transformation of our relationships. By delving into the essence of forgiveness, we have discovered that it is not merely a simple, one-time event, but rather a complex and multifaceted process that requires a deep understanding of our own emotions, the perspectives of others, and the intricate dynamics that shape our connections.

Through acknowledging the hurt, releasing resentment, and choosing compassion, we have seen how forgiveness can liberate us from the shackles of the past, allowing us to move forward with greater resilience, wisdom, and peace. We have also recognized that forgiveness is not about condoning or forgetting the hurtful behavior, but rather about reclaiming our own emotional well-being and creating space for positive change and growth.

Moreover, we have explored the crucial role of empathy and understanding in facilitating the forgiveness process, as these qualities enable us to see beyond our own pain and connect with the humanity in others. By cultivating empathy and seeking to understand the complex factors that contribute to hurtful actions, we open ourselves up to the possibility of genuine healing, reconciliation, and the restoration of damaged relationships.

As we move forward on our journeys of personal growth and relationship building, let us embrace the transformative power of forgiveness. Let us recognize that by choosing to forgive, we are not only healing ourselves but also contributing to a more compassionate, connected, and harmonious world. May we find the strength and courage to embark on this transformative path, knowing that it is through forgiveness that we can truly unlock the full potential of our relationships and our own personal growth.

Section 2: The Personal Benefits of Forgiveness

Forgiveness is a powerful tool that can transform not only our relationships but also our own lives. When we hold onto resentment, anger, and bitterness, we carry a heavy burden that can weigh us down and hinder our personal growth and well-being. However, when we choose to forgive, we open ourselves up to a world of positive possibilities and inner peace. In this section, we will explore the numerous personal benefits of forgiveness and how embracing this practice can lead to a more fulfilling and joyful life.

Forgiveness is not about condoning or excusing hurtful behavior; rather, it is a conscious decision to release the negative emotions associated with past wounds and move forward with a lighter, more compassionate heart. By letting go of the pain and resentment, we create space for healing, self-discovery, and renewed purpose. The act of forgiveness allows us to reclaim our power and take control of our own happiness, rather than allowing the actions of others to dictate our emotional state.

Throughout this section, we will delve into the various ways in which forgiveness can positively impact our mental health, emotional well-being, and overall quality of life. From reducing stress and anxiety to fostering greater self-awareness and personal growth, the benefits of forgiveness are far-reaching and transformative. We will explore how forgiveness can lead to increased resilience, improved relationships, and a more positive outlook on life, ultimately enabling us to navigate challenges with greater ease and grace.

As we embark on this journey of understanding the personal benefits of forgiveness, it is essential to approach the topic with an open mind and a willingness to engage in self-reflection. By examining our own experiences and emotions, we can begin to cultivate a more forgiving mindset and unlock the powerful potential for personal transformation that lies within each of us. So, let us dive in and discover how the practice of forgiveness can truly change our lives for the better.

Subsection 2.1: Emotional Healing and Reduced Stress

Forgiveness is a powerful catalyst for emotional healing and stress reduction. When we hold onto resentment and anger, we create a toxic emotional environment within ourselves that can lead to chronic stress, anxiety, and even depression. The negative emotions associated with unforgiveness can consume our thoughts, drain our energy, and hinder our ability to experience joy and contentment in life.

However, when we choose to forgive, we begin the process of emotional healing. By releasing the grudges and bitterness we harbor, we create space for more positive emotions to flourish. Forgiveness allows us to let go of the past and focus on the present, freeing ourselves from the burden of unresolved emotional pain.

Research has shown that forgiveness can have a profound impact on our mental health. Studies have found that individuals who practice forgiveness report lower levels of stress, anxiety, and depression compared to those who hold onto resentment. Forgiveness has also been linked to improved self-esteem, greater life satisfaction, and enhanced overall well-being.

The act of forgiveness is not about condoning or forgetting the hurtful behavior; rather, it is a conscious decision to release the negative emotions associated with the offense. By choosing to forgive, we take control of our own emotional well-being and refuse to let the actions of others dictate our happiness.

Forgiveness is a process that requires patience, self-reflection, and a willingness to let go. It may not happen overnight, and it may involve working through difficult emotions and memories. However, the benefits of forgiveness are well worth the effort. As we release the toxic emotions and resentment, we create space for emotional healing, inner peace, and renewed vitality.

In addition to reducing stress and promoting emotional healing, forgiveness can also have a positive impact on our physical health. Chronic stress and negative emotions have been linked to a range of health problems, including heart disease, high blood pressure, and weakened immune function. By practicing forgiveness, we can reduce the physiological toll of stress on our bodies and promote overall physical well-being.

Ultimately, forgiveness is a gift we give ourselves. It allows us to break free from the chains of anger, resentment, and bitterness, and embrace a life of emotional freedom and inner peace. By choosing to forgive, we open ourselves up to the possibility of healing, growth, and renewed vitality in all aspects of our lives.

Subsection 2.2: Increased Self-Awareness and Personal Growth

The journey of forgiveness is not only about releasing negativity and healing emotional wounds; it is also a profound opportunity for personal growth and self-discovery. When we choose to forgive, we embark on a path of introspection that encourages us to confront our own emotions, beliefs, and patterns of behavior. This process of self-reflection can lead to a greater understanding of ourselves, our values, and our relationships with others.

Forgiveness requires us to take an honest look at our own role in the situation, examining our thoughts, feelings, and actions. By doing so, we gain valuable insights into our own strengths, weaknesses, and areas for improvement. We may discover that we have been holding onto limiting beliefs or unhealthy patterns of behavior that have contributed to our struggles in relationships. Through forgiveness, we can begin to challenge these beliefs and patterns, replacing them with more positive and empowering ones.

As we navigate the process of forgiveness, we also develop a deeper sense of empathy and compassion, both for ourselves and others. We learn to recognize that everyone makes mistakes and that we all have the capacity for growth and change. This understanding can foster a greater sense of connection and understanding in our relationships, as we approach others with more patience, kindness, and grace.

Moreover, the act of forgiveness requires courage and vulnerability. It means letting go of our defenses and opening ourselves up to the possibility of healing and transformation. By embracing this vulnerability, we cultivate a greater sense of authenticity and self-acceptance. We learn to embrace our imperfections and to extend the same compassion and understanding to ourselves that we extend to others.

The personal growth that comes from forgiveness is not always easy, but it is always worthwhile. It requires us to step outside of our comfort zones, to face our fears, and to trust in the power of healing and transformation. As we do so, we develop greater resilience, self-awareness, and emotional intelligence – qualities that serve us well in all areas of life.

Ultimately, the process of forgiveness is a journey of self-discovery and personal growth. It invites us to look within, to confront our own emotions and beliefs, and to emerge stronger, wiser, and more compassionate. By embracing this journey, we not only heal our relationships with others but also deepen our relationship with ourselves, cultivating a greater sense of purpose, meaning, and fulfillment in life.

Subsection 2.3: Enhanced Resilience and Coping Skills

Forgiveness is not only a powerful tool for emotional healing and personal growth but also a key factor in building resilience and strengthening coping skills. When we practice forgiveness, we develop a greater capacity to navigate life's challenges, setbacks, and adversities with grace, adaptability, and a positive mindset.

Resilience is the ability to bounce back from difficult experiences, to withstand stress and adversity, and to adapt to changing circumstances. It is a crucial skill that enables us to thrive in the face of life's inevitable ups and downs. Forgiveness plays a significant role in fostering resilience by helping us let go of negative emotions, such as anger, resentment, and bitterness, which can drain our emotional resources and hinder our ability to cope with stress.

When we hold onto grudges and unresolved emotional pain, we create a constant source of stress and tension in our lives. This chronic stress can take a toll on our mental and physical well-being, making us more vulnerable to the negative effects of future challenges and setbacks. By practicing forgiveness, we release this emotional baggage and free up our mental and emotional energy to focus on problem-solving, self-care, and personal growth.

Moreover, forgiveness helps us develop a more flexible and adaptable mindset. When we forgive, we acknowledge that life is not always fair or perfect and that people, including ourselves, make mistakes. This understanding allows us to approach challenges with a more open and accepting attitude, rather than becoming rigid or defensive in the face of adversity. By cultivating a forgiving mindset, we become more resilient in the face of change and uncertainty, as we are better equipped to let go of expectations and adapt to new circumstances.

Forgiveness also strengthens our coping skills by promoting emotional regulation and self-awareness. When we practice forgiveness, we learn to recognize and manage our own emotions more effectively. We develop the ability to pause, reflect, and respond to challenging situations with greater clarity and composure, rather than reacting impulsively or lashing out in anger. This emotional intelligence enables us to cope with stress and adversity more effectively, as we are better able to identify and address the root causes of our distress.

In addition, forgiveness fosters a support network of strong, healthy relationships that can provide a buffer against stress and adversity. When we forgive others and cultivate compassion and understanding in our relationships, we create a network of support and encouragement that can help us weather life's storms. These positive relationships provide a source of emotional strength, practical assistance, and a sense of belonging that can enhance our resilience and coping skills.

Ultimately, forgiveness is a powerful tool for building resilience and strengthening our ability to cope with life's challenges. By releasing negative emotions, cultivating a flexible and adaptable mindset, developing emotional intelligence, and fostering supportive relationships, we become better equipped to navigate the ups and downs of life with greater ease and grace. As we practice forgiveness, we not only heal our past wounds but also prepare ourselves to face future challenges with resilience, courage, and a positive outlook.

Summary: Embracing Forgiveness for a Transformed Life

Throughout this section, we have explored the profound personal benefits of forgiveness and how embracing this practice can lead to a more fulfilling, joyful, and resilient life. Forgiveness is not about condoning hurtful behavior or forgetting the past; rather, it is a conscious decision to release the negative emotions that hold us back and to create space for healing, growth, and inner peace.

By choosing to forgive, we embark on a transformative journey of emotional healing, self-discovery, and personal growth. We learn to let go of the anger, resentment, and bitterness that weigh us down, freeing ourselves from the burden of unresolved pain and allowing more positive emotions to flourish. This process not only reduces stress and promotes mental well-being but also fosters greater self-awareness, empathy, and compassion.

Moreover, forgiveness strengthens our resilience and coping skills, enabling us to navigate life's challenges with greater ease and adaptability. By releasing emotional baggage and cultivating a forgiving mindset, we become better equipped to face adversity, regulate our emotions, and maintain a positive outlook in the face of setbacks.

As we have seen, the benefits of forgiveness extend far beyond our personal well-being, positively impacting our relationships and overall quality of life. By embracing forgiveness, we open ourselves up to the possibility of deeper connections, greater understanding, and more fulfilling interactions with others.

The journey of forgiveness is not always easy, but it is always worthwhile. It requires courage, vulnerability, and a willingness to confront our own emotions and beliefs. However, as we navigate this path, we emerge stronger, wiser, and more compassionate, with a renewed sense of purpose and inner peace.

So, let us embrace the transformative power of forgiveness and embark on a journey of personal growth and emotional freedom. By choosing to forgive, we not only heal our past wounds but also unlock the boundless potential for joy, resilience, and fulfillment in all aspects of our lives. Remember, forgiveness is a gift we give ourselves – a gift that has the power to transform our lives and the lives of those around us.

Section 3: Forgiveness in the Context of Relationships

Forgiveness is a powerful tool that can transform relationships, heal wounds, and create a foundation for lasting, meaningful connections. Whether it's a romantic partnership, a family bond, or a cherished friendship, the ability to forgive and let go of resentment is essential for maintaining healthy and thriving relationships. In this section, we will explore the role of forgiveness in various types of relationships and how it can help individuals navigate the challenges and complexities that arise when two people come together.

Throughout our lives, we encounter countless opportunities to practice forgiveness in our relationships. From minor misunderstandings to deep-seated hurts, the way we respond to these challenges can either strengthen or weaken our connections with others. By embracing forgiveness, we open the door to healing, growth, and a deeper understanding of ourselves and those we hold dear.

In the following subsections, we will delve into the dynamics of forgiveness in romantic relationships, family structures, and friendships. We will examine how forgiveness can help couples overcome conflicts, rebuild trust, and foster a more loving and supportive partnership. We will also explore the significance of forgiveness in mending estranged family relationships and creating a more harmonious family environment. Furthermore, we will discuss the role of forgiveness in maintaining and strengthening friendships, as well as how it contributes to more positive and compassionate social interactions.

Through real-life examples, expert insights, and practical advice, this section aims to empower readers with the tools and knowledge needed to cultivate a forgiving mindset and apply it effectively in their relationships. By understanding the transformative power of forgiveness, readers can unlock the potential for deeper, more meaningful connections and create relationships that stand the test of time.

Subsection 3.1: Forgiveness in Romantic Relationships

In the realm of romantic partnerships, forgiveness plays a crucial role in fostering a healthy, loving, and enduring connection between two individuals. When couples inevitably face conflicts, misunderstandings, and hurts, the ability to forgive and let go of resentment can be the key to overcoming challenges and strengthening the bond they share.

Forgiveness in romantic relationships is not about condoning hurtful behavior or forgetting the pain caused by a partner's actions. Instead, it is a conscious choice to release negative emotions, such as anger, bitterness, and resentment, and to work towards healing and reconciliation. By embracing forgiveness, couples demonstrate their commitment to the relationship and their willingness to grow together, even in the face of adversity.

One of the most significant benefits of forgiveness in romantic partnerships is its ability to help couples overcome conflicts. When partners are able to forgive each other for their mistakes and shortcomings, they create a safe space for open communication, vulnerability, and problem-solving. Instead of holding onto grudges or engaging in endless cycles of blame and defensiveness, forgiving couples can approach conflicts with empathy, understanding, and a shared desire to find resolution.

Moreover, forgiveness is essential for rebuilding trust in romantic relationships. Trust is the foundation upon which all healthy partnerships are built, and when it is broken, it can be incredibly challenging to restore. However, through the process of forgiveness, couples can gradually rebuild trust by demonstrating their commitment to honesty, transparency, and accountability. As partners work to forgive each other and prove their reliability and dependability over time, they can create a renewed sense of security and confidence in their relationship.

Beyond helping couples overcome conflicts and rebuild trust, forgiveness also has the power to deepen the emotional connection between partners. When individuals choose to forgive, they open their hearts to compassion, understanding, and vulnerability. They create a space for their partner to be imperfect, to make mistakes, and to grow alongside them. This level of acceptance and unconditional love can foster a profound sense of intimacy, as partners feel seen, heard, and valued for who they are, flaws and all.

It is important to note that forgiveness in romantic relationships is not always easy, and it is a process that requires patience, effort, and a willingness to work through difficult emotions. Couples may need to seek the guidance of a therapist or counselor to navigate the complexities of forgiveness and to develop the necessary skills for effective communication and conflict resolution.

However, the rewards of forgiveness in romantic partnerships are immeasurable. By choosing to let go of resentment and embrace compassion, couples can build a love that is resilient, enduring, and deeply fulfilling. They can create a partnership that not only weathers the storms of life but also grows stronger and more beautiful with each passing year.

Subsection 3.2: Forgiveness in Family Dynamics

Family relationships are often the most complex and emotionally charged connections we experience throughout our lives. The dynamics within a family can be influenced by a myriad of factors, including past hurts, unresolved conflicts, and deep-seated resentments. In this intricate web of relationships, forgiveness emerges as a powerful tool for healing, reconciliation, and fostering a more harmonious family environment.

Forgiveness in family relationships is not about forgetting the past or excusing hurtful behavior. Instead, it is a conscious choice to release the emotional burden of anger, bitterness, and resentment that can weigh heavily on the heart and mind. By embracing forgiveness, family members can begin to heal old wounds, mend estranged relationships, and create a foundation for a more loving and supportive family dynamic.

One of the most significant benefits of forgiveness in family relationships is its ability to break the cycle of pain and hurt that can be passed down through generations. When family members hold onto grudges and resentments, they inadvertently create a legacy of emotional baggage that can impact future generations. By choosing to forgive, individuals can put an end to this cycle and create a new path forward, one that is rooted in understanding, compassion, and healing.

Forgiveness is particularly crucial in the context of estranged family relationships. Estrangement can occur for a variety of reasons, such as unresolved conflicts, differing values, or a lack of communication. When family members become estranged, the emotional distance can feel insurmountable, and the prospect of reconciliation may seem daunting. However, forgiveness can serve as a bridge to reconnect and rebuild these fractured relationships.

The process of forgiveness in estranged family relationships often begins with a willingness to listen and understand the other person's perspective. By creating a safe space for open and honest communication, family members can begin to unravel the complex emotions and experiences that led to the estrangement. Through active listening, empathy, and a genuine desire to understand, individuals can start to see each other in a new light and find common ground upon which to rebuild their relationship.

Forgiveness in family dynamics also plays a vital role in fostering a more harmonious and supportive family environment. When family members are able to let go of past hurts and resentments, they create space for more positive and nurturing interactions. Instead of being weighed down by negative emotions, individuals can focus on building stronger, more meaningful connections with their loved ones.

To cultivate forgiveness within the family, it is essential to practice empathy and compassion. By putting ourselves in the shoes of our family members and seeking to understand their experiences and perspectives, we can develop a deeper sense of understanding and connection. This empathetic approach can help us to see past the hurt and pain and recognize the shared humanity that binds us together as a family.

It is important to note that forgiveness in family relationships is a personal journey, and each individual may have their own timeline and process for reaching a place of forgiveness. Some may find it easier to forgive, while others may struggle with the concept and require more time and support. It is crucial to respect each person's unique path and to offer patience, understanding, and encouragement along the way.

Ultimately, forgiveness in family dynamics is about choosing to prioritize love, healing, and connection over the pain of the past. By embracing forgiveness, we open the door to a more harmonious, supportive, and fulfilling family life. Through the power of forgiveness, we can break free from the cycles of hurt and resentment that have held us back and create a new legacy of love, understanding, and togetherness that will endure for generations to come.

Subsection 3.3: Forgiveness in Friendships and Social Interactions

Friendships and social interactions form the fabric of our daily lives, providing us with a sense of belonging, support, and connection. However, these relationships are not immune to conflicts, misunderstandings, and hurt feelings. Forgiveness plays a vital role in maintaining and strengthening friendships, as well as contributing to more positive and compassionate social interactions.

In the context of friendships, forgiveness is essential for navigating the inevitable challenges that arise when two individuals with different personalities, backgrounds, and opinions come together. Friends may inadvertently say or do things that cause hurt or disappointment, leading to feelings of anger, resentment, or betrayal. By embracing forgiveness, friends can work through these difficult emotions and find a path towards understanding, healing, and reconciliation.

Forgiveness in friendships requires open and honest communication, a willingness to listen and understand each other's perspectives, and a commitment to rebuilding trust. When friends are able to have difficult conversations, express their feelings, and take responsibility for their actions, they create a foundation for forgiveness and growth. By choosing to let go of resentment and focus on the positive aspects of the friendship, individuals can strengthen their bond and develop a deeper appreciation for each other.

Moreover, forgiveness in friendships can prevent minor conflicts from escalating into larger, more damaging issues. When friends hold onto grudges or engage in passive-aggressive behavior, they risk eroding the trust and intimacy that define their relationship. By practicing forgiveness, friends can nip potential problems in the bud and maintain a healthy, supportive dynamic that allows both individuals to thrive.

Beyond individual friendships, forgiveness also plays a crucial role in fostering more positive and compassionate social interactions. In our daily lives, we encounter a wide range of people, each with their own unique experiences, beliefs, and challenges. Misunderstandings, conflicts, and offenses can occur in any social setting, from the workplace to community gatherings to online interactions.

By cultivating a forgiving mindset, individuals can approach social interactions with greater empathy, patience, and understanding. Instead of reacting with anger or judgment when someone says or does something hurtful, a forgiving person can take a step back, consider the other person's perspective, and respond with kindness and compassion. This approach can diffuse tense situations, promote open dialogue, and create a more harmonious social environment.

Forgiveness in social interactions also has the power to inspire others and create a ripple effect of positivity. When individuals witness acts of forgiveness and compassion, they are more likely to adopt a similar mindset and approach in their own interactions. By modeling forgiveness, we can contribute to a culture of understanding, empathy, and respect, where people feel safe to express themselves, make mistakes, and grow together.

It is important to note that forgiveness in friendships and social interactions does not mean tolerating abuse, neglect, or unhealthy behavior patterns. Forgiveness should not come at the cost of one's own well-being or self-respect. In situations where a friendship or social relationship is consistently toxic or harmful, it may be necessary to set boundaries, limit contact, or even end the relationship altogether.

However, for the vast majority of friendships and social interactions, forgiveness is a powerful tool for building and maintaining strong, positive connections. By embracing forgiveness, we open ourselves up to deeper, more meaningful relationships, characterized by trust, compassion, and mutual understanding. Through the practice of forgiveness, we can create a more loving, supportive, and inclusive social world, one interaction at a time.

Summary: Embracing Forgiveness for Stronger, More Fulfilling Relationships

Throughout this section, we have explored the transformative power of forgiveness in various types of relationships, from romantic partnerships to family bonds and friendships. By embracing forgiveness, we open the door to healing, growth, and deeper, more meaningful connections with those we hold dear.

Forgiveness is not about forgetting the past or excusing hurtful behavior; rather, it is a conscious choice to release the emotional burdens that weigh us down and prevent us from moving forward. In romantic relationships, forgiveness helps couples overcome conflicts, rebuild trust, and foster a more loving and supportive partnership. Within family dynamics, forgiveness can break the cycle of pain and resentment, mend estranged relationships, and create a more harmonious and nurturing family environment. And in friendships and social interactions, forgiveness promotes understanding, compassion, and positive connections that enrich our lives.

The path to forgiveness is not always easy, and it requires patience, empathy, and a willingness to work through difficult emotions. However, the rewards of forgiveness are immeasurable. By letting go of anger, bitterness, and resentment, we create space for joy, love, and personal growth. We give ourselves and our loved ones the opportunity to learn, heal, and thrive together.

As you reflect on the insights and advice provided in this section, consider how you can incorporate forgiveness into your own relationships. Remember that forgiveness is a personal journey, and each individual may have their own unique path to follow. Be patient with yourself and others, and trust in the power of forgiveness to transform your relationships and your life.

By embracing forgiveness, you have the power to create a legacy of love, understanding, and connection that will endure for generations to come. So take a deep breath, open your heart, and embark on the beautiful journey of forgiveness. Your relationships, and your life, will be all the richer for it.

Section 4: The Process of Letting Go

Forgiveness is a powerful tool for healing and growth, but it is often easier said than done. The process of letting go of resentment, anger, and other negative emotions associated with past hurts can be challenging, especially when the wounds run deep. However, holding onto these emotions can be like carrying a heavy burden that weighs us down and prevents us from moving forward in our relationships and personal lives.

In this section, we will explore the process of letting go and provide guidance on how to navigate this difficult but rewarding journey. We will delve into the importance of acknowledging and validating our emotions, as well as the role of reframing our narratives and finding meaning in our experiences. By learning to practice self-compassion and self-care, we can create a supportive environment for ourselves as we work through the letting go process.

Throughout this section, we will emphasize the significance of acceptance and the power of focusing on personal growth and progress. By embracing the reality of our situations and releasing the need for control or retribution, we can free ourselves from the shackles of resentment and anger, allowing us to move forward in a more positive and constructive manner.

The process of letting go is not always linear, and it may involve setbacks and challenges along the way. However, by committing to this journey and utilizing the strategies and insights provided in this section, you can cultivate a greater sense of peace, resilience, and emotional freedom in your life and relationships. As you embark on this transformative path, remember that letting go is not about forgetting or condoning hurtful actions, but rather about reclaiming your power and choosing to focus on your own healing and growth.

Subsection 4.1: Acknowledging and Validating Emotions

The first step in the process of letting go is to acknowledge and validate the emotions you experience in relation to the hurtful event or situation. It is essential to recognize that your feelings are valid and that it is normal to experience a range of emotions, such as anger, sadness, disappointment, or betrayal, when you have been hurt.

Many people have a tendency to suppress or ignore their emotions, believing that acknowledging them will only intensify the pain. However, denying or bottling up your feelings can actually prolong the healing process and make it more difficult to move forward. By acknowledging your emotions, you give yourself permission to feel and express them in a healthy manner.

Validating your emotions involves accepting them without judgment and understanding that they are a natural response to the hurtful experience. It is important to remember that your feelings are not right or wrong; they simply are. By validating your emotions, you create a safe space for yourself to process and work through them.

One effective way to acknowledge and validate your emotions is to practice mindfulness. Take a moment to sit with your feelings, observing them without trying to change or suppress them. Notice how they manifest in your body, such as tightness in your chest or a knot in your stomach. Breathe deeply and allow yourself to fully experience the emotions without getting caught up in the stories or thoughts surrounding them.

Another helpful technique is to express your emotions through writing or talking to a trusted friend or therapist. Putting your feelings into words can help you gain clarity and perspective, as well as provide a sense of release. When expressing your emotions, be honest and authentic, avoiding the temptation to censor yourself or downplay the impact of the hurtful experience.

Remember that acknowledging and validating your emotions is not a sign of weakness, but rather a courageous act of self-compassion. By giving yourself permission to feel and express your emotions, you lay the foundation for healing and growth. This process may be uncomfortable at times, but it is a necessary step in letting go of the pain and moving forward in a positive direction.

Subsection 4.2: Reframing the Narrative and Finding Meaning

As you navigate the process of letting go, it is essential to reframe the narrative surrounding the hurtful event and find meaning or lessons learned from the experience. The way we perceive and interpret our experiences has a significant impact on our emotional well-being and ability to move forward. By consciously shifting our perspective and looking for growth opportunities, we can transform pain into wisdom and resilience.

One powerful strategy for reframing the narrative is to challenge the limiting beliefs and assumptions that may have arisen from the hurtful experience. For example, if you have been betrayed by a partner, you might find yourself thinking, "I can never trust anyone again" or "I am unworthy of love." These beliefs can keep you stuck in a cycle of negativity and hinder your ability to form healthy relationships in the future. By questioning the validity of these beliefs and replacing them with more balanced and empowering thoughts, such as "I have the capacity to trust again" or "I am deserving of love and respect," you can gradually shift your mindset and open yourself up to new possibilities.

Another effective approach to reframing the narrative is to focus on the lessons learned from the experience. While it may be difficult to see the silver lining in the midst of pain, every challenge we face has the potential to teach us something valuable about ourselves, others, or life in general. Take some time to reflect on the insights you have gained from the hurtful event. Perhaps you have discovered the importance of setting healthy boundaries, the value of self-love and self-respect, or the strength of your own resilience. By reframing the experience as an opportunity for growth and learning, you can find a sense of purpose and meaning that transcends the pain.

It is also helpful to consider the broader context of your life when reframing the narrative. Often, when we are in the midst of a difficult situation, it can feel all-consuming and overwhelming. However, by zooming out and looking at the bigger picture, we can gain a more balanced perspective. Remind yourself of the many positive aspects of your life, such as supportive friends and family, personal achievements, or cherished memories. Recognizing that the hurtful event is just one part of your complex and multi-faceted life story can help you maintain a sense of hope and perspective.

As you work on reframing the narrative, it is important to be patient and compassionate with yourself. Shifting deeply ingrained patterns of thinking and feeling takes time and practice. Be kind to yourself as you navigate this process, and celebrate the small victories along the way. Remember that every step you take towards reframing the narrative and finding meaning is a step towards healing and growth.

Ultimately, the power to reframe your story lies within you. By consciously choosing to focus on the lessons, insights, and opportunities for growth that arise from even the most painful experiences, you can reclaim your narrative and create a more empowering and resilient life story. As the author and activist Gloria Steinem once said, "The truth will set you free, but first it will piss you off." Embrace the truth of your experience, but also embrace the freedom that comes from reframing it in a way that supports your healing and growth.

Subsection 4.3: Practicing Self-Compassion and Self-Care

As you navigate the complex and often challenging process of letting go, it is crucial to prioritize self-compassion and self-care. These practices are essential for maintaining emotional well-being and fostering a supportive environment that allows for healing and growth. When we treat ourselves with kindness and understanding, we create a solid foundation from which we can better manage the difficulties associated with letting go of resentment, anger, and other negative emotions.

Self-compassion involves treating yourself with the same level of care, concern, and understanding that you would extend to a dear friend who is going through a tough time. It means recognizing that everyone makes mistakes, experiences hardships, and feels pain, and that these experiences are a natural part of the human condition. By cultivating self-compassion, you can develop a more balanced and nurturing approach to dealing with the challenges of letting go.

One key aspect of practicing self-compassion is learning to be mindful of your inner dialogue. Many people have a tendency to engage in self-criticism and negative self-talk, especially when faced with difficult emotions or situations. However, this harsh inner critic can exacerbate feelings of shame, guilt, and worthlessness, making it even harder to let go and move forward. Instead, try to cultivate a more compassionate and understanding inner voice, one that speaks to you with the same kindness and support you would offer to a beloved friend.

Another important component of self-compassion is allowing yourself to feel and express your emotions without judgment. When working through the process of letting go, it is normal to experience a wide range of feelings, including sadness, anger, fear, and confusion. Rather than trying to suppress or avoid these emotions, practice acknowledging and accepting them as valid and natural responses to your situation. By giving yourself permission to feel, you create space for healing and release.

In addition to practicing self-compassion, prioritizing self-care is essential for maintaining emotional and physical well-being during the letting go process. Self-care encompasses a wide range of activities and practices that help you nurture and support yourself on all levels – mentally, emotionally, physically, and spiritually. By consistently engaging in self-care, you can build resilience, reduce stress, and create a greater sense of balance and stability in your life.

Some examples of self-care practices that can be particularly helpful when working through the process of letting go include:

1. Engaging in regular physical exercise, such as walking, yoga, or swimming, to release endorphins and reduce stress.
2. Practicing relaxation techniques, like deep breathing, meditation, or progressive muscle relaxation, to calm the mind and body.
3. Spending time in nature, which has been shown to have a grounding and restorative effect on emotional well-being.
4. Nurturing supportive relationships with friends, family, or a therapist who can offer a listening ear and emotional support.
5. Engaging in creative activities, such as writing, painting, or playing music, as a means of self-expression and emotional release.
6. Making time for hobbies and activities that bring you joy, fulfillment, and a sense of accomplishment.
7. Establishing healthy boundaries and learning to say "no" to commitments or situations that drain your energy or compromise your well-being.

Remember, self-care is not a selfish act, but rather a necessary practice for maintaining the emotional and mental strength needed to navigate life's challenges, including the process of letting go. By consistently prioritizing self-compassion and self-care, you empower yourself to face difficulties with greater resilience, clarity, and grace. As you extend kindness and understanding to yourself, you cultivate a deeper capacity for healing, growth, and ultimately, the freedom that comes with letting go.

Subsection 4.4: Embracing Acceptance and Moving Forward

As you progress through the process of letting go, it becomes increasingly important to embrace acceptance and focus on moving forward in a positive, growth-oriented manner. Acceptance, in this context, does not mean condoning or agreeing with the hurtful actions or events that have taken place. Rather, it involves acknowledging the reality of the situation and recognizing that you cannot change the past, but you can choose how you respond to it in the present and future.

One of the most challenging aspects of acceptance is releasing the need for control or retribution. When we have been hurt, it is natural to want to seek justice or revenge, or to hold onto the belief that we can somehow change the outcome of the situation. However, clinging to these desires can keep us stuck in a cycle of anger, bitterness, and resentment, preventing us from healing and moving forward.

Embracing acceptance requires a conscious decision to let go of the need for control and to focus on what you can change – namely, your own thoughts, feelings, and actions. This process may involve grieving the loss of what could have been, or the idea of the relationship or situation that you had hoped for. Allow yourself to feel these emotions fully, but also recognize that holding onto them indefinitely will only prolong your pain and hinder your growth.

As you work towards acceptance, it can be helpful to practice mindfulness and self-compassion. Observe your thoughts and feelings without judgment, acknowledging their presence but also recognizing that they do not define you. Treat yourself with kindness and understanding, as you would a dear friend who is going through a difficult time. Remind yourself that everyone makes mistakes and experiences challenges, and that these experiences do not diminish your worth or value as a person.

Another key aspect of moving forward is focusing on personal growth and learning. While the hurtful experience may have been painful, it can also serve as a catalyst for self-discovery and transformation. Take time to reflect on the lessons you have learned, the strengths you have developed, and the insights you have gained about yourself and your relationships. Consider how you can apply these lessons to create positive changes in your life and to build healthier, more fulfilling connections with others.

Moving forward also involves setting new goals and cultivating a sense of purpose and direction. Rather than dwelling on the past or what could have been, focus on what you want to create in your life moving forward. Set intentions for personal growth, self-discovery, and the development of meaningful relationships. Engage in activities and pursuits that bring you joy, fulfillment, and a sense of accomplishment, and surround yourself with supportive, uplifting individuals who encourage your progress.

Throughout this process, be patient and compassionate with yourself. Embracing acceptance and moving forward is a gradual, non-linear journey that may involve setbacks and challenges along the way. Recognize that healing takes time, and that it is okay to have moments of sadness, anger, or grief, even as you work towards letting go. Trust in your own resilience and capacity for growth, and know that every step you take towards acceptance and forward movement is a step towards a more empowered, fulfilling life.

Ultimately, embracing acceptance and moving forward is about reclaiming your power and choosing to focus on the present and future, rather than remaining stuck in the pain of the past. By releasing the need for control or retribution, and instead focusing on personal growth, self-discovery, and the cultivation of meaningful connections, you open yourself up to new possibilities and opportunities for healing and transformation. As you navigate this journey, remember that you are not alone, and that there is always hope for a brighter, more fulfilling future ahead.

Summary: Letting Go and Embracing a Brighter Future

As we conclude this section on the process of letting go, it is important to recognize the transformative power of releasing resentment, anger, and other negative emotions associated with past hurts. By acknowledging and validating our emotions, reframing our narratives, practicing self-compassion and self-care, and ultimately embracing acceptance, we can free ourselves from the burden of emotional pain and move forward in a more positive, growth-oriented manner.

Throughout this journey, we have explored the significance of allowing ourselves to feel and express our emotions without judgment, while also challenging limiting beliefs and assumptions that may hinder our progress. By focusing on the lessons learned and the opportunities for personal growth, we can find meaning and purpose in even the most difficult experiences.

As you embark on your own path of letting go, remember to be patient and compassionate with yourself. Healing is a gradual process that requires time, effort, and self-reflection. Trust in your resilience and capacity for growth, and surround yourself with supportive individuals who encourage and uplift you along the way.

Ultimately, the power to let go and embrace a brighter future lies within you. By consciously choosing to release the pain of the past and focus on the present and future, you open yourself up to new possibilities for healing, growth, and fulfillment in your relationships and in your life as a whole. As you continue on this transformative journey, know that every step you take towards letting go is a step towards a more empowered, authentic, and joyful existence.

Section 5: Cultivating a Forgiving Mindset

Forgiveness is a powerful tool that can transform not only our relationships but also our own lives. It is a choice we make to let go of resentment, anger, and bitterness, and to embrace compassion, understanding, and peace. However, cultivating a forgiving mindset is not always easy, especially when we have been deeply hurt or betrayed. It requires a conscious effort and a willingness to see beyond our own pain and to recognize the humanity in others.

In this section, we will explore the various strategies and techniques that can help us develop a more forgiving mindset and incorporate forgiveness into our daily lives. We will delve into the importance of empathy and perspective-taking, and how these skills can help us understand and relate to others, even when they have wronged us. We will also discuss the role of gratitude and compassion in fostering a forgiving attitude, and how these qualities can help us find peace and healing in the face of adversity.

Moreover, we will examine the ways in which forgiveness can be integrated into our personal values and belief systems, becoming a guiding principle in our interactions with others and our decision-making processes. By making forgiveness a central part of our lives, we can create a more positive and harmonious environment for ourselves and those around us.

Throughout this section, we will provide practical tips and exercises that can help you cultivate a more forgiving mindset, even in the most challenging of circumstances. Whether you are struggling to forgive a past hurt or simply looking to bring more compassion and understanding into your relationships, the insights and strategies provided here will serve as a valuable guide on your journey towards greater forgiveness and inner peace.

Subsection 5.1: Practicing Empathy and Perspective-Taking

Empathy and perspective-taking are essential skills that can help us cultivate a more forgiving mindset. When we practice empathy, we strive to understand and share the feelings of another person, putting ourselves in their shoes and imagining how they might be experiencing a situation. This ability to connect with others on an emotional level can foster a deeper sense of compassion and understanding, even in the face of conflict or hurt.

Perspective-taking, on the other hand, involves actively considering a situation from another person's point of view. It requires us to step back from our own thoughts, beliefs, and biases and to examine a situation through the lens of someone else's experiences, motivations, and circumstances. By engaging in perspective-taking, we can gain valuable insights into the reasons behind someone's actions or words, which can help us approach the situation with greater empathy and openness.

Cultivating empathy and perspective-taking is a skill that requires practice and intentional effort. One effective way to develop these abilities is through active listening. When engaging in conversations with others, particularly during conflicts or disagreements, make a conscious effort to listen attentively and without judgment. Focus on understanding the other person's perspective, asking questions to clarify their thoughts and feelings, and validating their experiences.

Another powerful tool for developing empathy and perspective-taking is through the use of "I" statements. When expressing your own thoughts and feelings, use phrases such as "I feel" or "I understand," rather than "you" statements that can come across as accusatory or blaming. This approach helps to create a safe and non-judgmental space for open communication and understanding.

Engaging in regular self-reflection can also help cultivate empathy and perspective-taking. Take time to examine your own thoughts, feelings, and reactions to various situations, and consider how they might be influenced by your own experiences, biases, and assumptions. By gaining a deeper understanding of yourself, you can develop a greater capacity for understanding and relating to others.

Incorporating empathy and perspective-taking into your daily life can have a profound impact on your relationships and your ability to forgive. When we approach others with compassion and understanding, we create a foundation for more meaningful and positive connections. We become better equipped to navigate conflicts, to find common ground, and to extend forgiveness when needed.

Ultimately, practicing empathy and perspective-taking is a powerful way to cultivate a more forgiving mindset. By making a conscious effort to understand and relate to others, we can break down barriers, build bridges, and create a more compassionate and understanding world.

Subsection 5.2: Developing Gratitude and Compassion

Gratitude and compassion are two powerful emotions that can significantly contribute to a more forgiving and understanding outlook on life and relationships. When we cultivate a sense of gratitude, we shift our focus from what we lack to the abundance of blessings in our lives. This shift in perspective can help us approach challenges and conflicts with a more positive and resilient mindset, making it easier to extend forgiveness and understanding to others.

Practicing gratitude involves actively acknowledging and appreciating the good things in our lives, no matter how small they may seem. It can be as simple as taking a moment each day to reflect on the people, experiences, and opportunities that bring us joy and fulfillment. By regularly engaging in gratitude practices, such as keeping a gratitude journal or expressing appreciation to others, we train our minds to seek out the positive aspects of our lives, even in the face of adversity.

Compassion, on the other hand, is the ability to empathize with others' suffering and the desire to alleviate it. When we approach others with compassion, we recognize that everyone faces challenges and struggles, and we seek to understand and support them rather than judge or condemn. Compassion allows us to see beyond our own perspective and to connect with others on a deeper, more human level.

Cultivating compassion requires us to practice empathy and to actively seek to understand the experiences and emotions of others. It involves listening with an open heart, offering support and kindness, and recognizing that we all share a common humanity. By extending compassion to others, we create a more forgiving and understanding environment, one in which mistakes and conflicts can be addressed with patience, care, and respect.

Developing gratitude and compassion is a ongoing process that requires intentional effort and practice. One effective way to cultivate these qualities is through loving-kindness meditation, a practice that involves directing positive thoughts and well-wishes towards oneself and others. This type of meditation can help us develop a greater sense of connection and empathy, and can foster a more forgiving and compassionate mindset.

Another powerful tool for cultivating gratitude and compassion is through acts of kindness and service. By actively seeking out opportunities to help and support others, we shift our focus from our own concerns to the needs and well-being of those around us. This can help us develop a greater sense of perspective and empathy, and can foster a more forgiving and understanding approach to life and relationships.

Ultimately, developing gratitude and compassion is a transformative process that can have a profound impact on our lives and relationships. By actively cultivating these qualities, we create a more positive, resilient, and forgiving mindset that allows us to navigate challenges and conflicts with greater ease and understanding. We become more attuned to the experiences and needs of others, and we develop a greater capacity for empathy, kindness, and forgiveness.

Subsection 5.3: Incorporating Forgiveness into Personal

Values and Beliefs

Integrating forgiveness into one's personal values and belief system is a crucial step in cultivating a forgiving mindset. When we make forgiveness a guiding principle in our lives, it becomes more than just a one-time act or a response to a specific situation; it becomes a way of life, influencing our daily interactions, decisions, and overall outlook.

Incorporating forgiveness into our personal values involves recognizing its importance and making a conscious effort to prioritize it in our lives. This means taking the time to reflect on our beliefs about forgiveness, and considering how we can align our actions and attitudes with these beliefs. It may involve challenging long-held assumptions or biases, and being open to new perspectives and ways of thinking.

One way to make forgiveness a central part of our personal values is to actively seek out opportunities to practice it in our daily lives. This can involve making a conscious effort to let go of minor grievances or annoyances, and choosing to respond with understanding and compassion instead of anger or resentment. It can also involve being more forgiving towards ourselves, acknowledging our own mistakes and shortcomings with kindness and self-compassion.

Another important aspect of incorporating forgiveness into our personal values is recognizing its role in our spiritual or philosophical beliefs. Many religious and spiritual traditions emphasize the importance of forgiveness, viewing it as a key component of personal growth, healing, and enlightenment. By exploring the teachings and practices related to forgiveness within our own belief systems, we can gain a deeper understanding of its significance and find new ways to integrate it into our lives.

Ultimately, making forgiveness a guiding principle in our lives requires a willingness to embrace change and to let go of old patterns of thinking and behaving. It involves recognizing that holding onto anger, resentment, and bitterness only serves to harm ourselves and our relationships, and that true peace and happiness come from a place of compassion, understanding, and forgiveness.

By incorporating forgiveness into our personal values and belief systems, we create a foundation for more positive and meaningful interactions with others. We become more resilient in the face of challenges and conflicts, and we develop a greater capacity for empathy, compassion, and understanding. In doing so, we not only improve our own lives but also contribute to a more forgiving and compassionate world.

Summary: Embracing Forgiveness as a Way of Life

Throughout this section, we have explored the transformative power of cultivating a forgiving mindset and incorporating forgiveness into our daily lives. By practicing empathy and perspective-taking, we can develop a deeper understanding of others' experiences and emotions, fostering compassion and understanding in our relationships. Gratitude and compassion serve as powerful tools for creating a more positive, resilient, and forgiving outlook on life, allowing us to navigate challenges and conflicts with greater ease and grace.

Integrating forgiveness into our personal values and belief systems is a crucial step in making forgiveness a way of life. By recognizing the importance of forgiveness and making a conscious effort to prioritize it in our daily interactions and decisions, we can create a foundation for more meaningful and harmonious relationships. This process may require challenging long-held assumptions, exploring the teachings of our spiritual or philosophical traditions, and being open to new perspectives and ways of thinking.

Ultimately, cultivating a forgiving mindset is an ongoing journey that requires intentional effort, self-reflection, and a willingness to embrace change. By incorporating the strategies and insights discussed in this section, we can develop a greater capacity for empathy, compassion, and understanding, not only improving our own lives but also contributing to a more forgiving and compassionate world. As we move forward, let us embrace forgiveness as a guiding principle, allowing it to shape our interactions, decisions, and overall approach to life and relationships. In doing so, we open ourselves up to greater peace, happiness, and fulfillment, both within ourselves and in our connections with others.

Chapter Summary: Embracing Forgiveness for Personal Growth and Relationship Healing

Throughout this chapter, we have explored the transformative power of forgiveness and the importance of letting go of resentment for personal growth and relationship healing. By understanding the nature of forgiveness, its key components, and the distinction between forgiveness and condoning or forgetting, we can begin to cultivate a more forgiving mindset. The process of forgiveness involves acknowledging hurt, releasing negative emotions, and choosing compassion, all of which can be facilitated by empathy and understanding.

Forgiveness offers numerous personal benefits, such as emotional healing, reduced stress, increased self-awareness, personal growth, and enhanced resilience. When applied to relationships, forgiveness can help heal wounds, rebuild trust, and strengthen connections in romantic partnerships, family dynamics, and friendships. The act of letting go involves acknowledging and validating emotions, reframing the narrative, practicing self-compassion and self-care, and ultimately embracing acceptance and moving forward.

By incorporating forgiveness into our personal values and belief systems, we can develop a more empathetic, compassionate, and understanding approach to life and relationships. Through consistent practice and a commitment to personal growth, we can harness the transformative power of forgiveness to heal ourselves and our relationships, fostering a more positive and fulfilling life. Remember, forgiveness is a choice and a journey – one that requires patience, self-reflection, and a willingness to let go of the past and embrace a brighter future.

Chapter 14: Embracing Diversity and Inclusivity in Relationships

In the tapestry of life, relationships serve as the vibrant threads that weave together the unique experiences, perspectives, and identities of individuals from all walks of life. As we navigate the complex landscape of human connections, it becomes increasingly evident that embracing diversity and fostering inclusivity are not merely noble ideals but essential components of building strong, meaningful, and fulfilling relationships.

In a world that is beautifully diverse, our relationships have the power to bridge gaps, challenge stereotypes, and promote understanding and respect. When we open our hearts and minds to the richness of diversity, we create space for growth, empathy, and the celebration of our shared humanity. By actively seeking out and embracing relationships that span across various dimensions of diversity, such as race, ethnicity, gender, sexual orientation, age, and ability, we expand our horizons and enrich our lives in immeasurable ways.

However, building and maintaining diverse and inclusive relationships requires more than just good intentions. It demands a commitment to self-reflection, cultural competence, and a willingness to engage in sometimes difficult conversations. It involves recognizing and challenging our own biases, assumptions, and privileges, while actively listening to and validating the experiences and perspectives of others.

Throughout this chapter, we will embark on a journey of exploration and growth, delving into the transformative power of diverse and inclusive relationships. We will examine the benefits and challenges of cultivating connections across differences, and provide practical strategies for fostering understanding, respect, and equity in all of our interactions. By embracing the beauty of diversity and committing to inclusivity, we not only enrich our own lives but also contribute to building a more just, compassionate, and interconnected world.

So, let us approach this chapter with an open mind, a curious heart, and a willingness to learn and grow. Together, we will celebrate the incredible tapestry of human diversity and discover the profound joy and fulfillment that comes from building bridges of understanding and love across all boundaries.

Section 1: Understanding the Value of Diversity in Relationships

In the tapestry of life, relationships serve as the threads that weave together the diverse experiences, perspectives, and backgrounds of individuals. Just as a beautiful tapestry derives its richness from the variety of colors and patterns, our relationships thrive when we embrace and celebrate the diversity that exists within them. This section explores the profound value and importance of diversity in various types of relationships, from romantic partnerships to friendships, family bonds, and professional connections.

As we navigate the complexities of human interaction, it becomes increasingly clear that diversity is not merely a buzzword, but a fundamental aspect of building strong, resilient, and meaningful relationships. When we open our hearts and minds to the unique qualities and experiences that each person brings to the table, we create a space for growth, learning, and mutual understanding. Diversity in relationships allows us to challenge our assumptions, expand our worldviews, and cultivate a deeper sense of empathy and compassion for others.

Throughout this section, we will delve into the many facets of diversity and its impact on the health and longevity of our relationships. From the benefits of exposure to different cultures and belief systems to the importance of recognizing and respecting individual differences, we will explore how embracing diversity can enrich our lives and strengthen the bonds we share with others. By understanding the value of diversity in relationships, we can actively work towards creating a more inclusive, accepting, and harmonious world, one connection at a time.

Subsection 1.1: Defining Diversity and Its Many Forms

Diversity is a multifaceted concept that encompasses the vast array of differences among individuals, groups, and communities. At its core, diversity recognizes and celebrates the unique characteristics, experiences, and perspectives that shape our identities and enrich our interactions with others. To fully grasp the significance of diversity in relationships, it is essential to understand its various dimensions and how they intersect to create the vibrant tapestry of human existence.

One of the most visible aspects of diversity is race and ethnicity. These dimensions refer to the social constructs and cultural identities that are associated with an individual's ancestry, physical characteristics, and geographical origins. Recognizing and appreciating the richness of racial and ethnic diversity is crucial in building inclusive and equitable relationships, as it allows us to challenge stereotypes, overcome prejudices, and foster a deeper understanding of different cultural backgrounds and experiences.

Gender and sexual orientation are other significant dimensions of diversity. Gender diversity acknowledges the spectrum of gender identities, including but not limited to male, female, transgender, non-binary, and gender-fluid individuals. Sexual orientation, on the other hand, refers to an individual's emotional, romantic, and sexual attraction to others, such as heterosexual, homosexual, bisexual, or pansexual. Embracing gender and sexual orientation diversity in relationships promotes inclusivity, challenges heteronormative assumptions, and creates a safe space for individuals to express their authentic selves without fear of judgment or discrimination.

Age is another dimension of diversity that often shapes our experiences and perspectives. Each generation brings unique values, beliefs, and life experiences to the table, and embracing age diversity in relationships allows for the exchange of wisdom, knowledge, and fresh perspectives. By fostering intergenerational connections and understanding, we can bridge gaps, challenge ageist stereotypes, and create a more cohesive and supportive society.

Ability diversity encompasses the wide range of physical, cognitive, and psychological abilities that individuals possess. This includes visible and invisible disabilities, as well as neurodiversity, which refers to the natural variation in human brain function and behavioral traits. Embracing ability diversity in relationships involves recognizing and valuing the unique strengths, challenges, and contributions of individuals with different abilities, creating an inclusive environment that promotes accessibility, accommodations, and equal opportunities for all.

In addition to these core dimensions, diversity also encompasses a wide range of other factors, such as socioeconomic status, religion, language, education, and political beliefs. Each of these dimensions contributes to the complex and intersectional nature of diversity, highlighting the importance of adopting a holistic and inclusive approach to understanding and appreciating the unique qualities and experiences of others.

By recognizing and celebrating the many forms of diversity, we can cultivate relationships that are built on a foundation of mutual respect, empathy, and understanding. Embracing diversity allows us to expand our horizons, challenge our assumptions, and create a more just and equitable world, one connection at a time.

Subsection 1.2: The Enriching Power of Different Perspectives and Experiences

Diversity in relationships is not merely about accepting differences; it is about actively embracing and celebrating the unique perspectives and experiences that each individual brings to the table. When we open ourselves to the enriching power of diverse viewpoints, we unlock a world of personal growth, enhanced understanding, and expanded horizons.

Engaging with people from different backgrounds, cultures, and walks of life exposes us to a tapestry of ideas, beliefs, and ways of thinking that challenge our preconceived notions and broaden our worldviews. Through these interactions, we learn to appreciate the complexity and beauty of the human experience, recognizing that there is no single "right" way to navigate life's challenges and triumphs.

In the context of relationships, diverse perspectives serve as a catalyst for deeper understanding and empathy. When we listen to the stories and experiences of others, we gain insight into their struggles, joys, and aspirations, fostering a sense of connection and compassion that transcends superficial differences. By embracing diversity, we cultivate the ability to see the world through the eyes of others, developing a more nuanced and inclusive understanding of the human condition.

Moreover, engaging with diverse perspectives encourages personal growth and self-reflection. As we encounter ideas and experiences that differ from our own, we are prompted to examine our own beliefs, biases, and assumptions critically. This introspective process allows us to identify areas for personal development, challenge our limitations, and expand our capacity for empathy and understanding.

Diverse perspectives also serve as a source of creativity and innovation in relationships. When individuals from different backgrounds come together, they bring a wealth of unique experiences, skills, and knowledge to the table. This diversity of thought fosters an environment of collaboration and synergy, where new ideas can emerge, and innovative solutions can be found to the challenges that relationships inevitably face.

Furthermore, embracing diverse perspectives in relationships contributes to the creation of a more inclusive and equitable society. By valuing and celebrating the experiences of others, we actively work towards dismantling the barriers of prejudice, discrimination, and marginalization that can divide communities and hinder progress. In doing so, we build bridges of understanding, fostering a sense of belonging and unity that transcends our differences.

Ultimately, the enriching power of different perspectives and experiences lies in their ability to expand our understanding of ourselves, others, and the world around us. By embracing diversity in our relationships, we embark on a journey of personal growth, empathy, and connection, creating a more vibrant, compassionate, and inclusive world, one relationship at a time.

Subsection 1.3: The Role of Diversity in Building Resilient and Adaptable Relationships

In an increasingly interconnected and rapidly evolving world, the ability to build resilient and adaptable relationships is more crucial than ever. As we navigate the complexities of modern life, embracing diversity emerges as a key factor in fostering relationships that can withstand challenges, adapt to change, and thrive in the face of adversity.

Diversity, in all its forms, serves as a catalyst for personal and interpersonal growth. When we engage with individuals from different backgrounds, cultures, and perspectives, we are exposed to a rich tapestry of ideas, experiences, and ways of thinking. This exposure challenges our assumptions, expands our worldviews, and encourages us to develop a more flexible and open-minded approach to relationships.

By embracing diversity, we cultivate a deeper understanding and appreciation for the unique strengths, challenges, and contributions that each individual brings to the table. This understanding fosters empathy, compassion, and a sense of shared humanity, which are essential ingredients for building resilient relationships. When we recognize and value the inherent worth of every person, regardless of their differences, we create a foundation of mutual respect and trust that can weather the storms of life.

Moreover, diverse relationships provide a fertile ground for personal growth and development. As we navigate the challenges and opportunities that arise from interacting with people who are different from ourselves, we are pushed to expand our comfort zones, develop new skills, and adapt to unfamiliar situations. This process of continuous learning and growth enhances our emotional intelligence, communication abilities, and problem-solving skills, all of which are critical for building strong and resilient relationships.

Embracing diversity also contributes to the creation of more inclusive and equitable relationships. When we actively seek out and value diverse perspectives, we challenge the power imbalances and systemic inequalities that can undermine the health and longevity of our connections. By fostering an environment of inclusion, where every voice is heard and every experience is valued, we create relationships that are built on a foundation of fairness, justice, and mutual support.

Furthermore, diverse relationships are better equipped to adapt to the ever-changing landscape of our world. In a global society marked by rapid technological advancements, shifting social norms, and evolving cultural values, the ability to navigate and embrace change is paramount. Diverse relationships, with their rich tapestry of experiences and perspectives, provide a wealth of resources and strategies for adapting to new challenges and opportunities. By drawing on the collective wisdom and resilience of our diverse connections, we can build relationships that are flexible, adaptable, and capable of thriving in the face of uncertainty.

Ultimately, embracing diversity is not just a moral imperative, but a practical necessity for building resilient and adaptable relationships. By actively seeking out and valuing the unique qualities and experiences of others, we create a world where every relationship has the potential to be a source of strength, growth, and transformation. In doing so, we not only enrich our own lives but also contribute to the creation of a more just, compassionate, and inclusive society for all.

Summary: Embracing Diversity for Stronger, More

Fulfilling Relationships

Throughout this section, we have explored the profound value and importance of embracing diversity in various types of relationships. By recognizing and celebrating the unique qualities, experiences, and perspectives that each individual brings to the table, we open ourselves up to a world of personal growth, enhanced understanding, and expanded horizons.

Diversity, in all its forms, serves as a catalyst for building stronger, more resilient, and more fulfilling relationships. When we engage with people from different backgrounds, cultures, and walks of life, we challenge our assumptions, broaden our worldviews, and cultivate a deeper sense of empathy and compassion. This process of continuous learning and growth enhances our emotional intelligence, communication skills, and problem-solving abilities, all of which are essential for navigating the complexities of human connection.

Moreover, embracing diversity contributes to the creation of a more inclusive and equitable world. By actively seeking out and valuing diverse perspectives, we challenge the power imbalances and systemic inequalities that can undermine the health and longevity of our relationships. In doing so, we foster an environment where every voice is heard, every experience is valued, and every connection has the potential to be a source of strength, growth, and transformation.

As we move forward in our exploration of relationships, it is crucial to carry these insights with us. By embracing diversity as a fundamental pillar of healthy, thriving connections, we not only enrich our own lives but also contribute to the creation of a more just, compassionate, and inclusive society for all. So let us continue on this journey with open hearts and minds, ready to celebrate the beautiful tapestry of human diversity and build relationships that stand the test of time.

Section 2: Cultivating Cultural Competence and Sensitivity

In today's interconnected world, where relationships transcend borders and cultural boundaries, developing cultural competence and sensitivity has become more important than ever. As we navigate the rich tapestry of human diversity, it is essential to foster inclusive and respectful relationships that celebrate and honor the unique backgrounds, experiences, and perspectives of those around us.

Cultivating cultural competence and sensitivity is a lifelong journey that requires openness, curiosity, and a willingness to learn. It involves recognizing and acknowledging the inherent value and dignity of all individuals, regardless of their race, ethnicity, religion, gender identity, sexual orientation, age, or ability. By embracing diversity and actively seeking to understand and appreciate cultural differences, we can build bridges of understanding, empathy, and respect in our relationships.

However, developing cultural competence and sensitivity is not always an easy task. It requires us to confront our own biases, assumptions, and privileges, and to engage in ongoing self-reflection and growth. It means being willing to listen deeply, to ask questions with genuine curiosity, and to approach cultural differences with humility and an open mind.

Throughout this section, we will explore the key principles and practices of cultivating cultural competence and sensitivity in our relationships. We will delve into the importance of self-awareness, cultural knowledge, and effective communication skills in fostering inclusive and respectful connections. We will also examine common challenges and pitfalls, and provide practical strategies for navigating cultural differences with grace, empathy, and understanding.

By cultivating cultural competence and sensitivity, we not only enrich our own lives and relationships but also contribute to building a more just, equitable, and compassionate world. So, let us embark on this transformative journey together, with open hearts and minds, ready to learn, grow, and celebrate the beauty of diversity in all its forms.

Subsection 2.1: Understanding and Acknowledging Cultural Differences

In the rich tapestry of human relationships, cultural differences play a significant role in shaping our interactions and connections with others. Recognizing, understanding, and respecting these differences is essential for building inclusive, harmonious, and fulfilling relationships. Cultural differences encompass a wide range of factors, including race, ethnicity, religion, language, values, customs, and social norms. These differences influence how individuals communicate, express emotions, perceive the world, and navigate social situations.

To cultivate cultural competence and sensitivity in relationships, it is crucial to approach cultural differences with an open mind and a willingness to learn. This means setting aside preconceived notions, stereotypes, and judgments, and instead embracing curiosity and empathy. By actively seeking to understand and acknowledge the unique cultural backgrounds and experiences of others, we can bridge gaps, foster understanding, and create more meaningful connections.

One key aspect of understanding cultural differences is recognizing that there is no one "right" way to live, think, or behave. Each culture has its own set of values, beliefs, and practices that have been shaped by history, geography, and social contexts. What may be considered polite or appropriate in one culture may be viewed as rude or offensive in another. By acknowledging and respecting these differences, we can avoid misunderstandings, conflicts, and unintentional offenses in our relationships.

Another important aspect of acknowledging cultural differences is being aware of power dynamics and privilege. In many societies, certain cultural groups may hold more power and privilege than others due to historical, economic, and social factors. Recognizing and acknowledging these imbalances is crucial for building equitable and inclusive relationships. It involves being mindful of one's own cultural background and privilege, and actively working to create spaces where all individuals feel valued, respected, and heard, regardless of their cultural identity.

Acknowledging cultural differences also means being willing to engage in ongoing learning and self-reflection. As we navigate relationships with individuals from diverse cultural backgrounds, we may encounter situations that challenge our assumptions, beliefs, and worldviews. By remaining open to learning, asking questions, and seeking to understand different perspectives, we can expand our cultural knowledge and develop greater empathy and understanding.

Ultimately, understanding and acknowledging cultural differences is not about erasing or ignoring the unique aspects of our own cultural identities. Rather, it is about creating a space where all individuals can bring their whole selves to their relationships, and where differences are celebrated as sources of strength, resilience, and beauty. By embracing cultural differences with curiosity, respect, and empathy, we can build bridges of understanding, foster meaningful connections, and create a more inclusive and compassionate world.

Subsection 2.2: Developing Self-Awareness and Challenging Personal Biases

Cultivating cultural competence and sensitivity in relationships requires a deep commitment to self-awareness and a willingness to confront our own biases and assumptions. We all carry with us a unique set of experiences, beliefs, and values that shape our perceptions and interactions with others. These personal biases, whether conscious or unconscious, can significantly impact the way we navigate relationships, especially those that cross cultural boundaries.

Developing self-awareness is the first step in challenging our biases and promoting more inclusive interactions. It involves taking an honest look at our own thoughts, feelings, and behaviors, and recognizing how they may be influenced by our cultural background, upbringing, and life experiences. This process of introspection can be uncomfortable at times, as it requires us to confront aspects of ourselves that we may prefer to ignore or deny.

One effective way to cultivate self-awareness is through regular self-reflection and journaling. By taking the time to examine our thoughts, reactions, and experiences in various situations, we can gain valuable insights into our own biases and assumptions. We may discover patterns of thinking or behavior that are rooted in cultural stereotypes or prejudices, and begin to question their validity and impact on our relationships.

Another key aspect of developing self-awareness is actively seeking out diverse perspectives and experiences. By engaging with individuals from different cultural backgrounds, we can expand our understanding of the world and challenge our own preconceived notions. This may involve participating in cultural events, joining diverse communities, or simply having open and honest conversations with people whose experiences differ from our own.

As we become more self-aware, it is crucial to take active steps to challenge and overcome our biases. This requires a willingness to step outside of our comfort zones, to listen deeply and empathetically to others, and to be open to changing our perspectives and behaviors. It may involve unlearning long-held beliefs or confronting uncomfortable truths about ourselves and our society.

Challenging personal biases is an ongoing process that requires humility, courage, and a commitment to growth. It means being willing to admit when we are wrong, to apologize for our mistakes, and to continuously educate ourselves about the experiences and perspectives of others. It also means being an active ally and advocate for marginalized communities, using our privilege and platform to amplify diverse voices and challenge systemic inequities.

Ultimately, developing self-awareness and challenging personal biases is essential for building authentic, inclusive, and respectful relationships. By taking responsibility for our own growth and development, we can create a ripple effect of positive change in our personal lives, our communities, and the world at large. It is a lifelong journey that requires patience, perseverance, and a deep commitment to justice and equality for all.

Subsection 2.3: Practicing Cultural Humility and Openness to Learning

In the journey of cultivating cultural competence and sensitivity, practicing cultural humility and maintaining an openness to learning are essential. Cultural humility is a lifelong process of self-reflection and self-critique, recognizing that our own cultural perspectives are limited and that there is always more to learn from others. It involves acknowledging our biases, assumptions, and gaps in knowledge, and actively seeking to expand our understanding of diverse cultures and experiences.

Practicing cultural humility requires a willingness to step back from our own cultural lens and to approach others with curiosity, respect, and a genuine desire to learn. It means being open to hearing and valuing the stories, perspectives, and experiences of individuals from different cultural backgrounds, even when they challenge our own beliefs or worldviews. By embracing cultural humility, we create space for authentic dialogue, mutual understanding, and the building of trust and respect in our relationships.

Cultural humility also involves recognizing and addressing power imbalances that may exist in our interactions with others. It means being aware of our own privileges and how they may impact our relationships, and actively working to create more equitable and inclusive spaces. This may involve stepping back and allowing others to take the lead, amplifying marginalized voices, and being willing to engage in difficult conversations about race, ethnicity, gender, and other aspects of identity.

Alongside cultural humility, remaining open to learning is crucial for fostering inclusive and respectful relationships. This means recognizing that our cultural knowledge is always evolving and that there is no endpoint to learning. It involves actively seeking out opportunities to engage with diverse communities, attending cultural events, reading books and articles by authors from different backgrounds, and participating in workshops and trainings on cultural competence.

Engaging in ongoing self-education about diverse cultures and experiences is a key aspect of remaining open to learning. This may involve exploring the histories, traditions, and contemporary issues facing different cultural groups, as well as examining our own cultural identities and how they have been shaped by societal norms and expectations. By committing to continuous learning, we can deepen our understanding of the complexities and nuances of cultural diversity, and become more effective allies and advocates for social justice.

Practicing cultural humility and openness to learning is not always easy, and it requires a willingness to sit with discomfort and to challenge our own assumptions and biases. It may involve making mistakes, apologizing, and learning from our missteps. However, by embracing these practices with courage, compassion, and a commitment to growth, we can build more authentic, inclusive, and meaningful relationships that celebrate the richness of human diversity.

Summary: Embracing the Lifelong Journey of Cultural Competence

Cultivating cultural competence and sensitivity is a lifelong journey that requires ongoing commitment, self-reflection, and a willingness to learn and grow. By developing self-awareness, challenging personal biases, and practicing cultural humility, we can foster more inclusive, respectful, and fulfilling relationships with individuals from diverse backgrounds.

Throughout this section, we have explored the importance of acknowledging and understanding cultural differences, confronting our own assumptions and prejudices, and actively seeking out opportunities to expand our cultural knowledge and empathy. By embracing these practices with courage, compassion, and an open mind, we can build bridges of understanding, celebrate the richness of human diversity, and create a more just and equitable world.

As we continue on this journey of cultural competence, it is essential to remember that there is always more to learn and that our growth is never complete. By remaining curious, humble, and committed to ongoing self-education, we can deepen our understanding of the complexities and nuances of cultural diversity, and become more effective allies and advocates for social justice.

Ultimately, cultivating cultural competence and sensitivity is not just a personal endeavor, but a collective responsibility. By working together to create more inclusive, respectful, and equitable spaces in our relationships, communities, and society as a whole, we can harness the transformative power of diversity and build a world where all individuals feel valued, respected, and celebrated for who they are.

Section 3: Fostering Inclusive Communication and Connection

In a world that is becoming increasingly diverse and interconnected, the ability to communicate effectively and build genuine connections with people from different backgrounds is more important than ever. Embracing diversity in relationships not only enriches our lives but also promotes understanding, empathy, and personal growth. However, navigating the complexities of diverse relationships can be challenging, especially when it comes to communication and building meaningful connections.

This section explores practical strategies for fostering inclusive communication and building authentic relationships across diverse backgrounds. We will delve into the importance of active listening, empathy, and using inclusive language to create a safe and welcoming space for all individuals. By developing these skills, we can break down barriers, challenge stereotypes, and cultivate a deeper appreciation for the unique perspectives and experiences that each person brings to the table.

Through real-life examples and expert insights, we will examine how to celebrate and appreciate differences while finding common ground and shared values. We will also discuss how to navigate difficult conversations about diversity and inclusion, addressing misunderstandings and cultural miscommunications with sensitivity and respect. By embracing the principles of inclusive communication, we can foster more meaningful and authentic connections with people from all walks of life.

Whether you are seeking to build stronger friendships, create a more inclusive workplace, or cultivate a more loving and understanding family dynamic, the strategies and insights in this section will provide you with the tools you need to communicate effectively and build bridges of understanding across diverse backgrounds. So, let us embark on this journey together, learning how to celebrate the beauty of diversity and create a more inclusive and connected world, one relationship at a time.

Subsection 3.1: Active Listening and Empathy in Diverse Relationships

In the tapestry of diverse relationships, active listening and empathy serve as the golden threads that weave understanding and connection. When we engage with individuals from different backgrounds, cultures, and experiences, it is essential to approach these interactions with an open heart and a willingness to truly hear and understand their perspectives.

Active listening goes beyond simply hearing the words spoken; it involves being fully present and attentive to the speaker, both verbally and non-verbally. This means setting aside distractions, maintaining eye contact, and showing genuine interest through facial expressions and body language. By giving our undivided attention, we create a safe space for others to express themselves freely and authentically.

Empathy, the ability to understand and share the feelings of another, is a critical component of active listening in diverse relationships. It requires stepping into someone else's shoes and seeing the world through their lens. When we practice empathy, we suspend judgment and seek to comprehend the emotions, experiences, and challenges that shape an individual's perspective.

In the context of diverse relationships, active listening and empathy help bridge gaps in understanding and foster deeper connections. By validating and acknowledging the experiences of others, we create a foundation of trust and respect. This is particularly important when engaging with individuals from marginalized or underrepresented communities, as it demonstrates a genuine desire to learn and grow from their insights.

Practicing active listening and empathy also helps us navigate difficult conversations and sensitive topics that may arise in diverse relationships. When we approach these discussions with a non-judgmental and open-minded attitude, we create space for honest and constructive dialogue. By seeking to understand rather than to be understood, we can find common ground and build bridges of understanding.

Moreover, active listening and empathy enable us to challenge our own biases and assumptions. When we truly listen to the stories and experiences of others, we expand our worldview and gain a more nuanced understanding of the complexities and richness of diversity. This self-reflection and growth are essential for fostering inclusive and equitable relationships.

To cultivate active listening and empathy in diverse relationships, we must be intentional and consistent in our efforts. This involves practicing mindfulness, asking open-ended questions, and being willing to sit with discomfort or uncertainty. It also means being humble and acknowledging when we make mistakes or have blind spots in our understanding.

By embracing active listening and empathy as core values in our diverse relationships, we create a ripple effect of understanding, compassion, and connection. We become better allies, advocates, and friends, and we contribute to building a more inclusive and empathetic world, one conversation at a time.

Subsection 3.2: Using Inclusive Language and Avoiding Stereotypes

In the tapestry of diverse relationships, the words we choose have the power to either create a sense of belonging or reinforce barriers and divisions. Inclusive language is a crucial tool for fostering an environment where all individuals feel valued, respected, and heard, regardless of their background, identity, or experiences. By being mindful of the impact of our words and actively choosing language that embraces diversity, we can build stronger, more authentic connections with those around us.

Inclusive language involves using terms and phrases that are welcoming, respectful, and free from bias or discrimination. It means avoiding words that perpetuate stereotypes, marginalize certain groups, or make assumptions about an individual's identity or experiences. For example, instead of using gender-specific language like "policeman" or "stewardess," we can opt for gender-neutral alternatives such as "police officer" or "flight attendant." By making these small but significant changes in our language, we create a more inclusive space that acknowledges and celebrates the diversity of identities and experiences.

When interacting with individuals from diverse backgrounds, it is essential to be aware of the stereotypes and biases that may influence our language and perceptions. Stereotypes are oversimplified and often inaccurate generalizations about a particular group of people, based on characteristics such as race, ethnicity, gender, age, or sexual orientation.

These stereotypes can be harmful and limiting, as they fail to recognize the unique qualities and experiences of each individual.

To avoid perpetuating stereotypes, we must challenge our own assumptions and biases, and actively seek to understand and appreciate the complexity and richness of each person's identity. This involves being open to learning about different cultures, experiences, and perspectives, and being willing to listen with empathy and respect. By approaching diverse interactions with curiosity and a genuine desire to connect, we can move beyond stereotypes and build more authentic and meaningful relationships.

In addition to avoiding stereotypes, it is crucial to be mindful of the impact of our words on others. Language has the power to include or exclude, to uplift or demean, and to create a sense of belonging or alienation. When communicating with individuals from diverse backgrounds, we must consider how our words may be perceived and whether they may unintentionally cause harm or offense.

This requires a willingness to listen, learn, and adapt our language when necessary. It means being open to feedback and being willing to apologize and make amends when we make mistakes. By cultivating a sense of cultural humility and a commitment to ongoing learning and growth, we can become more effective communicators in diverse relationships.

To foster inclusive language and avoid stereotypes, we can take proactive steps such as educating ourselves about different cultures and identities, seeking out diverse perspectives and voices, and being intentional about the words we choose. We can also advocate for inclusive language in our personal and professional lives, challenging others when necessary and leading by example.

By embracing inclusive language and rejecting stereotypes, we not only build stronger, more authentic connections with those around us but also contribute to creating a more just and equitable society. We become agents of change, working towards a world where all individuals are valued, respected, and celebrated for their unique identities and experiences. Through our words and actions, we have the power to create a more inclusive and connected world, one interaction at a time.

Subsection 3.3: Celebrating and Appreciating Differences

In the vibrant tapestry of diverse relationships, celebrating and appreciating the unique qualities and contributions of individuals from different backgrounds is a fundamental aspect of fostering inclusivity and connection. When we genuinely recognize and value the richness of diversity, we create a culture of respect, understanding, and mutual growth.

Celebrating differences begins with a mindset of curiosity and openness. It involves actively seeking to understand and learn from the diverse perspectives, experiences, and cultural backgrounds that each individual brings to the table. By approaching diversity with a sense of wonder and appreciation, we can expand our own worldviews and gain valuable insights that enrich our relationships and personal growth.

One way to celebrate and appreciate differences is by creating spaces for sharing and storytelling. Encouraging individuals to share their unique stories, traditions, and cultural practices can foster a deeper understanding and appreciation of the diversity within our relationships. Whether it's through informal conversations, organized events, or creative projects, providing platforms for diverse voices to be heard and celebrated can strengthen the bonds of connection and empathy.

Another aspect of celebrating differences is recognizing and acknowledging the strengths and contributions of individuals from diverse backgrounds. This involves moving beyond stereotypes and assumptions and actively seeking to understand the unique skills, talents, and perspectives that each person brings to the relationship. By valuing and leveraging the diverse strengths within our relationships, we create a more inclusive and innovative environment that benefits everyone involved.

Appreciating differences also means being willing to challenge our own biases and assumptions. It requires a commitment to ongoing self-reflection and personal growth, as we strive to understand and overcome the unconscious biases that may influence our interactions with others. By actively working to dismantle stereotypes and prejudices, we can create more authentic and equitable relationships that truly celebrate the beauty of diversity.

In celebrating differences, it's essential to create an atmosphere of psychological safety and respect. This means fostering an environment where individuals feel comfortable expressing their unique identities and perspectives without fear of judgment or discrimination. By establishing clear guidelines for respectful communication and behavior, we can ensure that everyone feels valued and included, regardless of their background or experiences.

Moreover, celebrating differences involves actively seeking out opportunities to engage with diverse communities and cultures. This can include attending cultural events, participating in diversity and inclusion workshops, or volunteering with organizations that promote equity and social justice. By immersing ourselves in diverse experiences and perspectives, we can broaden our understanding and appreciation of the richness of human diversity.

Ultimately, celebrating and appreciating differences is about recognizing the inherent value and worth of every individual. It's about creating a culture of belonging, where everyone feels seen, heard, and respected for who they are. By embracing the unique qualities and contributions of individuals from diverse backgrounds, we not only enrich our relationships but also contribute to building a more inclusive and equitable world.

In the context of diverse relationships, celebrating and appreciating differences is an ongoing journey of learning, growth, and connection. It requires a willingness to step outside of our comfort zones, to listen with empathy and respect, and to actively champion diversity in all its forms. By making a conscious effort to celebrate and appreciate the unique qualities and contributions of individuals from diverse backgrounds, we can foster more authentic, meaningful, and inclusive relationships that truly reflect the beauty and richness of our diverse world.

Summary: Embracing Diversity for Stronger, More Authentic Connections

In this section, we have explored the vital role of inclusive communication in building genuine connections across diverse backgrounds. By actively listening with empathy, using inclusive language, avoiding stereotypes, and celebrating differences, we can foster relationships that are built on a foundation of mutual respect, understanding, and appreciation.

The strategies and insights discussed in this section serve as a roadmap for navigating the complexities of diverse relationships. By implementing these practices in our daily interactions, we can break down barriers, challenge our own biases, and create a more welcoming and inclusive environment for all.

It is important to remember that fostering inclusive communication and connection is an ongoing journey of learning and growth. It requires a willingness to step outside of our comfort zones, to listen with an open heart, and to continuously educate ourselves about the diverse experiences and perspectives of others.

As we move forward, let us embrace the power of inclusive communication to build bridges of understanding and create a more compassionate and connected world. By valuing and celebrating the unique qualities and contributions of every individual, we not only enrich our own lives but also contribute to a society that is more equitable, just, and inclusive.

So, let us take the insights and strategies from this section and apply them in our relationships, both personal and professional. Let us be the change we wish to see, leading by example and inspiring others to embrace diversity and foster genuine connections. Together, we can create a world where every voice is heard, every story is valued, and every relationship is a celebration of the beautiful tapestry of human diversity.

Section 4: Navigating Challenges and Building Bridges

In the journey of embracing diversity and inclusivity in relationships, it is inevitable that challenges will arise. Cultural differences, misunderstandings, and deeply ingrained biases can create barriers to genuine connection and understanding. However, these challenges also present valuable opportunities for growth, learning, and the development of stronger, more resilient relationships.

As we navigate the complexities of diverse relationships, it is essential to approach challenges with an open mind, a willingness to listen, and a commitment to building bridges of understanding. By fostering a culture of empathy, respect, and effective communication, we can create a solid foundation for addressing conflicts and finding common ground.

In this section, we will explore some of the most common challenges that may arise in diverse relationships, such as cultural miscommunications, difficult conversations about sensitive topics, and the impact of societal inequities on relationship dynamics. We will provide practical strategies and tools for navigating these challenges with grace, compassion, and a focus on building lasting connections.

Through real-life examples and expert insights, we will guide you in developing the skills necessary to engage in constructive dialogue, seek mutual understanding, and find shared values that transcend differences.

By learning to address challenges head-on and build bridges of understanding, you will be equipped to cultivate more inclusive, equitable, and fulfilling relationships that celebrate the beauty of diversity.

As we embark on this journey together, remember that navigating challenges in diverse relationships is an ongoing process of learning, growth, and self-reflection. With an open heart, a curious mind, and a commitment to building a more inclusive world, you have the power to transform challenges into opportunities for deeper connection and understanding.

Subsection 4.1: Addressing Misunderstandings and Cultural Miscommunications

In the tapestry of diverse relationships, misunderstandings and cultural miscommunications can often arise, creating tension and barriers to genuine connection. These challenges stem from differences in communication styles, cultural norms, and underlying assumptions that shape our interactions. However, by approaching these situations with empathy, openness, and a willingness to learn, we can transform potential conflicts into opportunities for growth and understanding.

When addressing misunderstandings and cultural miscommunications, the first step is to cultivate a sense of self-awareness. Recognizing our own biases, assumptions, and communication patterns allows us to approach interactions with greater sensitivity and adaptability. By taking a step back and examining our own cultural lens, we can begin to appreciate the diversity of perspectives and experiences that others bring to the table.

Active listening plays a crucial role in navigating misunderstandings and cultural differences. By fully engaging in the conversation, asking clarifying questions, and seeking to understand the other person's point of view, we create a space for genuine dialogue and mutual understanding. It is essential to approach these interactions with an open mind, suspending judgment and avoiding the temptation to make assumptions based on stereotypes or preconceived notions.

When misunderstandings or cultural miscommunications do occur, it is important to address them promptly and respectfully. This involves taking responsibility for our own actions, apologizing if necessary, and expressing a sincere desire to understand and resolve the issue. By approaching the conversation with a spirit of collaboration and a focus on finding common ground, we can work together to bridge the gap and find mutually beneficial solutions.

In some cases, cultural differences may require a more nuanced approach. It is helpful to educate ourselves about the cultural norms, values, and communication styles of those we interact with, while also being mindful not to generalize or stereotype. Seeking guidance from cultural experts, attending diversity and inclusion workshops, or engaging in open and respectful conversations with individuals from different backgrounds can deepen our understanding and enhance our ability to navigate cultural differences effectively.

Ultimately, addressing misunderstandings and cultural miscommunications requires a commitment to ongoing learning, self-reflection, and personal growth. By cultivating a mindset of curiosity, humility, and empathy, we can approach diverse relationships with greater understanding and resilience. Through open and respectful communication, a willingness to listen and learn, and a focus on building bridges of understanding, we can navigate the challenges that arise and create stronger, more inclusive connections that celebrate the beauty of our differences.

Subsection 4.2: Engaging in Difficult Conversations About Diversity and Inclusion

Engaging in conversations about diversity, inclusion, and social justice issues within relationships can be challenging, as these topics often evoke strong emotions and deeply held beliefs. However, having these difficult conversations is crucial for fostering understanding, growth, and positive change in our relationships and communities. By approaching these discussions with empathy, openness, and a commitment to learning, we can create a safe space for meaningful dialogue and build stronger, more inclusive connections.

One of the key strategies for engaging in difficult conversations about diversity and inclusion is to approach them with a mindset of curiosity and a willingness to listen. Rather than entering the conversation with the goal of proving a point or changing someone's mind, focus on understanding their perspective and experiences. Ask open-ended questions, actively listen to their responses, and seek to gain insight into their worldview. By demonstrating genuine interest and respect for their thoughts and feelings, you create an environment that encourages open and honest communication.

It is also essential to be mindful of your own biases, privileges, and limitations when engaging in these conversations. Recognize that your experiences and understanding of diversity and inclusion may differ from those of others, and be open to learning from their perspectives. Engage in self-reflection and educate yourself on the historical and systemic factors that contribute to inequality and discrimination. By acknowledging your own growth areas and committing to ongoing learning, you can approach these conversations with greater humility and effectiveness.

When discussing sensitive topics related to diversity and inclusion, it is crucial to use inclusive and respectful language. Avoid using offensive or derogatory terms, and be mindful of the impact your words may have on others. If you are unsure about the appropriate terminology or language to use, don't be afraid to ask for guidance or clarification. Remember that the goal is to create a safe and inclusive space for dialogue, and using respectful language is a fundamental part of that process.

During difficult conversations, emotions can run high, and it is essential to practice effective communication skills to navigate these moments.

Use "I" statements to express your own thoughts and feelings, rather than making accusations or generalizations. Avoid interrupting or dismissing others' experiences, and instead, validate their emotions and perspectives. If the conversation becomes heated or unproductive, suggest taking a break or revisiting the topic at a later time when emotions have settled.

It is important to recognize that engaging in difficult conversations about diversity and inclusion is an ongoing process, not a one-time event. Commit to continuing the dialogue and taking action to promote equity and inclusion in your relationships and communities. This may involve educating others, advocating for change, or working to dismantle systemic barriers that perpetuate inequality. By consistently engaging in these conversations and taking meaningful action, we can create a more inclusive and just society for all.

Ultimately, engaging in difficult conversations about diversity and inclusion requires courage, empathy, and a willingness to step outside of our comfort zones. By approaching these discussions with an open heart, a curious mind, and a commitment to growth and understanding, we can build bridges of connection and create more inclusive, equitable, and fulfilling relationships that celebrate the beauty of our differences.

Subsection 4.3: Seeking Common Ground and Shared Values

In the tapestry of diverse relationships, it is easy to focus on the differences that set us apart. Cultural backgrounds, life experiences, and personal beliefs can sometimes create barriers to understanding and connection. However, by actively seeking common ground and shared values, we can build bridges that transcend these differences and foster stronger, more meaningful relationships.

The journey of finding common ground begins with a willingness to look beyond surface-level differences and explore the deeper aspects of our shared humanity. It requires an open mind, a curious heart, and a commitment to understanding one another on a fundamental level. By approaching diverse relationships with empathy and a genuine desire to find points of connection, we create a foundation for building lasting bonds.

One powerful way to seek common ground is through the exploration of shared values. Despite our diverse backgrounds and experiences, there are often core values that unite us as human beings. These may include a desire for love, respect, compassion, justice, or personal growth. By engaging in open and honest conversations about the values that guide our lives, we can discover surprising points of alignment and build a sense of mutual understanding.

Actively listening to one another's stories and experiences is another essential aspect of finding common ground. When we take the time to truly hear and appreciate the unique perspectives of those around us, we gain a deeper understanding of their hopes, dreams, fears, and aspirations. Through this process, we often find that our own experiences and emotions are not so different from those of others, creating a sense of shared humanity that transcends surface-level differences.

It is important to approach the search for common ground with a spirit of humility and a willingness to learn. Recognizing that our own perspectives and experiences are limited, we must be open to the wisdom and insights that others bring to the table. By embracing a mindset of continuous learning and growth, we can expand our understanding of the world and build more inclusive, empathetic relationships.

In seeking common ground, it is also crucial to acknowledge and respect the differences that make each individual unique. Finding shared values and experiences does not mean erasing or minimizing the rich diversity that exists within our relationships. Instead, it is about creating a space where differences can be celebrated and appreciated, while simultaneously recognizing the fundamental threads that bind us together as human beings.

Ultimately, the process of seeking common ground and shared values is an ongoing journey that requires patience, persistence, and a commitment to building understanding. It may not always be easy, and there may be moments of discomfort or disagreement along the way. However, by approaching diverse relationships with an open heart, a curious mind, and a willingness to find points of connection, we can build bridges of understanding that lead to more fulfilling, inclusive, and meaningful connections.

In a world that often feels divided by differences, the act of seeking common ground and shared values is a powerful tool for building unity and understanding. By focusing on the aspects of our shared humanity that unite us, we can create a more compassionate, empathetic, and interconnected world, one relationship at a time.

Summary: Building Bridges of Understanding in Diverse Relationships

Navigating the challenges that arise in diverse relationships is an essential part of fostering inclusivity, understanding, and growth. By addressing misunderstandings and cultural miscommunications with empathy, openness, and a willingness to learn, we can transform potential conflicts into opportunities for deeper connection. Engaging in difficult conversations about diversity and inclusion requires courage, active listening, and a commitment to ongoing learning and self-reflection. Seeking common ground and shared values allows us to build bridges that transcend our differences and create a foundation for lasting, meaningful relationships.

Throughout this section, we have explored practical strategies and insights for navigating the complexities of diverse relationships. From cultivating self-awareness and cultural sensitivity to practicing effective communication and finding points of connection, these tools empower us to create more inclusive, equitable, and fulfilling relationships. By embracing the challenges as opportunities for growth and understanding, we can work together to build a more compassionate, empathetic, and interconnected world.

As we continue on this journey of embracing diversity and inclusivity in our relationships, remember that it is an ongoing process of learning, growth, and self-discovery. By approaching each interaction with an open heart, a curious mind, and a commitment to building bridges of understanding, we have the power to create positive change in our relationships and communities. Let us celebrate the beauty of our differences while recognizing the fundamental threads that bind us together as human beings, and work towards creating a more inclusive and harmonious world, one relationship at a time.

Section 5: Creating Inclusive and Equitable Relationship Dynamics

In our increasingly diverse and interconnected world, fostering inclusive and equitable dynamics in relationships has become more important than ever. Whether it's a romantic partnership, a friendship, a family bond, or a professional connection, creating an environment where all individuals feel valued, respected, and supported is crucial for building strong and meaningful relationships.

Inclusive relationships celebrate and embrace the unique qualities, backgrounds, and experiences that each person brings to the table. They are built on a foundation of mutual respect, understanding, and empathy, allowing all parties to feel heard, appreciated, and included. By actively promoting inclusivity, we can create relationships that are not only more fulfilling and enriching but also more resilient and adaptable in the face of challenges.

Equity, on the other hand, goes beyond mere inclusion and focuses on ensuring that everyone in a relationship has access to the same opportunities, resources, and support they need to thrive. It recognizes that different individuals may have different needs and challenges, and it seeks to address these disparities by providing tailored support and accommodations. By striving for equity in our relationships, we can create a more level playing field where everyone has the chance to succeed and reach their full potential.

In this section, we will explore various strategies and approaches for creating inclusive and equitable dynamics in different types of relationships. We will delve into the importance of recognizing and addressing power imbalances, promoting allyship and advocacy, and continuously learning and growing together. By implementing these practices and principles, we can cultivate relationships that are not only more inclusive and equitable but also more fulfilling, meaningful, and transformative for everyone involved.

Subsection 5.1: Recognizing and Addressing Power Imbalances

In the context of diverse relationships, power imbalances can arise due to various societal inequities, such as differences in race, gender, socioeconomic status, age, or ability. These imbalances can create an uneven dynamic, where one person holds more influence, control, or privilege over the other. Recognizing and addressing these power imbalances is crucial for fostering inclusive and equitable relationships.

Power imbalances can manifest in subtle ways, such as one person consistently making decisions for the relationship or having greater access to resources and opportunities. They can also be more overt, such as instances of discrimination, marginalization, or even abuse. When left unaddressed, power imbalances can lead to feelings of resentment, disempowerment, and erosion of trust within the relationship.

To create a more equitable and inclusive dynamic, it is essential for individuals in a relationship to openly acknowledge and discuss power imbalances. This requires a willingness to engage in honest and sometimes difficult conversations about privilege, oppression, and systemic inequalities. By bringing these issues to the forefront, partners can work together to identify how power imbalances may be impacting their relationship and explore ways to mitigate them.

One key aspect of addressing power imbalances is practicing active listening and empathy. The person holding more power should strive to understand the experiences and perspectives of their partner who may be facing marginalization or disadvantage. This involves creating a safe and non-judgmental space for open dialogue, validating their partner's feelings, and being receptive to feedback and criticism.

Another important step is actively working to redistribute power within the relationship. This can involve making a conscious effort to share decision-making responsibilities, ensuring equal access to resources and opportunities, and supporting each other's personal growth and empowerment. It may also require the person with more privilege to use their advantages to advocate for their partner and challenge systemic inequalities that contribute to power imbalances.

In some cases, addressing power imbalances may require seeking support from outside resources, such as couples therapy, diversity and inclusion workshops, or social justice organizations. These resources can provide valuable guidance, tools, and strategies for navigating the complexities of power dynamics in diverse relationships.

Ultimately, recognizing and addressing power imbalances is an ongoing process that requires commitment, self-reflection, and a willingness to grow and change. By actively working to create more equitable and inclusive dynamics, partners in diverse relationships can build stronger, more resilient connections based on mutual respect, understanding, and support.

Subsection 5.2: Promoting Allyship and Advocacy in Relationships

In the journey towards creating inclusive and equitable relationships, promoting allyship and advocacy plays a crucial role. Being an ally means actively supporting and standing up for individuals who face marginalization, discrimination, or oppression, even if you do not share their specific experiences or identity. Advocacy, on the other hand, involves using your privilege, voice, and resources to challenge systemic inequalities and push for positive change.

Promoting allyship and advocacy within relationships requires a commitment to ongoing learning, self-reflection, and action. It involves recognizing and acknowledging the unique challenges and barriers that individuals from diverse backgrounds may face, and taking proactive steps to support and uplift them. This can manifest in various ways, such as educating oneself about different cultures, identities, and experiences, listening to and amplifying marginalized voices, and speaking out against discrimination and injustice.

In the context of romantic relationships, being an ally and advocate means creating a safe and supportive space for your partner to express their thoughts, feelings, and experiences related to their identity. It involves actively listening to their concerns, validating their emotions, and working together to navigate the challenges they may face. This may require challenging your own biases, privileges, and assumptions, and being open to learning and growing alongside your partner.

Allyship and advocacy also extend beyond the confines of individual relationships and into the broader community. It involves using your platform and influence to raise awareness about diversity and inclusion issues, challenge stereotypes and prejudices, and advocate for systemic change. This can take many forms, such as participating in social justice movements, supporting diversity and inclusion initiatives in your workplace or community, or using your social media presence to amplify marginalized voices and perspectives.

It is important to note that being an ally and advocate is not a one-time action, but rather an ongoing commitment to learning, growth, and action. It requires a willingness to listen, learn, and adapt, as well as a readiness to take responsibility for your own mistakes and biases. It also involves recognizing that allyship and advocacy are not about personal gain or recognition, but rather about using your privilege and resources to create a more just and equitable world for all.

Promoting allyship and advocacy in relationships can have a profound impact on fostering inclusivity, understanding, and respect. By actively supporting and uplifting individuals from diverse backgrounds, we can create stronger, more resilient connections that celebrate and embrace our differences. Moreover, by advocating for systemic change and challenging inequalities, we can contribute to building a more just and inclusive society for everyone.

Subsection 5.3: Continuously Learning and Growing Together

Embracing diversity and inclusion in relationships is not a one-time achievement, but rather an ongoing journey of learning, growth, and commitment. It requires a willingness to continuously explore, understand, and appreciate the unique perspectives, experiences, and identities that each individual brings to the relationship. By viewing diversity and inclusion as a shared journey, partners can foster a dynamic of continuous learning and growth that strengthens their bond and enriches their connection.

One key aspect of this shared journey is a commitment to ongoing self-reflection and self-education. This involves taking the time to examine one's own biases, assumptions, and privileges, and actively working to expand one's knowledge and understanding of diverse cultures, identities, and experiences. By engaging in self-reflection and self-education, individuals can develop greater self-awareness, empathy, and cultural competence, which are essential for building inclusive and equitable relationships.

Another crucial element of continuously learning and growing together is open and honest communication. Partners should create a safe and non-judgmental space where they can openly discuss their thoughts, feelings, and experiences related to diversity and inclusion. This involves actively listening to each other, validating each other's perspectives, and being receptive to feedback and constructive criticism. Through open and honest communication, partners can deepen their understanding of each other's unique identities and experiences, and work together to navigate the challenges and opportunities that come with embracing diversity.

Continuously learning and growing together also involves seeking out new experiences and perspectives that broaden one's horizons and challenge one's assumptions. This can take many forms, such as attending cultural events, engaging in diverse social circles, or exploring new forms of art and media that represent diverse voices and experiences. By actively seeking out new experiences and perspectives, partners can expand their worldview, develop greater cultural awareness, and cultivate a more inclusive and equitable mindset.

It is important to recognize that the journey of continuously learning and growing together is not always easy or comfortable. It may involve confronting difficult truths, acknowledging past mistakes, and grappling with complex issues of power, privilege, and oppression. However, by approaching this journey with humility, openness, and a willingness to learn and grow, partners can build stronger, more resilient relationships that celebrate and embrace diversity in all its forms.

Ultimately, continuously learning and growing together is about recognizing that diversity and inclusion are not static endpoints, but rather dynamic processes that require ongoing effort, commitment, and collaboration. By viewing this journey as a shared endeavor, partners can create relationships that are not only more inclusive and equitable, but also more fulfilling, meaningful, and transformative. Through continuous learning and growth, partners can build a foundation of mutual respect, understanding, and appreciation that allows their relationship to thrive in the face of diversity and change.

Summary: Embracing Inclusivity and Equity for Stronger Relationships

Creating inclusive and equitable relationship dynamics is a vital aspect of building strong, healthy, and fulfilling connections with others. By recognizing and addressing power imbalances, promoting allyship and advocacy, and committing to continuous learning and growth, we can foster relationships that celebrate diversity and promote mutual respect, understanding, and support.

Throughout this section, we have explored the importance of acknowledging and discussing power imbalances that may arise due to societal inequities. By engaging in honest conversations, practicing active listening and empathy, and working together to redistribute power, partners can create a more equitable and inclusive dynamic that benefits both individuals and the relationship as a whole.

We have also emphasized the significance of promoting allyship and advocacy within relationships and beyond. Being an ally and advocate involves actively supporting and uplifting individuals from diverse backgrounds, challenging systemic inequalities, and using our privilege and resources to push for positive change. By incorporating these practices into our relationships, we can contribute to building a more just and inclusive society for all.

Finally, we have highlighted the ongoing nature of embracing diversity and inclusion in relationships. It is a shared journey of continuous learning, growth, and commitment that requires self-reflection, open communication, and a willingness to seek out new experiences and perspectives. By approaching this journey with humility, openness, and a desire to learn and grow together, partners can build resilient, meaningful, and transformative relationships that thrive in the face of diversity and change.

As we conclude this section, we encourage readers to reflect on the insights and strategies discussed and consider how they can apply them to their own relationships. By actively working to create inclusive and equitable dynamics, we can cultivate connections that not only enrich our lives but also contribute to a more just and compassionate world. Remember, embracing inclusivity and equity is an ongoing commitment, but it is one that holds the power to strengthen and transform our relationships in profound and lasting ways.

Section 6: Celebrating the Beauty of Diverse Love and Connections

Love knows no boundaries, and the tapestry of human relationships is woven with threads of countless colors, each representing a unique story of connection and affection. In a world that is increasingly diverse and interconnected, it is more important than ever to celebrate the beauty and value of love in all its forms. This section invites you to embark on a heartwarming journey that explores the richness and resilience of diverse relationships, showcasing the power of love to transcend differences and bring people together.

As we delve into the world of diverse love and connections, we will discover the transformative impact of representation and visibility. By seeing ourselves reflected in the stories and experiences of others, we find validation, inspiration, and a sense of belonging. From the trailblazing couples who have paved the way for greater acceptance to the everyday heroes who fearlessly love despite societal challenges, these narratives serve as beacons of hope and encouragement for all who seek to build meaningful connections across the spectrum of diversity.

Through the lens of empathy and understanding, we will explore the unique strengths and challenges that come with navigating relationships that defy traditional norms and expectations. Whether it's the unbreakable bond of an interracial couple, the tender love story of two individuals with different abilities, or the courageous journey of an LGBTQ+ partnership, each tale of diverse love is a testament to the resilience and beauty of the human spirit.

As we celebrate the kaleidoscope of love and connections, we will also reflect on the importance of creating a more inclusive and accepting world. By embracing diversity in all its forms and championing the rights of all individuals to love freely and openly, we can contribute to a society that values compassion, understanding, and equality. Together, we will explore how each of us can become an ally and advocate for diverse relationships, breaking down barriers and fostering a culture of respect and appreciation.

So, let us embark on this heartfelt exploration of diverse love and connections, opening our minds and hearts to the endless possibilities that arise when we embrace the beauty of our differences. Through the power of storytelling, shared experiences, and a commitment to understanding, we will discover that love truly has no limits and that the bonds we forge across the spectrum of diversity have the power to transform not only our own lives but the world around us.

Subsection 6.1: The Power of Representation and Visibility

In a world where diversity is the fabric of our society, the representation and visibility of diverse relationships in media, culture, and public discourse hold immense power. When we see ourselves reflected in the stories, images, and narratives around us, we feel validated, understood, and connected to a larger community. Representation serves as a mirror, affirming our experiences and reminding us that we are not alone in our journeys.

The visibility of diverse relationships in media and culture plays a crucial role in shaping public perception and fostering acceptance. When we are exposed to a wide range of love stories, from interracial couples to LGBTQ+ partnerships, we begin to recognize the universality of love and the beauty in our differences. These representations challenge stereotypes, break down barriers, and create space for empathy and understanding.

Moreover, the power of representation extends beyond the realm of personal validation. It has the potential to drive social change and influence policies that protect the rights and dignity of all individuals. When diverse relationships are normalized and celebrated in the public eye, it becomes harder to justify discrimination and marginalization. Visibility serves as a catalyst for progress, inspiring conversations, and demanding equality.

However, the journey towards authentic and inclusive representation is ongoing. It requires a conscious effort from content creators, media outlets, and society as a whole to ensure that the stories being told reflect the rich tapestry of human love and connection. We must strive for representations that go beyond tokenism and stereotypes, portraying diverse relationships with depth, complexity, and respect.

As we continue to advocate for greater visibility and representation, we must also acknowledge the courage and resilience of those who have paved the way. The trailblazers who have lived their truth openly, often in the face of adversity, have made it possible for others to see themselves reflected in the world around them. Their stories serve as a testament to the transformative power of love and the importance of being seen.

In celebrating the power of representation and visibility, we recognize that every story matters. Every love story, no matter how unconventional or diverse, deserves to be told and celebrated. By amplifying these narratives, we create a more inclusive and compassionate world, one where love knows no boundaries and where every individual feels seen, valued, and embraced for who they are.

Subsection 6.2: Sharing Stories and Experiences of Diverse Relationships

In the tapestry of human connections, the threads of love and companionship weave together to create a beautiful and diverse picture. Each relationship is unique, with its own set of joys, challenges, and triumphs. By sharing the stories and experiences of individuals in diverse relationships, we celebrate the richness of love in all its forms and gain valuable insights into the journeys of those who have navigated the path of love against the backdrop of societal norms and expectations.

One such story is that of Priya and Alex, an intercultural couple who found love across continents. Priya, born and raised in India, and Alex, hailing from the United States, met while studying abroad in Europe. Despite their different cultural backgrounds, they forged a deep connection based on shared values, mutual respect, and a willingness to learn from each other. Their journey was not without challenges, as they navigated the complexities of long-distance communication, cultural differences, and family expectations. However, through open and honest dialogue, a commitment to understanding, and unwavering support for one another, Priya and Alex built a strong foundation for their relationship. Their story serves as a testament to the power of love to bridge cultural divides and create a beautiful fusion of traditions and perspectives.

Another inspiring tale is that of Emma and Olivia, a same-sex couple who fought for their right to love openly and proudly. Growing up in a small, conservative town, both Emma and Olivia struggled with accepting their sexual orientation and finding acceptance within their community. When they met in college, they found solace and strength in each other's company. Together, they embarked on a journey of self-discovery, activism, and advocacy for LGBTQ+ rights. Despite facing discrimination and challenges along the way, Emma and Olivia remained committed to their love and to creating a world where all individuals can love freely and without fear. Their story is one of resilience, courage, and the transformative power of love to break down barriers and inspire change.

The story of Liam and Sophie, a couple with different abilities, is one of love that transcends physical limitations. Liam, an accomplished artist who uses a wheelchair, and Sophie, a passionate educator, met through a mutual friend. From the moment they first connected, they recognized in each other a kindred spirit and a deep appreciation for life's beauty.

Their relationship blossomed as they discovered shared interests, a love for adventure, and a determination to live life to the fullest. While navigating the challenges of accessibility and societal perceptions, Liam and Sophie found strength in their bond and in their commitment to supporting each other's dreams. Their story reminds us that love has the power to see beyond surface-level differences and celebrate the unique qualities that make each individual special.

These are just a few examples of the countless stories of diverse relationships that exist in our world. Each story is a reminder that love knows no boundaries and that the beauty of human connection lies in its diversity. By sharing these experiences, we create a space for empathy, understanding, and celebration. We recognize that every relationship, regardless of its form or the challenges it faces, is a testament to the resilience and power of the human heart.

As we continue to share and celebrate the stories of diverse relationships, we contribute to a more inclusive and accepting world. We break down stereotypes, challenge prejudices, and inspire others to embrace love in all its forms. These stories serve as a reminder that, at the core of every relationship, lies the universal human desire for connection, understanding, and acceptance. By honoring and uplifting these diverse narratives, we create a world where love is celebrated in all its beautiful and varied forms.

Subsection 6.3: Embracing the Unique Strengths and Resilience of Diverse Connections

In the rich tapestry of human relationships, diverse connections shine as vibrant threads that strengthen the fabric of our society. These relationships, born from the union of individuals with different backgrounds, experiences, and identities, possess a unique set of strengths and an unparalleled resilience that have the power to transform lives and foster positive change.

One of the most remarkable strengths of diverse relationships is their ability to bridge gaps in understanding and cultivate empathy. When two individuals from different walks of life come together, they bring with them a wealth of perspectives, values, and experiences. Through open and honest communication, they have the opportunity to learn from each other, challenge preconceived notions, and expand their worldviews. This exchange of ideas and insights fosters a deeper understanding of the complexities and nuances that shape our diverse world, promoting compassion and empathy for those whose lives may differ from our own.

Diverse relationships also exhibit an extraordinary resilience in the face of adversity. Couples who navigate the challenges of cultural differences, societal prejudices, or discrimination often develop a strong bond forged through shared struggles and a commitment to their love. They learn to lean on each other for support, find strength in their unity, and develop effective strategies for overcoming obstacles. This resilience not only strengthens their relationship but also serves as an inspiration to others, demonstrating that love can thrive despite the barriers erected by society.

Moreover, diverse relationships have the transformative power to effect social change. When individuals from different backgrounds come together in love and partnership, they challenge the status quo and dismantle stereotypes. They become living examples of the beauty and value of diversity, showing that love knows no boundaries and that our differences can be a source of strength and unity. By openly celebrating their love and sharing their stories, these couples contribute to a more inclusive and accepting society, inspiring others to embrace diversity in their own lives and relationships.

The unique strengths and resilience of diverse relationships also extend to the families and communities they create. Children raised in diverse households benefit from exposure to multiple languages, cultures, and ways of thinking, developing a broader perspective and a deeper appreciation for diversity. These families become microcosms of the world we strive for, where differences are celebrated, and love and respect are the guiding principles. As these children grow and interact with others, they carry with them the values of inclusivity and acceptance, becoming agents of change in their own right.

In embracing the unique strengths and resilience of diverse connections, we recognize the immense potential they hold for fostering understanding, empathy, and social progress. By supporting and celebrating these relationships, we contribute to the creation of a more inclusive and compassionate world. We acknowledge that diversity in love is not a weakness but a powerful force for good, capable of breaking down barriers, healing divides, and inspiring positive change.

As we move forward in our journey to build a more equitable and harmonious society, let us draw strength from the resilience and transformative power of diverse relationships. Let us stand in solidarity with those who love bravely and authentically, recognizing that their stories and experiences are valuable threads in the rich tapestry of human connection. Together, by embracing the beauty and strength of diversity in all its forms, we can create a world where love truly conquers all, and where every relationship is celebrated for the unique and precious bond it represents.

Summary: Embracing the Tapestry of Love

As we conclude this exploration of diverse love and connections, we are reminded of the incredible beauty and strength that lies within the tapestry of human relationships. Each story we have encountered serves as a thread, woven together to create a rich and vibrant picture of love in all its forms. From the heartwarming tales of intercultural couples navigating the complexities of their backgrounds to the inspiring journeys of LGBTQ+ individuals fighting for their right to love openly, these narratives have illuminated the transformative power of love to transcend boundaries and bring people together.

Through the lens of representation and visibility, we have seen how the presence of diverse relationships in media, culture, and society can have a profound impact on fostering acceptance, understanding, and social change. By celebrating and amplifying these stories, we contribute to a world where every individual feels seen, valued, and free to love authentically. The power of representation extends beyond personal validation; it has the potential to shape public perception, challenge stereotypes, and inspire future generations to embrace the beauty of diversity in all its forms.

Moreover, the unique strengths and resilience demonstrated by diverse relationships serve as a testament to the indomitable nature of love. These connections, forged in the face of adversity and societal challenges, remind us that love has the power to overcome barriers, heal divides, and create a more inclusive and compassionate world. By supporting and celebrating these relationships, we recognize their immense potential to foster empathy, understanding, and positive change.

As we move forward, let us carry the lessons and insights gained from these stories of diverse love and connection. Let us continue to advocate for greater representation, visibility, and acceptance of all forms of love. By embracing the beauty and strength of diversity in our relationships, we contribute to the creation of a world where every love story is celebrated, and every individual is free to love without fear or judgment. Together, we can weave a tapestry of love that is as rich, vibrant, and enduring as the human spirit itself.

Chapter Summary: Embracing the Tapestry of Love

As we navigate the intricate tapestry of relationships, it becomes clear that diversity and inclusivity are not merely ideals to strive for, but essential threads that strengthen the fabric of our connections. Embracing the beauty of diverse relationships opens our hearts and minds to a world of possibilities, where differences are celebrated, and understanding and respect form the foundation of every interaction.

By cultivating cultural competence, practicing empathy, and engaging in open and honest communication, we can foster relationships that transcend boundaries and bring people together. It is through these diverse connections that we gain new perspectives, challenge our own biases, and grow as individuals and as a society.

However, the journey towards inclusivity is not without its challenges. It requires a willingness to have difficult conversations, confront power imbalances, and actively work towards creating equitable spaces for all. But in the face of these challenges lies an opportunity for profound growth and transformation.

As we continue to weave the tapestry of our relationships, let us embrace the unique strengths and resilience that diversity brings. Let us celebrate the stories and experiences of those whose love knows no bounds, and let us be inspired by their courage and determination to create a more inclusive world.

In the end, embracing diversity and inclusivity in our relationships is not just a noble pursuit; it is a fundamental aspect of building a society where every individual feels valued, respected, and celebrated for who they are. By opening our hearts to the beauty of diverse connections, we not only enrich our own lives but also contribute to the creation of a more compassionate and understanding world.

Chapter 15: The Journey of Continuous Growth and Learning

In the realm of relationships, growth is not a destination but an ongoing journey. It is a path paved with self-discovery, learning, and the willingness to embrace change. As we navigate the complexities of human connections, we come to understand that the key to building and maintaining fulfilling relationships lies in our commitment to personal development.

Throughout our lives, we encounter a myriad of experiences that shape our understanding of love, trust, and intimacy. Each relationship, whether romantic, familial, or platonic, presents us with unique challenges and opportunities for growth. By approaching these experiences with an open mind and a curious heart, we can extract valuable lessons that contribute to our overall well-being and the health of our relationships.

The journey of continuous growth and learning is not always easy. It requires us to confront our own limitations, fears, and vulnerabilities. It calls upon us to step outside of our comfort zones and explore uncharted territories within ourselves and our relationships. However, it is through this process of self-reflection and self-improvement that we cultivate the skills and qualities necessary to build strong, resilient, and deeply meaningful connections.

In this chapter, we will delve into the importance of embracing a growth mindset, investing in personal development, and seeking inspiration and guidance along the way. We will explore the role of continuous learning in relationships, and how it can help us navigate the inevitable challenges and changes that arise over time. By committing to a lifelong journey of growth and self-discovery, we open ourselves up to the possibility of creating truly authentic and fulfilling relationships that stand the test of time.

So, let us embark on this transformative journey together, armed with the knowledge that every step we take towards personal growth is a step towards building the relationships we have always dreamed of. With courage, compassion, and a willingness to learn, we can unlock the full potential of our connections and create a life filled with love, joy, and endless possibilities.

Section 1: Embracing a Growth Mindset

Imagine a world where every challenge is an opportunity for growth, where setbacks are merely stepping stones to success, and where the power to transform your relationships lies within your own mindset. Welcome to the world of the growth mindset – a powerful concept that has the potential to revolutionize the way you approach personal development and cultivate thriving connections with others.

In this section, we will embark on a journey of self-discovery and explore the profound impact that embracing a growth mindset can have on your life and relationships. We will delve into the fundamental differences between a fixed mindset and a growth mindset, and uncover how your beliefs about your own abilities and potential can shape the course of your personal growth and the quality of your interactions with others.

Through a combination of scientific research, real-life anecdotes, and practical insights, we will unravel the secrets to cultivating a love for lifelong learning, reframing failures as valuable opportunities for growth, and harnessing the power of a growth mindset to build deeper, more meaningful connections with the people in your life.

Whether you are seeking to improve your communication skills, strengthen your emotional intelligence, or simply become the best version of yourself, embracing a growth mindset is the key to unlocking your full potential and creating the fulfilling relationships you deserve. So, let us embark on this transformative journey together, and discover the incredible possibilities that await you when you open your mind to the power of growth and self-discovery.

Subsection 1.1: Understanding Fixed vs. Growth Mindsets

At the core of personal development and relationship success lies a fundamental concept that shapes the way we perceive ourselves, others, and the world around us: mindset. Our mindset is the lens through which we view our abilities, challenges, and opportunities for growth. It is the driving force behind our thoughts, beliefs, and actions, and it has the power to either propel us forward or hold us back.

In her groundbreaking research, psychologist Carol Dweck identified two distinct types of mindsets: the fixed mindset and the growth mindset. Individuals with a fixed mindset believe that their abilities, intelligence, and talents are static, predetermined traits that cannot be significantly altered. They view success as a validation of their inherent abilities and failure as a direct reflection of their shortcomings. As a result, they often avoid challenges, fear criticism, and feel threatened by the success of others.

In contrast, those with a growth mindset embrace the belief that their abilities, intelligence, and talents can be developed and expanded through dedication, hard work, and continuous learning. They view challenges as opportunities for growth, failure as a stepping stone to success, and the success of others as inspiration for their own self-improvement. Individuals with a growth mindset are more resilient, adaptable, and open to feedback, as they understand that their efforts and learning experiences shape their progress and achievements.

The impact of these two mindsets extends far beyond personal development; it also plays a crucial role in the realm of relationships. Those with a fixed mindset often view relationships as a means to validate their own self-worth, leading to a focus on performance and a fear of vulnerability. They may struggle with open communication, constructive criticism, and the inevitable challenges that arise in any relationship.

On the other hand, individuals with a growth mindset approach relationships as opportunities for mutual growth, learning, and connection. They value open communication, embrace vulnerability, and view conflicts as chances to strengthen their bond and understanding. They are more likely to foster healthy, supportive relationships built on a foundation of trust, empathy, and continuous self-improvement.

By understanding the distinction between fixed and growth mindsets, we can begin to cultivate a more empowering and adaptive perspective on ourselves and our relationships. Embracing a growth mindset allows us to break free from self-limiting beliefs, foster resilience in the face of challenges, and create an environment where both personal and interpersonal growth can flourish. In the following subsections, we will explore practical strategies for nurturing a growth mindset and harnessing its power to transform our relationships and lives.

Subsection 1.2: Cultivating a Love for Lifelong Learning

In the pursuit of personal growth and relationship success, cultivating a love for lifelong learning is an essential strategy. By fostering a genuine passion for continuous self-improvement, you can unlock your full potential, enhance your interpersonal skills, and navigate the ever-changing landscape of relationships with greater ease and confidence.

Embracing lifelong learning begins with a fundamental shift in perspective. Rather than viewing education as a finite journey with a clear beginning and end, it is crucial to recognize that learning is an ongoing process that extends far beyond the walls of a classroom. Every experience, interaction, and challenge presents an opportunity to acquire new knowledge, skills, and insights that can enrich your personal and professional life.

One effective way to cultivate a love for lifelong learning is to identify your areas of interest and curiosity. By focusing on subjects and skills that genuinely captivate you, the process of learning becomes intrinsically rewarding and self-motivating. Whether you are passionate about psychology, communication, or personal development, pursuing knowledge in these areas can provide a sense of fulfillment and purpose that fuels your desire to continue growing.

Another key strategy for fostering a love for lifelong learning is to embrace a diverse range of learning opportunities. In the digital age, access to educational resources has never been more abundant or convenient. From online courses and webinars to podcasts and books, there is a wealth of knowledge available at your fingertips. By exploring various formats and platforms, you can discover the learning styles that resonate with you and create a personalized education plan that fits your goals and lifestyle.

Cultivating a love for lifelong learning also involves surrounding yourself with individuals who share your passion for growth and self-improvement. Engaging with like-minded people, whether through study groups, workshops, or mentorship programs, can provide a supportive and stimulating environment that encourages you to push beyond your comfort zone and explore new ideas. By learning from and alongside others, you can gain valuable perspectives, challenge your assumptions, and accelerate your personal development journey.

To truly embrace lifelong learning, it is essential to reframe your relationship with failure and setbacks. Rather than viewing mistakes as a reflection of your worth or abilities, approach them as valuable opportunities for growth and self-discovery. By cultivating a resilient and adaptable mindset, you can transform challenges into stepping stones toward greater understanding and success.

Ultimately, cultivating a love for lifelong learning is a deeply personal and transformative journey. By nurturing your natural curiosity, seeking out diverse learning experiences, and embracing the power of continuous self-improvement, you can unlock your full potential and build the foundation for rich, fulfilling relationships. As you embark on this lifelong adventure, remember that the greatest investment you can make is in yourself and your capacity to grow, learn, and thrive in all aspects of life.

Subsection 1.3: Reframing Failures as Opportunities for Growth

Failure. It's a word that often evokes feelings of shame, disappointment, and self-doubt. In a society that places a high value on success and achievement, it's easy to view failures and setbacks as personal shortcomings or indications of inadequacy. However, to truly embrace a growth mindset and unlock your full potential in both personal development and relationships, it is essential to reframe the way you perceive and respond to failures.

At its core, failure is simply feedback – a message that your current approach or strategy is not yielding the desired results. Rather than interpreting this feedback as a reflection of your inherent abilities or worth, a growth mindset encourages you to view failures as valuable opportunities for learning, growth, and self-discovery. By shifting your perspective and embracing the lessons that failures have to offer, you can cultivate resilience, adaptability, and a deeper understanding of yourself and others.

One of the most significant benefits of reframing failures as opportunities for growth is that it allows you to develop a more resilient and adaptable mindset. When you view setbacks as temporary challenges rather than permanent obstacles, you are more likely to persevere in the face of adversity and continue pursuing your goals with determination and enthusiasm. By embracing the idea that failures are a natural and necessary part of the learning process, you can approach new experiences and challenges with greater confidence, knowing that each setback brings you one step closer to mastery and success.

Moreover, reframing failures as opportunities for growth can have a profound impact on your relationships and interpersonal interactions. When you embrace the idea that mistakes and setbacks are a valuable part of the learning process, you become more open to feedback, constructive criticism, and the perspectives of others. This openness fosters a culture of continuous improvement and collaboration, as you and your loved ones work together to identify areas for growth and support each other in overcoming challenges.

To effectively reframe failures as opportunities for growth, it is important to cultivate a curious and reflective mindset. Rather than dwelling on the negative emotions associated with setbacks, approach each failure with a sense of curiosity and a desire to understand what went wrong and what you can learn from the experience. Ask yourself questions such as, "What can I do differently next time?" or "What skills or knowledge do I need to acquire to overcome this challenge?" By engaging in self-reflection and analysis, you can extract valuable insights and lessons from each failure, using them as stepping stones toward personal and interpersonal growth.

Another key strategy for reframing failures is to celebrate the progress and growth that results from setbacks. Rather than focusing solely on the end goal or desired outcome, take time to acknowledge and appreciate the small victories and improvements that emerge from your failures. Recognize that each setback brings you closer to your ultimate objectives and that the lessons you learn along the way are just as valuable as the final destination.

Ultimately, reframing failures as opportunities for growth is a powerful tool for cultivating a growth mindset and building strong, resilient relationships. By embracing the idea that setbacks are a natural and necessary part of the learning process, you can approach challenges with greater confidence, extract valuable lessons from each experience, and foster a culture of continuous improvement and collaboration in your personal and interpersonal life. As you navigate the inevitable ups and downs of life and relationships, remember that each failure is an invitation to grow, learn, and become the best version of yourself.

Summary: Unlocking Your Potential Through a Growth

Mindset

Embracing a growth mindset is a transformative journey that empowers you to unlock your full potential in both personal development and relationship success. By recognizing the distinction between fixed and growth mindsets, you can break free from self-limiting beliefs and cultivate a perspective that fosters resilience, adaptability, and continuous learning.

Through nurturing a genuine passion for lifelong learning, you can expand your knowledge, skills, and self-awareness, creating a solid foundation for building strong, healthy relationships. By actively seeking out diverse learning opportunities and surrounding yourself with individuals who share your commitment to growth, you can create a supportive and stimulating environment that propels you forward on your journey of self-discovery.

Moreover, by reframing failures and setbacks as valuable opportunities for growth, you can develop a resilient and adaptable mindset that allows you to navigate challenges with greater ease and confidence. By approaching each obstacle with curiosity and a desire to learn, you can extract valuable lessons and insights that contribute to your personal and interpersonal growth.

As you embrace a growth mindset, remember that the journey of self-improvement is an ongoing process that requires dedication, patience, and self-compassion. By celebrating your progress, learning from your experiences, and maintaining a commitment to continuous growth, you can cultivate a more fulfilling and authentic life, both individually and in your relationships with others.

In the following sections, we will delve deeper into the practical strategies and techniques for applying a growth mindset to your personal development and relationship goals. By integrating these insights into your daily life and interactions, you can unlock your true potential and create the meaningful, lasting connections you desire. Embrace the power of a growth mindset, and embark on a transformative journey of self-discovery and relationship success.

Section 2: Investing in Personal Development

The journey of continuous growth and learning is not only essential for nurturing fulfilling relationships but also for cultivating a deep sense of self-awareness and personal satisfaction. By investing time and energy in personal development, you unlock the door to a more authentic, confident, and empowered version of yourself. This, in turn, has a profound impact on the quality and depth of your relationships with others.

Embarking on a path of self-discovery and growth requires courage, introspection, and a willingness to step outside your comfort zone. It involves taking an honest look at your strengths, weaknesses, values, and aspirations, and using this self-knowledge as a foundation for positive change. Through this process, you gain a clearer understanding of your own needs, desires, and boundaries, enabling you to communicate more effectively and foster healthier connections with others.

Investing in personal development is not a selfish endeavor; rather, it is a gift that extends far beyond the self. As you grow and evolve, you become better equipped to show up as a more present, compassionate, and supportive partner, friend, and family member. You develop the emotional intelligence and resilience necessary to navigate the inevitable challenges and conflicts that arise in relationships, and you inspire others to embark on their own journeys of self-discovery and growth.

Throughout this section, we will explore the myriad benefits of prioritizing personal development and provide practical strategies for identifying areas for self-improvement, setting meaningful goals, and cultivating a lifelong love for learning and growth. By embracing the transformative power of self-discovery and investing in your own personal evolution, you lay the foundation for building and maintaining truly fulfilling relationships that stand the test of time.

Subsection 2.1: Identifying Areas for Self-Improvement

The first step in investing in personal development is to identify areas where you can grow and improve. This process requires honest self-reflection and a willingness to acknowledge both your strengths and weaknesses. By taking a candid look at yourself, you can pinpoint the aspects of your life that need attention and create a roadmap for self-improvement.

One effective way to begin this self-assessment is to reflect on your values, goals, and aspirations. Ask yourself what matters most to you and what you hope to achieve in your personal and professional life. This introspection can help you identify areas where you may need to focus your growth efforts, such as developing specific skills, overcoming limiting beliefs, or improving your communication and interpersonal abilities.

Another valuable tool for identifying areas for self-improvement is seeking feedback from others. Ask trusted friends, family members, or colleagues to provide honest and constructive input on your strengths and weaknesses. This external perspective can offer valuable insights into blind spots you may have overlooked and help you gain a more well-rounded view of yourself.

In addition to personal reflection and external feedback, consider using self-assessment tools and personality tests to gain a deeper understanding of your traits, preferences, and tendencies. Instruments such as the Myers-Briggs Type Indicator (MBTI), the Big Five personality test, or the StrengthsFinder assessment can provide valuable information about your unique characteristics and help you identify areas where you can leverage your strengths and address your weaknesses.

As you identify areas for self-improvement, it's essential to approach the process with self-compassion and a growth mindset. Remember that everyone has room for growth, and acknowledging your weaknesses is a sign of strength, not failure. By embracing the opportunity to learn and develop, you set the stage for personal transformation and more fulfilling relationships with others.

Once you have identified your areas for self-improvement, the next step is to prioritize them based on their potential impact on your life and relationships. Focus on the areas that will yield the greatest benefits and align with your values and goals. This targeted approach will help you allocate your time and energy effectively and ensure that your personal development efforts are meaningful and purposeful.

Subsection 2.2: Setting Meaningful Goals and Action Plans

Setting meaningful goals and creating action plans are crucial components of successful personal development. Without clear, well-defined objectives and a roadmap to guide your efforts, it's easy to lose focus and motivation, leading to stagnation and unfulfilled potential. By taking the time to establish purposeful goals and develop strategic action plans, you empower yourself to make significant strides in your personal growth journey.

The process of setting meaningful goals begins with self-reflection and introspection. Take a moment to consider your values, passions, and long-term aspirations. What do you want to achieve in your personal and professional life? What skills or qualities do you wish to cultivate? By aligning your goals with your core values and desires, you infuse them with a sense of purpose and significance, making them more compelling and motivating.

When crafting your personal development goals, it's essential to ensure that they are specific, measurable, achievable, relevant, and time-bound (SMART). Vague or overly ambitious goals can lead to frustration and disappointment, while well-defined, realistic objectives provide a clear target to work towards. For example, instead of setting a general goal like "improve my communication skills," a SMART goal might be "attend a public speaking workshop and deliver a 10-minute presentation to my colleagues within the next three months."

Once you have established your goals, the next step is to create a detailed action plan. Break down each goal into smaller, manageable tasks and milestones, outlining the specific steps you need to take to achieve them. This process helps you stay organized, focused, and accountable, reducing the risk of becoming overwhelmed or discouraged.

Your action plan should include a timeline for each task, as well as any resources, support, or tools you may need along the way. Consider potential obstacles or challenges you may face and develop contingency plans to address them proactively. By anticipating and preparing for setbacks, you increase your resilience and adaptability, enabling you to stay on track even when faced with adversity.

As you work towards your personal development goals, it's crucial to maintain a flexible and adaptable mindset. Life is unpredictable, and circumstances may change, requiring you to adjust your plans accordingly. Regularly review and reassess your goals and action plans, making modifications as needed to ensure they remain relevant and aligned with your evolving needs and priorities.

Remember to celebrate your progress and accomplishments along the way, no matter how small they may seem. Acknowledging your successes and milestones helps maintain motivation and reinforces the value of your efforts. Share your achievements with supportive friends, family, or mentors, and don't hesitate to seek guidance or encouragement when needed.

By setting meaningful goals and creating comprehensive action plans, you lay the foundation for transformative personal growth and development. This proactive approach to self-improvement not only enhances your own sense of fulfillment and purpose but also empowers you to show up as a more authentic, confident, and capable partner in your relationships. As you navigate the path of continuous learning and self-discovery, your dedication to personal growth will inevitably enrich and strengthen the connections you share with others.

Subsection 2.3: Balancing Self-Improvement with Self-Acceptance

In the pursuit of personal growth and self-improvement, it is essential to strike a delicate balance between striving for change and practicing self-acceptance. While investing time and energy in developing oneself is commendable, it is equally important to approach this journey with self-compassion and a healthy dose of self-love.

Many individuals embark on a path of self-improvement with the belief that they must fix or change everything about themselves to be worthy of love and acceptance. However, this mindset can lead to a never-ending cycle of self-criticism and feelings of inadequacy. When we constantly focus on our flaws and shortcomings, we risk overlooking the unique qualities and strengths that make us who we are.

Practicing self-acceptance does not mean settling for mediocrity or resigning oneself to a life without growth. Instead, it involves acknowledging and embracing our inherent worth as human beings, regardless of our imperfections or areas for improvement. It means treating ourselves with the same kindness, understanding, and compassion that we would extend to a dear friend or loved one.

Self-acceptance is the foundation upon which genuine personal growth can take place. When we approach self-improvement from a place of self-love and self-compassion, we create a safe and nurturing environment that allows us to explore our weaknesses and challenges without fear of judgment or self-condemnation. We become more willing to take risks, step outside our comfort zones, and learn from our mistakes, knowing that our worth is not contingent upon our successes or failures.

Moreover, practicing self-acceptance can help us maintain a healthy perspective on our personal development journey. It reminds us that growth is a lifelong process and that setbacks and challenges are a natural part of the human experience. By embracing our imperfections and celebrating our progress, no matter how small, we cultivate resilience and a growth mindset that enables us to navigate life's ups and downs with greater ease and grace. Balancing self-improvement with self-acceptance also has profound implications for our relationships with others. When we learn to love and accept ourselves unconditionally, we become better equipped to extend that same love and acceptance to those around us. We develop greater empathy, compassion, and understanding for the struggles and imperfections of others, fostering deeper, more authentic connections built on a foundation of mutual respect and appreciation.

To strike a healthy balance between self-improvement and self-acceptance, it is important to engage in practices that nurture both aspects of our being. This may involve setting meaningful goals and taking action towards personal growth while also carving out time for self-care, reflection, and self-compassion. It may mean surrounding ourselves with supportive individuals who encourage us to be our best selves while also accepting us for who we are in the present moment.

Ultimately, the key to balancing self-improvement with self-acceptance lies in recognizing that our worth as individuals is inherent and unchanging. By approaching personal growth from a place of self-love and self-compassion, we open ourselves up to a more fulfilling, authentic, and joyful life, one in which we can embrace our imperfections while continuously striving to become the best versions of ourselves.

Summary: Embracing the Lifelong Journey of Personal Growth

Investing in personal development is a lifelong journey that requires dedication, self-awareness, and a willingness to embrace change. By identifying areas for self-improvement, setting meaningful goals, and creating actionable plans, you lay the foundation for a more fulfilling and authentic life. However, it is equally important to approach this journey with self-compassion and acceptance, recognizing that growth is an ongoing process and that setbacks are a natural part of the human experience.

As you navigate the path of self-discovery and personal growth, remember to celebrate your progress and accomplishments along the way. Embrace the challenges and opportunities that arise, knowing that each experience contributes to your overall development and resilience. By cultivating a growth mindset and a commitment to continuous learning, you not only enhance your own sense of purpose and well-being but also enrich the relationships you share with others.

Ultimately, investing in personal development is a powerful way to show up as your best self in all aspects of life. By prioritizing self-awareness, setting meaningful goals, and balancing self-improvement with self-acceptance, you create a solid foundation for building and maintaining authentic, fulfilling relationships. As you continue on this lifelong journey of growth and self-discovery, trust in the process and have faith in your ability to transform your life and relationships for the better.

Section 3: Continuous Learning in Relationships

In the ever-evolving landscape of human connections, one truth remains constant: the most fulfilling and enduring relationships are those that embrace continuous learning and growth. Just as individuals thrive when they invest in personal development, relationships flourish when partners actively seek opportunities to learn, adapt, and evolve together.

Imagine a relationship as a shared journey, where two people embark on a path of discovery, not only of each other but also of themselves. By approaching relationships with a growth mindset, couples can cultivate a deep understanding, empathy, and appreciation for one another, strengthening the bond that unites them.

In this section, we will explore the transformative power of continuous learning in relationships. We will delve into the importance of learning from past experiences, developing essential interpersonal skills, and fostering a culture of shared growth and mutual support. By embracing the idea that relationships are not static but rather dynamic entities that require ongoing nurturing, couples can unlock the key to building and maintaining healthy, resilient, and deeply satisfying connections.

As we embark on this exploration, it is essential to recognize that the journey of continuous learning in relationships is not always a smooth one. It requires vulnerability, openness, and a willingness to step outside of one's comfort zone. However, the rewards of this journey are immeasurable, as it enables couples to navigate challenges, deepen their understanding of one another, and create a love that stands the test of time.

So, let us dive into the fascinating world of continuous learning in relationships, armed with an open mind, a curious heart, and a commitment to growth. Together, we will uncover the strategies, insights, and wisdom that can transform your relationships into a source of endless inspiration, joy, and fulfillment.

Subsection 3.1: Learning from Relationship Experiences

The journey of continuous learning in relationships is greatly enriched by the wisdom gained from past experiences. Every relationship, whether it be a romantic partnership, a friendship, or a family bond, offers valuable lessons that can inform future growth and decision-making. By taking the time to reflect on these experiences, individuals can cultivate a deeper understanding of themselves, their patterns, and the dynamics that shape their connections with others.

One of the most powerful ways to learn from relationship experiences is through self-reflection. This process involves taking an honest, introspective look at one's own thoughts, feelings, and behaviors within the context of past relationships. By examining the successes, challenges, and failures encountered along the way, individuals can gain insight into their strengths, weaknesses, and areas for personal growth. This self-awareness is crucial for making positive changes and avoiding the repetition of unhealthy patterns in future relationships.

Another key aspect of learning from relationship experiences is the willingness to seek feedback from others. Often, the people closest to us can offer valuable perspectives on our interactions and the impact of our actions. By actively listening to the insights and observations of trusted friends, family members, or even former partners, we can gain a more well-rounded understanding of our relational strengths and blind spots. This feedback, when approached with an open mind and a commitment to growth, can be a catalyst for positive change and personal development.

It is important to recognize that learning from relationship experiences is not about dwelling on the past or assigning blame. Rather, it is about embracing the lessons that each relationship offers and using them as a foundation for future growth. By approaching past experiences with curiosity, compassion, and a willingness to learn, individuals can transform even the most challenging relationships into opportunities for self-discovery and personal evolution.

Ultimately, the journey of continuous learning in relationships is a deeply personal and ongoing process. It requires a commitment to self-reflection, a willingness to embrace feedback, and the courage to make positive changes. By consistently seeking to learn from past experiences, individuals can cultivate the self-awareness, emotional intelligence, and relational skills necessary to build and maintain healthy, fulfilling relationships throughout their lives.

Subsection 3.2: Developing Interpersonal Skills and Emotional Intelligence

In the journey of continuous learning in relationships, developing interpersonal skills and emotional intelligence plays a pivotal role. These essential skills form the foundation of healthy, resilient, and fulfilling connections with others. By consistently working on improving communication, empathy, and conflict resolution abilities, individuals can navigate the complexities of relationships with greater ease and effectiveness.

One of the cornerstones of strong interpersonal skills is effective communication. This involves not only expressing oneself clearly and authentically but also actively listening to and understanding others. To continuously improve communication skills, individuals can practice techniques such as paraphrasing, asking clarifying questions, and using "I" statements to express their thoughts and feelings. By honing these skills, partners can foster a deeper sense of connection, trust, and mutual understanding.

Empathy, the ability to understand and share the feelings of another, is another crucial component of emotional intelligence in relationships. Developing empathy requires a willingness to step into the other person's shoes, to see the world through their eyes, and to validate their experiences. Practicing active listening, asking open-ended questions, and demonstrating genuine curiosity about a partner's perspective can help cultivate empathy. By consistently exercising empathy, individuals can create a safe and supportive environment where both partners feel heard, understood, and valued.

Conflict resolution skills are equally important in maintaining healthy relationships. Disagreements and conflicts are inevitable in any partnership, but how couples navigate these challenges can make all the difference. To continuously improve conflict resolution skills, individuals can learn to approach conflicts with a problem-solving mindset, focusing on finding mutually beneficial solutions rather than assigning blame. Practicing effective communication techniques, such as using "I" statements and active listening, can help de-escalate tensions and promote understanding. Additionally, learning to regulate one's own emotions, practice self-soothing techniques, and take timeouts when necessary can help prevent conflicts from escalating and allow for more constructive discussions.

Developing interpersonal skills and emotional intelligence is an ongoing process that requires consistent effort and practice. One effective strategy is to seek out educational resources, such as books, workshops, or online courses, that focus on building these skills. Engaging in self-reflection, journaling, and seeking feedback from trusted friends or a therapist can also provide valuable insights and opportunities for growth. By proactively working on these skills, individuals can cultivate a greater capacity for empathy, communication, and conflict resolution, leading to more fulfilling and harmonious relationships.

It is important to recognize that developing interpersonal skills and emotional intelligence is a deeply personal journey. Each individual brings their own unique experiences, strengths, and challenges to the table. By approaching this process with self-compassion, patience, and a willingness to learn, individuals can gradually transform their relationships and create a more loving, supportive, and connected world, one interaction at a time.

Subsection 3.3: Growing Together as a Couple

In the tapestry of a long-term relationship, the threads of shared growth, learning, and mutual support are intricately woven, creating a beautiful and resilient bond that stands the test of time. When couples embrace the idea of growing together, they embark on a transformative journey that not only strengthens their connection but also allows them to evolve as individuals.

At the heart of growing together as a couple lies a commitment to continuous learning. This learning encompasses not only the acquisition of new skills and knowledge but also the deep exploration of each other's thoughts, feelings, and aspirations. By actively seeking to understand and appreciate one another's unique perspectives and experiences, couples create a safe and nurturing space for growth.

Shared growth in a relationship is a dynamic process that requires open communication, vulnerability, and a willingness to step outside of one's comfort zone. It involves setting common goals, supporting each other's dreams, and celebrating milestones along the way. When couples approach challenges and opportunities as a team, they foster a sense of unity and resilience that allows them to weather any storm.

Mutual support is the cornerstone of growing together as a couple. It is the unwavering belief in each other's potential, the encouragement during times of doubt, and the compassion in moments of vulnerability. By being each other's greatest cheerleaders and sources of comfort, couples create a foundation of trust and security that allows them to take risks, pursue their passions, and grow in ways they never thought possible.

Growing together as a couple also involves embracing change and adapting to the inevitable shifts that life brings. As individuals evolve and circumstances change, couples who are committed to shared growth learn to navigate these transitions with grace and flexibility. They understand that growth often involves letting go of old patterns and embracing new ways of being, both individually and as a partnership.

One of the most beautiful aspects of growing together as a couple is the opportunity to learn from each other. Each partner brings a unique set of strengths, experiences, and insights to the relationship, creating a rich tapestry of knowledge and wisdom. By actively seeking to learn from one another, couples expand their horizons, challenge their assumptions, and gain a deeper appreciation for the complexities and beauty of the human experience.

To foster a culture of shared growth and learning in a relationship, couples can engage in a variety of activities and practices. Setting aside dedicated time for meaningful conversations, exploring new hobbies and interests together, attending workshops or classes, and engaging in self-reflection and personal development are all powerful ways to cultivate growth. By making a conscious effort to prioritize shared experiences and learning opportunities, couples can create a relationship that is vibrant, fulfilling, and continually evolving.

Ultimately, growing together as a couple is a beautiful and transformative journey that requires commitment, patience, and a deep love for one another. It is a recognition that the greatest adventures and the most profound lessons often lie not in the destination but in the shared path of discovery. By embracing the idea that relationships are living, breathing entities that require nurturing and growth, couples can create a love that not only endures but also flourishes, inspiring each other to become the best versions of themselves.

Summary: Embracing the Lifelong Journey of Learning and Growth in Relationships

The journey of continuous learning in relationships is a lifelong pursuit that requires dedication, openness, and a willingness to grow. By learning from past experiences, developing essential interpersonal skills and emotional intelligence, and committing to shared growth as a couple, individuals can cultivate resilient, fulfilling, and deeply meaningful connections.

Throughout this section, we have explored the transformative power of embracing ongoing learning and growth in relationships. We have seen how reflecting on past experiences can provide valuable insights and opportunities for self-discovery, enabling individuals to break free from unhealthy patterns and make positive changes in their lives. We have also highlighted the importance of continuously developing communication, empathy, and conflict resolution skills, which form the foundation of strong, healthy relationships.

Furthermore, we have emphasized the significance of growing together as a couple, setting common goals, supporting each other's dreams, and celebrating milestones along the way. By creating a culture of shared learning and mutual support, couples can navigate life's challenges and transitions with grace, flexibility, and a deep sense of connection.

As we conclude this section, it is essential to remember that the journey of continuous learning in relationships is not always easy, but it is infinitely rewarding. It requires vulnerability, courage, and a commitment to self-reflection and personal growth. By embracing this lifelong pursuit, individuals and couples can unlock the full potential of their relationships, creating a love that not only endures but also flourishes.

So, let this section serve as an invitation to embark on a journey of endless discovery and growth in your relationships. Embrace the lessons that each experience offers, nurture your interpersonal skills and emotional intelligence, and cherish the opportunity to learn and evolve alongside your loved ones. In doing so, you will create a legacy of love, resilience, and connection that will inspire and enrich your life for years to come.

Section 4: Seeking Inspiration and Guidance

As we navigate the complex tapestry of relationships, it's essential to recognize that we don't have to embark on this journey alone. Throughout history, countless individuals have shared their wisdom, experiences, and insights, offering valuable guidance to those seeking to cultivate meaningful connections and foster personal growth. In this section, we'll explore the various sources of inspiration and support available to us as we strive to build stronger, more fulfilling relationships.

Whether you're facing challenges in your personal life or simply looking to deepen your understanding of human connections, seeking guidance from others can provide a fresh perspective and illuminate new paths forward. From the sage advice of mentors and role models to the collective wisdom found in books, workshops, and online resources, there's a wealth of knowledge waiting to be discovered.

By opening ourselves up to the experiences and insights of others, we can gain a more comprehensive understanding of the intricacies of relationships and the many ways in which we can nurture and strengthen our connections with those around us. Through this process of learning and growth, we not only enhance our own lives but also become better equipped to support and inspire others on their own journeys.

As we delve into the various sources of inspiration and guidance available to us, we'll explore the transformative power of mentorship, the value of engaging with personal development resources, and the importance of surrounding ourselves with growth-oriented communities. By actively seeking out these opportunities for learning and self-discovery, we can cultivate the skills, knowledge, and mindset necessary to build the kind of relationships we've always dreamed of having.

So, let us approach this section with an open mind and a willingness to learn, knowing that every insight gained and every connection made brings us one step closer to the fulfilling, joyful relationships we all deserve.

Subsection 4.1: Learning from Mentors and Role Models

In our quest for personal growth and relationship development, we often find ourselves seeking guidance and inspiration from those who have walked the path before us. Mentors and role models serve as invaluable sources of wisdom, offering insights and perspectives that can help us navigate the complexities of our own journeys.

When we open ourselves up to the guidance of mentors and role models, we gain access to a wealth of knowledge and experience that can accelerate our own growth and development. These individuals have often faced similar challenges and obstacles, and their stories of resilience and triumph can provide us with the motivation and encouragement we need to persevere through our own struggles.

One of the key benefits of learning from mentors and role models is the opportunity to gain a fresh perspective on our own experiences. By sharing our thoughts, feelings, and challenges with someone who has been there before, we can gain new insights and ideas that we may not have considered on our own. This exchange of knowledge and experience can help us break through limiting beliefs, overcome obstacles, and develop new strategies for success.

Moreover, mentors and role models can serve as powerful sources of accountability and support. When we share our goals and aspirations with someone we trust and respect, we are more likely to follow through on our commitments and take the necessary steps to achieve our objectives. This sense of accountability can be particularly valuable when it comes to relationship growth, as it can help us stay focused on our priorities and avoid falling back into old patterns of behavior.

Of course, finding the right mentor or role model is not always easy. It requires a willingness to step outside of our comfort zones and seek out individuals who embody the qualities and values we aspire to cultivate in ourselves. This may involve reaching out to someone we admire in our personal or professional lives, joining a mentorship program or support group, or simply being open to the guidance and wisdom of those around us.

Ultimately, the key to learning from mentors and role models is to approach these relationships with an open mind and a willingness to learn. By listening carefully to their stories, asking thoughtful questions, and reflecting on their insights and advice, we can gain valuable knowledge and inspiration that can help us navigate the challenges and opportunities of our own journeys.

As we continue to grow and evolve in our relationships and personal lives, the guidance and support of mentors and role models can serve as a powerful catalyst for positive change. By seeking out these invaluable sources of wisdom and inspiration, we can accelerate our own growth and development, and cultivate the kind of fulfilling, meaningful relationships we all desire.

Subsection 4.2: Engaging with Personal Development Resources

In our modern world, access to information and resources for personal growth and self-improvement is more abundant than ever before. From books and workshops to online courses and podcasts, there is a wealth of knowledge available to those seeking to enhance their understanding of relationships and cultivate the skills necessary for success.

One of the most powerful tools for personal development is the written word. Books have long been a source of inspiration, guidance, and practical advice for those navigating the complexities of human connections. Whether you're seeking to improve your communication skills, deepen your emotional intelligence, or simply gain a fresh perspective on the nature of relationships, there is likely a book out there that can help.

When selecting books for personal development, it's important to choose titles that align with your specific goals and interests. Look for authors who have established themselves as experts in their field, and don't be afraid to step outside your comfort zone and explore new ideas and approaches. Some popular titles in the realm of relationship development include "The 5 Love Languages" by Gary Chapman, "Attached" by Amir Levine and Rachel Heller, and "Crucial Conversations" by Kerry Patterson, Joseph Grenny, Ron McMillan, and Al Switzler.

In addition to books, workshops and seminars can provide a powerful opportunity for learning and growth. These events often bring together experts and individuals from diverse backgrounds, creating a dynamic and engaging environment for learning and self-discovery. Whether you attend in person or participate online, workshops can provide a structured and supportive space to explore new ideas, develop new skills, and connect with like-minded individuals.

When considering workshops and seminars, look for events that are led by experienced facilitators and that offer a clear and comprehensive curriculum. Some popular topics in the realm of relationship development include effective communication, conflict resolution, and emotional intelligence. Be sure to read reviews and testimonials from past participants to get a sense of the quality and impact of the event.

Online courses and digital resources have also emerged as powerful tools for personal development in recent years. Platforms like Udemy, Coursera, and LinkedIn Learning offer a wide range of courses on topics related to relationships, communication, and personal growth. These courses often include a mix of video lectures, interactive exercises, and downloadable resources, making it easy to learn at your own pace and on your own schedule.

When selecting online courses, look for programs that are taught by experienced instructors and that offer a clear and engaging curriculum. Be sure to read reviews and ratings from past students to get a sense of the quality and effectiveness of the course. Some popular online courses in the realm of relationship development include "Effective Communication" by Dr. Paul Glaser, "Resolving Conflict" by Donna Bowman, and "Emotional Intelligence" by Dr. Travis Bradberry.

Ultimately, the key to engaging with personal development resources is to approach them with an open mind and a willingness to learn. Whether you're reading a book, attending a workshop, or taking an online course, the insights and knowledge you gain can have a profound impact on your relationships and your overall well-being.

As you explore the various resources available to you, remember that personal growth is an ongoing journey. There will always be new skills to develop, new perspectives to consider, and new challenges to overcome. By making a commitment to continuous learning and self-improvement, you can cultivate the kind of fulfilling, meaningful relationships that bring joy and purpose to your life.

Subsection 4.3: Joining Growth-Oriented Communities and Support Groups

In our journey of personal growth and relationship development, surrounding ourselves with like-minded individuals who share our values and aspirations can be a powerful catalyst for positive change. Growth-oriented communities and support groups provide a unique opportunity to connect with others who are also committed to self-improvement and nurturing meaningful relationships.

These communities come in many forms, from online forums and social media groups to in-person meetups and workshops. By joining a growth-oriented community, you gain access to a wealth of knowledge, experiences, and perspectives that can broaden your understanding of relationships and provide valuable insights into your own journey.

One of the key benefits of participating in these communities is the sense of belonging and support they provide. When you surround yourself with individuals who are also striving to grow and improve, you create a positive and uplifting environment that encourages you to push beyond your comfort zone and embrace new challenges. This supportive atmosphere can be particularly valuable during times of struggle or uncertainty, as it reminds you that you are not alone in your journey and that there are others who understand and relate to your experiences.

Moreover, growth-oriented communities offer a rich tapestry of experiences and expertise that can accelerate your own learning and development. By engaging in meaningful conversations, sharing your own stories and insights, and seeking guidance from those who have walked a similar path, you can gain new perspectives and strategies for navigating the complexities of relationships. This exchange of knowledge and ideas can be incredibly empowering, as it helps you realize that the challenges you face are not unique and that there are proven strategies for overcoming them.

In addition to the personal growth benefits, joining a supportive community can also have a profound impact on your relationships themselves. As you learn and grow alongside others who share your values and goals, you become better equipped to communicate effectively, resolve conflicts, and build deeper, more meaningful connections with the people in your life. You may even form new friendships and relationships within the community itself, further expanding your network of support and inspiration.

When seeking out a growth-oriented community or support group, it's important to find one that aligns with your specific needs and goals. Consider factors such as the group's focus, the experience and expertise of its members, and the format and frequency of its interactions. Some communities may be more structured, with regular meetings and guided discussions, while others may be more informal and self-directed.

Regardless of the specific format, the key is to approach these communities with an open mind and a willingness to engage. By actively participating in discussions, sharing your own experiences and insights, and supporting others in their own journeys, you can maximize the benefits of being part of a growth-oriented community.

As you embark on this path of personal growth and relationship development, remember that the connections you make and the communities you join can have a profound impact on your journey. By surrounding yourself with like-minded individuals who share your commitment to self-improvement and nurturing meaningful relationships, you create a powerful support system that can help you navigate even the most challenging of times. So, take the time to seek out and engage with these communities, knowing that every connection you make brings you one step closer to the fulfilling, joyful relationships you deserve.

Summary: Illuminating the Path to Growth and Fulfillment

As we conclude this section on seeking inspiration and guidance for personal growth and relationship development, it's important to recognize the transformative power of the insights and strategies we've explored. By actively engaging with mentors, personal development resources, and growth-oriented communities, we open ourselves up to a world of wisdom and support that can profoundly impact the quality and depth of our relationships.

The journey of continuous learning and self-discovery is not always easy, but it is undeniably rewarding. As we navigate the challenges and opportunities that arise in our relationships, having access to a diverse array of resources and perspectives can make all the difference. Whether we're seeking guidance on effective communication, conflict resolution, or cultivating emotional intelligence, the knowledge and tools we acquire through these channels can help us build the kind of strong, healthy, and fulfilling connections we all desire.

It's important to remember that growth is an ongoing process, and there will always be new insights to gain and skills to develop. By embracing a mindset of continuous learning and remaining open to the wisdom of others, we position ourselves for success in both our personal and relational lives. The connections we make, the communities we join, and the resources we engage with all contribute to the rich tapestry of our growth and development, empowering us to create the relationships and lives we've always envisioned.

As we move forward on this path, let us do so with a sense of curiosity, courage, and commitment. By actively seeking out the guidance and inspiration that resonates with our unique needs and goals, we take a proactive stance in shaping the trajectory of our relationships and our personal evolution. With each step we take, each insight we gain, and each connection we make, we move closer to unlocking the full potential of our relationships and ourselves.

So, let us embrace the journey of continuous growth and learning, knowing that the rewards are well worth the effort. As we continue to explore the various sources of inspiration and guidance available to us, we can trust that we are laying the foundation for a lifetime of rich, meaningful, and fulfilling relationships. With an open mind, a willing heart, and a steadfast commitment to personal development, there is no limit to the heights we can reach and the connections we can create.

Section 5: Overcoming Obstacles to Growth and Learning

The journey of personal growth and relationship development is rarely a smooth, uninterrupted path. Along the way, we encounter various obstacles and challenges that can hinder our progress and test our resolve. These barriers, whether internal or external, can lead to feelings of frustration, self-doubt, and stagnation, causing us to question our ability to grow and improve our relationships.

However, it is essential to recognize that these obstacles are not insurmountable. With the right mindset, strategies, and support, we can navigate through these challenges and emerge stronger, wiser, and better equipped to cultivate meaningful connections with others. In this section, we will explore some of the most common obstacles to personal growth and relationship development, and provide practical guidance on how to overcome them.

From identifying and challenging limiting beliefs that hold us back, to navigating the discomfort of change and uncertainty, we will delve into the psychological and emotional barriers that can impede our progress. We will also discuss the importance of maintaining motivation and commitment to growth, even in the face of setbacks and disappointments.

By addressing these obstacles head-on and developing the skills and resilience needed to overcome them, we can unlock our full potential for personal growth and create the foundation for healthy, thriving relationships. So, let us embark on this transformative journey together, armed with the knowledge, tools, and determination to break through any barriers that stand in our way.

Subsection 5.1: Identifying and Challenging Limiting Beliefs

One of the most significant obstacles to personal growth and learning is the presence of limiting beliefs. These deeply ingrained, often subconscious beliefs about ourselves and the world around us can hold us back from reaching our full potential and cultivating healthy, fulfilling relationships. Limiting beliefs may manifest as negative self-talk, self-doubt, or a fixed mindset that hinders our ability to embrace change and growth.

To overcome these self-imposed barriers, it is crucial to develop the ability to identify and challenge limiting beliefs. The first step in this process is self-awareness. By taking the time to reflect on our thoughts, emotions, and behaviors, we can begin to recognize patterns and underlying beliefs that may be holding us back. This can be achieved through practices such as journaling, meditation, or engaging in honest self-reflection.

Once we have identified our limiting beliefs, the next step is to challenge them. This involves questioning the validity and accuracy of these beliefs, and seeking evidence to support or refute them. For example, if we hold the belief that we are not capable of forming meaningful relationships, we can challenge this by examining past experiences that contradict this belief or by seeking feedback from trusted friends and family members.

Another effective strategy for overcoming limiting beliefs is to reframe them in a more positive and empowering light. By consciously replacing negative self-talk with affirmative statements and focusing on our strengths and potential, we can gradually shift our mindset and build a more resilient and growth-oriented outlook.

Surrounding ourselves with supportive, growth-minded individuals can also play a crucial role in challenging limiting beliefs. By engaging in open, honest conversations with others who are committed to personal development, we can gain new perspectives, insights, and encouragement that help us break free from self-imposed limitations.

Ultimately, the journey of overcoming limiting beliefs is an ongoing process that requires patience, self-compassion, and a willingness to step outside of our comfort zones. By consistently identifying and challenging these beliefs, we can unlock our full potential for growth and cultivate the mindset necessary for building and maintaining healthy, thriving relationships.

Subsection 5.2: Navigating Resistance to Change and Uncertainty

Change and uncertainty are inevitable companions on the path of personal growth and relationship development. As we strive to improve ourselves and our connections with others, we often find ourselves facing the discomfort and fear that come with venturing into uncharted territory. Resistance to change, both within ourselves and from those around us, can create significant barriers to growth and progress.

To successfully navigate resistance to change and uncertainty, it is essential to first acknowledge and accept their presence. Recognize that feeling uncomfortable or anxious when faced with new challenges or unfamiliar situations is a natural human response. By embracing these emotions rather than trying to suppress or avoid them, we can begin to develop the resilience and adaptability needed to push through resistance and thrive in the face of uncertainty.

One effective strategy for overcoming resistance to change is to focus on the potential benefits and opportunities that lie on the other side of discomfort. By keeping our eyes on the prizes—such as improved self-awareness, stronger relationships, and greater personal fulfillment—we can find the motivation and courage to take the necessary steps forward. Visualizing positive outcomes and celebrating small victories along the way can help maintain momentum and counteract the pull of resistance.

Another key aspect of navigating change and uncertainty is cultivating a support system of trusted friends, family members, or mentors who can offer encouragement, guidance, and accountability. Surrounding ourselves with individuals who are committed to personal growth and who understand the challenges we face can provide a vital source of strength and inspiration during times of doubt or struggle.

It is also crucial to approach change and uncertainty with a growth mindset, viewing obstacles and setbacks as opportunities for learning and development rather than as insurmountable barriers. By embracing a spirit of curiosity and experimentation, we can reframe the discomfort of change as an exciting challenge to be tackled head-on. This shift in perspective can help us maintain a sense of control and agency, even in the face of uncertainty.

Practicing self-compassion and patience is equally important when navigating resistance to change. Recognize that growth is a gradual, non-linear process, and that setbacks and missteps are a natural part of the journey. By treating ourselves with kindness and understanding, we can maintain the emotional resilience needed to persevere through difficult times and continue making progress towards our goals.

Ultimately, the key to successfully navigating resistance to change and uncertainty lies in developing a toolbox of strategies and mindsets that allow us to embrace discomfort, maintain perspective, and keep moving forward. By consistently applying these tools and techniques, we can cultivate the adaptability and resilience needed to thrive in the face of change and create the conditions for lasting personal and relationship growth.

Subsection 5.3: Maintaining Motivation and Commitment to Growth

The journey of personal and relationship growth is an ongoing process that requires consistent effort, dedication, and perseverance. However, maintaining motivation and staying committed to this path can be challenging, especially during times of adversity or when progress seems slow. It is essential to develop strategies and mindsets that help us stay focused, energized, and determined to continue growing, even in the face of obstacles and setbacks.

One key factor in maintaining motivation is setting clear, meaningful goals that align with our values and aspirations. By having a strong sense of purpose and direction, we can tap into a deep well of intrinsic motivation that fuels our commitment to growth. Breaking down larger goals into smaller, achievable milestones can also help us maintain momentum and celebrate progress along the way, providing a sense of accomplishment and reinforcing our dedication to the journey.

Another crucial aspect of staying motivated is cultivating a support system of like-minded individuals who share our commitment to personal and relationship development. Surrounding ourselves with people who inspire, encourage, and hold us accountable can provide a powerful source of motivation and help us stay on track when our own resolve wavers. Engaging in regular discussions, sharing experiences, and celebrating successes with our support network can help reinforce our commitment and provide valuable perspectives and insights.

Maintaining a growth mindset is also essential for staying motivated and committed to ongoing development. By viewing challenges and setbacks as opportunities for learning and improvement, rather than as failures or indictments of our abilities, we can maintain a sense of resilience and adaptability in the face of adversity. Embracing the idea that our skills and relationships are not fixed, but rather malleable and capable of continuous growth, can help us approach obstacles with curiosity, creativity, and a willingness to experiment and take risks.

Incorporating regular self-reflection and self-care practices into our routines can also play a vital role in sustaining motivation and commitment to growth. Taking time to assess our progress, acknowledge our strengths and areas for improvement, and celebrate our achievements can help us maintain a positive outlook and renew our dedication to the journey. Engaging in activities that promote physical, emotional, and mental well-being, such as exercise, meditation, or pursuing hobbies and interests, can help us recharge, reduce stress, and maintain the energy and focus needed to continue growing.

Finally, it is important to recognize that motivation and commitment are not constant states, but rather fluctuating experiences that ebb and flow over time. Accepting that there will be periods of heightened enthusiasm and periods of doubt or struggle can help us develop a more compassionate and realistic approach to growth. By practicing self-forgiveness, patience, and understanding, we can navigate the inevitable ups and downs of the journey with greater ease and resilience.

Ultimately, maintaining motivation and commitment to ongoing personal and relationship development requires a combination of clear goals, supportive relationships, a growth mindset, self-care practices, and a compassionate, realistic approach. By consistently applying these strategies and mindsets, we can cultivate the inner resources and outer support needed to stay dedicated to the lifelong journey of growth and transformation.

Summary: Embracing the Challenges of Growth and Learning

Throughout this section, we have explored the various obstacles and challenges that can hinder personal growth and relationship development. From identifying and challenging limiting beliefs to navigating the discomfort of change and uncertainty, and maintaining motivation and commitment, the journey of growth is rarely a smooth one.

However, by recognizing these obstacles as natural and inevitable parts of the process, we can develop the mindset, strategies, and resilience needed to overcome them. By consistently applying the tools and techniques discussed in this section, such as self-awareness, reframing, seeking support, and practicing self-compassion, we can cultivate the inner resources and outer support necessary to push through barriers and continue making progress.

It is essential to remember that growth is not a destination, but rather a lifelong journey of learning, self-discovery, and transformation. By embracing the challenges and opportunities that arise along the way, we can develop the adaptability, resilience, and wisdom needed to thrive in the face of adversity and create the conditions for lasting personal and relationship growth.

As we move forward on this path, let us approach each obstacle as an invitation to deepen our self-understanding, strengthen our relationships, and expand our capacity for growth and change. By staying committed to the journey and trusting in the process, we can unlock our full potential and create the fulfilling, authentic lives and relationships we desire.

Section 6: Celebrating Progress and Milestones

In the journey of continuous growth and learning, it's essential to take a moment to acknowledge and celebrate the progress you've made and the milestones you've reached. Too often, we become so focused on the challenges ahead that we forget to recognize the valuable lessons we've learned and the positive changes we've implemented in our lives and relationships.

Celebrating your progress, no matter how small, serves as a powerful motivator and reinforces your commitment to personal and relationship growth. It helps you maintain a positive outlook, boosts your self-confidence, and provides a sense of accomplishment that fuels your desire to continue improving.

Moreover, sharing your victories and insights with others can inspire them on their own journeys of self-discovery and relationship development. By openly discussing your experiences, you create opportunities for meaningful connections, mutual support, and the exchange of wisdom.

In this section, we'll explore the importance of recognizing and appreciating the small victories along the way, reflecting on the lessons learned, and inspiring others through your shared experiences. We'll discuss strategies for maintaining a growth-oriented mindset, even in the face of challenges, and how to use your progress as a springboard for further development.

As you read through this section, remember that every step forward, no matter how small, is a cause for celebration. Embrace the journey of continuous growth and learning, and let your progress be a source of pride, motivation, and inspiration for yourself and those around you.

Subsection 6.1: Recognizing and Appreciating Small Victories

In the pursuit of personal growth and relationship development, it's easy to overlook the small victories and focus solely on the larger milestones. However, recognizing and appreciating the seemingly minor successes along the way is crucial for maintaining motivation, building momentum, and fostering a sense of accomplishment.

Small victories can take many forms, such as successfully implementing a new communication technique with your partner, showing empathy in a challenging situation, or taking a step outside your comfort zone to try something new together. These moments may not feel groundbreaking, but they represent significant progress in your journey of continuous growth and learning.

By acknowledging and celebrating these small victories, you reinforce the positive changes you're making and create a sense of pride in your efforts. This recognition helps to build self-confidence and encourages you to continue pushing forward, even when faced with obstacles or setbacks.

Moreover, appreciating small victories allows you to maintain a balanced perspective on your growth journey. Instead of becoming discouraged by the distance between where you are and where you want to be, you learn to find joy and satisfaction in the incremental progress you're making.

This mindset shift can help alleviate stress, reduce self-criticism, and promote a more positive outlook on your personal and relationship development.

To make the most of your small victories, consider keeping a growth journal where you record your successes, no matter how minor they may seem. Regularly revisit these entries to remind yourself of the progress you've made and to draw inspiration during challenging times. You can also share your victories with your partner or a trusted friend, creating opportunities for mutual celebration and support.

Remember, every small victory is a testament to your commitment to growth and learning. By recognizing and appreciating these moments, you not only enhance your own sense of accomplishment but also inspire others to embrace the power of continuous self-improvement in their lives and relationships.

Subsection 6.2: Reflecting on Growth and Lessons Learned

Reflecting on personal and relationship growth is an essential practice that allows you to gain valuable insights, maintain perspective, and continue making progress on your journey of continuous learning. By regularly taking the time to look back on your experiences, you can identify patterns, celebrate successes, and extract meaningful lessons that will guide you in your future growth and decision-making.

One effective way to reflect on your growth is to keep a journal or diary. Writing down your thoughts, feelings, and experiences can help you process your emotions, clarify your thoughts, and track your progress over time. As you review your journal entries, you may notice recurring themes, challenges, or successes that you can learn from and build upon.

Another powerful reflection tool is to engage in open and honest conversations with your partner, family, or close friends. Sharing your experiences and listening to their perspectives can provide valuable insights and help you see your growth from different angles. These conversations can also strengthen your relationships by fostering a sense of mutual understanding, support, and accountability.

When reflecting on your growth, it's essential to approach the process with a non-judgmental and compassionate mindset. Recognize that growth is not always linear, and setbacks are a natural part of the learning process. Instead of focusing on perceived failures or shortcomings, try to reframe these experiences as opportunities for learning and self-discovery.

As you reflect on your lessons learned, consider how you can apply these insights to your current and future relationships. What strategies have worked well for you in the past, and how can you adapt them to new situations? What challenges have you faced, and what skills or resources do you need to overcome similar obstacles in the future?

In addition to personal reflection, seeking feedback from others can provide valuable insights into your growth and areas for improvement. Consider asking your partner, family members, or trusted friends for their honest and constructive feedback on your communication skills, emotional intelligence, or other aspects of your relationships. Be open to their perspectives and use their input to inform your ongoing growth and development.

Remember that reflection is not a one-time event but an ongoing practice that requires commitment and dedication. By making reflection a regular part of your routine, you can cultivate a growth-oriented mindset, stay attuned to your progress, and maintain a sense of perspective on your journey of continuous learning and self-discovery.

Subsection 6.3: Inspiring Others Through Shared Experiences and Wisdom

As you navigate your own journey of personal growth and relationship development, it's important to recognize the power of sharing your experiences and insights with others. By openly discussing your triumphs, challenges, and lessons learned, you have the opportunity to inspire and support others who may be facing similar situations or seeking guidance on their own paths.

Sharing your story can be a deeply empowering experience, both for yourself and for those who hear it. When you vulnerably share your struggles and how you've overcome them, you normalize the challenges that many people face in their relationships and personal lives. This can help others feel less alone and more understood, creating a sense of connection and community.

Moreover, by sharing the strategies, tools, and mindset shifts that have helped you navigate difficult times and foster positive change, you provide valuable resources and inspiration for others. Your experiences and wisdom can serve as a roadmap, offering hope, encouragement, and practical guidance to those who are seeking to improve their own relationships and personal growth.

When sharing your experiences, it's essential to do so from a place of authenticity, humility, and compassion. Recognize that everyone's journey is unique, and what has worked for you may not necessarily be the best solution for others. Instead of presenting your insights as universal truths, frame them as personal reflections and suggestions, encouraging others to adapt and apply them in ways that resonate with their own circumstances and values.

It's also important to create a safe and non-judgmental space when sharing your experiences. By fostering an atmosphere of openness, respect, and empathy, you encourage others to share their own stories and insights, creating a rich tapestry of shared wisdom and support. This exchange of experiences can lead to powerful connections, collaborations, and mutual growth, as individuals learn from and inspire one another.

There are many ways to share your experiences and inspire others on their journeys. You might consider writing a blog, hosting a podcast, or creating social media content that focuses on personal growth and relationship development. You could also lead workshops, support groups, or mentorship programs, where you can directly engage with others and offer guidance and encouragement.

Ultimately, by sharing your experiences and wisdom, you have the power to make a positive impact on the lives of others. Your story has the potential to inspire, uplift, and empower those who are navigating their own challenges and seeking to build stronger, more fulfilling relationships. By openly discussing your journey, you not only support others but also reinforce your own commitment to continuous growth and learning, creating a ripple effect of positive change in the world around you.

Summary: Embracing the Journey of Growth and Celebration

Celebrating progress and milestones is an essential aspect of the journey of continuous growth and learning in relationships. By recognizing and appreciating the small victories, reflecting on the lessons learned, and sharing your experiences with others, you cultivate a growth-oriented mindset that fuels your motivation and inspires positive change.

Remember that every step forward, no matter how small, is a testament to your commitment to personal and relationship development. Embrace the power of celebration, and let your progress be a source of pride, encouragement, and inspiration for yourself and those around you.

As you continue on this path of continuous growth, maintain a compassionate and non-judgmental approach, acknowledging that setbacks and challenges are natural parts of the learning process. Use these experiences as opportunities for self-discovery and growth, and trust in your ability to overcome obstacles and build stronger, more fulfilling relationships.

By openly sharing your journey with others, you create a ripple effect of positive change, inspiring and empowering those who may be facing similar challenges or seeking guidance on their own paths. Your story has the power to normalize struggles, provide hope, and offer practical guidance, fostering a sense of connection and community.

Embrace the journey of growth and celebration, and remain committed to the ongoing process of learning, reflection, and self-improvement. As you do so, you not only enhance your own relationships but also contribute to a world where empathy, understanding, and love can flourish.

Chapter Summary: Embracing the Journey of Lifelong Growth for Thriving Relationships

Throughout this chapter, we have explored the importance of embracing the ongoing journey of personal growth, learning, and self-discovery as a key to building and maintaining fulfilling relationships. By cultivating a growth mindset, investing in personal development, and continuously learning from relationship experiences, we can foster a strong foundation for healthy and thriving connections with others.

We have discussed the significance of seeking inspiration and guidance from mentors, role models, and personal development resources, as well as the value of connecting with growth-oriented communities and support groups. Overcoming obstacles to growth and learning, such as challenging limiting beliefs and navigating resistance to change, is an essential part of the journey.

As we progress on this path of continuous growth and learning, it is crucial to celebrate our progress and milestones, no matter how small they may seem. Recognizing and appreciating our personal growth and the lessons we have learned along the way can provide motivation and encouragement to continue on this transformative journey.

Ultimately, embracing the journey of lifelong growth and learning is not only beneficial for our personal development but also for the health and vitality of our relationships. By consistently striving to become the best versions of ourselves, we can create a ripple effect of positivity and growth in our connections with others, inspiring and supporting them on their own journeys of self-discovery and relationship success.

As we conclude this chapter, remember that the journey of continuous growth and learning is an ongoing process that requires dedication, patience, and self-compassion. Embrace the challenges, celebrate the victories, and remain open to the endless possibilities for personal and relationship growth that lie ahead. By doing so, you will be well-equipped to build and maintain fulfilling, loving, and enduring relationships that stand the test of time.

Afterword: Embracing the Journey of Lifelong Growth and Connection

As we conclude this exploration of relationships and personal growth, it's important to recognize that the journey of self-discovery and connection is an ongoing one. Throughout the chapters of this book, we've delved into the many facets of building and maintaining healthy, fulfilling relationships with others and with ourselves. From understanding the foundations of strong connections to navigating challenges and embracing diversity, we've covered a wide range of topics that contribute to the richness and complexity of human relationships.

One of the key takeaways from this journey is the importance of continuous learning and growth. By adopting a growth mindset and investing in personal development, we open ourselves up to new experiences, insights, and opportunities for positive change. This commitment to lifelong learning allows us to evolve as individuals and to bring our best selves to the relationships we cherish.

Another crucial aspect of this journey is the power of empathy, vulnerability, and authenticity. By cultivating these qualities within ourselves and our interactions with others, we create space for deeper, more meaningful connections. When we approach our relationships with an open heart and a willingness to understand and support one another, we build the trust and resilience necessary to weather life's storms and celebrate its joys together.

As you reflect on the insights and strategies shared in this book, remember that the path to fulfilling relationships and personal growth is not always a straight or easy one. There will be challenges, setbacks, and moments of uncertainty along the way. However, by embracing the journey with curiosity, compassion, and a commitment to learning, you'll find that these obstacles become opportunities for growth and transformation.

Take the time to integrate the lessons you've learned into your daily life and interactions with others. Experiment with new communication techniques, practice empathy and active listening, and dare to be vulnerable in your connections. Celebrate the progress you make, no matter how small, and be gentle with yourself when you stumble or face difficulties. Remember that growth is a process, and every step forward is a testament to your resilience and dedication.

As you continue on this path of lifelong learning and connection, know that you are not alone. Seek out the support and guidance of trusted friends, family members, or professionals when needed, and don't hesitate to reach out for help when facing particularly challenging situations. Surround yourself with individuals who inspire and encourage your growth, and be that source of support for others in turn.

Finally, embrace the beauty and diversity of the relationships in your life. Celebrate the unique qualities and experiences that each person brings to your world, and strive to create inclusive, equitable spaces where all individuals feel valued and respected. By fostering a sense of belonging and understanding in your relationships, you contribute to a more compassionate and connected society as a whole.

As you close this book and embark on the next chapter of your journey, carry with you the knowledge, insights, and tools you've gained. Trust in your ability to navigate the complexities of relationships and personal growth with wisdom, empathy, and resilience. And most importantly, never stop learning, growing, and cherishing the connections that make life a rich and meaningful adventure.

Don't miss out!

Visit the website below and you can sign up to receive emails whenever Sandy Y. Greenleaf publishes a new book. There's no charge and no obligation.

https://books2read.com/r/B-A-HNUEB-OVZZC

Connecting independent readers to independent writers.

Also by Sandy Y. Greenleaf

AI's Take on Personal Growth
AI's Take on Relationships